THE WITHDRAWAL OF RIGHTS

SYNTHESE LIBRARY

STUDIES IN EPISTEMOLOGY,

LOGIC, METHODOLOGY, AND PHILOSOPHY OF SCIENCE

VOLUME 314

THE WITHDRAWAL OF RIGHTS

Rights from a Different Perspective

by

OVADIA EZRA

Tel Aviv University,
Tel Aviv, Israel

KLUWER ACADEMIC PUBLISHERS

DORDRECHT / BOSTON / LONDON

A C.I.P. Catalogue record for this book is available from the Library of Congress.

ISBN 978-90-481-6127-0

Published by Kluwer Academic Publishers,
P.O. Box 17, 3300 AA Dordrecht, The Netherlands.

Sold and distributed in North, Central and South America
by Kluwer Academic Publishers,
101 Philip Drive, Norwell, MA 02061, U.S.A.

In all other countries, sold and distributed
by Kluwer Academic Publishers,
P.O. Box 322, 3300 AH Dordrecht, The Netherlands.

Printed on acid-free paper

TABLE OF CONTENTS

ACKNOWLEDGEMENTS

I would like to express my deep gratitude to some of those who have helped me in writing this study.

First, I want to thank Prof. Jacob Joshua Ross from Tel Aviv University, for years of wholehearted involvement and guidance. His wisdom, patience and tolerance were an immense contribution to my philosophical development, and to the quality of this book.

Prof. Alan Gewirth from The University of Chicago for having such an interesting, challenging and fruitful theory, and for his invaluable comments and advices on a previous version of this book.

Prof. Joel Feinberg from University of Arizona at Tucson for his illuminating comments on the different issues that were raised in this book.

Prof. Carl Wellman from Washington University at Saint Louis for his priceless comments and notes which made this book much more accurate, consistent and clear.

Prof. Anat Biletzki, whose patience and determination made an immense contribution to the publication of this book, for being so helpful throughout the years.

Ms. Ingrid Krabbenbos from Kluwer Academic Publishers for her substantial help in solving many technical issues involved in the publishing of this book.

Mrs. Sandy Bloom for the wonderful job she did in linguistic editing.

Finally I want to thank my teachers, colleagues and friends whose support and encouragement assisted in the formation this book. Dr. Zvi Tauber, Prof. Shlomo Biderman, Prof. Yoav Ariel, Dr. Anat Matar and Prof. Yael Tamir, all from Tel Aviv University.

INTRODUCTION

This study seeks to participate in, and to advance, a widespread tradition in the contemporary ethical-political discussion, which is usually called "rights-talk". This tradition has gathered momentum during the last two generations, mainly as a result of the dissatisfaction with some conclusions that follow from consequentialist or utilitarian attempts to resolve moral dilemmas or moral conflicts. Such attempts might well result in some decisions that seem morally monstrous in certain cases, where a pure utilitarian calculation may justify the cause of a minor injustice, in order to avoid a major harm or hardship. A utilitarian consideration might justify, for example, the injury of an innocent person, in order to save the lives of some (or even many) others. However, such conclusions strike at some of our fundamental beliefs regarding justice, fairness and humanity. We have the feeling that in these borderline cases, there is an irreparable conflict between consequentialist theories and some of our accepted moral values.

As a reasonable way to overcome such conflicts, we assume that people have, as individuals, some basic interests that must be protected and should not be denied even for the sake of social utility, great as it may be. These interests, when they receive the acknowledgement of the social framework as valid, are considered as rights, and as rights they protect the individual's interests, and can compete with other moral considerations such as the common good or the rights of other individuals. A theory in which the normative codes are used as instruments for protecting interests and rights of individuals is usually called a "right-based theory".[1] Although there are many possible justifications for protecting rights of individuals (such as duty-based or goal-based theories), right-based theories are those that serve most frequently for this purpose.

In my view, when we base rights on interests, we do not wish to imply that only those interests which are protected by rights are more important than other interests. We also do not mean that these interests have a lexical priority over other interests (that is, that these interests should be fully satisfied before fulfilling the other interests). We mean that the rights that protect those interests are not merely "side constraints" on actions of others, as Nozick considers them. We intend to say that they can function as grounds for explicit and obligatory demands from certain individuals or bodies.[2] In Dworkin's terminology, we can say that a possessor of a right has a "trump", which can override other moral considerations.

This study adopts the Rawlsian concept of the role of rights in society. According to this concept, rights function as a final court of appeal in ordering conflicts between claims of moral individuals.[3] This means that rights confer upon their possessors a valuable moral status that can justify the imposing of duties and burdens upon others, including limitations upon the liberties of others. Such an approach towards rights requires that the main part of any discussion regarding rights will be dedicated to defining the legitimate restrictions that may be imposed on others, when exercising these rights.

However, in order to discuss the benefits involved with the moral status of a possessor of rights, as also the burdens it imposes upon the duty-bound persons (or corporations which are considered, for our purposes, as "artificial persons"[4]), we must set out the semantic realm within which rights acquire their meaning and validity. In this realm the term "right" is only one of many moral terms which, when considered as a whole, create its sense and its obligatory status. To this realm belongs our understanding of norms, aims, desires, justification, validity, etc. Our concept of a right is derived from our understanding of its relation to the other normative terms within this realm.[5] This entails that the sense and validity of a right will be coherent with the ethical and political theory, within which this right is claimed.

We assume that validating a right is possible only within a normative system, whether this system is legal or moral. This validity should reflect our moral and political view, which is the collection of our normative beliefs joined into a coherent and consistent set. When we consider a right as valid, we at once define the identity of its possessor and what is to be done in order to enable her to exercise and capitalize on this specific right. This includes the range and weight of the right, and the mutual linkage between the possessor and the other partners to the social interaction. Most of our acknowledgement of the validity of a right, relates to the efforts to ensure the possessor the ability to gain the benefit from her moral status, and to guarantee that she is aware of her moral status, which entitles her to possess this right. The more people recognize the significance of rights to their coexistence, the more will there be interests, which are acknowledged as rights in that society.

The desire to internalize the idea, that rights are moral assets that people should acquire in the course of their membership in a common framework (a state or a community), also finds its expression in the theoretical discussion of rights. Most of the discussions within rights-talk concentrate on the significance of conferring, bestowing and possessing rights. They deal intensively with the sets of safety and protection constraints required for a successful exercising of rights. The main goal of these discussions is to inquire into the validity of right-claims, and the range of their applicability. Most of the participants in rights-talk intend to minimize the possibility of violating or denying people's rights, and try to support the goal of providing as many rights to as many people as possible.

In this study I address another issue, and deal with rights from the point of view of their withdrawal. I want to inquire into the conditions and circumstances under which rights lose their validity, and in which it is justifiable to withdraw these rights from possessors who already possess them (by taking them back or limiting their range), or deny them to potential possessors who claim to have them (by not bestowing them). This does not mean to say that I ascribe less importance to the possession of rights, or try to reduce their significance and status within the community. The opposite is true. In order to prevent the erosion of their role in society, and to encourage their obligatory status, I think that we should prevent unjustifiable or excessive use of rights. This would strengthen the reality of possessing rights by those who justifiably exercise them. The stringent application of the conditions for the possession of rights, would strengthen the validity of the possessor's claims, and increase the obligation of the community to guarantee the possessor's ability to capitalize on her rights. On the other hand, this stringency increases the commitment of the community, to avoid situations where people enjoy rights that they are not entitled to possess. This would add some additional significance to the possession of rights.

However, in order to define the conditions and circumstances under which rights lose their validity, we must form a framework within which rights are valid. This framework defines the relations that a right establishes between its possessor, respondent and their surroundings. It also defines the content of a right, its conditions of validity, and the mutual linkage between the moral concepts that create the moral status of a right. I deal with these issues in the first chapter of this study.

The first chapter lays down the conceptual framework within which I discuss, in the following chapters, the possession and the withdrawal of rights. In that chapter I present my overview of the content of rights, which I presume can exist solely within a normative system, whether moral or legal, and apply only to things that are valuable to their owners. Among the different ways of regarding rights, I prefer, in this study, to consider them as "affirmative claims". The main reason for this is my desire to consider interests as rights, only when there is a specified respondent, who is duty-bound because of this interest, and is obliged to fulfill it. I also prefer not to consider rights merely as justified claims, but to accept Joel Feinberg's concept of rights as "valid claims" – that is a justification within a system of rules.[6]

Another characteristic of the view that is presented in the first chapter is the assumption that the possession of a specific right includes the possession of all the necessary conditions for exercising this right. Here I follow Henry Shue, who expresses this view by saying: "If everyone has a right to y, and the enjoyment of x is necessary for the enjoyment of y, than everyone has a right to x".[7] This expresses the desire that the possessor of a certain right will be able to capitalize on (that is, to successfully exercise) her right whenever she prefers to, and also the desire that this right will not turn out to be an abstraction that exists only in theory. Such an attitude places welfare and human rights at its center and insists that these rights should be concrete and applicable.

The second chapter continues to develop the conceptual framework within which this study takes place. It deals with the identity of possible right-holders, or with the question: who is capable of possessing rights? To this question there are two leading answers. One is to define a possessor of rights in individual terms. I use the term "agent-relative" to identify this approach, whose main idea is to ascribe rights to persons according to some individual characteristics, that mainly relate to the perceptual, cognitive or mental abilities of the agents. As a representative theory of this approach I choose Alan Gewirth's theory of rights, as introduced in his book *Reason and Morality* (1978). This theory concentrates on the moral agent, and ascribes rights to an agent because of her following the Principle Of Generic Consistency (PGC). According to Gewirth, being a purposive-prospective (that is, "rational") agent entitles a person to possess the generic features of action: freedom and welfare (which are necessary for the definition of an event as an action). When such an agent also acts in accordance with the PGC, she is entitled to possess rights. Since the rights of a person are based on her mental capacities (and more specifically on her following the PGC), she possesses them regardless of her social status or social role.

The other leading answer that is discussed in the second chapter, considers moral agents as members in the moral community. I use the term "communitarian" for describing such theories, and choose A.I. Melden's theory, as this was introduced in his book *Rights and Persons* (1977), as a representative theory. In this theory, those who share a certain set of moral and normative conventions, principles and rules, are considered as members in the same moral community. This status bestows upon them certain rights, but requires their fulfilling of some duties and obligations that they bear as members. Within the community there must be sincere mutuality and reciprocity between the members, in order to enable all of them to exercise and capitalize on their rights. However, this makes the moral status of the members, as possessors of rights, conditional to their fulfillment of their commitments and obligations towards the community within which they "transact", that is, actively pursue their rights and duties.

My preference in the second chapter is for the communitarian approach, mainly because it gives a better guarantee for the fulfillment of rights, by those called upon to respect them. In my view, the community is necessary in order to ensure its members the ability of exercising their rights, and in this sense it functions as a guarantor of these rights. This function is crucial especially with regard to human and welfare rights, which are my main interest. These rights are usually addressed to the community or the state. Prior to the existence of the community, these rights have no respondent, and hence cannot be exercised by their possessors. Additional confirmation for the significance of the community to welfare and economic rights is to be found in Gewirth's more recent book: *The Community of Rights* (1996). Even Alan Gewirth, whose basic position is Kantian (and this makes his theory an outstanding representative of agent relative theories), acknowledges the significance of the community for the welfare of human beings. In this book he considers "The Community of Rights" as:

> "A society whose government actively seeks to help fulfill the needs of its members, especially those who are most vulnerable, for the freedom and well-being that are the necessary goods for human agency, when persons can not attain this fulfillment by their own efforts".[8]

However, in order to identify who can have an "entry-ticket" to the community, I use the terminology that is used in agent-relative theories. I determine some individual or subjective requirements, that function as the criteria for assessing the extent of agency to which the agent can attain, when entering the community. To these criteria I add some communitarian requirements for moral agency, which together with the subjective requirements, create the status of a moral agent who can possess rights. The extent, to which a member is entitled to possess rights, depends on the extent to which this member actually fulfills both kinds of requirements. In essence, this is an expansion of Gewirth's Principle of Proportionality, which originally referred only to the subjective requirements. Here, this principle is used also for the communitarian requirements, which can change the moral status of the member, when they are not sufficiently fulfilled.

The main idea of my concept of possessing rights is that the actual measure of their possession by the moral agent, as a member of the community, should be conditional and proportionate to the actual fulfillment of each requirement (individual or communitarian) by this possessor. Whenever there is an incompatibility between a member's entitlement to have a certain measure of rights, and the actual measure of possession, the community has to rectify this by matching the correct measure of rights to the member's entitlement. When a member possesses fewer rights than she deserves, the community must bestow upon her the missing rights. On the other hand, when she possesses more rights than her measure of fulfillment of the requirements for having these rights entitles her to possess, the community has to take away the excessive rights from this member. This matter is the topic of the third chapter.

In the third chapter I present my view concerning the conditions and circumstances within which rights do not apply, or should be withdrawn. This chapter continues the line of argument of the previous chapters, and considers the validity of a person's claims (that is, regarding her rights), as resulting from the acknowledgement of these claims by the community. This acknowledgement is given according to the fulfillment of the necessary conditions that were defined as bestowing these rights. The extent to which these conditions are fulfilled, determines the extent to which the community allows the possessor to have her moral status. In this chapter I argue, that since the possession of rights results from interrelations between members of the community under certain conditions and circumstances, changes in these relations or circumstances affect the moral status of the possessors, and accordingly, affect their possession of rights.

The components of a fully specified right, namely the conditions of possession and engagement, its weight, addressee and range, create both the conditions where this right can be exercised, and where this right does not apply. When the community decides that one or more of these conditions are not sufficiently satisfied, the possessor's entitlement to keep his right is reduced, and accordingly the range, scope or power of this right may be reduced or canceled. If so, it is the community's obligation to withdraw the excessive part of the exercising of this right, or even to completely withdraw the right. This may be clear and easy to implement with regard to legal rights, whose validity results from clearly stated rules. However, when dealing with moral rights, whose validity results from principles, the assessment of both, the extent to which the above conditions are fulfilled, and the appropriate measure of rights that should be conferred or withdrawn, will always be approximate and uncertain. This fact entails that the community should be very careful and cautious, when deciding on the withdrawal of moral or human rights.

The next two chapters (chapters 4 and 5) are used as test cases for my position regarding the withdrawal of rights. In these chapters I try to implement the guidelines for the withdrawal of rights in specific issues. I deal with these issues from a right-based point of view, but try to show how my position relates to the main approaches to these issues, which have been discussed in the literature. This requires of me that I offer an exposition of these existing approaches at least as background for my discussion, at the beginning of each of these chapters.

The fourth chapter of this study deals with the most frequent case of the withdrawal of rights, which is the case of punishment. I offer an exposition of the two leading approaches to the matter of punishment: the forward-looking, that is, mainly based on utilitarian considerations, and the backward-looking, which is based on retribution. I argue that the justification of punishment is best considered at two levels. The first of these is the justification of the very *practice* or *institution* of punishment, which deals with the question, why do we punish at all. The second is the matter of the justification of a *specific case* within this practice, and thus answers the question, why do we punish a specific offender. The forward-looking approach suggests a reasonable answer to the first question, while the backward-looking approach provides a better answer to the second question. So, it becomes apparent that in order to justify punishment in general and in particular cases of punishment, we have to provide a justification that includes both forward and backward-looking considerations.

This method of dealing with punishment leads me to prefer an approach that has been called "fair-play retributivist" or "right retributivist". According to this approach, there must be an equal share of burdens among the members of the moral community, and every participant has to respect his obligations as a member. When an offender commits a crime, he disturbs the balance between the obligations and rights among the community, inasmuch as he enjoys the benefits of the social cooperation without shouldering its burdens. Hence, he enjoys rights that he should not have, and these rights should be withdrawn from him. This way of justifying punishment answers the questions why there is a duty to punish, and why this duty is imposed upon the community. The community, as the authority that allocates and controls the balance of rights and duties among its members, has to guarantee the proper use of rights, and the sufficient fulfillment of obligations within the community. In cases of distortion in the use of rights or in fulfilling duties, it has to reassess the possession of rights by those who cause this distortion, and confer rights according to the possessors' new entitlement.

This method of justification is also used for the case of capital punishment, which is also discussed in the fourth chapter. I suggest certain conditions and circumstances within which this punishment may be considered as legitimate. After presenting the main arguments used by Abolitionists, who oppose this penalty, and Retentionists, who support it, I offer my view regarding capital punishment. I maintain that this penalty may be imposed for cruel and vicious crimes that are committed by culprits who were sentenced to life imprisonment, prior to the crime for which they are sentenced now. This is because we want to preserve a balance between the severity of the crime and the gravity of the punishment. Imposing another life imprisonment for the additional crime, will be, in fact, abstaining from punishing the offender, because he then enjoys the same rights that were possessed by him before the additional crime. This would be a distortion of the principle that requires a correlation between the rights that a person is entitled to possess, and the rights that this person actually possesses. This would also be unfair towards the other prisoners who are sentenced to life-imprisonment but did not commit another crime. The "fair play retributive" or "right retributive" approach, which imposes upon the community a duty to punish offenders, demands that the community will not ignore the additional crime, and thus must withdraw the only right that is yet possessed by the offender. Of course, there must be some constraints that arise from the irreversibility of capital punishment, such as the demand for a unanimous decision among judges and jury, and the possibility of appealing to a higher instance before the execution. In my opinion, the death penalty may, in certain circumstances, be considered legitimate.

The last part of the fourth chapter deals with social (as opposed to legal) withdrawal of rights. In this part I examine the phenomenon of "outing" (i.e. the exposure of the sexual orientation of homosexuals and lesbians) and its ethical aspects, from a right-based point of view. I argue there, that a person's right to privacy with regard to his sexual orientation should be respected even when this person is a public figure. However, when this person attempts to insult, hurt or strike at homosexuals or at their rights, while he is himself a homosexual, his "outing" is justifiable. This is based on the fair play retributive attitude towards the withdrawal of rights. A person, who wishes to injure or violate the rights of others, should suffer by being deprived of some of his rights. In a case where the appropriate way to punish him is by exposing him to the dangers and threats from which other homosexuals suffer, his homosexuality should be disclosed.

The fifth chapter deals with cases where rights are denied to possible or future right-holders, who are not yet considered as full-fledged members of the moral community. These possible right-holders do not sufficiently fulfill the subjective requirements for agency, and hence they can be considered only as partial members of the community. In other words, their "entry ticket" to the moral community is only partly valid. The extent to which they possess the subjective requirements for agency, entitles them to possess some, but not all, of the rights that full-fledged agents enjoy. Other rights are denied to them, permanently or temporarily, in order to adjust their actual possession of rights to their correct level of agency.

The fifth chapter examines three issues. The first is children's rights. These rights should be limited to the extent to which the children can be considered as responsible, or the extent to which they possess the subjective requirements for agency. This means that during their maturation, children gradually acquire more rights and liberties, according to their moral and mental development. When they are fully mature they enjoy the status of full members of the moral community, and should enjoy all the rights that such a status entitles.

The second issue that is discussed in the fifth chapter is the rights of fetuses, in the context of the morality of abortion. The discussion of this issue requires the discussion of two different aspects. The first is the alleged blow at the sanctity of human life, and this matter is discussed only in brief. The second is the ostensible violation of the fetus' right to well-being. I deal with this issue as a conflict between the mother's rights to freedom, well-being, autonomy and self-determination, and the fetus' right to existence and well-being. However, this conflict is usually of a forced-choice kind, where the rights of the two parties cannot coexist, and the fulfillment of one of them abolishes the right of the other. The community, as the respondent of these rights cannot provide for the fulfillment of both, and hence has to decide in general, and perhaps also in specific cases, which right overrides the other. I argue that this conflict should be resolved according to the possessor's moral status within the community. Accordingly, since the mother is an actual (and a full-fledged) member of the moral community, while the fetus is only a future member (and hence is considered as placed in a lower moral status), the mother's rights in general override those of the fetus, and abortion is legitimate. In cases where there is a possibility of responding to both claims and saving the fetus' life (cases of late abortion which is, in fact, early delivery), the community has to make as many efforts as it can to respect the fetus' rights and give it life.

The third issue discussed in the fifth chapter is that of the rights of mentally retarded persons. The limitation of their liberty rights is based on a justification, which is similar to the limitation of children's rights, namely, the ascription of only limited responsibility and autonomy to mentally retarded persons. This explains why we deny them some liberty rights. However, while children's rights are usually denied only temporarily, the rights of mentally retarded persons are usually denied permanently. This difference requires that we should be much more careful with regard to the denial of the rights of mentally retarded persons. I discuss a few cases where such rights are in doubt. The first one concerns their right to consent or refuse to medical treatment, where I argue that the only case where this right should be withdrawn from them is when the treatment is necessary for saving their lives. The next issue that is questioned is their reproduction rights. This issue is divided into two questions. One is whether they have a right to parenthood, in the sense of giving birth to babies. My answer to this question is strictly positive. This means that I oppose compulsory castration or sterilization, and even the compulsory use of contraceptives. The second question, whether mentally retarded people who have children have a right to bring them up by themselves, is much more complicated, because a new factor appears: the right of the newborn babies. My answer to this question is less decisive. I argue that when all possible assistance of the community will not be sufficient to guarantee the children's decent growth and development, the community should consider removing the children from their parents' guardianship. I think that this should be the last resort to be considered, in order to protect the children's right to a secure future, as Joel Feinberg calls this basic right, because this act brutally strikes a blow at the parents' rights. However, in serious or acute cases of mentally retarded parents, this has to be done, in order to guarantee the children's welfare, well-being and even safety and security.

As the reader will probably notice, this study has been deeply affected by Alan Gewirth's theory, which inspired me to start dealing with rights in the first place. I use many of his ideas, even though not always in a way that he would agree with. This mainly refers to the implementation of his terminology and his principle of proportionality in a basically communitarian right-based theory, which he principally rejects. However, even though his epistemological project that establishes moral agency, and hence the possession of rights on the basis of consistency is logically valid, I choose not to content myself with only the subjective requirement of rationality, in order to possess rights.

Gewirth argues that since the agent's right-claim is based on his own agency needs, it is "prior to and independent of a community or social rules, except in a certain minimal sense".[9] He assumes that the addressees of a person's claim can understand this claim and comply with it, and this understanding and ability do not involve social rules or institutions, that would incorporate or sanction these claims. I will not enter here too deeply into the debate with MacIntyre, Frankena, Ross and others[10] whether a claim-right can *exist* prior to the existence of a community or not. Instead, I will deal with a related question, whether we can *ensure* or *guarantee* the fulfillment of a right, prior to the existence of the community. In this matter, I think that the respondents' understanding is not sufficient for their acceptance of the burdens to fulfill their duty. I think that a person's understanding of himself as being theoretically *obligated* by a duty, is different from his readiness to see himself as genuinely *bound* by the duty.

The question of whether a person's innate desire to be consistent obliges her to do what she morally ought to, depends on our meaning and understanding of the terms "consistency" and "ought". However, in the sort of the pre-communal understanding to which Gewirth presumably refers, it is the person's free choice to comply with her obligations to others, or to abstain from doing so. A similar argument has been raised by Jacob Joshua Ross who claims that from the fact that a person's action logically requires that she will have generic rights, it does not follow that she has a moral right to demand the fulfillment of her needs. This is because rights are not derived from logic, but from the moral relations accepted by the community. Ross regards Gewirth's assumption that if a person logically has to have something, then she also has a moral right to demand this thing, as merely an example of what Joel Feinberg calls "rights in the manifesto sense". These are valid claims to something, but as yet constitute no claim against any respondent whose duty it is to provide for these claims.[11] I think that in order to make such rights concrete or applicable, we need the community to function as their guarantor or bailor. If the community recognizes them as valid claims, it has to either nominate their respondents and make sure that they fulfill their duties, or to be itself the respondent who is duty-bound to fulfill these rights. This is, in fact, the case for moral rights, human rights, welfare rights and economic rights; without the existence of the community, these rights do not have a respondent. If we want these rights to be concrete or "real", we must have the community's acknowledgement of them as valid claims. Thus the desire to ensure the actual fulfillment of rights, and to guarantee that their possessors will be able to exercise and capitalize on them, leads me to the communitarian approach, where the community exists even prior to the possession of any right. When the community acknowledges the validity of human rights or welfare rights, it simultaneously acknowledges that these rights impose duties on the community itself. When we deal with claim-rights whose respondent is not the community, and their respondent denies her correlative duty, the community has to intervene in order to force her, either by law or by public opinion, to fulfill her obligation as a respondent. The existence of a framework, which has the authority to control the transactions that take place within it, and to realize rights so as to enforce the fulfillment of duties, makes the ability to exercise rights more substantial.

However, this authority of the community to intervene in the members' rights and obligations is crucial to my issue, which is precisely the withdrawal of rights. For this I am inevitably drawn into the communitarian approach, since I have to identify the framework or institution, which is capable of withdrawing rights from individuals. The desire to authorize the community to withdraw rights requires that I recognize it as the framework that exclusively allocates rights and duties. Without its existence, I might have the legitimacy to withdraw rights, but will not have the actual possibility of doing so. Thus, the existence of the community not only ensures the possibility of exercising rights, but also makes sure that the inappropriate use of rights will not be allowed, or will even be prevented.

In any event, despite this disagreement, I use Gewirth's theory as the foundation of my view, and consider it as very inspiring and fruitful. I hope that I have not made crucial distortions in my use of this theory, by providing it with a communitarian basis. I think that the integration of the agent-relative and the communitarian approaches enables us to deal both with the possession and the withdrawal of rights in a more effective way. A significant step in this direction has already been taken by Gewirth himself in his recent book. However, my own espousal of the communitarian basis seems to me far more substantial than what is apparently implied by Gewirth himself. I maintain that the whole discussion of rights should relate to the people's ability to enjoy them, and this definitely involves the matter of applicability and communal acceptance. I hope this study contributes something not only to rights-talk, but also to the internalizing of the idea of rights, as a final court of appeal in ordering conflicting claims between moral agents. It is my belief that the recognition of the significance of rights in social and moral life, will encourage human-rights activists to struggle both for the possession of rights, as well as for the correct and appropriate use of rights, including also the right to withdraw them when this is justified.

CHAPTER 1

THE CONCEPT OF RIGHTS

The most decisive issue in formulating a theory of rights (or a theory of the withdrawal of rights) deals with the question: "What can be conceived as rights?" This question relates to the epistemological, ontological and normative status of rights. The present study concerns itself mainly with the social function of rights: it therefore skirts epistemological and ontological matters, and concentrates on the ethical and political status of rights. Accordingly, I do not address the question regarding what kinds of entities rights are. At most I relate to the questions of how do we recognize rights, their content and validity.

However, any discussion regarding the content, validity, scope or practice of rights has its meaning within a certain "semantic realm"[12]. This realm is attached to a normative system, which includes its fundamental notions, rules, common beliefs and conventions. Judith Jarvis Thomson describes this metaphorically by:

> "Thinking of morality as a continent and of rights as a territory or realm somewhere in it; understanding what is within the realm of rights requires getting a sense of where in the continent it lies".[13]

By saying this she means that:

> "The concept of a right is only one among many moral concepts, and understanding what it is to have a right requires us to get a sense of how that concept is related to the others".[14]

This idea is widely accepted in different variations, and it became a reference point in most of the arguments in and around rights-talk. Ronald Dworkin, for example, assumes that a theory of rights has to be related to other elements of political theory[15], and expresses the commonly held axiom regarding the dependence of rights on the political, social and moral basis that constitute the meaning and validity of rights. This attitude brings the discussion about rights to the realm of norms[16], goals, aims and, essentially, powers and liberties – which are the main elements of human interrelations and conflicts.

Having a right gives its owner some kind of what Thomson denominates as “valuable moral status”[17], or what Melden calls the “normative status a human being has with respect to others”.[18] The content and category of that status are, however, determined by an overall legal, moral and political world-view. This view locates the right in the appropriate context of social life, as a conclusion of some fundamental decisions about the nature of rights. Among these decisions are our resolutions to questions about the connections between rights and interests, the correlation between rights and duties, and briefly, what do we mean by a right. Additional decisions we should make are whether rights are (affirmative) claims, entitlements, side constraints upon others’ actions, “trumps”, established ways of acting, etc.

Another decision to be made is this: at what level of urgency should we begin to consider the need to fulfill rights? On the lowest level, rights can be considered as important interests that get more weight than interests that are not protected by rights. Here, rights are considered as special interests whose fulfillment gets high priority. A more stringent level gives interests protected by rights, a “lexical priority” over other interests (which means that they have to be fully satisfied before other interests are taken into consideration). At this level, interests, which are protected by rights, have to be taken more seriously, and be fully fulfilled before we turn to the fulfilling of other social or moral obligations or requirements. The third and highest level of obligation at which we can consider the fulfillment of rights, sets up rights as an obligatory basis for strict constraining requirements on others’ actions[19] or even a basis for limiting the freedom of others.[20] At this level, rights can also impose limitations on the actions of others, or even impose requirements that others should abstain from certain actions. However, there is another way to evaluate rights, without a direct reference to interests. From this aspect of evaluation we have to decide whether we consider rights as “trumps”, in Dworkin’s terminology, and hence function as what Rawls defines as a “final court of appeal for ordering the conflicting claims of moral persons”.[21] Such an attitude toward rights sometimes requires us not only to impose constraints on others, but also to take concrete actions to fulfill the rights. This concept of rights involves, at least, “some sort of normative direction on the behavior of others”, as Rex Martin carefully formulates this demand.[22] Such an understanding of rights means that the acknowledgement of one’s claim as a right includes, inter alia, the assurance that the relevant respondent will carry out the requirements that are demanded by that right. Otherwise the fulfillment of the above right may be subject to the respondent’s good will or benevolence. At this level, possessing a right also includes having all the necessary conditions and means to capitalize on that right. It means that the owner of a right has a real capability of exercising his right. Henry Shue, who holds such a position, maintains that: "If everyone has a right to y, and the enjoyment of x is necessary for the enjoyment of y, than everyone has a right to x".[23] The acceptance of such a sense of rights, urges the participant of rights-talk to accurately define each element and component of the concept of a right, and to create a scheme in which having a right means having some moral status or moral assets.

In the coming pages I map the semantic realm in which my discussion takes place, and present my concept of a right. In brief, I give reasons for my preference for considering rights as valid claims that exist within a normative order and are justified within a system of rules or principles. I also regard them as interest-related and as including their "conditions of engagement", that is, having a right includes having all that is necessary to exercise it.

1.1 SOME AGREEMENTS ABOUT RIGHTS

In the broadest sense, rights can be conceived in accordance with Tibor Machan's formulation: "*social conditions that ought to be maintained,* [or] moral principles pertaining to aspects of social life"[24]. These expressions capture the implication that rights are a set of normative rules or demands that must be retained in order to sustain the social framework and to make social interactions possible. Besides such a general description, there are many details that can be accepted as common characteristics of rights, as discussed in different sorts of rights-talk.

The basic convention about rights is that they "belong within normative orders"[25], or have a substantial meaning within common and acknowledged normative frameworks. This gives rights not only validity, but also an obligatory status. Without the existence of a normative system, there cannot be any power, force or authority to rights or to right-holders. (In chapter 2, I discuss the significance of rules and principles to the existence and validity of rights). Their colleagues can simply disregard or ignore the rights or the duties that are imposed by these rights. The normative order within which rights are claimed, ensures the possessor of a right that her claim is not only recognized but also respected. The postulate of having a normative system as a preliminary demand is parallel to the claim that rights need a background (and an endorsement) to which they refer, and from which they get their meaning and validity (the "realm of rights"). At the theoretical level this postulate is the basis of rights-talk, but at the practical level, the normative system is equivalent to the alignment of moral and political beliefs shared by all the participants of the social framework.

Another common feature of rights is that they belong to individuals, and this, according to Raz[26], can also include an "artificial person" or "whatever counts as an individual within a given normative order (human being, company, trade union, club, football team, etc.)",[27] as Neil MacCormick says. Although there is an accepted sense, according to which we give priority to individual rights over corporation rights[28], it is agreed that corporations can and does have rights.

It is significant that although the ascription of rights to their possessors depends on universal rules and principles, it varies with particular individuals.[29] This means that one holds a right because one has the properties defined as bestowing a certain right. The principles define a state of affairs whose occurrence bequeaths a right to whoever suits that state of affairs, or the description that is acknowledged as sufficient to bestow a right.

The most obvious characteristic of rights (that is sometimes neglected in the discussions, mostly because it is so evident) is that rights apply to things that are valuable to their possessors. Someone who has a right to something must value this thing as good or essential to him in normal conditions or, at least, that this thing is considered as such in the society where he lives. In some theories of rights (e.g., that of Raz) rights are derived from interests, and this character is an essential part of the definition of rights in many theories. Such an attitude towards rights avoids the dispute as to whether individuals have rights to evil things, such as becoming slaves, for example.[30] The general consensus (and I am part of this consensus) is that rights are part of one's welfare, benefit, or well-being, and not of one's affliction.

1.2 THE MORAL STATUS OF RIGHTS

1.2.1 Rights As Claims

The most familiar description of the moral status of a right is that of "a claim" or, in Hohfeldian terms "an affirmative claim"[31] which Hohfeld considers as the correlative of a "duty". The basic structure of a claim right (and sometimes I simply use the term "a claim") is the following:

"A has a right to X against B by virtue of Y".[32]

This structure includes five variables:

First, the person who has the right, or "the owner" of the right (A). He is the *subject* of the right.[33]

Second, the *nature* of the right. This includes the modality, stringency and the meaning of the statement that someone has a right. This component defines what we mean by ascribing a right to its possessor (for example, we assume that she has an affirmative or valid), how we express this (by holding someone as being under a correlative duty, etc.), and to what extent we assume that this right competes with other moral considerations.

Third, the *object* of the right – what is the right to (X).

Fourth, the *respondent* (or addressee) of the right – the person against whom the subject has a right. In other words, the one who is under a correlative duty (B).

Fifth, the *justifying basis* or *grounds* (in another version Gewirth uses the term *justifying reason*) of the right. This means that by virtue of which the right is had (Y).

Recognizing rights as claims has some repercussions. First, is the creation of the correlation between rights and duties. Hohfeld calls rights, duties, immunities, etc. "relations". His example to explicate the correlation between a right and a duty, is:

> "If X has a right against Y that he shall stay off the former's land, the correlative (and equivalent) is that Y is under a duty toward X to stay off the place".[34]

A similar relation is manifested in the definition that Raz gives to a right-holder:

> "X has a right if and only if X can have rights, and, other things being equal, an aspect of X's well-being (his interest) is a sufficient reason for holding some other person(s) to be under a duty".[35]

Even though Hohfeld defends the logical correlativity of rights and duties, while Raz only conceives of them as reasons for duties, they both intend to say that when someone has a right, there is always someone else who is under a duty.

This linkage between rights and duties is essential to the concept of a right as a claim, in legal and formal systems. However, in ethics, understanding a moral right as "a kind of a claim", and a claim as "an assertion of a right", comes predominantly to "use the idea of a claim in informal elucidation to the idea of a right".[36] Joel Feinberg, who argues this, perceives claiming as an elaborate sort of rule-governed activity (this will lead, later on this chapter, to an amended identification of rights as "valid claims" – that are justified within a system of rules), which is public, familiar and open to our observation.[37] Having difficulties with defining a claim, Feinberg explains instead what it means: "to make a claim". He lays stress on the performative sense of "to make a claim" and tries to clarify his position through this sense.

Feinberg says that making a claim is in fact, demanding something as due by virtue of a supposed right. In other words, making a claim is applying for what is recognized as one's due – because one satisfies the conditions specified by a rule for the ownership of what one demands. It is worth mentioning that making a claim can only be done by the person who has the right or has qualified for it, or as Feinberg expresses this: "*Having a claim consists in being in a position to claim, that is, to make claim to,* or *claim that*".[38] Being in a position to claim does not entail that the owner of a claim is actually claiming, but only that she has the title that makes the claim valid. She does not even need to be aware of being in a position to claim, or she may be unwilling to exploit that position. Being in a position to claim – namely having a valid claim – makes one an owner of a right.

1.2.2 Valid And Justified Claims

Among many possible ways to connect rights and claims, the most frequent ones are either to consider rights as justified or justifiable claims, or to consider them as valid claims. Following Feinberg, I use the latter description for reasons I will explain. Feinberg refers to validity as a certain kind of justification – namely within a system of rules.[39] He regards a person as having a right, when recognition of his claim (as valid) is called for: a legal right – by the governing legal rules; a moral right – by the principles of enlightened conscience.

A similar position is held by Eugene Kamenka who considers rights as:

> "Claims that have achieved a special kind of endorsement or success: legal rights by a legal system; human rights by widespread sentiment or an international order...Claims presented as rights are claims that are often, perhaps usually, presented as having a special kind of importance, urgency, universality, or endorsement that makes them more than disparate or simply subjective demands".[40]

Those who equate rights with justified or justifiable claims assert that the justification of claims is what turns them into rights. They distinguish claims from mere demands by the legitimate grounds that the claimant needs to have, for having her right.[41] Most of them, when specifying the kind of justification, use the concept of a system of rules in one way or another. For them, rights exist only when there are rules and principles that specify the conditions according to which rights are given (to those who satisfy these conditions).[42] In all these ways of justification, the necessity of a system of rules (either rules or principles)[43] that turns claims into rights, limits the range of rights to what Feinberg entitles "valid claims". Even Neil MacCormick, who speaks explicitly about having rights as having "justified claims", starts his argument by proclaiming that "*rights belong within normative orders*"[44]. He argues that the normative order assures the right-holder that her claim is recognized and respected. This, virtually, can be regarded as making her claim valid, despite the fact that MacCormick does not use the term "validity" in his argument. Concluding that rights are valid claims binds us to assume an intimate linkage between norms and rights. It is not necessary to identify rights with a special kind of norms (as Robert Alexy, for example, does), but, at least, it presupposes the existence of some normative system.[45]

Before summing up the discussion about the relations between rights and claims, I want to mention a similar but slightly different position that is held by George Rainbolt. He conceives rights as "normative constraints on others". By saying "constraints" he refers to "something that restricts or limits a person's action".[46] Rainbolt argues that among all the Hohfeldian relations, there are only two that impose constraints on others, and these two are Hohfeld's "Claims" and "Immunities". He concludes this from the analysis of their correlatives: "Duties" and "Disabilities" that are both normative constraints (on those to whom they apply). The acceptance of this position leads him to the conclusion that the correlatives of "Duties" and "Disabilities", namely "Claims" and "Immunities", entail normative constraints on others.[47] Even though Rainbolt's idea sounds attractive at first sight, I prefer to maintain the standard position that identifies rights as valid claims. The main reason for this is that despite the complexity of the correlation theory (that Rainbolt points out clearly), the correlation between rights and duties has a prominent function. It not only entails normative constraints on others, but also imposes duties that sometimes force the others to affirmative acts. Being bound by duties involves more commitment than mere constraints, on the addressees of the rights. The difference between the two options will become clear, when I discuss specific questions such as whether possessing rights includes also having the conditions of engagement of these rights. Another related question is whether having rights entails the possession of the necessary conditions to enjoy these rights. The conclusion that rights are valid claims leads to positive answers to these two questions, and imposes on the addressees of rights the duties to provide all the facilities for capitalizing on the rights.

1.3 THE MEANING OF HAVING RIGHTS

Rights usually determine the conditions under which one is considered as a "right-holder". James Nickel calls them "conditions of possession", and says that they fix the identity of the person who acquires the moral status that is given by the right. Since the second chapter of this study deals with this topic, I just mention it here, without discussing it in detail. A more significant component of a right for the discussion here is what Nickel calls "conditions of engagement". These conditions determine: "when does the right apply and what (if anything) has to be done to bring it into play?"[48]. In other words, we can describe the conditions of engagement as the circumstances under which we can put the rights into practice or implement it. Those who use a more detailed taxonomy distinguish between some other notions, which apply to the use and the practice of rights. For them "to exercise" is simply to invoke the right, without dealing with the question whether anything has been achieved by doing so. A successful use of a right – meaning effectively exercising (or using) the right (when the right-holder gets what she deserves to), is "to capitalize" this right.[49]

My view is that having a right must incorporate one's ability not only to exercise it, but also one's ability to capitalize on it. The main justification for this view is that there is equivalence between all the conditions that are recognized as essential to the fulfillment of a right. Even those who insist that rights are distinct from their conditions of engagement, agree that one's right to X entails that others will not prevent one from getting X (without depriving one of one's right to X). That means that withholding X from a person violates one's right, sometimes to the extent of prevention or even denial of this right. This leads to the conclusion that recognition of one's right to X, entails the refrainment of others from denying one's right to X. I consider this refrainment a necessary condition to the existence of one's right to X, as something recognized and acknowledged by the community. I emphasize the element of recognition, because I consider it as central to the conception of the right of a human being, as a normative status that one has with respect to others[50]. If it is legitimate to see the necessary condition of refrainment as an integral part of the right, it is the same with the other necessary conditions. Denying them negates the ability to exercise the right, and, in fact, its actual existence. The idea here is that rights constitute a moral status that needs to be concrete and not abstract.

A very similar position is held by Rex Martin, and presenting his view may clarify the significance I ascribe to the social acknowledgement of a right to its applicability. Martin thinks that a practice can be said to be a right insofar as it is backed up – that is, endorsed and accredited – by social recognition. He suggests that: "this factor of social recognition or ratification is actually a constituent of rights – that is, our characterization of something as a right".[51] Martin assumes, at least in his discussion of legal rights, that any recognized – affirmed and acknowledged – right, also consists in practices of governmental promotion and protection. This additional feature of promotion and maintenance, must supplement that of recognition in order to have more than a nominal right. This feature, according to Martin, is not merely another characteristic of a legal right, but an ingredient in the very notion of such a right, excepting those rights that are merely nominal.[52] The promotion and maintenance of rights are presupposed when a right is recognized as such, and this makes this right applicable and concrete. The presupposition of the promotion and maintenance of a right in order to make it concrete and not merely nominal in Martin's theory, is equivalent to my presumption of Nickel's "conditions of engagement" as an integral part of the acknowledgement of a right, and to Henry Shue's claim that the right to X includes the right to what is necessary for the enjoyment of it.

This attitude toward rights confirms that with respect to some kinds of rights – especially welfare, special and positive rights – the conditions of engagement of these rights are essential to their existence. My special interest in welfare and human rights as urgent interests of people, leads me to look for a theory in which rights are justified on the basis of protecting and promoting interests of individuals. Such a theory is usually classified as "right-based". [53] In the next paragraphs I will try to clarify the linkage between rights and interests.

1.3.1 Rights And Interests

Jeremy Waldron refers to three central rights that can be grounded on interests. In the most straightforward model, says Waldron, rights are important interests that get more weight than other interests (according to utilitarian or other welfarist calculations). They can be overridden for utility considerations. In the second model, interests that are protected by rights have "lexical priority" over other interests – meaning that they have to be fully fulfilled and promoted, before other interests are even considered. The utility considerations are relevant here only when rights conflict *inter se.*[54]

These levels cannot support the view that rights are claims. For this we need the third model of justifying rights on the basis of interests. In this model, rights can be used as justifying grounds for limiting the freedom of other persons. And for making the fulfillment of the interests more real, this limitation is understood more extensively in such a way that it can even impose duties on the respondents of the rights, which are based on these interests.

One of the most familiar definitions, which directly connects between rights and interests, is one mentioned earlier, that of Joseph Raz, who conceives of rights as grounds for duties. According to this definition, rights are ground requirements for actions due to the interests of other beings. The fact that a right is considered sufficient grounds for holding someone bound to a duty, gives it a significant (and John Rawls thinks this even an ultimate[55]) role in settling conflicting demands of individuals or institutions. The relevant considerations to settle these conflicts are the urgency and necessity of the interests, which are claimed as rights, to their possessors.

Raz's position indicates his preference of the concept of rights as claims rather than that of entitlements. Insofar as we deal with welfare rights, it becomes crucial to have a specific addressee of a right, in order to be able to protect or promote the interests of right-holders. When conflicts concerning interests of individuals (or institutions) arise, rights may become meaningless unless there is someone to claim against, or from whom to demand the realization of the interests, which are protected by rights. The significance of claiming, especially in welfare rights, results from the fact that these rights are of the kind that D.D. Raphael entitles "rights of recipience". The meaning of such rights is first and foremost "rights against" – in the sense of the existence of duties on the part of the addressees of these rights (as it is in Hohfeld's correlation theory).[56] Welfare rights also include what Alan Gewirth calls "action-related goods".[57] Here we have something that should be received by the right-holder, and given by the addressee. Otherwise capitalizing on welfare rights becomes impossible.

When Hart insists that rights are conceived of as *possessed* or *owned by* or *belonging to* individuals, he considers rights as a kind of moral property of individuals, to which they are entitled as individuals.[58] His view transforms the moral status of a right into the concept of a property. This property is truly formed by moral rules, and in that sense it is recognized and respected as owned by everyone. However, as we have seen before in Martin's theory, respect (or recognition) alone does not yet entail any obligation or commitment to provide anything to the possessor. Property should only be respected by others, but nothing else. Interests establish a different kind of obligation. They regard the possession of rights as having a moral status that should not only be respected, but also something that should be fulfilled. The foundation of rights on interests gives them an obligatory moral status, rather than demonstrating them as a property. The need to fulfill the interests holds the addressee as an integral component of the moral relations created by the rights.

The position that argues that rights must be interest-related claims stands at the foundation of most of the theories that demand welfare rights. In such theories (i.e., Dworkin's "trump" theory), the protection of rights (especially of welfare rights) becomes crucial when individual interests oppose a collective interest. In such a clash the ability to find a solution is increased, when both sides seek to ground their claims on the same kind of justification. The evaluation of the weight that should be given to each conflicting claim turns out to be the estimation of the significance and urgency of the fulfillment of the interests of each side, considering the cost of it to each side.

In brief, the idea of rights as derived from interests, places welfare and human rights – as high priority interests – in the center of the discussions within rights-talk. Accordingly, all the "positive" rights (that require some kind of actions from the addressees) get their strength more effectively within it. The fact that the concept of rights as affirmative claims establishes definite moral relations between the possessor and the addressee also helps to determine the expiry conditions of these relations. For this, the concept of rights as claims has a significant role in the withdrawal of rights.

I assert that the concepts of rights I defend – as claims, as interest-related and as including their conditions of engagement – are linked. These three concepts reflect a social attitude that wishes to sustain people's well-being. In this view, the right to life, for example, is not merely the right not to be killed. It includes all the necessary conditions for living: food, shelter, health care, etc. The same is the case with other rights such as education or work. These are not merely rights to look for a job, or not to be prevented from seeking an education. The acknowledgement of these basic goods as rights entails the demand to provide employment and education, and to make them accessible to the right-holders. Otherwise these rights are considered as void. This explains the desire to regard rights as claims. Understanding them as affirmative claims (or as "rights against") defines the identity of those who are duty bound to support us to exercise these rights, or (in the rights mentioned above), to provide the means for capitalizing on these rights. The conclusion of the last paragraphs is that the concept of rights is tied to a set of social and political beliefs that, as will be discussed later, determine the normative and social commitments of the one who discusses rights in any context. Accordingly, the selection of positions and concepts to be discussed in this study, will be done in a way will be coherent with a comprehensive world-view, within which rights are bestowed or withdrawn.

1.4 CONDITIONS OF ABSENCE OF RIGHTS

Important components of any conceptual framework that accompany the classification of rights, are the terms that indicate their measure of applicability. In section 1.3 I mentioned Tara Smith's terminology for making use of rights. She distinguishes between "having", "exercising", "capitalizing" rights, etc. These terms indicate different levels of using or actualizing rights. Corresponding terms within "rights-talk" apply to their opposites – situations where rights do not hold or apply. Adopting Hohfeld's position that identifies rights with affirmative claims, I am committed to the correlative theory (despite its difficulties), and hence, obliged to use an adequate terminology, when turning to specify the terms in question. I found Alan Gewirth's terms suitable and relevant to my aims. According to Gewirth, a right *is fulfilled*, when its correlative duty has been carried out, and *infringed* when the correlative duty has not been carried out. One's right is fulfilled when the action required by the right is performed, or when the prohibited action is not performed. An infringement of a right can appear on various occasions. When a right is unjustifiably infringed, Gewirth calls it a *violated* right. When there is a sufficient justification for the infringement of a right (meaning that the right is justifiably infringed) this right is said to be *overridden*. When a right cannot be overridden at all, that is to say, its infringement can never be justified, this right is regarded as *absolute*.[59]

For Gewirth, the absoluteness of rights concerns criteria of justification. His view maintains that there are rights that are based on the supreme principle of morality, and hence absolute. Although I accept his terminology, I argue that there are no such rights, and this term only has theoretical status because it represents an empty group of rights. I deal with the main argument for this in the third chapter of this study. However, for the time being I just want to say that the sources of the difference between my view and Gewirth's, is that his theory is Kantian-oriented (as a conclusion of his PGC), while mine (following Melden) integrates communitarian elements into the discussion, that make the infringement of any right legitimate (of course, under the proper conditions and circumstances).

1.4.1 *Prima-Facie* Rights

The possibility of justifiable infringements of rights – that is to say, "overriding" them – leads us to the distinction between "absolute" and "prima facie" rights. This is one of the most widespread distinctions that are discussed, when dealing with the withdrawal or the waiving of rights. The origin of this line of discussion was W.D. Ross' idea of "prima facie" duties. That idea, jointly with the idea of the correlation between rights and duties, created the notion of "prima facie" rights. Although there are difficulties (and sometimes ambiguities) in the original notion of "prima facie" duties, it provides a very efficient way to clarify the idea of duties and rights that sometimes do not hold or apply.

The idea of absolute rights, according to Gewirth, refers to rights that cannot be justifiably infringed, and hence, must be fulfilled without any exceptions. Carl Wellman (following Joel Feinberg) perceives absolute rights as rights that hold in all possible circumstances (without exception). Such rights can never be overridden.[60] When we talk about rights that do not hold on certain occasions, we presuppose that these rights are not absolute, and that they are conditional.

When W.D. Ross speaks about duties, he denies the notion of "absolute" duties, because he thinks that any duty might be outweighed under exceptional circumstances. Therefore he speaks instead of "actual" duties, and distinguishes them from "prima facie" duties. The latter are duties that hold in ordinary circumstances – meaning that they are morally obligatory – unless there are special circumstances that override them. This is to say that these duties hold so long as they can be morally justified. When there are circumstances that make it justified to abstain from fulfilling these duties, they cease to obligate. The implication that Wellman draws from this is that an "actual" duty is one that it is not in fact overridden, even though it could be overridden.[61] Alternatively, Ross explains "prima facie" duties as "conditional duties", that hold so long as there are no other stringent considerations that make it morally better to refrain from these duties. Many objections have been argued against the consistency and efficiency of Ross' position. Even Ross himself admits that sometimes this distinction is somewhat misleading.[62] However, the idea of duties that can be outweighed under certain circumstances enables us to resolve conflicts between duties, by a calculation of the moral value of any particular selection. It also enables us to determine whether a certain duty is valid, holds or exists, on a particular occasion.

The distinction between "prima facie" and "actual" duties easily gave rise to the analogous distinction between "actual" and "prima facie" rights.

Similar to "actual" duties, which were understood as real and not only presumed or apparent, there are "actual" rights that are real and not merely alleged or apparent.[63] The analogy to "prima facie" duties, that is assumed by Wellman as grounds of what may well be duties, or "duty-imposing reasons", are "prima facie" rights. According to this analogy, rights are to be understood as grounds of rights, meaning reasons that, if not outweighed by other contrary reasons, confer rights. On this view, prima facie rights are reasons for rights (and maybe for other Hohfeldian positions), but not *conclusive* reasons. Wellman explains his view by giving an example that is taken from Aristotle. In this example, a captain of a boat throws people's goods out of his boat, because of a storm that might sink the boat. Wellman thinks that it is widely recognized that throwing people's goods overboard infringes their moral property rights; but the danger to the lives of both passengers and crew, justifies the overriding of these rights.[64] Wellman brings other examples to support his view that rights can be overridden not merely by other rights, but also by other moral considerations like (in the example given by Aristotle) necessities (whether private or public) or important interests.

Wellman emphasizes that the fact that rights can be overridden, does not mean that these rights are limited, or that their scope is limited so that the rights are inapplicable to the cases at issue. It does not also mean that exceptions are built into the definition or content of these rights. It means that there are some authoritative sources in certain cases, for considerations sufficient to override the rights that do apply in these cases. Wellman insists that to override a right is neither to nullify or extinguish it, nor to say that this right does not exist. It might even mean the contrary: that the reality of the right is presupposed, and this is what makes it necessary for the right to be overridden. If this right were not applicable, it would not be considered to exist, in the first place. Then we could not say, that although it was applicable we override it by considering necessities or other interests. When we override a certain right (as a reason for holding someone under a duty), we outweigh it in practice, for moral considerations that we find stronger than the interests that are protected by that particular right. When a right is overridden, it is so in some respect or with regard to some specified implication. But this right remains to be considered as a reason in other situations. This brings Wellman to think that the title "prima facie" for such a right is misleading, because it might seem to say that this right ceases to play a role when it is overridden. He suggests that the title "prima facie" would apply to the implications of the right, and indicates that when some considerations override a right, they simply outweigh the right as a reason (for others being under a duty), in the specified situation.[65]

Although Wellman's analysis prefers the idea of "prima facie" implications of rights, rather than that of "prima facie" rights, he illustrates the way in which rights that are conceived as valid under usual circumstances, lose their obligatory status in particular situations. They are overridden only in the particular case in which moral considerations outweigh them. The idea of "prima facie" rights, then, conforms more or less to Wellman's illustration of "prima facie" implications. This idea has been widely discussed and interpreted, and has also come under severe criticism. It is based on the concept that rights are not absolute, and can be justifiably infringed because of other moral considerations.

1.4.2 A Different Attitude Towards The Absence Of Rights

The idea of understanding rights as "prima facie" may be useful for solving conflicts between clashing interests or necessities. However, my aim in this study is to define the circumstances and conditions under which it is legitimate and justifiable to withdraw a person's rights, that is, to take back rights that are already possessed by their holder. For this purpose, the idea of classifying rights as "prima facie" will not fit, because my concern is for the cases in which the withdrawal of rights is due to the public identity of the right-holder. In order to make this possible, I prefer to say that the alleged right-holder lacks the necessary qualifications for the possession of that right, or that part of the components of her right are not sufficiently fulfilled. Using this argument properly, requires an appropriate definition of the identity of a potential right-holder, and of what is needed for becoming an actual right-holder. This entails the construction of a framework within which rights get their validity and moral status, and of the conditions under which they are conferred upon particular individuals. This is the content of the coming chapter.

1.5 SUMMARY

In this chapter I briefly sketch the semantic domain within which the present discussion takes place. The foundational presumption of the position I introduce is that rights exist solely within a normative system. This system establishes the validity, scope and power of rights within it, due to a comprehensive acknowledgement that was given to them, by all the participants in the social interaction. Among various ways in which the moral status of rights could be expressed, I preferred the understanding of rights as valid claims (in the sense of being justified within a system of rules), and by doing so I commit my position to the correlation theory between rights and duties.

Another conclusion of this chapter is, that rights and their conditions of possession and engagement are inseparable. That is to say that the necessary conditions that are needed for capitalizing on any right, are an integral part of the existence of the right, and without them this right is considered to be a nullity. This view is connected to another relevant aspect of rights that I represent. This is the understanding of rights as interest-related. The reason for this results mainly from the significance I ascribe to welfare rights, which otherwise, lose part of their strength and power of conviction. An indispensable implication of our concentrating on welfare rights is considering them as "rights of recipience". This is to say that having a right entails that other people will carry out actual actions in order to capitalize on this right.

In the coming chapter I deal with the identity of possible possessors of rights (or right-holders), in order to establish an appropriate background for the withdrawal of rights. As a preparation for this, I mentioned situations where rights lose their validity (for example, "prima facie" rights). My approach is to concentrate on the possessors of rights, and after defining their identity and the conditions of possession and engagement of the rights they presume to hold, I define the conditions under which their rights lose their validity. So, the coming chapter will deal with the identity of possible and actual right-holders.

CHAPTER 2

THE IDENTITY OF RIGHT-HOLDERS

In this chapter I review some of the familiar theories about the identity of possible right-holders. The main purpose of this is to examine the characterization of those who are presumed to have rights. A fundamental assumption of this discussion is that a presumed right usually includes its "conditions of possession". This means that each right defines the conditions under which one is considered to fit the description that makes him a right-holder. Being a right-holder means that one has a moral status bestowed by the right, because he meets the qualifications needed for holding that right. These qualifications are defined as an integral part of each particular right. If we examine Gewirth's analysis of the structure of a claim right, we can easily perceive this.

Gewirth analyzes the structure: **"A has a right to X against B by virtue of Y".** When he specifies the components of this structure he identifies A as the *subject* of the right, or the owner (or the possessor) of it. Gewirth defines Y as the *justifying reason* (or *ground*) of the right, i.e. that by virtue of which the right is had.[66] The justifying reason is supposed to determine the characteristics, so that the person who bears them, will be considered qualified to be the *subject* of that right.

However, this is only a formal analysis that does not, by itself, indicate the identity of the subject. For this we need a particular content for the right. We realize that the subject of the right must have certain reasons that bestow upon him his moral status, and that these reasons are included in the content of the right. Joseph Raz, among many others, formulated the definition of a right, which identifies a possible possessor of a right that suits his formulation. His definition has been much discussed, partly because of its innovative approach, but mainly because of its commitment to a welfarist conception of rights. According to Raz:

> "*Definition*: 'X has a right' if and only if X can have rights, and, other things being equal, an aspect of X's well-being (his interest) is a sufficient reason for holding some other person(s) to be under a duty.

> *Capacity for Possessing rights*: An individual is capable of having rights if and only if either his well-being is of ultimate value or he is an 'artificial person' (e.g. a corporation)".[67]

Raz's definition views a possessor of a right as an individual whose welfare has a moral value, and this value should be considered within the social framework. Such a view assumes some presuppositions regarding the persons who interact within the social scheme, which creates the moral value of one's interests. One's recognition as a right-holder identifies him as being in a position, where his interests are to be morally considered. Raz's definition refers to entities whose well-being can be considered of ultimate value (and we can roughly say that he refers to people and corporations). This question is different from the question regarding what a particular right-holder actually possesses. The answer to the latter question is to be found in the specific interest that is considered sufficient reason for holding the respondent as duty-bound (as in interest-related theories). The possessor has a claim against the addressee to act in a way that will fulfill his interest. The first question about the identity of a possible right-holder relates to the subject of a right, while the second question relates to the moral status held by the possessor, with regard to the object of the right.

When discussing legal rights, it is assumed that one's claims are valid only if one is considered a citizen, a resident, or at least a visitor of the political framework, within which the particular legal system exists. In this case, the legal system usually defines the range of its jurisdiction, and this includes the identity of the individuals who are supposed to obey its rules, and to be protected by them. Joel Feinberg, who considers rights as "valid claims", namely, justified within a system of rules, clarifies the point discussed here. His distinction between legal and moral rights concerns the kind of justification both kinds of rights should have. According to Feinberg, legal rights are valid when their official recognition is called for by the legal rules that apply. Moral rights are valid when the recognition of their claim is called for by moral principles, or what Feinberg calls "**the principles of an enlightened conscience**".[68] A similar position is held by Eugene Kamenka, who considers rights as claims that have achieved a special kind of endorsement or success. He argues that legal rights get their endorsement from the legal system, while human rights (which can be conceived, for our purpose here, as equivalent to moral rights) get their endorsement from the "**widespread sentiment of an international order**".[69] In both positions the justifying grounds of legal rights is the legal system (and more specifically, the legal rules), and it is easy to assume that their range of validity is clearly defined. The identity of the possessors of such rights is clearly recognized.

However, this is not the case when discussing moral rights. Feinberg's term of "an enlightened conscience" does not have an acknowledged sense, which is recognized and accepted by a considerable part of society. It involves faith, belief, ideology and sometimes a religious stance, on the part of every participant of the social process, who may give her own interpretation to this term. There are some presumptions here, about some common normative principles, that reflect some shared moral beliefs which constitute what John Rawls called "our public political culture".[70] Only on the basis of these presumptions, rights can acquire their justification, and be acknowledged as valid. The identity of their possessors depends on the question who is considered as part of the normative system, or who is recognized as belonging to the shared political culture. To this question, many different answers have been given.

The definition of Raz, that we have already considered, is one of the best known in the field. But there are some other alternative definitions. The common denominator of all the answers to the question: who belongs to the common political culture, lies in their attempt to connect their concept of a right-holder, or to their own concept of a person. Each theory of rights ascribes rights to those who are part of the same reference group of the theory. A theory of legal rights will refer only to those who are the subjects of the legal system. A theory of human rights will refer to human beings in general, and needs an appropriate definition of a person, to whom those rights are granted. A theory of moral rights refers to those who are the reference group of morality, and this may be a very loosely defined group.

2.1 SOME ACKNOWLEDGED CHARACTERISTICS OF RIGHT-HOLDERS

Traditional attitudes towards the appropriate concept of a person who is capable of possessing rights, have assumed that a human being has an essential nature, in the sense that human nature has a specific quality (or a set of qualities) that is common to all human beings. This nature was supposed to include the essential features that encompass all arbitrary differences between individuals. Part of these essential features was biological, and concerned the belonging to a certain class of creatures, namely *Homo sapiens*. However, these traditional attitudes did not express the uniqueness of the human being who is capable of possessing rights. Hence, other cognitive features were added, in order to characterize more precisely what constitutes a human being. Among the suggestions raised was the capacity to choose, to use concepts, to reason, etc.[71]

These are basically normative assumptions regarding man's nature, more than they are descriptive qualities that may simply be ascribed to people. They reflect Kantian tendencies that connect humanity with certain mental faculties that give human beings their uniqueness and their moral status.[72] The main purpose of these tendencies is to associate morality with responsibility. However, all the attempts to specify an essential nature of the human being, that would be relevant for a moral judgment (and hence for ascribing moral rights to subjects of this nature), did not yield satisfactory results. For this reason, a better solution for identifying individuals who can be recognized as the subjects of a moral reference group was needed, and a more flexible attitude was preferred. According to this line of thought, human nature was taken to be a "potentiality for a certain range of qualities and activities".[73] Within this range, the potential for a perfected perceptual apparatus, and for reasoning and cognitive abilities, are the most central for considering a creature as human.

However, when considering who is worthy (and not only capable) of possessing rights, even one's recognition as a human being is not sufficient. It is sufficient to characterize one as a potential possessor, but the moral status of a right-holder is not guaranteed, until some additional conditions are present (for there is a difference between being capable of possessing rights and being worthy of possessing rights, which requires some additional normative requirements). These conditions distinguish between one's being considered a "human being" (which is basically a biological classification), and one's recognition as "human" (this difference will be central in the continuation of this chapter, in the distinction between an "agent" and a "moral agent", or a "full-fledged member of the moral community").

The recognition of an individual as "human" is necessarily normative and includes, according to Blackstone, "not only factual characteristics but also a notion of what man should be and how man should be treated". Blackstone's attitude emphasizes that considering a person as human, does not merely classify him according to certain descriptive criteria, but prescribes a general mode of treatment for him.[74] Acknowledging this assumption transforms theories of rights into a matter of the conditions, under which an individual becomes capable of having rights, or the matter of the "conditions of possession" of rights. This is also the thrust of the present chapter. The identity of a presumable right-holder will reflect, in fact, the appropriate conception about the circumstances, under which a person is regarded as capable of possessing rights, and then the conditions and circumstances under which she actually possesses these rights. In the next section I will introduce some of the common views regarding these matters.

2.2 A FEW REMARKS ON THE CONCEPTS OF POSSIBLE RIGHT-HOLDERS

I have already mentioned Raz's definition of the capacity for having rights, that requires right-holders to be creatures that have interests. A more familiar way of identifying possessors of rights is to ascribe to them some moral characteristics. In most of the modes of rights-talk, these characteristics define right-holders as "moral agents", or as "members of the same moral community". Generally, these two ways of ascribing (moral) rights to people, represent the main traditions of moral referring to human beings as possessors of rights. The former approach, which I will entitle (for reasons of convenience) "Kantian" or "Agent Relative", puts the idea of a rational – and hence a free person – in the center, and derives morality from this characteristic (including moral abilities like responsibility, free choice, etc.). According to this approach, a person realizes her rational essence through her moral activity as an individual. The latter approach, which I entitle "Communitarian", assumes that a person realizes her moral abilities within a moral community, and hence her moral status is derived from her participation and transactions within the community. A main part of this chapter will examine these two approaches, in order to clarify their basic principles. This is because my theory combines the requirements of these two approaches, in order to establish my concept of a possible right-holder and my concept of an actual possessor of rights. My theory, which is basically communitarian, incorporates some components that usually belong to agent-relative theories. So, for my purposes I need to introduce the reader to these two modes. The representative of the former approach is Allan Gewirth's PGC theory, while the latter is represented by A. Melden's "moral community" theory. First, however, I want to make a few introductory remarks concerning these approaches, which serves as a clarifying background to the following theories.

2.2.1 The Idea Of A Free Person

When we consider freedom as an essential requirement for a moral judgment, and therefore for holding someone as capable of possessing moral rights, we assume a prescriptive and not a merely descriptive attitude towards her. We ascribe independence to her, in the sense that she is capable of self-rule, self-government, and other capacities that are included in the comprehensive term "autonomy".[75] The most significant factors of her ascribed autonomy are her awareness of her capacities, and her consciousness of herself as a free person. This is similar to Rawls' idea, that free persons consider themselves as the self-originating source of their valid claims. Such an approach considers free persons as capable of taking responsibility for their ends and of adjusting their aims and aspirations.[76] In this sense, the freedom we ascribe to them means the freedom of "self-direction". The assumption that this sense of freedom is essential for regarding individuals as capable of possessing rights associates the idea of a free person with the concepts of aims, purposes, aspirations and interests. This association presumes that a free person can morally judge and assess, both the intentions and consequences of the acts in which she is involved, or by which she is affected. Here, we approach the concept of "an agent", which is central to the first theory I review, namely Alan Gewirth's theory of the PGC.

2.3 ALAN GEWIRTH'S THEORY OF RIGHTS

The main goal of Gewirth's right-based theory is to set up a supreme moral principle. His concept of a right is derived from certain moral assumptions regarding human actions and their generic features. He believes that the necessary content of morality is to be found in these moral assumptions. According to Gewirth, a human "action" has, in the strict sense relevant to moral precepts, two generic features: voluntariness or freedom, and purposiveness or intentionality. The first feature means that the performance of the action is under the agent's control, in the sense that she chooses to act the way she does out of her own free will. The second feature means that the agent acts for some ends or purposes, which constitute her reason for acting.[77] In order to assume this, Gewirth presumes that both features are associated with a certain minimal aspect of rationality and normativeness. The precepts that express these features in human actions are presented as reasoned commands, meaning that they lead to the correct action, from the agent's point of view. The reasons also have a teleological aspect, namely that they lead the agent to act in a way that leads to her ends and goals. This involves an intrinsic reference to the ends and goals the agent envisages for her action.[78] The purposiveness of actions, then, involves the substantive aspect of these actions, namely their specific content.

The character of the agent who is the subject of such a mode of action, is considered to be rational, in the sense of having the abilities of understanding and implementing her choices. She is regarded as capable of selecting and revising her choices, and able to reason and justify her selections. In this sense she is considered responsible for her actions, their performances, and their consequences. This is similar to the "Kantian" concept. Similar to Kant, Gewirth also associates the concept of rationality with the concept of freedom. The way he does it, is by assuming that agents make evaluative judgments about the integrity of their purposes, and about the freedom and welfare, which they regard as necessary conditions for their action to achieve their purposes. The agents' judgments about their integrity, implicitly evaluate the generic features of actions as significant for their attempts to gain it, and hence as necessary goods.[79] On this assumption Gewirth establishes his argument for what he considers as the supreme moral principle, namely *"the Principle of Generic Consistency" (PGC).* In this argument he uses another Kantian principle: the logical principle of universalizability. I now briefly sketch Gewirth's argument, before analyzing it.

2.3.1 The Establishment Of The Principle[80]

Considering freedom as the *procedural* generic feature of action, and welfare as the *substantive* feature (in the sense of having the general abilities and conditions needed for achieving one's purposes), Gewirth establishes two main theses. The first is that every agent must accept that he has rights to freedom and well-being. The second is much more crucial: that every agent must accept that all other agents have the same rights he claims for himself, and this means that the existence of universal and equal moral rights must be accepted, within the whole context of action.

The argument for the first thesis is as follows:

Every agent must regard freedom and well-being as necessary goals for himself (since they are necessary conditions for actions in general, and without them he is not able carry out his objectives).

This forces him to accept:

(1) "I must have freedom and well-being" (where "must" has a practical-prescriptive sense).

Accepting this obliges him to accept:

(2) "I have rights to freedom and well-being".

The agent has to accept this, because rejecting this would require him to reject:

(3) "All other persons ought at least to refrain from removing or interfering with my freedom and well-being".

Rejecting (3) entails him to accept:

(4) "Other persons may (i.e. it is permissible that other persons) remove or interfere with my freedom and well-being".

By accepting (4) the agent has to accept:

(5) "I may not (i.e. it is permissible that I not) have freedom and well-being".

But (5) contradicts (1).

Gewirth says that since every agent must accept (1), he has to reject (5). And since (5) follows from the denial of (2), every agent must reject that denial, so that he must accept (2):

"I have rights to freedom and well-being".

This is the first thesis Gewirth wants to establish. Its main point is, that every human action is necessarily connected with the concept of rights. It follows from the assumption that every agent must accept that he has rights to the necessary conditions of action.[81]

The argument for the second thesis, the generalization that every agent must accept that all other agents have the same generic rights that he has, is based on the principle of universalizability. Briefly, this principle says that if some predicate P, belongs to some subject S, because he has some quality Q, (as a sufficient condition), then, P logically must belong to all other subjects who have the quality Q. Accordingly, if an agent holds that he has generic rights because he is a prospective purposive agent, then this agent logically must also hold, that every other agent has the same generic rights.

According to the previous paragraphs, and following the conclusion of (1) to (5), every agent has to accept:

(6) "I have rights to freedom and well-being, because I am a prospective purposive agent".[82]

And considering the principle of universalizability, every agent is forced to generalize his claim, and hence to accept:

(7) "All prospective purposive agents have rights to freedom and well-being".

Here Gewirth turns to the prescriptive aspect of his analysis. He argues that universalized judgments set prescriptive requirements for actions, made by those who maintain them. According to these requirements every agent must consider the status of others, who might be affected by his actions. Considering them as prospective purposive agents, leads the agent to accept a moral principle, formulated as follows:

(8) "Act in accord with the generic rights of your recipients, just as yourself".

Gewirth calls this the Principle of Generic Consistency – or PGC – because it combines the formal considerations of consistency, with the material considerations of the generic features and rights of action. He considers this a principle of human rights, since it forces every agent to accept that all other agents have rights equal to his own.[83]

2.3.2 The Derivation Of Right-Claims From The Principle of Generic Consistency

For my purposes here, the most relevant aspect of the Principle of Generic Consistency, is the derivation of right-claims from this principle. Gewirth maintains that when the agent holds that he has rights to the generic features of his action, he implicitly makes a corresponding right-claim.[84]

This claim establishes the requirement that others ought, at least, to refrain from interfering with the necessary conditions to which the agent has a right. This is evident when discussing liberties. But when Gewirth considers claim-rights, he argues for a positive component of this right, namely, that others ought to assist the agent to achieve freedom and well-being. Here he has to show that all the components of the structure of a claim-right exist, in order to make the claim concrete, or even valid.

Gewirth shows, at the level of the individual, why an agent must admit that she has generic rights, and that others have them too. According to the structure of a claim right, every right has someone against whom it is claimed. In the case of human rights or welfare rights, we cannot consider any one individual as being their respondent, or as being duty-bound to fulfill them. This is because we cannot establish justifying grounds for holding that a particular respondent is under a duty to fulfill the requirements of a specific welfare or human right. Addressing this right precisely against him cannot be justified under any circumstances. We also cannot, alternatively, impose this duty collectively on all other individuals or "the world", because practically we will not be able to claim against all the individuals together (since each of them can ignore any private duty, and claiming against everyone is practically equivalent to claiming against no-one, considering, inter alia, the principle: "ought implies can") and we will remain, again, without a real respondent.

Thus, in the absence of specified addressees to fulfill their claims, people must direct their claims to some abstract addressee, let us say, the community. The community is the first candidate to function as the addressee of human and welfare rights since it embodies the common and shared moral principles and social norms of its members. As such we can assume that it bears the common responsibility and obligation to provide the members primary goods and basic rights and liberties. This presupposes the existence of a community to which such claims are addressed, and which includes the framework of common rules that provide the justification and legitimacy of these rights.

When we assume that human rights and welfare rights are addressed against the community, we must presume its existence, in order to have a respondent to right-claims that is concerned with the economy, welfare and freedom. In Gewirth's book *The Community of Rights* (published in 1996), he emphasizes the role of the government and the community in protecting human rights. He insists that human rights "warrant serious and active governmental concern for protecting and promoting the freedom and well-being of all humans, especially those who are most deprived".[85] Gewirth considers human rights as rights that belong to every human being, but at the same time every human being is also the respondent of the human rights of others.[86] However, when we consider economic rights as being claimed against the government and the community as a whole, we need to have it as an integral part of these claim-rights (and more specifically: the addressee or the respondent of these rights). In any event, even from the agent's point of view, she needs to recognize the existence of a legitimate or acknowledged system of rules to claim against, before making any claim. In the coming paragraphs I try to resolve this argument and explain why rights cannot be valid prior to the existence of a system to rules or principles. I will do so through a dispute with Gewirth's theory that insists that the agent right claim is logically prior to or independent of a community that shares social rules (precisely because it is based on the possessor's agency needs).[87]

2.4 THE PRIORITY OF A SYSTEM OF RULES

In the first chapter I briefly explained the reasons for preferring to conceive rights as valid claims, over the other possible ways of understanding them. In the next sections I specify and recapitulate this preference, and bring further arguments for supporting the view that requires the existence of a moral community, for making the actualization of rights possible.

There are two critical approaches that dispute Gewirth's theory. The first regards the impossibility of actualizing rights without having a definite addressee, who is obliged to fulfill the content of the right, according to the structure of a claim right. Since in Gewirth's theory, the existence of rights is independent of the actual existence of the community, no one is regarded as committed to the framework within which the right is claimed. In the absence of a community, the mutual acknowledgement of the members, as liable and responsible for the realizing of each member's rights and interests, is missing. This bases the duties of those who are regarded as addressees of the rights, merely on good will or supererogation, and may turn the rights into something without substance. The compelling force, which is sometimes needed for the enforcement of the correlated duties, and which is usually vested in the community, does not exist. When there is no actual community to provide human rights, and there is no way to impose the correlative duties on any individual, there is no one else who is duty-bound to provide for them. In this case, what Gewirth himself regards as the necessary conditions for action, will become empty of content.

However, even if it is not logically necessary to have a community in order to establish people's rights, or to receive the approval of all the participants to mutually respect each other's rights, we must have a community to ensure the exercising of rights within it. Even if the principle of solidarity (or integrity) is respected by people prior to the existence of the community (and Gewirth thinks that through the recognition of mutuality entailed by human rights, the society becomes a community), still, the fulfillment of rights is based on the respondent's good will. After all, consistency may morally oblige the respondent to respect others' rights, but, as a free person, she can renege on this obligation. For ensuring rights, even in such cases, we need the community, as a guarantor for the exercising of these rights.

The second criticism of Gewirth's theory, results from the original motivation for this study, namely the difficulties involved in providing for the withdrawal of rights within agent-relative theories. This subject is the main topic to be discussed in the next chapter. Here I just note the main point: in a theory that bases the possessing of rights upon generic (or natural) features, the status of the right-holder does not change, so long as he maintains the features that bestow rights upon him. In Gewirth's theory, with which we are dealing, the rights to freedom and well-being are parts of one's agency (inasmuch as they are the necessary conditions of successful actions). The way the agent acts, does not affect his need for the necessary conditions to accomplish his actions, and hence his rights to freedom and well-being. When this is carried out we will see that this might, sometimes, have unbearable consequences. This is especially true when an agent decides, logically and consciously, to act wickedly. His generic rights remain his own, and there cannot be any justification for their denial or withdrawal. Gewirth is aware of this kind of problem, and tries to overcome it. His treatment of this topic is explained within the context of the detailed discussion in the next chapter.

The main problem with agent-relative theories is how to define who has the authority to withdraw rights from people. Unless we acknowledge a framework, and ascribe to it the authority to allocate rights, we cannot impose on it the responsibility to withdraw rights when it is necessary. In order to ordain any institution to withdraw rights, we must acknowledge it as the authority that bestows or allocates rights, and that is also responsible for the exercise of them.

However, at this stage I want to concentrate on the first line of criticism, and clarify the necessity of an actual community, as a precondition for having rights. Simultaneously I will explain why the ascribing of rights solely on the basis of generic features of action is insufficient. The main point here is the desire to ensure the durability, integrity and actuality of rights, and of their applicability. When considering welfare rights, we need to have the community as their respondent, and hence we regard the community as an integral part of the structure of these claim-rights. But even when we consider rights *in personam*, that have specific respondents, we need to have an authority that ensures them, and that will compel the addressees to respond to these rights, and to fulfill their correlative duties. This is necessary, because consistency can oblige the agent to fulfill his duties only when he has good will. However, in the absence of good will, we need an authority that will regulate rights and duties, and ensure their fulfillment, in cases where the respondents renege on their obligations.

2.4.1 The Superiority Of The Communitarian Approach

The alternative to agent-relative theories of rights (of which Gewirth's theory is one of the most prominent) is based on what Raz calls "the reciprocity theory".[88] At the core of such theories, there is an assumption that only members of the same moral community can have rights. Those who adopt this idea, think that rights cannot be bestowed solely because of the personal identity or the generic features of their possessors. In this alternative approach, a right to something is created by the rules and principles of an actual community, which specify certain conditions of possession for each right, and declare that only those who satisfy them are entitled to have this right.[89] Such an approach assumes that without the public acknowledgement of these rules and principles, social life becomes impossible. Social life is based on the mutual reliance of society's participants one upon the other, and on the participants' awareness of this reliance. Unless they discover their mutual reliance, and acknowledge the shared rules and principles that assure their commitment to the continuity of their cooperation in the social life, they do not commit themselves to respect and to value others' interests. In such a situation, they do not consider themselves as addressees of any claim, in the sense of being under a duty towards the possessors of any right. Their commitment to others' interests starts when they regard all the participants of the social interaction as belonging to the same normative system, at least to the extent that they share the same norms of conduct and the same set of moral principles. When they do share a common value system, they create a community. From this stage, the members of the community can reasonably expect that their interests will be considered and respected. Prior to that, however, they could only consider themselves as entitled to have something, but no one except them, necessarily accepts their demands. Their ability to claim their rights appears when their claims reach some measure of recognition and acknowledgement.[90]

2.5 MELDEN'S THEORY OF RIGHTS

A.I.Melden's theory can be considered as a typical paradigm of a communitarian conception of rights, even though Melden had no occasion to think of it in this manner, since the idea of "communitarism" had not yet gained the acceptance that it has achieved since then. In the center of his view there is a general assumption about every kind of social interaction. He assumes that in each level of social life, some segments of the lives of the participants are joined together, and the linkage caused by this joining, creates the moral relations between them. In Melden's discussion, he examines the relation between a promiser and a promisee, as a kind of moral relation. His conclusion of this discussion, is that in order to find what imposes the duty and obligation upon the promiser, we have to focus attention, not only upon the promiser, but rather upon the whole conceptual complexity of the moral relations between a promiser and a promisee. These relations are established in the making and acceptance of the promise.[91] The act of promising creates the rights of the promisee, and the correlative duty of the promiser. Within such an approach, both rights and duties of the participants in social life, are created by the moral relations and conventions acknowledged and confirmed by them.

Melden bases his concept of rights on the idea, that the status of a person as a moral agent is created by the moral and social context, within which the connections between a person's public life and that of the others, take place. In the same way that he examined the promise, as an institution that constitutes a special moral obligation between its participants, Melden presents the family as an institution of the same kind. In both cases, he thinks that the rights of the parties are based on their mutual understanding of their obligations towards each other, because of their belonging to a certain normative environment, namely the one associated with the same institution. Melden expresses this in the following way:

> "What is essential, not only in the case of a promise, but also in the case in which the lives of siblings are joined in such a way that rights and obligations may have application, is the mutual understanding that exists between the parties and that certain performances of sorts of performances – the performance described in the promise locution or those brotherly and sisterly actions in which siblings give each other special consideration (e.g. the sharing of their resources with each other) – which support each other in their endeavors, and in normal cases at least are assured as anything that the recipient of the special consideration can do on his own".[92]

Like in the case of a promise, Melden regards the family as a social institution that defines the moral relations between its members, including the rights and obligations involving its practice. His basic approach insists that this is the way rights are established. According to Melden: "the conception of the right of a human being is the conception of a normative status that he has with respect to others, and it is to be understood, if at all, only in terms of its place in the scheme of related concepts in which it has its place."[93] But the most important grounds for rights which people have (either created by a promise or by belonging to an institution such as a family), is the way in which they join their lives as individuals, with the lives of the other members of the community. This joining of lives, takes place against the background of normatively appropriate settings, and relates to their exercise and enjoyment of the rights that such individuals have (as human beings). In Melden's theory, the agency of people is to be measured according to their sensitivity to the variety of circumstances and situations, in which their lives are joined with those of others.

This suggests a fine distinction, which can be drawn between two possible ways of regarding a person. The first is to conceive a person's status as an individual, with her hopes, aspirations, ends, etc. This understanding can be seen as a generic, natural or even normative characterization. In this sense, we can understand this kind of comprehension of the concept of a person, as referring to Gewirth's notion of a prospective agent. Gewirth himself does not distinguish between prospective agents and actual agents. For him, both prospective and actual agents possess rights. The second way is to consider Melden's concept of a person, as referring to actual agents only. This view distinguishes the aspect of being an agent, from being a mere person. Here, a person needs to have some measure of social surroundings, in which her life is joined to lives of others, in order to attain her agency, and hence to be able to claim her rights. This becomes crucial when discussing the possession of rights. Gewirth's lack of differentiation between a prospective and an actual agent, bestows upon both kinds of agents their generic rights. In Melden's theory, a person needs to become an agent before she has any actual rights. In the next sections of this chapter, I return to the distinction between these kinds of agents, and argue that the difference between Melden's and Gewirth's theories, raises the question whether every prospective agent is automatically to be considered as an actual agent, as in Gewirth's theory, or whether there is a process within which a person becomes an agent (the position I wish to defend). The absence of such a process, in Gewirth's theory, saves him the necessity of positing any primary conditions for having generic rights. Melden's theory, on the other hand, forces him to assume the existence of a community, in which a person actually receives her rights. The coming paragraphs discuss the creation of the status of an agent in Melden's theory, and explicate the concept of "a member in the moral community", which is the subject of rights in this theory.

2.5.1 The Communal Aspects Of Having Rights

Like Gewirth, who assumes voluntariness and purposiveness as the generic features of an action, and hence concludes that every agent has generic rights to freedom and well-being (as necessary conditions of action), Melden starts his argument from a similar basic right that every moral agent has. He contends that any person, as a moral agent, has the basic right to go about his affairs in the pursuit of his interests. This right is regarded as the core of one's agency, and the infringement of it, means subverting his moral status as an agent.[94] Every specific right, including a right that was given by a promise, needs the acknowledgement and appreciation of the mentioned basic right, by those who are involved in exercising or implementing this right. The recognition of this basic right obligates the participants to follow the form of conduct that is required for the fulfillment of that specific right. In the case of a bona fide promise, for example, it is required that the parties involved will conduct their affairs with each other, with a proper concern for each other as agents. This requires that those who promise, be concerned with the desires of those who receive the promise, and are prepared to support them in their efforts to achieve their ends. This requirement follows from the conception of the promise as an agreement, where those involved in the transaction of that promise, are aware of the obligations and burdens which are created by the recognition of the basic right every agent has.

However, that is only one part of the framework within which rights get their validity. Besides the existence of the agreement (which is stipulated by the fulfillment of obligations), there must be a:

> "Community of understanding of the complex array of moral concepts, within which the concepts of a right and an obligation have their place, and, paradigmatically, when the setting appropriate for the enjoyment and exercise of rights is present".[95]

The agreement does not have any validity, without the "logical substratum that lies in the background of the...transaction of promising".[96] According to Melden, then, the basis for the existence of any agreement, or even an obligation, is possible only consequent to the existence of the normative and conceptual framework, within which there is comprehensive consent. Those who voluntarily share the normative demands, and understand the sense and meaning of the shared set of concepts, can be regarded as belonging to the same moral community. Considering them in this way, essentially means that they regard their lives as joined to those of others, within the same social unit. Their mutual reciprocity, when interacting within that unit, results from their maintaining of a defined social institution.

Melden explicates the way this substratum functions, in creating rights and obligations within the most typical social unit – the family. Here, the lives of the participants are joined together, in a way that affects most aspects of their common existence. Their mutual concern and support extend along a variety of enterprises in which they are engaged, and the rights and obligations they have towards each other, are the essential part of their regarding themselves as belonging to the same family. These rights are not derived from the character of the family as a social institution, but rather from the character of the way of life, in which members of the family are involved. An important conclusion of Melden's view is that within dysfunctional or broken families, this substratum does not exist, despite the fact that the formal structure of a family might exist. If the lives of the members of such families are unsuitably joined together, namely without concern for each other's goods and endeavors, they do not have any obligation towards their relatives, and do not have rights to claim against their relatives.

The same structure exists not only within families, but also within any institution, within which rights and obligations take place. Institutional rights are not derived from the character of the social arrangements that define the institutions under discussion. What makes them obligatory is the way the participants within the institutions view their lives as joined – at least in some spheres – to the lives of their partners. The point mentioned above, regarding the disruption of rights in families where the connections between their members are weak, is relevant also to larger social units. In such units, where their members do not have – at least to some extent – any commitment to others, and do not feel any solidarity or concern to the interests of others, the whole system of rights and obligations loses its meaning. When we appreciate these relations regarding the existence of rights and obligations between participants of social units, we can generalize these circumstances regarding having rights, and say that people cannot actually have rights, where they do not show any concern for others' interests. In order to have rights, they need to maintain and be part of the social order that enables the possession of rights. Possessing rights within a community by an individual, then, is dependent on the extent to which the possessor performs his obligation to the other members of the community, and, as will be shown later, to the community itself. This point is discussed in detail in the next chapter, but it is worth noting here, that the mutual linkage between possessors of rights, and the way they join their lives with those of the others, will be found crucial for the assessment of their rights.

2.5.2 Preserving The Community As A Basis For Having Rights

The significance of the moral community, as the framework where moral relations take place, and where the complex array of moral concepts has applications, brings Melden to conclude that the preservation of the community is of paramount value for its members. In the moral community, members are bound to one another, and hence must preserve the respect they have for the rights of others, and maintain the continued willingness to join their lives together. Above all, they must preserve the core of what defines them as a community, namely, the common understanding of moral considerations, according to which they bear their moral burdens and adopt their moral stance towards the others. The preservation of these conditions of the moral community, from those faults that might threaten or weaken the community, becomes the ultimate mission of those who wish to have rights within the community.[97]

A.J.M.Milne, who regards the community as central to every aspect of people's lives, takes a more decisive stance regarding this issue. For him, the interests of a community, which enables its members to live, are reducible to the common interests of its members. Thus, the necessary conditions for the existence of the community (including material conditions) have precedence over the self-interests of each member, whenever there is a conflict between the interests of the community and self-interest of any member. This obliges each member to assist in promoting the community's interests, as part of her social responsibility. Without the obligation to the interests of the community, the continued existence of the community as a social unit would be in danger.[98] The rationale that lurks behind Milne's view, is that since the community is the basis for one's survival, one is committed to its continuity, in order to keep on existing within it. The preservation of the community is her ultimate interest, and when discussing morality, it is her duty to preserve the morality of the community. If the existence of the moral community is the basis for her moral rights, she has to protect its interest, in order to be able to have those rights. The relations between the status of a person as an agent (and hence as capable of possessing rights) and her integration within the moral community, is the topic of the next paragraphs.

2.5.3 The Acquirement Of Moral Agency In Melden's Theory

The manner through which a person is defined as an agent, is probably the issue which distinguishes most clearly between individualistic and communitarian theories of rights. While in the former theories, like Gewirth's for example, the status of an agent is almost directly constructed into the definition of one's being a person, in the latter theories, agency is acquired through a process during which a person needs to internalize some values and norms, in order to become a member of the moral community, and accordingly to deserve his moral agency. The transformation of a person into a moral agent is caused not only by generic or natural features, but also by the way she treats her partners in the given social interaction, and by the concern she shows for the stability and morality of the social framework. Communal theories of rights distinguish between prospective and moral agents when discussing the possession of rights. They assume a gap between a moral and a prospective agent, and regard the latter as only a candidate for being a moral agent. This categorizes her as a possible partner in the social framework, in the sense that she is regarded as capable of integrating within the social interaction. In order to become a full-fledged member of the community, however, she has to conduct her interests in a way that considers her obligations towards the community and its members. Showing disregard for her responsibility as a full member in the community, strikes at the morality of her agency and reduces her moral status, and accordingly, her possession of rights.

In order to clarify the main difference between the two theories, we can say, roughly, that in individualistic theories, being an agent is sufficient for one to possess rights, and from this point of view (the capability of possessing rights) there is no difference between being an agent and being a moral agent. The morality of one's agency is a descriptive or classifying character of the agent, namely a certain ability or potential the agent naturally possesses. Her morality is included in her being an agent, and accordingly in her possession of rights. For communitarian theories, being an agent does not yet grant a right. It just indicates the capability of possessing rights. For actual possession of a right, one needs to follow the requirements of being a moral agent, which now gets a prescriptive sense, namely fulfilling some norms, rules and principles whose fulfillment bestows upon agents the status of moral agent. In short, the difference between being an agent (which only indicates the potential of possessing rights) and being a *moral* agent is the way the agent acts within the community.

Melden deals broadly with the question of the appropriate reasons for regarding people as capable of being moral agents, or possessors of moral rights. His rejection of the "sentimental" position, which suggests the capability of feeling pleasure and pain, as a reason for having moral rights, is therefore quite understandable and clear. The feature of capability of feeling pleasure and pain exists in animals too, and we usually do not regard them as moral subjects (unless we anthropomorphize them).[99] Another version of this position, which suggests the capability of feeling sympathy for others as a reason for possessing rights, is rejected for similar reasons. Sympathy does not seem a sufficient reason for possessing rights, because we do not see the relevance of such a feeling to our possession of moral rights. The fact that people can feel sensations or emotions of various kinds, does not express the uniqueness of being capable of possessing moral rights. Even though it contains the element of intentionality or purposiveness towards others, it lacks the element of voluntariness of actions, and thus seems insufficient for justifying the possession of moral rights. So Melden drops this "Humean" position, and looks into the "Kantian" stance, as something more prevalent and concrete, which stands at the basis of most individualistic and agent-relative theories, including that of Gewirth.

Melden investigates the attempt to ascribe rights to people because of their rationality, a property that is often supposed to be characteristic of human beings, but not to animals. He argues that this attempt will not help in identifying a person as a moral agent, or as deserving to possess rights.

Melden concentrates in his argument, on the problems caused by the gap that exists between being rational, and being moral (which in Kantian theories, for example, are not differentiated, or sometimes not even identified). His main point is that rationality is equally compatible either with immorality, or with amorality. He maintains that we can imagine intelligent beings, that have the ability to think, form concepts and reach conclusions, but have totally different considerations that move them to act the way they do. According to Melden, however much they might resemble to us in the way they think, we will not treat them as human beings, in the sense that they are part of our moral community, or as beings with which we can carry on our affairs.[100]

In a similar way Melden rejects the idea that people have rights because of their autonomy, namely, their ability to decide and to choose the way they go about their affairs. This characteristic might equally be a fitting description of sociopaths, who do not care about anyone's interests or welfare, and choose and decide according to their own selfish concern. We do not find them deserving of any ascription of moral rights, and their capacity for rationally choosing and deciding, is irrelevant for determining their moral status, and for assessing their morality. On the other hand, says Melden, this characteristic might exclude some agents to whom we do ascribe rights, like children or wives of despotic husbands, who make their choices according to the prohibitions and restrictions that their parents or husbands impose upon them.

We want to ascribe rights, according to our judgment of the merit of those whom we find as having respect for the interests of others, and to consider their conduct according to the extent of the responsibility they fill towards the social and moral framework, within which they claim their rights. The lack of mutual obligation (when it is from the person's unforced choice and not under duress), creates a failure in the attempts to identify agency with rationality. Rationality may affect the way a person understands situations, and even may impose moral responsibility upon her, but it is not sufficient for persuading her to act according to moral demands. The desirable reason for ascribing moral rights to a person, must consider her moral relations and associations, according to which she transacts with her partners in the social unit, within which this transaction takes place. This entails not only the ability to understand, but also the will and volition to cooperate with those whom the agent regards as joining their lives with her own life. In other words, this requires the element of reciprocity or mutuality in the agent's life, that was lacking in the attempts to ascribe rights to a person, merely according to the person's rationality. The Kantian suggestion that human beings have an intrinsic worth, that might be the source or grounds for the possession of human rights, is not a better solution than the previous attempts, which make rights dependent on mental capacities. Both value-talk and capacity-talk apply to concepts, rather than rights. The only reasonable choice left for Melden as grounds for possessing rights, thus, as he says, is to regard rights as dependent upon membership in a moral community, within which all members are equal. This makes the community, the reasonable object of the moral interest of all its members.[101] The community functions as the framework, within which members mutually transact with each other. The fact that they need the respect of others for their interests, in order to realize these interests, places them in the same – and hence equal – status, in their claims towards one another, and each one towards the community. The equal weight that is given to each member's claims requires everyone within the community to respect the interests of all the others, even when striving for their own interests. Here, membership in the moral community means a certain kind of behavior and treatment of the other members and the community as a whole. It is not merely nominal membership, but active and normative membership.

The equality that Melden ascribes to members of the moral community does not imply that all should be given an equal share of the common goods or resources. Nor does it imply that they are all equally capable of enjoying the same goods. It only implies that within the moral community, everyone has the equal right to pursue their interests. From this it follows, that each person, even the most advantaged and powerful, is accountable to everyone else – including the lowliest and most disadvantaged – for any infringement or violation of the latter's rights. Each person has the same moral authority with respect to anyone else, to respect and accord him these rights. If these rights are denied, each person has the authority to demand for redress for the damage he suffers.[102] This authority is the meaning of the recognition of a person as a member of the moral community, and this person is to be treated, as a moral agent, in accordance with this authority.

Moral agency, and hence the possession of rights, according to Melden, is based on the acknowledgement of all persons within the moral community, that they all share an enormously complicated form of life. These partners view their lives as joined to the lives of others, despite the varied ways each of them reveals himself as a moral human being. They understand that essentially, they all share some common features of their lives. In accordance with this understanding, persons realize that they all have interests in the pursuit of their goods, that their lives, like those of their partners, are bound together by ties of love and affection with their families and friends, and that there are numerous spheres of their lives that they find themselves sharing with others of the community. When persons internalize the idea that their lives are joined to others in some essential respects and segments of their existence, they come to treat the others as agents. This chiefly means a respect for the basic rights of all, to go about their affairs in the pursuit of their interests. And an essential part of this respect is to show consideration for others' interests, when pursuing their own interests.

The last statement, about the way persons internalize the communal form of life and become moral agents, is symptomatic of the idea that the acquisition of moral agency is attained through a process of moral development. This idea is central in most of the communitarian approaches towards moral agency. A.J.M. Milne, for example, thinks that "people become agents as they grow up in, and become members of, their community".[103] During their growth and maturation, people acquire the common values that enable their coexistence. They learn that some ways of acting are right, and others are wrong. They also learn that their mutual reliance one upon the other requires them to do the right things, and to refrain from doing the wrong things. They gradually discover that mutual reliance requires them to tell the truth, to keep agreements and promises, to refrain from violence, theft and deception, and particularly not to take unfair advantage of one another. During the course of their moral development, members of the community acknowledge that they share, and are aware of their sharing, common ideas about right and wrong. They also assume that the other members of the community acknowledge the same. This is, in essence, the expression of their entitlement for moral agency. Implementing this acknowledgement, expresses their agency.[104]

Melden emphasizes this idea in his discussion of the way children realize the moral import of a promise-locution.[105] At the beginning, they do not understand that actions like making and carrying out promises deal with rights that are conferred, and obligations that are assumed. With the developing of their moral understanding, they learn the differences between promises and other kinds of verbal expressions, and realize that the former impose moral requirements upon the parties involved, confer rights and obligations. Melden mentions that this process is gradual, and there is no sharp line that can be drawn between regarding children's expressions as promise-locutions or non promise-locutions. During the development of their moral understanding, they learn to distinguish different sorts of conduct and circumstances, within which the full array of moral concepts, including the concept of a promise, applies without any qualification. A fuller grasp of what is involved in promising, develops the understanding of the appropriate way, in which morally mature persons need to deal with those with whom they transact. Their awareness of the significance of the mutuality in keeping promises (and agreements), for their lives and for their ability to maintain the common institutions and the community as a whole, obliges them to treat their partners with respect and concern. They learn that breaking a promise might undermine their ability to carry on their affairs, with those with whom their lives are joined together. As the recognition of their mutual dependence develops, they learn that this dependence includes not only the advantages that can be gained from appropriate conduct with others, but also the risks and harms that might result from inappropriate treatment of others.

For Melden, the most significant implication of our moral development is not merely the increasing awareness of facts about ourselves and others, but a change in our moral concepts. [106] This is to say that not only are our moral judgments changed, but also that the whole conceptual framework within which acts are assessed as right or wrong has been modified. I prefer to call it a transformation from being merely agents, to actually becoming moral agents. One of the varied implications of this change is the acknowledgement of the moral community not only as functional, but also as having some moral virtues. It is to recognize that the obligations that are imposed upon agents within the community, result not only from the responsibility that they all feel towards each other's interests, but also from their respect and appreciation of each other's dignity and integrity. Their being entitled to the status of moral agents invests their self-esteem and self-respect as with dignity and integrity. Their view of their lives as joined to the lives of the other members of the community, in such a way that they all are equal – at least in the respect already mentioned, of having the same basic right – requires them to ascribe the same status to their partners. This interpretation of Melden's view is very close to his own expressions regarding the sense of being moral agents, in the last chapter of his book. The only shift from his explicit stance is my distinction between mere agents and moral agents. I am inclined to believe that he would largely agree with this distinction. The status he ascribes to moral agents, as full members of the moral community, is about the same as was presented in the last paragraphs, and the acquisition of this status occurs through the development of the agents in the community, and their integration within it.

2.5.4 The Relevant Differences Between The Two Approaches For The Current Discussion

As we see, there is an essential difference between individualistic or agent-relative theories, and communitarian theories of rights. This difference relates mainly to the features, according to which persons are considered as capable of possessing rights. We can summarize this difference by saying that in individualistic theories, the justifying grounds for moral agency – and hence for the possession of rights – are the generic (or natural) features of the prospective agent. In communitarian theories, on the other hand, the justifying grounds for possessing rights is the way the agent actually performs her social transactions. A better way to present this difference is to say that in the former theories, rights are bestowed according to the personal features of the agent, while in the latter theories, rights are bestowed according to the person's actions and behavior. Agent-relative theories view agents as individuals, whose rationality is a necessary and sufficient condition for considering them as moral agents. In communitarian theories rationality is indeed necessary, but not sufficient for possessing rights. In these theories, rationality (or any other personal feature) might be a necessary but not a sufficient condition, for bestowing what Melden entitles "an admission ticket", to the moral community.

The reason I refer to the "Kantian" approaches to agency, is my assumption that even though personal features such as rationality cannot by themselves justify the possession of rights, they must be considered as necessary for regarding certain kinds of beings as capable of participating in the social interaction. The position I support in the coming sections, distinguishes between mere agents and moral agents. The possession of rights is ascribed only to moral agents. Hence, there is a difference between mere agency and moral agency. The personal features that are sufficient for serving as grounds for the possession of rights in agent-relative theories such as Gewirth's, are regarded as sufficient for being capable of only the former kind of agency. This is to say that they can serve as an "admission ticket" to the former category. In my view, to be a moral agent – and hence to be capable of possessing rights – means to fulfill two different sets of requirements, that, in Rawlsian terminology, are to be ranked in a serial or "lexical" order.[107] The first set – which is basically the having of some mental and cognitive capacities – identifies one as a mere agent that is capable of entering the moral community (or as a prospective agent in agent-relative theories). Such an agent can be moral and possess rights when she fulfills the second set of requirements, which is basically the following of some normative and moral rules, norms and principles within an actual community. If this agent does not follow this set of requirements, she is not considered as moral, and hence not entitled to possess the rights that are bestowed upon full-fledged members of the moral community. In a more familiar terminology, a mere agent is equivalent to a possible right-holder, while a moral agent (or a full-fledged member of the moral community) is equivalent to an actual possessor of rights. Another way to explicate this distinction is to say that a possible right-holder or an agent is one who can have an "entry ticket" (that is to be considered as capable of possessing rights) to the moral community, and an actual possessor of rights or a full-fledged member of the moral community is one who fulfills the social and normative requirements that bestow the status of a moral agent. In the coming paragraph I try to present the two sets of requirements that, as said before, are to be ranked in lexical order.

The first set of requirements refers to what Carl Wellman calls "grounds of competence".[108] These are essentially generic features, regarding the person's mental and moral abilities, and their possession represents, in some sense, an agent-relative attitude. A person must have them (or at least potentially has them), in order to be considered as capable of fulfilling the second set of requirements. This expresses their "lexical" priority over the second set of requirements. Following Rawls, "lexical" order entails that the first set in the ordering, must be fully satisfied before we can move to the second. Accordingly, the second set of requirements does not come into play, before the first set is fully met. The fact that the first set of requirements includes not only actual abilities, but also a potential for having these abilities, moderates the demand for "full satisfaction" of the first set, before applying to the second set. It allows us to be content with "some measure of satisfaction" of this set, and not necessarily a complete satisfaction. On the other hand, the extent to which these requirements are fulfilled, affects the moral status of the ascribed agent, and hence the extent to which she possesses rights. However, this will be discussed at more depth, in the coming sections. So, for the time being, I leave this matter, and turn to the second set of requirements, and to its relations to the first.

While the first set of requirements represents a "Kantian" approach, which has a lot in common with Gewirth's concept of a prospective agent (even though, in my view, the person under concern is not yet regarded as moral), the second set of requirements represents a "communitarian" approach. Hence, it has some common denominators with Melden's view. Metaphorically, we can think of the relation between the two sets as comparable to the relation between being a human being, and being a citizen of a state. The first feature, in this example, is a necessary but not sufficient condition for being considered as capable of acquiring citizenship. Everyone who desires to belong to the second category must fulfill the requirements of the first category, namely, to be a human being. However, this is not sufficient. Even though this person belongs to the only group whose members are considered as possible candidates for entering the second category, she is still lacking some requirements and conditions that bestow the status of a citizen. Such a would-be citizen needs, for example, to remain in the state a minimal period of time, to pass criminal and health inspections and so on. Sometimes the individual needs to pass exams in order to show that she is familiar with the law, or with some basic elements of participation within the society (for example, in the USA, she needs to learn the national anthem by heart). Some of the conditions a person needs to fulfill, concern her capability to take part in social interactions, and to follow the conventions, rules and norms that are prevalent in that specific social unit. Some of these norms are acquired through practice and take time before being internalized. One needs to perform them with proficiency and learn their social value and function, during the process of integration. After showing appropriate conduct towards both, the social unit and also its members, this person can be regarded as a citizen (of course, after she settles the formal and legal arrangements and procedures). Among various aspects of "appropriate conduct", the most significant requirements are responsibility, accountability, and loyalty towards the common interests. The fulfillment of these requirements, expresses the view that the person who takes part in the communal activities, views her existence as bound, in some features, to the social framework, and hence, she is committed to its preservation. Such a commitment involves the concern not only for the common interests, but also for the self-interests of her partners to the social unit. Lacking such a concern endangers the common framework, and hence undermines the justification for accepting that person to the society, with the status of a citizen.

The same process takes place, in my theory, with the move from the first stage of prospective or mere agency to the second: the moral agency. A person needs to be acknowledged as a prospective or mere agent, namely, having the potential of being a moral agent, in order to be considered as capable of taking part in the moral community. This means that she possesses some moral and social abilities, whose development and elaboration take place within the community. The moral agency is acquired through the process, during which these abilities are advanced. The person concerned, becomes a moral agent in the course of exercising and performing her moral abilities. The point is that these abilities, that were only in potential at the beginning, become practiced within the concrete social transactions in the community. However, because the acquisition of the moral status is dependent on a process, it follows that the process must be continuously maintained.

In my view, membership in the moral community has some correlation with moral agency, and hence with the possession of rights. The extent to which members possess rights is dependent on the extent of their contribution to the proper functioning of the community. They must demonstrate some active involvement, whose interruption has negative effects on the possession of rights. Fixing hierarchical levels of possessing rights, which are dependent on the measure to which the member fulfills a set of requirements, enables a gradual withdrawal of rights, later on. In general, the content of this set refers to the way members bear their obligations towards the community, but its particular content will be specified in the relevant discussion, regarding the precise identity of a moral agent.

2.6 THE INTEGRATED CONCEPTION OF A MORAL AGENT

The idea of considering the status of persons, who mutually transact within the social framework, as combining both individual and communitarian elements, is quite frequent in political theories. Considering social life a manifestation of social cooperation entails the regarding of the individuals that create society, as having some common interests and values, which identify them as a reference group, rather than a random collection of individuals. Such a group is still not a collective, but rather a framework within which the individuals are able to realize some of their self-interests. When discussing the possession of rights, and especially human rights, there is an additional reason for regarding a person as an individual who is part of a community.

This reason is alluded to, in Gewirth's remark that human rights are claim-rights. He says that many of these rights require the enforcement, or at least, the protection of the government in order to be secured. The main reason for this is that these are rights to certain especially important objects and goods. In order to possess them, it is necessary that others refrain from interfering with the possessor's having these objects, and in certain circumstances, that others assist the possessor to acquire these objects. This requirement (to assist the possessor to acquire these objects) often involves a framework of institutional, especially governmental, rules.[109]

The structure of a claim-right entails that there be a definite respondent (or addressee) for a right, in order for it to be concrete. When we discuss moral rights as valid claims, we need to presuppose the existence of a moral community, in order to have an explicit respondent for these rights. This is because we cannot justify the imposing of the correlative duty on any other entity, rather than the community or the state. No individual can justifiably be considered as the respondent of human rights, mainly because no individual can provide their contents or objects. Considering the individual as independent of the community would abolish the obligation of the community to satisfy the individual's claims. Since such independence takes place in both directions, it frees the community from obligations towards the individual who is not part of it. Thus, even from Gewirth's point of view, human rights (which I consider as an essential part of moral rights) entail the existence of a framework, within which they can apply. My argument supposes a more binding connection between the individual and the community, but is grounded mainly on this attitude. The desire to realize moral rights, brings me to consider the community as the addressee of these rights, and hence, to assume its existence as an integral part of moral rights.

However, this point is part of my entire conception of the person, whenever dealing with moral or political issues. In this issue I accept Rawls' view that:

> "Since Greek times, both in philosophy and law, the concept of the person has been understood as the concept of someone who can take part in, or who can play a role in, social life, and hence exercise and respect his various rights and duties. Thus we say that a person is someone who can be a citizen, that is, a fully cooperating member of a society over a complete life".[110]

Rawls' concept of the person, for moral or political discussions, is actually the concept of a citizen. His attitude towards the person is to consider her as a free individual who cooperates with other individuals, who are considered as equal to her. They all have their own features as individuals, but as citizens we refer only to their "public identity", namely their identity as the subjects of the basic law.

Rawls refers mainly to the legal status and the legal aspects of rights and the other kinds of relations between the cooperating participants of the social framework. When we adopt Rawls' approach in the context of the moral status of rights, we still preserve the idea of the "public identity", but there we refer to this identity as connected to norms and principles, rather than to the basic law. This is the framework within which rights get their validity. However, the idea of regarding individuals according to their public identity for the matter of possessing rights, presumes some personal features that are necessary for participating in the common system. My move towards the identifying of adequate possessors of moral rights starts from the features that are necessary for individuals to become members of the moral community (and I bring their correlatives in Rawls' theory). Then, I turn to identify the communal conditions, whose fulfillment qualifies individuals as right-holders. These conditions also have correlatives, in other communitarian theories including those of Rawls and Melden, and I bring the relevant justifications from such theories.

2.6.1 The Concept Of A Prospective Or Mere Agent

The idea that rights get their validity and substance from the moral community, or at least from a system of rules, leads us to identify the possible possessor of rights in social or communitarian terms. The structure of a claim-right, which imposes a correlative duty upon the addressee, entails a certain measure of cooperation from his side. A lack of such cooperation reduces the possibility of fulfilling the claimed right, and this significantly reduces the possibility of exercising and capitalizing on the right. This makes the right less concrete and less applicable. Of course, there must be a sanction that the possessor of this right can activate against the addressee, but this may only be a way to punish the addressee. For in order to realize the content of the right, the possessor needs the cooperation of the respondent (I use Gewirth's terminology that employs the term "addressee" as a synonym of the term "respondent"). Such an interpretation of the relations that are needed between the "subject" or the "possessor" of the right and its "respondent", means that even the first set of requirements that were mentioned before (regarding the mental abilities), will have some social and communitarian aspects. Even though these were supposed to be "Kantian" or "generic" characteristics (like rationality or consistency), they will be estimated according to their social implications. At first sight this seems to conflict with Gewirth's position, but this is not completely so. This is a comprehensive interpretation of both the rational and moral abilities, as referring to the way people should treat one another. Gewirth's idea of consistency refers to the person's understanding that her demands and expectations from others have the same weight as their demands from herself. Accordingly, a person's generic rights are established with her acknowledgement of others' rights. This means that even Gewirth's "Kantian" concept of a moral agent, relates to the way the prospective agent maintains her interactions (or in Melden's terminology – her transactions) with other agents. This is my way of referring to the first set of requirements that are necessary to be capable of possessing rights.

The reference to Rawls shows that some other "Kantian" positions regard the concept of a person in terms of her social abilities, and not merely her individual characteristics. Rawls' concept of a person, as "someone who can take part in, or play a role in social life" presents a position that combines the "agent-relative" aspects of the person, with her social involvement. I hold a similar concept of a person, and regard her as a "prospective agent" (or "mere" agent to distinguish from "actual" or "moral" agent), or one who is capable of entering the moral community (or as a candidate for being a moral agent). I sketch this concept immediately below:

Most of the attempts to identify and describe the kind of entities to which one can ascribe moral rights, refer, more or less, to a similar sort of being. The most explicit expression of this kind is Joel Feinberg's identification of "normal adult human beings", as "the sort of beings of whom rights can meaningfully be predicated".[111] These kinds of entities can have rights because of generic reasons (like in Gewirth's theory). These entities are basically capable of perception, cognition or in general, having some cognitive characteristics. In such agent-relative theories, the right-holder gets her moral status from her essential nature that constitutes grounds for the possessor's claim. This approach emphasizes the individual aspects of the possessors of rights, as grounds for their claims. In the alternative approach, (or what I call communitarian, e.g., Melden's), human beings get their moral status from their participation in a social framework. Such theories emphasize the mutual and common aspects of people, when they are respected as right-holders. However, they still refer, first of all, to the same kind of entities, that Feinberg describes, namely "normal adults". They do not define the individual characteristics that are needed for belonging to the social framework, but impose normative requirements upon those who are members of the moral community. These requirements refer to the common segments of the participants' lives, and their fulfillment provides the moral grounds for the possessors' claims. These requirements are, in fact, the normative sense of being a "normal adult", and they have only an incidental reference to biological age. They may describe a mature behavior or conduct, but refer essentially to comprehension abilities, that we usually ascribe to adults.

My aim is to combine these two attitudes in such a way, that the agent-relative approach serves as an admission ticket to the social framework. This is to say that the possible members of the community need to fulfill some requirements regarding their cognitive and rational capabilities, which proves that they are capable for joining some segments of their lives with those of others. The actual practice of these requirements (which is specifically defined), bestows the status of "a member of the moral community". In order to become a possessor of rights, a member of the moral community is required to keep on maintaining her obligations towards the social framework. Here, being a mere "normal adult" is not sufficient for being regarded as a right-holder. For the most, it is sufficient for being considered as a "prospective" right-holder, or "mere" agent.

2.6.2 The Individual Requirements Of A Prospective Agent

At the foundation of my view there is an assumption that follows Carl Wellman's view about the kinds of beings who might possess rights. Wellman says that any conclusion about this, hinges both upon the nature of that kinds of beings, as also upon the nature of human rights.[112] Hence, the ascription of rights to their possessors must be correlative to the essential functions of these rights in society. Wellman lists some grounds for moral rights, the first of which can be used as a starting point for my attempt to identify prospective right-holders.

Wellman starts his identification of a possible right-holder from the requirement of dominion (within which he includes freedom and control). He argues that since the essential function of moral rights is to confer dominion on the right-holder, the latter must be capable of exercising dominion.[113]

An explication of the idea of dominion may be found in John Rawls' idea of the political conception of a person. Rawls ascribes freedom and rationality to moral persons, as their fundamental and essential characteristics. As moral persons, Rawls describes people as having two moral powers, and as having two corresponding highest-order interests, in realizing and exercising these powers. These capacities represent the rational abilities to understand, and a sufficient measure of freedom and unforced choice, to express what is contained in Wellman's notion of dominion. The first moral ability that Rawls ascribes to a moral person is "the capacity for an effective sense of justice, that is the capacity to understand, to apply and to act from (and not merely in accordance with) the principles of justice". The second capacity is formulated in a similar way, and applies to people's capacity "to form, to revise and rationally to pursue a conception of the good". Correspondingly, moral persons are said to be moved by two highest-order interests: "to realize and exercise these capacities".[114] Rawls says that the moral powers and the powers of reason, thought and judgment that are connected to them, are the grounds for our ascription of freedom to people.

The statement that expresses Rawls' intention by ascribing freedom and rationality to moral persons, in the most extensive sense, is his description of such persons, as those who view themselves as the self-originating source of their valid claims.[115] This means that they are not tied to any specific position, and are free to revise their conceptions of the good, or to pursue their changeable ends whenever they want. The responsibility for these ends is carried by them as part of their being the self-originating source of their claims.

The Rawlsian form of interpretation to Wellman's notion of "dominion", might serve as a basis for giving a sense to Raz's definition of a right-holder, that was mentioned at the beginning of this chapter. There, Raz suggests X as having a capacity for possessing rights, if his welfare is of ultimate value. We can start realizing that what gives one's welfare an ultimate value, is one's freedom in the "Kantian" sense, namely – one's supposed autonomy. When we ascribe full autonomy to agents, namely, consider them as the self-originating source of their valid claims, we place them in a moral status that acknowledges their entitlement to have claims. This is, essentially, an interpretation of Raz's expression of "can have rights", that applies to those who can be considered as possible right-holders.

Alan Gewirth assumes that human agency requires rationality in at least two senses. The first is being able to calculate that the agent has rights to the necessary means for the pursuit of her ends and purposes. The second refers to the agent's understanding that consistency requires her to accept that other agents have the same rights. The difference between Gewirth's view and that of Rawls is that the latter stipulates freedom as an essential characteristic of the agent, while the former regards freedom as the aim of a human being.[116] However, besides this dispute regarding the metaphysical status of freedom (whether it is a basic requirement for being able to become a prospective agent, or whether it is the main goal and purpose of having rights), both conceptions regard the agent's autonomy as the basis of her moral abilities. Gewirth's notion of "rational autonomy", in the sense of "self controlling" and "self developing", has an almost identical meaning to Rawls' notion of autonomy, that is manifested in his concept of the person. When Gewirth refers to autonomy, he connects it, like Wellman does, to the notion of dominion, but in the negative use of this idea. The person's autonomy includes her freedom to control her own life without being subjected to domination from others.[117]

When Gewirth responds to the criticism regarding the inequality between people in their abilities, that could justify a corresponding inequality in their rights, he indicates two crucial points that are very useful for my aims. The first answer says, that his argument for generic rights requires only a minimal rationality as sufficient for acquiring agency, and this minimum is held by all normal human adults. The required ability is that the agent knows who she is and what she is doing, that she can control her behavior for the sake of her purposes, and can recognize elementary forms of consistency and empirical connections.[118] The second answer says that the agent's claims are not based directly on her rationality or on any ability of agency, but on her having purposes she wants to fulfill. This having of purposes pertains equally to all prospective agents. The first answer, regarding minimal requirements of rationality, or minimal generic capabilities in general, raises the thought that this minimum can be understood as having only a potential for such abilities. This thought will get some supporting arguments later. One of them deals with the second answer, regarding having purposes. If we understand having purposes, as existing even when there is no full awareness of them, we can also ascribe purposes to those who will be able to realize their purposes, in the right conditions and circumstances. This leads us again, to prefer the idea that the content of mental requirements will be only in potential, and that this will be a sufficient basis for being a prospective agent.

Gewirth responds to another criticism, regarding the equality of possessing rights, between people with different amounts of capabilities for agency. He says that the fact that the qualities that justify having rights are unequally distributed, entails that the rights should be unequally distributed too. When human beings lack the minimal abilities that enter into normal agency, they have the generic rights to the degree to which they approach having these abilities. Gewirth calls this the *Principle of Proportionality (PP)*, and defines it as follows:

> "When some quality Q justifies having certain rights R, and the possession of Q varies in degree in the respect that is relevant to Q's justifying the having of R, the degree to which R is had is proportional to or varies with the degree to which Q is had".[119]

This principle seems to imply that the mere *potential* of having certain qualities, may be sufficient for becoming a prospective agent. Gewirth interprets the comprehensive implications of this principle, and reaches the conclusion that:

> "Insofar as there is any biological possibility that the human in question will attain the normal abilities of agency, they have rights to the fostering of these abilities. Even when such attainment seems hopeless, they still have the rights to be helped to attain as close an approximation of these abilities as possible".[120]

Here we see a trend towards the conception I want to maintain. This view gives up the attempts to ascribe to prospective agents, any specific quality that uniquely bestows their moral status upon them. Nor does this view assume an essential nature that is shared by all prospective agents. I prefer to speak of a prospective agent as having a potentiality for a certain range of qualities and activities.[121] These qualities refer to the agent's potentiality for reasoning, and the agent's perceptual tools.

When I specify the most representative qualifications to which this potentiality refers, I place Rawls' demand for autonomy, at the top. This demand, to ascribe to the prospective agent *the potential to become a self-originating source of valid claims*, seems the most fundamental requirement for being recognized as a prospective agent. This requirement is of ultimate value, for ascribing to prospective agents the capabilities of having responsibility and dominion.

M.P.Golding details some more specific requirements, whose potential possession I regard as essential for being a prospective agent. The first is *the capacity to engage in voluntary activities.*[122] This is a very similar requirement to Alan Gewirth's first notion of the generic feature of an action, namely, voluntariness or freedom. The significance of this capacity for ascribing responsibility, or for determining the agent's autonomy was discussed earlier, but I want to remark here that it is the core of the uniqueness of agency.

The second essential capacity that Golding mentions is *having desires and interests.* This is similar to Gewirth's second generic feature of action, namely, purposiveness or intentionality. Golding broaches the idea that desires and interests, may be included in the very meaning of acting voluntarily. Such a conception exists in most agent-relative theories (i.e. Raz's that bases rights on interest), but is central especially in welfarist theories of rights.

The third requirement relates to the last two just mentioned, but goes further beyond them. This is formulated by Golding as *the capacity to engage consciously in purposive activities.* This requirement implies some mental abilities such as (a certain minimum of) intelligence, memory, etc. The two capacities just mentioned, certainly entail some mental abilities for being able to have desires or for being involved in voluntary actions. The point of the third capacity is that it emphasizes the aspect of awareness to the purposes and the purposive activities. This requirement limits the range of the possible kinds of purposive activities that can be counted as justifying grounds for ascribing agency. This means that activities that are purposive, but lack the awareness of the performer, do not function as describing a prospective agent.

The fourth capacity is more specific, and concerns right-issues directly. It is *the capacity to communicate demands.* When the direct identification of rights is that of valid claims, the ability to claim entails communicative abilities, at least on a minimal level, for being in a status of claiming. This ability can be expressed either orally (or any kind of explicit utterance) or by expressive (deliberate or not) behavior. A view that refers to rights as an obligatory moral relation between parties, entails that the parties can communicate to one another in order to express their claims or to demand their rights. The obligation of the respondent cannot be effective (or even may not be possible) without being informed, and being able to communicate with the claimant. This rationale is also relevant to the next necessary capacity.

The fifth capacity is *the capacity for conscious response to demands.* Similar to the previous one, this capacity is demanded by holding a prospective agent, not only as an alleged possessor of rights, but also as bound by duties. For being able to be under a duty (or to become a "respondent" of rights), the ability to comply, or even to respond to the claimant's demand is an essential requirement. Golding indicates that the required response involves not only a certain kind of receptivity, but also predominately, a realizable capacity to fulfill some of the demands already mentioned.

As said before, Golding suggests these capacities (together with some others) as "significance conditions" for rights-talk. He refers to these requirements as part of the natural environment, within which the discussion of rights takes place. His basic attitude says that these are essential respects of the human way of life.[123] I use this description as a foundation of my concept of a prospective agent. However, there is a fundamental difference between the function of these requirements in my view, and in Golding's. For Golding, these are the subjective conditions that are necessary for a conception of human rights. I use Golding's view as a general description of the characteristics, to which a prospective agent needs to have a potential for, in order to acquire his moral status. The most significant aspect of this status is that it fulfills the primary subjective individual demands for entering the moral community. This is to say, that to be able to join the moral community, the prospective agent needs to have a potential for some perceptual, cognitive, (or "mental") and behavioral capacities. The potential to follow Rawls' concept of the person as autonomous, with the two moral abilities and two highest order interests, is the essential requirement needed for being considered as a candidate to enter the moral community. The main aspect of this requirement is to be considered, as a self-originating source of valid claims. The potential to have Golding's capacities are the actual requirements, to be considered as a candidate for entering the moral community.

This is, more or less, the "Kantian", or "generic" (both Rawls and Gewirth regard their conceptions as "Kantian") aspects of my concept of a prospective agent, who is the kind of being that can be a possible member, or a candidate to become a member of a moral community. A prospective agent still does not possess any rights. The only entitlement he might have (if at all) is to be under consideration to enter the moral community, but this is only a merit, yet not a valid claim or right. This follows from my understanding of a moral right as a valid claim, i.e., something which exists and can be justified only within a system of rules, and more specifically, within a moral community.

There is still a need to explain why I prefer to regard the characteristics that are necessary for a prospective agent as only in potential, rather than actual. I mentioned earlier, when I described the acquirement of agency in Melden's theory,[124] that a sharp line cannot be drawn between a locution of a promise and a non-promise locution, when discussing children's expressions. Melden's idea is that when we understand the acquirement of agency as a process, we cannot point to any stage of this process as the critical or singular point that determines the transformation between not bearing responsibility and being responsible. In our case, when we consider some measure of the above capabilities as sufficient for regarding one as a prospective agent, and we cannot point out the exact measure, we refer to the minimum as sufficient. This hypothesis is quite similar to Gewirth's idea in the last quotation, regarding those who have any biological possibility to attain the abilities of agency. Gewirth ascribes to them the rights of the fostering of these abilities. In my view, regarding these people as having the potential to become agents has the same meaning as when discussing their entitlement to be considered as prospective agents. However, the main difference between my view, which finds it sufficient to have only the potential of some mental and perceptual capacities, and other views that demand the actual possession of these capacities, is the fact that in the other theories, these capacities function as a justification, or as grounds for possessing rights. That is to say that other theories derive the possession of rights, directly from the possession of the generic features of action. This entails that the reasons for possessing rights, do actually exist. In my view, those who have the potential to the suggested capacities are not considered as actual agents but only as prospective agents, who still do not possess rights. This is the main reason to be content with only a potential, and not with actual possession of these capacities. The potential to possess these capacities is a way of describing the kind of beings, who are capable of taking part in social interactions (or of getting an "entry ticket" to the moral community, within which rights are bestowed). This "entry ticket" does not assure membership (definitely not a *full* membership) in that community, but merits its owner to be considered as part of it. His membership, and hence his (moral) agency and possession of rights, will be determined according the way he maintains his moral abilities (or carries out his potential), within the moral community. The process of acquiring the status of a member of the moral community will be introduced in the following paragraphs.

2.6.3 The Acquiring Of Moral Agency Within The Community

In the beginning of this chapter, I said that in my opinion, exercising rights is possible only within a moral community. In this section I want to show how the prospective agent gets her moral status and becomes an actual or moral agent, during her development in the moral community, where she develops her moral consciousness.[125] Here, I explicate the implications of the assertion that exercising rights in possible only within a community.

W.T.Blackstone, when discussing the necessary conditions for rights-talk, hints at a position that assumes that the notion of persons who make claims about their interests against other persons, clearly implies the notion of a human community.[126] He indicates that any elucidation of the notion of a right requires a detailed statement of the significant conditions, within which this notion takes place. I briefly brought Golding's view about the subjective conditions, which he holds as significant for any rights-talk. I accepted them as requirements for prospective agency (in addition to some "Rawlsian" requirements), and indicated that they function as an "entry ticket" to the moral community. Now I introduce the "environmental" (or social) requirements, which Golding holds as significant for any rights-talk.

Like Melden and other "communitarian" theorists, Golding considers the existence of the community, as one of the most significant conditions for any rights-talk.[127] He insists that in the absence of any type of community, as the social environment within which demands are called for, a rights-discourse "has no foothold". Outside the community it is pointless to even speak of human rights, because there is no respondent who is obliged to fulfill anyone's demands. Golding presents this argument mainly in the context of demanding rights, which seems to be impossible in the absence of communicating partners. However, when considering rights as valid claims, we regard the moral relation between the components of this claim as bilateral, namely not only A has a claim against B, but B is obliged to respond to A's claim. This is to say that the one who is the respondent (or addressee) of the right is bound by a duty, that is created by the social acknowledgement of A's claim as a right. The social acknowledgement is crucial, not only for the validity conditions of the right, but mainly for the "guarantee" of its fulfillment. The compelling power of the right, which forces the respondent to fulfill his correlative duty, comes from the social acknowledgement of the possessor's claim as a right. This acknowledgement requires the existence of a community, whose mutuality and solidarity create the social agreements, that function as the mentioned guarantee.

The necessity of a community becomes crucial especially when discussing human rights, because in such rights the "respondent" is the community itself, and it is the community's duty to fulfill them. In such a situation, the community must view itself as being under a duty. This requires that its members be committed to their common interests, and respect other's claims with the same strictness, that they expect their claims to be respected. Without such a commitment, there are no grounds for the mutuality required between claimants and respondents. The main cause for the mutuality is the members' recognition of themselves, as sharing some fundamental beliefs and principles. This recognition brings them to acknowledge themselves as belonging to the same reference group – or a community of some kind. This hypothesis brings Golding to conclude that:

> "We cannot speak of rights existing anterior to or outside of a community. Furthermore, rights are always 'possessed' in relation to a community. 'Right' is a forensic term, and all claimings of rights are directed to, and are made in relation to, an audience".[128]

The understanding of rights as valid claims, places this discussion in the context of what Raz calls the "reciprocity theories", because the structure of claiming dictates mutual acknowledgement of the participants' moral status. The context, within which this status is established, is the moral understandings shared by both parties, the claimant and the respondent. When they do not share any of these understandings, there cannot be any acknowledgement of the justification or the validity of any right, and hence, of its correlative duty. Nor is there any recognition of the obligation to respond to any right. This process was illustrated earlier, with reference to the example of the minor social unity: the family. There, the parental rights were valid within this unit, as a result of the acknowledgement of the complicated relations between the components of the family. These relations define the rights and duties of the parties, and have no compelling meaning outside the framework of the family.

We can speak, in a similar way, of rights within society. The best way to explain this is to discuss human rights. Even in agent-relative theories, Gewirth's for example, there is an agreement that human rights are claim-rights.[129] The main justification for this conception is that these rights are claimed against the government or society, which are the addressees of these rights. The validity and justification of these rights, that impose duties on the government and society, are created by the common acknowledgement of the interests that are protected and promoted by these rights. This social acknowledgement is possible only within a framework that accepts some common principles and beliefs, as normative guidelines of the members' conduct. Such an acceptance is, in practice, the mutual sharing of some compelling norms, so that those who carry them out can be considered as a community. The absence of common conventions and shared norms, nullifies the mutual commitment of the parties to each other, and as a result of this, the validity of the communal institutions. The source of the convincing (and also the compelling) force of social institutions is their being justifiable in the eyes of those who are involved in them. With the lack of this justification, the social institutions that function as the guarantors for the fulfillment of (at least human) rights, become weak, and virtually fade away. When the social institutions, including their common conceptual grounds, fade away, we cannot talk about an existing community. Thus, we lose the ability to claim, or to protect and promote interests, by defining them as rights.

The inevitable conclusion of the above argument is that it is baseless to speak of exercising or capitalizing on rights prior to, or apart from, a community. This brings us to the second kind of desideratum, for the possessing of rights. This is not a mere set of requirements, but represents the communal (or communitarian) aspect of possessing rights. While the first set of desiderata referred to the subjective or individual requirements for possessing rights, and included mainly cognitive abilities, the second refers to the way the prospective agent maintains the first set, within the conceptual and practical environment, that enables the possession of rights: that is, within the moral community.

As I have said before, my view is that prospective agency is not a sufficient condition for possessing rights. It shows only that the one who owns this prospective agency, fulfills the requirements for entering the moral community, and can be considered as a candidate for membership in that community. To be respected as a member of the community, the prospective agent has to show respect both for other members, and for the community itself. The demand for respecting others' interests exists in both agent-relative and communitarian theories. In agent-relative theories it is an intrinsic and integral part of one's agency, since the demand for consistency, which results from the agent's rationality, forces him to treat others' interests the way he expects them to treat the agent's own interests. In communitarian theories, the demand for respecting others' interests is an intrinsic and integral part of the member's moral agency, since his moral status is dependent upon the fulfillment of this demand. Gewirth derives this demand from the Principle of Generic Consistency, and argues that consistency demands the agent's recognition of the others' agency, and this requires the agent to bestow upon their interests the same weight she bestows upon her own interests. For Melden, who regards the whole process of exercising rights as resulting from an agreement (such as when he derives the obligations and duties from their correlation to the institution of the act of promising), the notion of mutuality is more crucial. All agreements entail that the parties involved view themselves as belonging to the same normative framework, within which they arrange their agreement. It is this viewing of themselves, which is the foundation upon which the agreement is based. And the framework within which this agreement is valid, is the moral community. So, it is quite clear that a communitarian theory, like Melden's, presumes the existence of the community as a necessary condition for the validity of claims. This idea is the basic assumption of my discussion.

However, besides the necessity of a community for creating substantial grounds for the possession of rights, Melden mentions another aspect that he considers crucial for the durability of rights and duties. This aspect is the consideration and respect that the prospective agent demonstrates towards her partners, and towards the community as a whole. Melden insists that the persons who are involved in rights and obligations: "are mindful of each other's interests, and concerned in some way to lighten each other's burdens, and promote each other's good."[130] This introduces an additional factor to the complexity of transactions between participants of the social unit. It is not a neutral intention towards the interests of the others, but an intention that includes some element of benevolence. Melden holds that good will towards others is required of those who have rights, or those who are duty-bound to fulfill them, and this benevolence is far from being independent of rights and obligations. He concludes his discussion regarding this issue by saying:

> "There could not be the sense of obligation in the absence of the concern for others, no respect for the rights of anyone without an interest in his well-being, and no sense of guilt or feeling of remorse because of the violation of the right of anyone, without an involvement in his interests, a concern to promote his good. The idea that rights and obligations impose no requirement of good will towards others is incoherent. Far from it being the case that a consideration of the rights of persons occupies a separate moral domain from that of benevolence, it *depends* upon it; for in the absence of a concern with the well-being of others there could be no sense of the

important role that the rights of persons, our own and those of others, play in our life".[131]

I use a similar idea that connects between certain intentional requirements, and the embodiment of rights and obligations. Being less optimistic and more skeptic about human nature than Melden (that is why I deal with the withdrawal of rights while Melden deals with their possession), I do not stipulate benevolence or good will from a prospective agent, in order to become a member of the moral community, but have somewhat different – though more temperate – intentional requirements. What I demand from a prospective agent is only to abstain from the opposite of Melden's requirements. Following most of the theorists of rights, I consider the concern for others' interests as an indispensable part of any social arrangement. However, I minimize the motivation for this concern to only functional or instrumental reasons, and give up generosity or benevolence as the cause of it. For me, the desire for gaining the social advantages from the membership in the community is the main reason to uphold the obligations towards other members, or towards the community as a whole. I content myself with a minimal intentional requirement, mainly because what is important for me in the possession of rights is their applicability, or the ability to exercise and capitalize on rights. Good will definitely contributes towards this aim, but an abstention from the opposite, that is, the absence of ill will is sufficient for this aim. The important condition for making rights applicable is that the members of the moral community must cooperate, and it does not really matter whether their motivation to cooperate results from benevolence or from purely utilitarian calculation. The acknowledgement that it is the agent's interest to protect and to preserve the community, in order to enable the individual to promote and realize her self-interests, should be sufficient for persuading her to carry out her part of the social agreement. Her denial of her obligations would enfeeble the social agreement, and threaten its continuity and even its existence. So, in some sense, the preservation of the moral community can be understood as a protection of some necessary conditions for the ability to exercise rights, or even for discussing their validity.

At this point I come closer to my concept of a moral agent. For me the notion of an actual or moral agent (which is to be distinguished from that of Gewirth, who joins this notion with the notion of a prospective agent, at least for the matter of moral agency, or for the possession of generic rights), has some communitarian characteristics. This is to say that in my view, an actual or moral agent is a prospective or mere agent, who views himself as part of the community, or more accurately, who views himself as taking part in, or playing a role in, the community's social life. This status, of an actual or moral agent, implies that he practically (and not only consciously) admits his obligations as a member of the moral community, and is bound to fully cooperate with its demands and restrictions. In this case the prospective agent becomes an actual agent, or a member of the moral community. This is to say that a moral agent follows and fulfills his obligations as a member of the community. Taking the previous concept of a prospective agent and adding to it the communal commitments the agent accepts, brings about the concept of an actual or moral agent. A prospective agent is one who has the potential for some perceptual, cognitive (or "mental") and behavioral capacities (that were mentioned in the last section with regard to Rawls' concept of a person), who has, in addition, the communicative capacities demanded by Golding. Accordingly, an actual or moral agent (or a member of the moral community) is a prospective agent who does not intentionally harm, endanger or threaten the existence, integrity and morality of the community. And this agent, who is a member of the moral community, can be considered as a moral agent, and hence can possess rights, if he fulfills the intentional requirement that I mentioned earlier (that was distinguished from Melden's).

Melden holds that benevolence and good will are essential for the possibility of exercising rights, or for the creation of obligations and duties. For me the absence of the opposite (i.e. a lack of malice or evil intent), is sufficient for the possession of rights. A moral agent, in my view, is a member of the moral community who does not, of her own free will, renege on her obligations as a member. This kind of a member is entitled to possess rights, namely, can make valid claims and impose duties upon others. I do not require the agent to carry out her obligations beyond the call of duty, or out of good will. It is sufficient that she fulfills her obligations for any reason. The only necessity here is that she does not sustain ill will; that she does not intentionally renege on her obligations. Such a reneging, transforms her from being a moral agent to an immoral one. It is not a return to the status of a mere agent, who does not possess any normative judgment. The status of a moral agent is gained for some normative reasons, and entitles its bearer the rights that are bestowed upon moral agents. Intentional reneging of the obligations that are imposed upon members of the moral community, abolishes the status of moral agency. The status of moral agency is easy to attain, since it is bestowed merely for not reneging on the membership obligations within the community. So, a moral agent is merely an agent who does not intentionally carry out immoral actions against the community or its members, and more accurately, against her part of the social agreement. The absence of evil or malice in the agent's intentional conduct is the moral aspect that bestows upon the person her moral status as a moral agent, and as a result of this, her status as a possessor of rights. This is connected somehow to Melden's idea, of demanding benevolence and good will from members of the moral community. I minimize this demand and content myself with requiring the abstention from its opposite, so that the lack of "bad will" or wickedness, is sufficient for considering one as possessing moral agency. An agent who fulfills her part of the social agreement, willingly or not, will be considered as a moral agent, and entitled to possess the rights that are bestowed upon those, who are acknowledged as having this status.

The difference that is worthy of note between this conception and Melden's is that the latter unifies the notion of a moral agent, with that of a fully-fledged member of the moral community. In my view, a member of the moral community can lose all or part of her status of moral agency, and still be regarded as a member of the community. It is just her moral status that she has lost, but not her agency as such. This seems to be a nuance, but has a significant role in the withdrawal of rights. I said before, that a moral agent is one who bears her obligations within the moral community. This should be enough for regarding her as a moral agent, because she does not renege on her obligations. But this raises a fine distinction between "a moral agent", and "a member of the moral community". A mere or prospective agent needs only to be acknowledged of her obligations at the epistemological level. Her practicing and exercising of these obligations – at the practical level – turn her to be a member of the moral community. This member can then be a moral agent or she can become immoral, when, purposely, she threatens or injures the community, or its members. While in Melden's theory there is a full correlation between membership of the moral community and moral agency, in my view there is only a partial correlation. This correlation is continued, so long as the member of the community sustains her obligations, and ceases when she intentionally disregards them.

In some sense, we can say that my notion of a moral agent can be reducible to her innocence. In this sense, the innocence can function as a criterion for the assessment of the agent's morality, and hence serves as a measure of possessing rights. This criterion can be understood not only as a metaphor, but also as an elucidation of the distinction between being a member of the community, and being a moral agent. We can roughly say that a moral agent is an innocent (or blameless) member of the moral community. What is clarified here, is that, as distinct from Melden's view, the possession of rights is bestowed, essentially because of one's innocence, and not only because of one's membership in the community. This difference is significant for the matter of the withdrawal of rights. There, we shall find that the criterion of innocence has a crucial role. Here, it has mainly an explanatory role.

2.6.4 The Proportionality Of Moral Agency

When I presented Gewirth's theory, I mentioned his Principle of Proportionality in the context of the individual requirements for agency, and stressed his idea regarding different levels of possessing rights. According to Gewirth, when a certain quality justifies a possession of some rights, and this quality is varied in degree, it affects the degree of the possession of these rights. Gewirth illustrates his argument by saying that if x units of some quality Q justify one's possession of x units of some rights R, then y units of Q justify one's possession of y units of R. He adds that such proportionality is "a pervasive feature of traditional doctrines of distributive justice".[132] This principle is of substantial value when discussing welfare rights, but has an important function in any rights-talk. Its practical implications extend over the whole range of distributing and bestowing rights, especially in the assessment of the amount of rights that one's claims demand. This assessment refers to the numbers of rights one possesses, the scope of these rights, the weight that is given to each right, etc.

The evaluation of the extent to which one's justified claims can be considered as fulfilled, is one of the most problematic issues in rights-talk. The solution to this problem is connected to the extent to which the claims are justified. This is most workable when considering rights that are based on interests (this is why the Principle of Proportionality is so important for welfare rights). There, we need to estimate the extent of urgency of a certain interest, and the extent of its necessity. Then, according to these assessments, we set the correct amount of rights that follow from this interest. With human rights, it is much more difficult. We need to find the grounds for these rights, and according to the Principle of Proportionality, to match the amount of rights to one's entitlement. This is quite complicated, but it is, more or less, what we need to do, when trying to evaluate the degree of one's possession of rights.

Implementing Gewirth's Principle of Proportionality in my theory requires that I follow the process, according to which a person gets her moral status as a possessor of rights. This process has at least two steps. First, one must be considered an agent. Second, one must be a moral agent – namely, one who is integrated within the moral community. Correspondingly, the assessment of the extent to which the moral agent possesses her rights, should follow these steps as well. The extent to which one possesses rights is measured according to one's possession of the capacities that define one as an agent. This is the first step. We assess the level of potentiality regarding the intellective and communicative capacities that were mentioned before, and the level of actualizing these capacities, and fix the appropriate level of agency that these levels entitle.

Let us discuss this first step a little more. We have seen that in my theory, one's agency combines the abilities that arise from Rawls' conception of the self, while its detailed characterization was expressed by Golding's capacities. Considering this, we can say that the levels of agency vary according to the range of autonomy or dominion that we ascribe to the prospective agent. When we ascribe full autonomy to someone we consider her claims to be fully self-originating, and hence, she can become a full member of the moral community. That is to say that, her two Rawlsian moral abilities are developed to the necessary level that enables this prospective agent to fully cooperate in society. However, we can also determine that someone has only partial autonomy, and her claims have some heteronymous influences, and they are not fully self-originating. Similarly, we can say that she has only a certain amount of the Rawlsian moral abilities. We can say that she has only some "sense of justice" (regarding the first capacity), or that she has only some capacity "to form, to revise and rationally to pursue a conception of the good" (with regard to the second capacity). It does not much matter that we are satisfied with only a potential for having these abilities, or a potential for being a self-originating source of valid claims, because we can also rank both the potential, and its measure of realization. We can say, in the same way, that the prospective agent has some given measure of potential for these moral abilities, or some given potential to become a self-originating source of her valid claims. These can be reasons for considering her prospective agency as partial, and the extent to which she can take part in, or play a role in social life, as partial too.

The same procedure needs to be followed, when assessing one's range of capacities to each of Golding's requirements. Each of them can be extended over a wide range from partial to full possession, and this fixes different levels of prospective agency. Although we can hardly recognize different levels of the potential to have interests and desires (Golding's first requirement), we can easily observe different levels of the capacity for conscious response to demands (Golding's fifth requirement), among different prospective agents. The same procedure can take place when assessing one's potential for having the capacity to communicate demands (Golding's fourth requirement). The ability to evaluate the potential of having Golding's requirements enables us to fix the appropriate level of prospective agency, because this agency results from having this specific potential. However, this is only the first, and the least important, step since the measurement of potential has a lesser role in assessing one's agency.

Now we turn to the second step, which is the more important one, and concerns the **realization** of this potential. The extent to which a prospective agent realizes his potential is, virtually, the justifying grounds for his taking part in the moral community. Different levels of actualizing the mental (and also the moral) abilities create different levels of membership in the community. The differences can be caused by many factors. Not unintentionally I mentioned Joel Feinberg's identification of "normal adult human beings", as "the sort of beings of whom rights can meaningfully be predicated".[133] This classification can be the paradigmatic characteristics of what Golding calls "a full member of the community".[134] The reference to "normal adults" reveals at least two groups that are supposed to be considered as less than full-fledged members of the community. These are the groups, whose members are not adults or not "normal". Both groups (together with many other groups) lack some of the qualifications, or possess an insufficient amount of these qualifications, that usually confer the status of a full-fledged member in the community. According to the Principle of Proportionality, they can be given only partial membership in the community in the sense I used earlier: they may enjoy fewer rights, or their rights will have lesser scope or lesser weight than those of full-fledged members of the community. We can say about the members of these two groups, that their moral understanding has not been sufficiently developed, and hence, they are not considered as full members of the moral community. We can also say, more generally, that they do not sufficiently fulfill the requirements that are demanded from moral agents, or from full-fledged members of the community.

The first group, those who are not yet adults, have not sufficiently developed or actualized their potential to possess some mental abilities, and hence are considered as partial members of the community, or their level of membership is lower than full-fledged. The more they actualize their potential during their maturity, the more their moral status will grow. In any event, their possession of the potential to have some capacity, confers upon them their "entry ticket" to the moral community, although with less than a full membership, and hence with the possession of some, but not all, the rights that full-fledged members acquire. At least, they possess a certain amount of rights that are necessary for the fostering of these abilities.[135]

The issue of the second group is more complicated. We cannot responsibly decide whether those who are "not normal", completely lack the potential for certain mental capacities, or have some measure of them. Gewirth solves this problem by taking a decisive position, according to which even when there is no chance that some human beings can attain the abilities of agency, they still have the rights to attain "as close an approximation of these abilities as possible".[136] In this sense he confers upon them, more or less, the same basic rights we want to bestow on children, in order to enable their moral development. However, even here we realize that rights that are not concerned with the attainment of moral abilities, and rights that are somewhat less elementary, are not guaranteed to these prospective agents. It seems that some of these rights, which are grounded on the possession of some moral abilities within the moral community, cannot be warranted with regard to those who do not possess the mentioned requirements. The question whether our denying of some rights to these prospective agents, results from their lesser potential of having some moral abilities, or merely from not exercising them in one way or another, is very difficult to answer. We can skirt this question by saying that we bestow rights for a complex of reasons, which together create a conglomerate of justification for possessing rights. This answer may dim the problem, at least for the matter of the withdrawal of rights, which is the main topic of the next chapter. But it still requires us to assess the range of possessing the potential for each of the capacities, which are the grounds for the prospective agency. This issue refers mainly to mentally retarded or incapacitated persons, who possess some range of mental abilities, and hence are entitled to a set of welfare rights, that enable them at least a minimal level of self-respect, self-esteem and self-confidence. They cannot be considered as full-fledged members of the community, and may lose some of their rights (like property rights that are sometimes transferred to the agent's guardian or patron). The range of their possession of rights, although very difficult to assess, is matched to the approximate level of their agency. This is essentially an approximation of the level to which we ascribe to them the Rawlsian moral abilities, and their ability of being the self-originating source of their valid claims.

The way each participant of the social framework actually maintains her social obligations as a member of the community, is a more significant part of her being regarded as a member. The potential is the core of the reason for ascribing one's agency, but one's actualizing of this potential is the essence of that specific reason. The justification of the treatment of a member of the community with respect and appreciation, results mainly from the respect and appreciation she shows towards the community and the other members. Accordingly, the amount of agency we assume that a person has, and hence the extent to which we pay attention to her interests, is dependent on the amount of respect and appreciation with which she treats others' interests.

And this is an easier matter to assess, and respectively an easier way to grade her level of membership in the community.

Here, we get closer to the dominant factor that limits one's membership in the moral community: the range of one's being moral. I mentioned earlier, that one's morality is dependent on one's innocence. This brings us to the stage where we assess a person's membership in the moral community, and accordingly, her possession of rights, in accordance with her intentional reneging on her moral status as a member of the moral community. In the cases I earlier described as referring to **immoral** agents, there is a clear and obvious reason for a decrease in one's assumed moral agency. These are the most frequent cases where the withdrawal of rights becomes relevant. Here, there are reasons not only for not bestowing certain rights on the alleged agent, but for the denial of rights that she already possesses. Her level of moral agency has been reduced, and correspondingly, her degree of membership in the community. Her potential for having some moral abilities remains the same as before, but the way she actualizes this potential turns her to become an **immoral** agent, and hence impairs the validity of some of her claims. Thus, it also strikes at her position of claiming for these rights. This seems to be the easiest case of implementing the Principle of Proportionality, because it would give rise to a comprehensive agreement, about the justification for the decrease of the moral status of the agent. In any event, for the matter of assessing one's level of possessing rights, I say that the Principle of Proportionality functions as a measure for each aspect of the justifying grounds for moral agency. Whether it is the potential for mental abilities, the actualization of this potential, or even the actions that express the opposite of a specific actualization, we can grade in each of these aspects, the level to which one is entitled to one's assumed moral agency. Accordingly, we match the appropriate level of membership in the moral community, to the appropriate level of possessing rights. This "formula" serves as the foundation for the justification of the withdrawal of rights, in the coming chapter.

2.7 SUMMARY

In this chapter I tried to form the identity of a possessor of rights (or a right-holder) that would suit my view of possessing rights. I summarize two of the leading conceptions of possessing rights, and indicate my preference for one of them over the other. One conception is the "agent-relative" or "individualistic" approach that is represented by Alan Gewirth, which characterizes a possessor of rights as a moral agent, who acquires this status because of her following the Principle of Generic Consistency. This attitude places the prospective agent in the center, and considers her individual mental qualifications as the justifying grounds of her moral status. Gewirth himself calls this approach "Kantian", because of its rational aspects that are considered as the essential character of man's actions. According to this approach, the identity of a possessor of rights is identified with a prospective agent, as a result of her rationality. Since her rights are based on her mental capacities, she possesses them independently of her social status, or social role.

The second approach is "communitarian", and is represented by A.I. Melden's theory. According to this approach, the relevant moral attribute for the matter of possessing rights is one's membership in the moral community. Such an approach regards the notion of a right as resulting from the interrelations within an acknowledged (if not always clearly defined) social framework, which is based on common and shared normative and ethical rules and principles. The validity and the justifying grounds for rights, in this second approach, take place within an agreement that obligates those who participate in it. This obligation is created through the transactions between those who are involved in the social agreement. Here, their claims have a defined context within which they get their meaning and validity. This context is a set of moral and normative conventions, principle and rules, and those who share them can be considered as members of the moral community. These members have the moral status that bestows upon them certain rights, and turns them into possessors of rights. However, their membership requires their fulfilling of some social obligations that they bear as members, and depends on the way they assume their roles within the community.

The mutual dependence between the possession of rights, and the way members of the community maintain their transactions, place this approach within the domain of "reciprocity theories". Such theories entail the existence of sincere mutuality and reciprocity between those who commonly share a set of social obligations. The existence of normative principles and their acceptance by the participants, are considered as necessary conditions for exercising rights, or even for rights-talk. Hence, the existence of the moral community is required as a necessary condition for exercising rights. In this case, the preservation of the community and its members gets priority over one's self interests, when considering the individual's entitlement to possess rights. And since we assume that the fulfillment of the obligations towards the community is necessary for its preservation, we regard this fulfillment as a precondition for membership in the community, and for possessing rights within it. Therefore, in communitarian theories of this sort, the possession of rights, even when this is identified with membership in the moral community, requires more than merely possessing some generic or mental features. There must be a commitment to maintain a form of life that is appropriate to certain social normative standards.

The next step of my argument is the justification of my preference of the communitarian approach towards rights, over the agent-relative approach. The main reason for this is the decision, in the previous chapter, to regard rights as valid claims rather than entitlements. There, I preferred to consider rights as claims, essentially because this is the only way to guarantee welfare rights and human rights.[137] The idea that the ability to exercise and capitalize on rights entails considering them as valid claims is based on the assumption that some (especially human or welfare) rights, are to be given by the community. The only way to convince the community to bear its obligations, or to fulfill the demands of the mentioned rights, is to define the relations between the possessors of these rights and the community, according to the structure of a claim-right (the same structure that was taken from Gewirth). This is to say that when we deal with these rights, we consider the community as their addressee (or their respondent). And in order to be able to maintain this structure and its internal relations between its components (the claimants or possessors, and the respondent – the community itself), we need to regard the community as a necessary condition for the exercising of rights. Hence, the existence of the community is regarded as prior to the actual existence of rights, and as a necessary condition for their exercise. This analysis makes it groundless to speak of real rights prior to, or apart from, a community. Those who can enjoy rights within the moral community need to be considered as members of it. When they are regarded as such, they have some obligations towards the community, which actually establishes their ability to have rights. Then, their possession of rights is dependent on the way they bear these obligations.

The necessity of the existence of a moral community for exercising rights requires some clarifications regarding those who can have an "entry-ticket" to the moral community. For this matter, I used an agent-relative course and determined some agent-relative requirements, that function as the criteria for identifying those who can enter the moral community. The fulfillment of these requirements is the first step of justifying one's possession of rights. I call them the "individual" or "subjective" requirements. In addition to these, I mention those requirements, which result from the communitarian aspects of possessing rights: those requirements, which concern one's transactions within the community. They include the way one carries out one's obligations, and the absence of intentional harmful tendencies in one's conduct.

Both agent-relative and communitarian requirements, lexically ordered, together create a conglomerate of justification for regarding one as a moral agent. This status confirms the validity of one's claims, and enables one to possess rights. Every deviation from the conditions that constitute one's moral status, affects one's moral position, and changes the level to which one is entitled to one's moral status, and accordingly, the range of one's possession of rights. The extent to which one is considered as a possessor of rights, depends on the extent to which one fulfills the various requirements of each aspect of her being considered a member of the moral community. This is, virtually, an expansion of Gewirth's Principle of Proportionality, although the original idea referred to only one aspect of assessing one's agency.

The individual and communitarian aspects of identifying a moral agent, establish practicable grounds for discussing the withdrawal of rights, which is my main interest and the focus of this book. When there is a clear sense of the identity of the supposed possessor of rights, and of the justifying grounds and reasons for regarding her as a member of the moral community (and hence as a moral agent), we can question the conditions and circumstances within which this agent loses her moral status. The withdrawal of one's rights expresses a reduction of a person's moral status, and correspondingly one's possession of rights. In some sense we can regard this process as a re-examination or a reassessment of one's moral agency. The reconsideration of one's fulfillment of each requirement of agency, fixes one's current entitlement to one's moral status, to the extent of fulfillment of each set of requirements. Whenever there is an incompatibility between a person's morality and her moral status, we need to adjust her possession of rights to her new moral status. This theory regards the possession of rights within the community, as a result of different considerations regarding the moral relations between the components of the structure of a claim-right. Modifications in these relations affect the moral status of each component towards the other, and changes the validity of one's obligations, liabilities, burdens and duties on the one hand, and of one's privileges, rights, immunities and concessions on the other. The effects of some modifications of one's moral status, on one's possession of rights, are the topic of the coming chapter. There I deal with the guiding principles of what I, following Gewirth, call **overriding** rights – which are the justified infringement of rights – as opposed to **violating** rights – which is the unjust infringement of rights.

CHAPTER 3

THE WITHDRAWAL OF RIGHTS

The framework within which this study takes place, considers rights as valid claims, that is, claims that are justified within a system of rules. The validity of these claims is grounded on a certain description, which is held sufficient for justifying the claims, of those who fit this description.[138] In this sense, the possessor of rights can simply be considered as the person holding a set of qualifications, which certifies her status as a right-holder. The way I describe a possessor of rights entails the possession of some individual mental capacities, together with some normative requirements, that are part of the agent's membership of the moral community. Both individual (or "agent-relative", or "Kantian") and communitarian requirements, so lexically ordered, create justifying grounds, which is not only the necessary but also the sufficient condition, for ascribing moral agency to someone. Of course, both kinds of requirements need to coexist, since the moral agency results from the existence of an aggregate of characteristics, whose combination creates the moral agency. Each of these sets of characteristics can be considered as a necessary condition, but only their conjunction creates the validity of the claims, or the justifying grounds for possessing rights.

When the conditions and circumstances, under which one becomes a possessor of rights, are fully defined, we can decide to what extent that person should possess her rights. The possibility of determining degrees of possession of each component of the qualifications for possessing rights creates the possibility of determining the degrees of one's possession of rights. An absence of some components, or insufficient measure of any of them, undermines the validity of the claims that are supposed to be justified by the existence of these components. This is the starting point of my discussion about the withdrawal of rights. When considering the level of a person's moral agency, we actually determine the level of the possession of rights to which she is entitled, and if there is incompatibility between these levels, we have to adjust and regulate them. The adjustment might be performed in both directions: on the one hand, we can bestow rights that one is entitled to have but as yet does not actually possess. However, on the other hand, we can withdraw rights that the person is not entitled to possess.

The withdrawal of rights can be justified in different ways. At one level, rights can be denied temporarily, until one fulfills some requirements lacking at the moment. When this situation is changed, and these requirements are sufficiently fulfilled, these rights are returned or given to the person. This is the case when considering children's rights. The quantity of rights that children possess, should be correlative to their moral and mental development, and be dependent on it. This level is quite clear in the domain of legal rights, where the required qualifications for the possession of each right are clearly defined. For example, a person cannot have the right to vote for the government or to drive a car, before reaching a certain age. At the appropriate age she can vote (when age is the only requirement), or apply for a driving license (in addition to the fulfillment of some other requirements). Another example is the legal right to citizenship. An immigrant has to live for a certain amount of time in the country, before being entitled even to apply for citizenship. After the required stay in the country, she can receive citizenship (after fulfilling some additional requirements).

At another level, rights can be permanently denied, when certain requirements will never be fulfilled. The easier way to clarify this idea is, again, to look at legal rights. The right to be elected for presidency in the USA is given only to those who are born in the USA. Hence, this right will never be held by an American citizen who arrived in the USA as an immigrant, even though he possesses all the other citizenship rights. When considering moral rights, this situation is analogous to assessing the rights of mentally retarded persons. These prospective agents may never possess the mental requirements necessary for full membership in the moral community. Thus, we may not ascribe to them some capabilities that are considered necessary for the possession of certain rights (some of the requirements that belong to the first or "subjective" set of requirements for agency). In these cases we may not bestow upon them certain rights, even though they can enjoy other rights.

These two levels can be regarded as a simple manifestation of Dworkin's "trump" theory.[139] The prospective agent does not have, temporarily or permanently, a trump card that overpowers certain other considerations. However, there is also a third level of withdrawing rights. At this level we withdraw some of the actual rights, which the agent already possesses. This happens when an agent possessed some rights before, and ceased to maintain the justifying grounds for their possession. These are the cases where the agent fulfilled the requirements that justified her possession of some rights, and at a certain time ceased to fulfill these requirements. At this stage the reassessment of her rights, requires that those rights which she is no longer entitled to have, will be withdrawn from her. The typical circumstance, in which this procedure takes place in rights-talk, is the case of punishment. There, the agent intentionally reneges on her obligations as a member of the moral community, and undermines the justifying grounds for her moral status, and accordingly, her entitlement to possess rights. We can, therefore, use Dworkin's terminology, and consider this agent as one who lost her trump card or, in effect, lost her rights. We can justify this withdrawal of her right, by saying that she does not follow the description that created her former moral status and bestowed upon her the rights that this status usually entitles.

Each of these levels of withdrawing rights, requires its detailed arguments and separate justifications. Part of them, at least in principle, can have an accepted justification, and the discussion can turn around the specific cases of withdrawing rights (some of which may, sometimes, be found insoluble). Although the solutions of such discussions are always partial and not satisfactory, and sometimes they are only a compromise between conflicting interests, we can agree on the way we should try to solve them. More interesting but much more difficult to discuss, are those cases where the conflicts are not between the community and an individual within it, but rather between two members of the moral community. Here the question: who holds a trump against the other, is very complicated. The interests of both parties are sometimes hard to measure, and sometimes have the same weight. We cannot merely say that one's rights were overridden by the other's rights. We need to show how the other's interests (that are protected by his rights) were found more urgent, or got more weight, and thus justified the overriding of someone else's rights (that are supposed to protect her interests). Here, a more complicated procedure is needed, in order to decide which one of the conflicting interests gets priority over the others. For this, we need to turn to the social function of rights, and to the moral aspect of their possession.

The position regarding the concept of a right, nearest to the one I want to promote in this study, is to be found in Rawls' attitude towards their status. He says:

> "A conception of a right is a set of principles, general in form and universal in application, that is to be publicly recognized as a final court of appeal for ordering the conflicting claims of moral persons".[140]

Although there are differences between the Rawlsian concept and mine, I found his view regarding the social function of rights, very useful and clear. This is the format for settling conflicts between claims. Settling conflicts between claims of different persons should be performed by appealing to the interests that each claim represents. This involves the assessment of the validity of each claim, and the weight and range of each. Then we can decide which claim overrides the other. This is, in essence, a reassessment of each claim under the new circumstances (when it conflicts with other rights). When we deal with the withdrawal of rights of individuals within the community, we need only to assess the agent's fulfillment of certain kinds of requirements. We need to assess the agent's level of membership in the moral community, and the level of damage and threat that the agent imposed upon the community. However, when we discuss a conflict between rights of different agents within the community, it is a lot more complex to determine whose rights override the others. In such cases we need to assess each one's agency, on one hand, and the measure of urgency of the fulfillment of her interests, on the other. However, this reassessment can generate obscure and uncertain decisions regarding the conflict between rights, especially in controversial decisions.

These are the cases where an applicable theory of rights, can offer guidelines for solutions of conflicts between rights of different individuals.[141] To this kind of cases belong the disputes regarding abortions, where the mother's rights conflict with the fetus' rights. Here we cannot withdraw any of both sides' rights, without having some weighty arguments that support our decision. The conflicting interests in such cases are not only of different weight, but also of a different quality and a different category. For example, the mother's exclusive right to decide what will happen to and be done with her body, conflicts with the fetus' rights to be developed into a prospective agent. These are different kinds of rights, with different kinds of claimants, or, at least, claimants who have different kinds of moral standing. Any decision that comes out of this conflict between rights entails, first and foremost, a persuasive explanation, if not a justification, for choosing the particular methodology, that was used in order to solve this conflict. This is to say that before discussing an issue, we need to show that the way we examine this issue, is the one appropriate for such a discussion.

Similar principles apply to most of the questions regarding conflicts between rights or interests: issues such as the parental rights of mentally retarded persons, where the conflicts are between their right to pursue their own happiness or good, and the children's right to security and proper care and treatment.[142] These kinds of conflicts between rights, can (if at all) find their solution within rights-talk, only after an agreement about the fundamental principles of the right-based theory within which they are to be solved.

In the following sections, I try to defend the method I suggest to solve such conflicts between rights. I continue the line of argument of the previous chapter regarding the possession of rights, and use the same principles that were used for the assessment of one's possession of rights, in order to examine the case of the withdrawal of rights. I suggest that these conflicts will find their solution, by using the same method that was used in order to determine the agent's level of possessing rights. When there is a conflict between rights or interests, the solution should express the proportions between the level of agency of each side, and the level of possession of the alleged or assumed rights. Of course, the content (or the "object" in Gewirth terminology) of the conflicting rights (or the kind of interests to be protected by the conflicting rights) will play a substantial role in the decision. But the level of the moral status of the parties will be the basis, upon which we decide, if and to what extent, the overriding of a person's rights can make sense, or be justified.

Such a way of resolving conflicts between rights can be understood as a re-examination of the justifying grounds and reasons, for each of the conflicting rights. These justifications determine the extent to which one possesses the rights under discussion, and the extent to which these rights can be overridden by other rights, or can override other rights. The appeal to the justifying grounds of one's rights assists us to "quantify" the validity and soundness of a person's rights, and to assess the moral weight that is given to her claims, when these conflict with the claims of others. If the justifying grounds are considered as the foundation of one's rights, then it seems to be the relevant component to assess not only for the possession, but also for the withdrawal of rights.

In the course of setting out my theory, I mention some alternative views regarding the withdrawal of rights, and assess the extent of their agreement or disagreement with my view.

3.1 SOME RELATED POSITIONS REGARDING THE WITHDRAWAL OF RIGHTS

3.1.1 Gewirth's Position

The idea that the withdrawal of rights can be understood as a kind of removal of rights has various forms. We can find such a position in Gewirth's theory, which deals with the withdrawal of rights in the context of criminal law. Gewirth wants to show that the rules of criminal law are instrumental to the PGC. He explains this by saying that the PGC requires an equal distribution (of rights to well-being), between the agent and those affected by her action. When an agent causes harm to someone else, she violates this equality. Her punishment, which is prescribed by the criminal law, is justified, according to Gewirth, as a way of restoring this equality. Although Gewirth uses a different justification for the criminal law than that of retributive justice, he makes use of a similar idea. Gewirth says that the punishment of an agent, who inflicts a basic harm on another agent, redresses the previous balance that was disturbed by the harm that this agent caused. This, of course, requires that the penalties that are inflicted on the agent, should be proportional to the seriousness of her crimes, so that the equality involved is reasonably (even though not accurately) balanced. Gewirth views this as an application of the Principle of Proportionality: "although the penalties that are its contents, are not rights, but rather certain removals of rights".[143] We can see that the method of regarding the withdrawal of rights as a removal of them, in order to establish a balance between one's level of entitlement to certain rights, and the level to which one actually possesses them, is used even in some agent-relative theories.

The Principle of Proportionality is also used in Gewirth's discussion of the rights of children, mentally deficient persons and fetuses. He argues that the degree to which different groups approach the generic features of action, determines the degree to which they have or approach having generic rights. He does not regard children as prospective agents (who already have, according to his terminology, the proximate abilities of the generic features of action), but as potential agents (who, with normal maturation, will attain these features). Hence, they are not included among those whose right to freedom is required to be fully respected, according to the PGC.[144] This means that some of their rights are withdrawn from them, or not bestowed upon them. The rights they do possess are only those, which are preparatory for their acquiring the generic rights pertaining to full-fledged agency.

With mentally retarded persons, this matter is more complicated. They will never be able to attain all the capabilities that normal adults possess. Hence, they do not possess the same measure of rights to the necessary conditions required for moral agency. Their rights to freedom, according to Gewirth, are limited only to the extent that their conduct will not interfere with their own well-being, or with the generic rights of others. Here, again, Gewirth makes use of the idea that "the lesser practical abilities of such persons justify their having lesser rights".[145] The Principle of Proportionality determines the extent to which a person is entitled to possess generic rights, and enables us to deny her the possession of rights, which are beyond her capacities.

In the same way, Gewirth deals with the conflict between the fetus' rights to welfare and well-being and the mother's rights to freedom. I do not want to recount his whole argument here, but I briefly mention the main idea. He says that since the mother has the abilities that justify generic rights much more than does the fetus, she can be regarded as having more rights than the fetus. Here, the explanation for priority of the mother's rights is given because she possesses more rights than the fetus, since the fetus does not possess any rights to freedom, while the mother does. In other theories, when this issue is examined as a conflict between the mother's right to welfare and the fetus' same right, we may justify the priority of the mother's right because she possesses it to a higher degree than does the fetus. In any event, in Gewirth's theory, the fetus lacks a significant part of the abilities that justify generic rights, and lacks any purposes, and hence, is less than a full-fledged prospective agent. His generic rights, by comparison to his mother's generic rights, are minimal. This leads to the conclusion that abortion, under some additional conditions (like the age of the fetus, etc.), can be morally justified, since the mother's generic rights take priority over those of the fetus.[146]

The idea of limiting (or in the case of abortion – demolishing) rights, as a result of regulating and adjusting one's possession of rights, to the level she possesses the justifying reasons for them, has been discussed at some length. Gewirth's theory, as somehow deontological, determines one's agency according to one's personal abilities, and accordingly bestows rights upon this agent. Rights that one does not have justifications to possess are withdrawn. A communitarian theory, that measures one's agency according to the extent to which one fulfills her obligations as a member of the community, similarly determines her level of possessing rights. This theory withdraws her rights, whenever she does not fulfill these obligations, whether because she lacks the personal abilities for full membership in the community, or because she intentionally reneges on her obligations.

3.1.2 This Issue From The Communitarian Point Of View

The basic assumption of communitarian theories of rights identifies moral agency with membership in the moral community.[147] Hence, in such theories, the possession of rights results from this membership, and the level to which one is entitled to possess specific rights, is determined by the level of one's membership. As we saw earlier, such a membership consists of different elements. Some of them are personal or individual (for example, some mental abilities), and others relate to the agent's transactions within the community. The former elements are quite similar to their equivalents in agent-relative theories. The hierarchic order and grading of membership in the community are established in the same manner as in Gewirth's, or other agent-relative theories. It is clear that children or mentally retarded persons, are not regarded as full members of the moral community, and hence do not possess the same rights as normal adults. When regarding the acquiring of moral agency as a process, during which people become moral agents as they grow up and become full-fledged members of their community, we presuppose that there are some intermediate degrees in the moral development of people within the community. At each of these levels we ascribe a different level of morality and of moral agency, and bestow the equivalent measure of rights. In this sense, we can say that the denial of some rights (or their limitation), is simply not bestowing them. This is different from withdrawing rights in the sense that we withdraw rights that are already possessed by their holder, while in the case of children we do not yet bestow upon them rights that they may have in the future. The method of justification that was used for this earlier, of adjusting the possession of rights to the fulfillment of the requirements that entitle them, is equally relevant here.

The additional communitarian element of the justifying grounds for moral agency is the fulfillment of the communal requirements. However, this provides a wide range of reasons for the withdrawal of rights. These are the cases where the agent loses part of her agency because of her conduct. The main reasons for the withdrawal of rights within the community are the agent's disrespect for the interests of either the community as a whole, or for the interests of other members. When the agent does not observe the requirements of mutual concern and support, which are essential for the existence of the community, her moral status within the community is diminished. Her obligations towards other members are the essential part of her belonging to the same moral reference group (or the same moral community). Disrespect for them, undermines the conceptual substratum that lies in the background of the reciprocal transactions within the community. Another reason for the withdrawal of rights, results from the necessity to preserve the existence of the community in general, and its preservation as a moral system in particular. According to Melden, the preservation of the community is of paramount value for its members, since this is the only framework within which moral relations take place, and have (if at all) any application. Hence, the protection of the moral community from those actions or omissions, that might threaten or weaken its existence or its morality, becomes the ultimate mission of those who wish to have rights within the community.[148] When the existence or the morality of the community is damaged or endangered by an intentional activity of an agent, her part of the social agreement is not fulfilled, and some of her moral agency is taken from her. As a result of this, some of her rights are withdrawn.

This procedure can, more or less, find its counterpart even in Gewirth's theory, as far as this is concerned with the violation of the generic rights of other agents. But the essential difference between the two kinds of theories is that in some communitarian views (Milne's for example), whenever there is a conflict between the interests of the community (those which are regarded as necessary conditions for the existence of the community), and the self-interests of any particular member, the former have precedence over the latter.[149] In this case, rights can be withdrawn from agents, because these rights conflict with some interests of the community as a whole. In such cases, the overriding of these rights results from the superiority, which we ascribe to the rights that protect the fundamental interests of the community. This is a new dimension with respect to rights, when compared with agent-relative theories. What we have seen so far is that rights are bestowed according to one's moral status, or one's level of agency (and in communitarian theories, also according to the level of one's membership). It would seem that in this case the possession of rights is somewhat disconnected from one's agency, and become dependent on considerations that are external, from the agent's point of view (e.g., the needs of the community).

One way to skirt this problem is to say that the withdrawal of rights is due to the desire to protect the framework that enables the very existence of rights, and the regarding of their possessor as having any moral stance or status. This can be explained in terms of necessary and sufficient conditions, as I briefly note in the previous chapter. Such an explanation assumes that the essential prerequisites for the existence of a certain framework have precedence (or priority) over particular outcomes, which we wish to achieve from the existence of this framework. If we want the community to continue existing as a prerequisite for the members' ability to possess rights, we have to subordinate the rights of the members to the prerequisites of the existence of the community (for example, its basic principles, rule, unity, stability, etc.). Otherwise, we may "pour out the baby with the bath water", or we put an end to the members' ability to be considered as members, and consequently as possessors of rights at all. We assume that the destruction of the framework within which we exercise and capitalize on rights, abolishes the ability to enjoy them. Hence we agree to sacrifice some rights of a particular member, in order to secure the rights of the other members, and even the other rights of the members whose rights we sacrifice. In other words, we give priority to the foundation rather than the roof. We cannot do the reverse: to give priority to the member's interests over the fundamental or ultimate interests of the community, since after doing this the individual will not have the framework within which she can validate her claims, or give them any obligatory sense.

However, this partial solution is more appropriate to the concept of rights as entitlements, than as valid claims. This is because when the agent has a valid claim against the community, it is not easy to release the community from its obligation to fulfill this claim. This is not different from the more simple case, where the community has a valid claim against the agent, which demands that she waive some of her rights. We need a more persuasive justification to withdraw a person's rights in order to preserve the community.

Another way to ameliorate the problem is to follow Milne, and regard the interests of the community as reducible to the common interests of its members. Milne explains this by saying that a community consists of its members, and nothing apart from this. His position identifies the interests that the members have in common, with the interests of the community as a whole, and regards the expression "the interests of the community", as if it were an abbreviation for "the common interest of the members of the community".[150] He, of course, stresses that the common interest of agents as members of the community is different from their common self-interests as individual persons. Nevertheless, Milne's hypothesis may reduce the conflict between the interests of the community, and the interests of a particular agent, to a conflict between the agent's self interests, and the interest (although common) of the other members. However, this solution is unsatisfactory, since it is based on a somewhat problematic assumption. The identification of the common interests of the members with the interests of the community is not so easy to accept. Moreover, the idea that an agent as a member of the community, has some common interests that are in conflict with her own self-interests, is much more difficult to accept.[151] This is because this idea makes her membership in the moral community somehow nonremunerative. Her entering into the moral community was done in order to protect her interests, through their recognition as valid claims or as rights by the community. The situation where she finds her actual interests overridden by abstract ones (even when they are hers as well) creates alienation between herself and the community, or between her self-interests as an individual and her interests as a member of the community. This may weaken her obligations towards the community, and create further reasons to withdraw additional rights from her: this time, due to the more familiar reasons, such as non-fulfillment of her obligations as a member.

The only way to justify the withdrawal of rights through this method, is by limiting the range of the identification of the agent's self-interests with the community's interests, only to those interests required for the preservation of the wholeness and the morality of the community. Here, the agent's interests in sustaining the community are not abstract, and she regards its preservation as a protection of her ability to have rights at all. This brings us back to the previous discussion, regarding the sufficient and necessary conditions to possess rights. The solution that I suggest in the coming section utilizes this idea, but with some modifications. I argue that the withdrawal of rights can be justified, not only when the wholeness and morality of the community are in danger, but also for more comprehensive moral considerations. It will be justified not only according to the agent's individual conduct, or her level of membership in the moral community, but also according to the fulfillment of all the conditions of a fully defined and specified right.

3.2 TOWARDS A NEW CONCEPTION OF THE WITHDRAWAL OF RIGHTS

Most of the right-based theories relate to the issue of the withdrawal of rights, as a marginal section of the theory. The main part of their theories deals with the content of rights and their conditions of possession. It is necessary, then, to deal with the justifying grounds of rights (especially moral rights) and its applications, within a comprehensive theory of rights. The first and most urgent purpose of such a theory, is to formulate the semantic realm within which rights take place, and acquire their validity, their compelling force and moral status. This is the conceptual stage. The next purpose is to determine the identity of those who are capable of having rights, and the circumstances and conditions under which they are entitled to possess rights. The main question to be asked in a right-based theory is, "in virtue of what do persons possess their rights or get their moral status?" This is the justifying stage of the theory. The next purpose is to fill this moral status with content, which is the application stage of the theory. At this stage a theory defines the moral relations and, sometimes, the compelling mechanism or sanctions that possessors of rights can activate, in order to exercise or capitalize on their rights. Here we deal mainly with the modality and stringency of rights.[152] An important part of this stage is the guarantees that a possessor of rights has, as part of her rights (whether they are correlative duties that are imposed upon the respondents, or some other guarantees). Besides the questions regarding these guarantees, we deal at the application stage with the question, whether the possession of rights also includes their conditions of engagement.

In short, some of the most important right-based theories (Rex Martin's, for example) dedicate the essential part of their discussion to the necessity of ensuring rights, that is, to the guarantees of their possession, their exercise, and their fulfillment. This has almost become a tradition in the political discussion regarding rights and liberties, as a part of the traditions of liberal and social democratic thought. Whether the right-based theories belong to the tradition that Rawls associates with Locke, or to the tradition that Rawls associates with Rousseau, they continue the same tendency of both traditions: the desire to protect and promote rights, and the moral status of their possessors. According to Rawls, the tradition associated with Locke gives greater weight to what Constant calls "the liberties of the moderns". These are the freedoms of thought and conscience, some basic rights of the person, some property rights, and the rule of law. On the other hand, the tradition associated with Rousseau, gives greater weight to what Constant calls "the liberties of the ancients". These are the political liberties and the values of the political life.[153] In any event, each of these traditions, and the tradition of rights-talk as their inheritor, concentrates on the achievement and attainment of rights, as part of the struggle to enable as many people as possible, to enjoy rights to the highest possible measure. Those traditions functioned as the theoretical substratum of the long-lasting and painful process, during which human and welfare rights became an essential part of social life. The desire to internalize the idea of possessing rights, as an essential component of people who view themselves as belonging to, and taking part in, the social and moral community, was the main incentive of those traditions. Hence, their central pursuit was to define the conditions and circumstances under which rights are bestowed or conferred, rather than withdrawn or forfeited.

The question of the limits of the moral status of the possession of rights is usually discussed towards the end, and sometimes in the margins of right-based theories. This is usually the final part of the application stage of such theories. To this section belong the questions regarding the withdrawal of rights. However, this is the continuation of the application stage of these theories, and usually is not discussed as a separate issue, apart from the conditions of engagement and the conditions of possession of rights. Most of the issues at this stage pertain to the question, when do rights cease to hold or become invalid. The tenor of such debates is similar to those I expressed earlier, when I introduced the relation of agent-relative and communitarian theories, to the issue of the withdrawal of rights. Principally, they deal with the extent to which agents fulfill the requirements, due to which they get their moral status, and accordingly, possess rights. When there are incompatibilities between the extents to which agents are entitled to their moral status and between their actual possessions of rights, those theories justify the withdrawal of rights. This is, more or less, my way of studying the issue, but from a slightly different point of view.

My starting point is that the idea that regards rights as an essential part of social life, at least at the theoretical level, is widely accepted in contemporary rights-talk. Even though in practice this idea is not so widely accepted, and there are struggles for human and welfare rights in every country and society all over the world, there is a comprehensive consensus among theorists, about the significance of rights in modern political and social life. On the other hand, while the withdrawal of rights became, in practice, frequent and decisive in so many domains, this issue has been very under-discussed at the theoretical level. My position is that we can be equally decisive when discussing the withdrawal of rights, as when discussing the possession of rights, without threatening the significance we ascribe to their possession within modern society. In fact, the opposite may be true. The withdrawal of rights (in situations where it is justified and necessary), both in its practical and theoretical aspects, should be performed precisely from the desire to sustain and guarantee the status of rights, as a final court of appeal for ordering the conflicting claims of moral persons.[154] It categorically does not undermine the possession of rights, when agents justifiably possess them. On the contrary, when we prevent agents from using rights that they are not entitled to possess, we actually strengthen the ability of those who are entitled to possess rights, to exercise and capitalize on their own rights. In the coming sections I try to clarify my view, and present the conditions and circumstances under which the withdrawal of rights are justified.

3.2.1 Some Terminological Clarifications

Within rights-talk, when discussing the cases and circumstances where rights do not hold, there is a widespread use of terms, which assign different meanings to different kinds of such cases. I have already mentioned Gewirth's terminology, which distinguishes between different kinds of infringements of rights. According to his terminology, a right is *infringed* when the correlative duty is not carried out, whether justifiably or not. A right is *violated* when it is unjustifiably infringed, and is *overridden* when it is justifiably infringed.[155] However, these terms have different meanings and uses in different theories, and it is worthwhile to note other uses of similar, synonymous and equivalent terms.

Joel Feinberg deals with the nuances that differentiate between the uses of these terms within the semantic realm of alleged rights that lost their validity. He recalls Judith Thomson's distinction between *infringing* and *violating* one's right. Thomson's use of these terms is quite similar to Gewirth's: however she emphasizes that we violate another person's right, "if and only if, we do not merely infringe it, but more, are acting wrongly, unjustly in doing so".[156] Feinberg introduces some other distinctions between similar terms, and offers his clarifications of their meanings. Among many ways of regarding rights, he chooses those terms that he finds significant to clarify, and explicate their specific meaning and use.[157]

His first distinction is between *alienating* and *forfeiting* rights. A forfeitable right, according to Feinberg, is not possessed unconditionally in all circumstances, but rather, it is a right that one must qualify for, by meeting certain conditions of proper conduct. When the conduct of the possessor of such a right falls below the qualifying standards, she loses her right. This is to say that when the possessor of such a right misbehaves, she disqualifies herself for continued possession of her right, and becomes liable to its annulment. What Feinberg means, is that a forfeited right is not arbitrarily cancelled or withdrawn, nor it is voluntary relinquished or transferred. Rather, it is a consequence of the possessor's wrongdoing, which enables the right to be withdrawn from her (we can roughly say that "she brought it upon herself"). Hence, a *nonforfeitable* right is one that a person cannot lose through her own blundering or wrongdoing. On the other hand, an *inalienable* right is one that its possessor cannot give away or dispense with, through her own deliberate choice. So, from this definition we can recognize that an *alienable* right is one that its possessor **can** give away or dispense with, through her own deliberate choice.[158]

Feinberg's next distinction is between *inalienable* and *indefeasible* rights. An inalienable right is a right that one cannot give away or dispose of, even when she wishes to. Accordingly, an alienable right can be given away by its possessor, when she wishes to. An indefeasible right, in contrast, is a right that its possessor cannot be deprived of without her consent. Thus, a defeasible right is a right that one can be deprived of without her consent. In this case we speak of *annulling* her right.

Feinberg differentiates between the following similar terms in order to clarify them: *waiving* and *relinquishing* rights. Waiving a right relates to discretionary rights. When I waive my right, I actually exercise the power to release others from the correlative duty, which they bear towards me as the possessor of this right. Waiving a right can be understood in two contexts. The first is when the renouncing of a certain right is permanent and irrevocable. Here, the one who renounces her right can never get it back, even if she changes her mind. Another possibility is when the right is irrevocably renounced for *a fixed period of time.* During that period, no change of mind can restore the right to its original owner. However, after the expiration of that interval, the right can be repossessed. The weaker application of waiving a right, that Feinberg considers more natural or common, is to give up a right but retain the prerequisite to change one's mind at any time and at any point. In this sense, says Feinberg, whenever the renouncer wishes, he can nullify the transaction of his right. Thus, the waiving of a right is inherently revocable.[159] Both uses can be understood as relinquishing a right, but at different levels and in different senses.

Feinberg's distinctions relate to several cases where rights are not activated, either because of the absence of validity, or because of the absence of an interest or desire to exercise them. Carl Wellman calls such cases "*unreal rights*". There are several cases in which rights are considered "*unreal*". Wellman cites some examples. First, he recalls the cases where the alleged right-holder lacks the qualifications to possess a certain right (or all rights). In these cases the alleged rights are unreal, or we can even say that there are no such rights at all. The second argument for regarding rights as unreal is that their implications are false or unacceptable. Another way to regard rights as unreal is to argue that there are no grounds for those rights. This can be a result of the fact that the alleged grounds do not exist, or the specific grounds are inapplicable. Wellman's next case relates to derivative rights. In this example, some specific right is unreal because the more general right from which it is allegedly derived, is limited in such a way as to exclude this specific right. Similarly, we can say that some concrete right is unreal, because the more abstract right on which it is grounded, is outweighed by other conflicting abstract rights.[160] Wellman illustrates each of these cases, and some of his examples will be discussed later, in a different context. What is important for my purposes, is to mention that one of his ways of settling conflicts between rights, is not simply by withdrawing one of them, but by defining it as unreal, and hence as no longer existing. In this case, its withdrawal does not need any justification. I use a similar idea in my solution, adapted to my concept of a right-holder, but without being committed to define whether the withdrawn right is real or unreal.

3.2.2 Some Conceptual Clarifications

As we have seen, there are different forms or types of the withdrawal of rights, or to the situation that Judith Jarvis Thomson calls: "ceasing to have rights".[161] First and foremost, are those cases where right-holders bring themselves to cease to have rights.[162] These cases can result from various reasons. First, they can result from a promise, whose outcome creates a claim that the receiver acquires, and this claim annuls the possessor's right. Second, it can be a result of the possessor's consent. An outcome of this consent is that the consent-receiver acquires a privilege, that annuls the consent-giver's claim, and hence, her right.

Similar situations of ceasing to have rights can be the waiving of them, where the possessor divests herself of her rights. Thomson describes different mode of rights divestiture. The possessor can waive her rights by an intentional act, or by simply letting them lapse and refraining from action. In this case she can be said to have forfeited her rights.[163]

My purpose is not to deal with the cases where agents, from their own choice or free will, waive their rights. My basic view is that rights not only include their conditions of engagement, but also the possessor's privilege (precisely according to Hohfeld's meaning of the term[164]) to decide whether she exercises them or not. Of course, there are interesting and complicated cases of waiving rights, where we weigh and re-consider whether these rights can be forfeited. Cases like children's rights to a decent and appropriate education are, in my opinion, doubtful in this manner because we ascribe to children almost all the acknowledged rights of those members of the moral community, which we do not regard as full-fledged members. When the status of a prospective agent approaches (or gets closer to) the status of a moral agent, the questions whether and to what extent she is in a position to waive some of her basic rights, become more complicated and hard to answer.

However, I am most concerned with those cases in which the possessor of a right loses her right against her wishes, or at least, without her consent. This is to say that I leave aside the whole issue of waiving rights, together with the various ways of doing so: whether intentionally or not, and whether by active efforts or simply by letting them lapse. Instead I concentrate on those cases whereby rights are withdrawn from their possessors when they (the possessors) do not want to relinquish them. Other cases that enter my discussion are rights that are temporarily denied under specific circumstances, in order to bestow them when the time is right – like certain children's rights, which will be bestowed upon them in the course of their maturity. These cases are not the typical cases of *withdrawing* rights, but of *withholding* them. However, I include them in my discussion since the common denominator of these cases is that in all of them, we did not obtain the possessor's consent for waiving her rights. The other variables of withdrawing rights among these cases are different, and the reasons and grounds for the withdrawal of each right are different. But they all belong to the same category I have just mentioned.

The main reason I concentrate on these cases is due to my adoption of Rawls' concept of rights as "a final court of appeal for ordering the conflicting claims of moral persons".[165] This is a functional or instrumental concept of rights, but determines the most significant role they have in settling conflicts. Such an attitude towards rights, place the cases where there are conflicts between claims, in the center of the discussion. At this stage of my discussion, it does not matter whether the conflicts are real or feigned. This may be part of their solution. What interests me is that prima facie, there are conflicts between claims that require solutions of some kind. When one of the parties waives her rights or forfeits her claims, the conflict disappears and there is no longer any conflict between claims. This leads me to focus my discussion on the withdrawal of rights, when their possessors, at least theoretically, have interests in retaining possession of these rights. Here we need to judge which of the claims is valid, whether and to what extent it can override the opposing claim, under which conditions and for what duration. The considerations for this decision, can relate to one or many components of the justifying grounds of the conflicting claims, but they must be subordinated to the rules, regulations and principles, on which the possession of rights is determined. This means that to some extent, the withdrawal of rights can be viewed metaphorically as a fluctuating position on the scale of possessing rights.

My main idea is that in the same way that we measured, in the second chapter, a person's entitlement to possess her rights, or her level of membership in the moral community (which expresses her level of moral agency), we now readjust her level of possessing rights to her new entitlement. When we examine her level of moral agency, we do so according to her level of fulfillment of both individual and communitarian requirements for moral agency. What we actually do in this process, is to examine a person's fulfillment of the justifying grounds of her moral status, or her possession of rights. Whenever the level of fulfillment of the justifying grounds of her rights, stands higher than, or exceeds, her actual possession of some rights, we award her the missing rights. In the same way, when her level of fulfillment of the justifying grounds of her rights, stands below or is less than her actual possession of some rights, we withdraw from her the excessive rights. The component that is not sufficiently fulfilled, can be any condition of one's justification for having her rights, and the extent to which these rights are withdrawn, is proportional to the weight this component has when considering one's rights. In other words, the same component that justifies one's rights can be used, when improperly fulfilled, for justifying the withdrawal of these rights. I explain this in the paragraphs below.

3.2.3 Possible Directions For Justifying The Withdrawal Of Rights

Before discussing my theory of the withdrawal of rights, I want to present my concept of the general components of a fully specified right, in order to identify possible justifying grounds for its withdrawal. Some of these components were already mentioned before, but here I specify their role in bestowing and withdrawing one's rights. For this matter I refer to James W. Nickel's analysis,[166] and use his terminology for explicating my theory of the withdrawal of rights. To begin with, I introduce their "positive" role, namely their function in establishing one's possession of rights.

First, Nickel speaks of the conditions that give one the right, or that make one a right-holder. Nickel calls them *Conditions of Possession*, and says that they are determined by the right itself. These conditions determine who has the right (or who is the *subject* of the right, in Gewirth's terminology), and specify not only the possession of the right, but, sometimes, the procedures for permanently withdrawing the right. They can, for example, specify the procedures through which this right can be sold, repudiated or forfeited.

The second component of a right is that of the *Conditions of Engagement.* These conditions specify the circumstances, under which the purported right can be brought into play. They define the appropriate circumstances under which this right really generates a correlative duty, when it is claimed or invoked. This means that a right is *engaged* when it is not only appropriately, but also successfully, claimed or invoked. These conditions do not determine when one has the right, but only when the right applies, and what has to be done in order to bring it into play. One can have a right without invoking it, but one cannot engage it, without claiming it first.

The third component is the *weight* of the right. This specifies the rank or importance the right has, in relation to other norms or requirements. In other words, the weight of a right specifies how strong or weighty it is, in relation to other considerations. This pertains mainly to the question, whether a certain right can be overridden by other considerations in cases of conflicts, and to the conditions, circumstances and permissible limits of such an overriding.[167]

The fourth component is the *addressees* of the right. This is the corresponding term of Gewirth's notion of "the respondents" of the right. These are the parties who bear obligations or other burdens because of the right. In the terminology I use throughout this study, the addressees are those who are under the correlative duty of the right, or those who are bound to make available the prescribed benefit that is included in the right.

Nickel's last component is the scope of the right. This is what I call "the content" of the right, or, in Gewirth's terms, "the object" of the right. Nickel explains the scope of a right, as the freedom or benefit that must be made available, under certain circumstances, to the right-holder. In simple words, the scope of a right specifies what this is a right to, or what the right-holder is entitled to have, by virtue of possessing this right.[168] To this aspect also belong the boundaries and restrictions on the enjoyment of this right.

Nickel gives an example that clarifies and illustrates his terms. In his example:

–All residents of the United States *(the Conditions of Possession, that specify who has the right)*,

–who are charged with a serious criminal offence and request a trial by jury *(the Conditions of Engagement, that specify when does the right apply)*,

–have a right of a certain weight or priority *(the weight that specifies how strong or weighty is the right in competition with other considerations)*,

–against the government of the United States and its states *(the addresses that specify who bears obligations or other normative burdens because of the right)*,

–to a trial by jury *(the scope, that specifies to what is the right-holder entitled by virtue of having the right)*.[169]

These five components, that classify the conditions under which one has a right, can also be used for explaining the non-exercise of this right. One's right-claim can fail because of a lack (or improper fulfillment) of each of these conditions. To begin with the first component, namely the conditions of possession, one can be considered as not qualified for possessing rights, because of different reasons related to the fulfillment of these conditions: a person's right has been transferred, sold, repudiated or forfeited.

Right-claims can also fail with regard to the second component: the conditions of engagement. In this case, there are circumstances where these rights do not apply to the situation where they are claimed, or where they have been waived, or even were not invoked. Here we say that the conditions of engagement are not appropriately fulfilled for some reason, and this causes the right-claims to fail.

The third component – the weight of the right – relates mainly to the conflict between claims, each of which has some moral justifying grounds. In this case the alleged right applies, but is outweighed by other considerations. This issue is often the key to the solution of moral dilemmas that include conflicts between rights, that Carl Wellman would have seen as "real" in different situations. Many of the current discussions regarding abortions, privacy and medical secrecy (especially the recent debates regarding AIDS sufferers), apply to the measurement of the weight of each party's rights, when they are in conflict with the rights of others.

The fourth component is a bit problematic. Nickel presents a situation where the right-claim fails, because its addressee is unable to comply with its fulfillment. According to his view, the right-claim indeed fails, but it raises some questions about the status of the addressee's correlative duty. These questions relate, inter alia, to the principle, which says that "ought" implies "can".[170] However, this is not my main interest here, so I shall simply remark that one's right can fail, because of reasons that are included in the fourth component of a right – its addressee. Sometimes when the addressee is the community, and the fulfillment of one's right includes the infringement of the rights of others, we might say that the community is "unable" to comply with one's right-claim. But this case can equally be presented as belonging to the previous component, where rights of the others override one's right, and hence it is connected to the question of the weight of the right. Nevertheless, this can be one of the cases of a failing of a right-claim, that Nickel ascribes to the addressee's inability to respond to the right, or to fulfill the correlative duty.

The fifth component of a right – its scope – comprises the right-claims that fail, as a result of falling short of their constraining requirements. This means that a right-claim fails, because the benefit that is being claimed falls outside the scope of the rights. In other words, one's claim is for something that is not included in the range of entitlements that the specific rights bestow or confer upon that person.

Each of these components justifies the withdrawal of rights in the same manner as it justifies the exercising of one's rights. The core of this way of thinking is, that just as each right specifies the conditions of its validity, scope, duration, range of application, etc., it also specifies its limits. This means that it determines not only the identity of its possessor and the circumstances under which this right should be conferred, but also prescribes when and under what circumstances, the right should be taken away or withdrawn. To use a different terminology, we can say that just as rights include, in their definition, their moral validity and justification, and hence the justification for establishing correlative duties, so too do they include their "conditions of expiration".[171] Our previous decision to regard rights as valid claims, leads us to say that rights include not only their conditions of validity, but also specify the conditions under which they lose their validity. When a person stops fulfilling the requirements that make her claim valid (and hence protected and guaranteed by a right), she is no longer entitled to the moral status, that comes with the possessing of this right. Hence, the withdrawal of this right can be justified.

From all the aforesaid, we reach the conclusion that a given right may have to yield to different sorts of considerations, and not only to the demands of another right.[172] We may find ourselves involved in the infringement of a person's rights, without being suspected of wrongdoing, even when we do not justify our infringement with the claim that we are protecting other people's rights. We can simply point to the lack of the validity of a right, or the lack of one of the components that establish the justifying grounds for this right. Despite the difficulties involved in the attempt to give a full and precise specification of each of these components, we can easily imagine situations where the lack of any of them, would support a justifiable case for withdrawing a person's rights.

Many attempts have been made to define or specify "absolute rights" or at least "inalienable rights". H.L.A.Hart speaks of the equal right of all men to be free, as a natural and hence an absolute right.[173] Stuart M. Brown Jr. regards the right of all to the protection of their moral interests, persons and estates, as an inalienable right. Hence, he insists that this right cannot be denied, waived, conveyed, delegated or voided.[174] However, all these attempts end in moot and controversial conclusions that have been comprehensively criticized. Generally these rights were found to be merely prima facie. William Frankena, for example, analyzes Hart's purported natural right, namely, the equal right to be free, and says that it actually breaks down into two prima facie rights: a right to equality, and a right to freedom.[175]

The fundamental assumption of this study rejects the claim that there are inalienable rights. I accept the criticism that has been made of such alleged rights.[176] Actually, most cases of withdrawing rights from others, relate to rights that are not considered as inalienable in any context. Whenever I discuss a case that is concerned with a right that is said to be inalienable, I will bring some of the arguments against the conceptions that assume that these rights are inalienable.[177] Regarding rights that are not claimed to be absolute, or that are usually regarded as alienable, their withdrawal will be justified not merely by considering them to be merely prima facie rights, but by pointing out that they are regarded as non-existent under certain conditions, where their claimings are justifiably not allowed.[178] This means that I regard the possession of all kinds of rights as conditional. The claim for their exercise is dependent upon the possessor's fulfillment of the requirements, through which the claim can be acknowledged by the community as valid. The validity of one's claim is, then, circumstantial and limited in duration. So long as the conditions that validate the claim exist, the claim is acknowledged as a right. Whenever any of these conditions is absent or incomplete, the right may vanish or be withdrawn. The essential question here, is who has the authority to decide that the justifying grounds for one's right are not present, and hence that the right can justifiably be withdrawn. In other words, I am concerned here with the question who is authorized to withdraw rights, or by whom a right can justifiably be withdrawn. I deal with this question in the coming section.

3.3 WHO HAS THE AUTHORITY TO WITHDRAW RIGHTS?

In order to use the method of adjusting the level or degree, to which a person may justifiably claim to possess rights, to the equivalent level to which she fulfills the requirements that bestow upon her the moral status involved in possessing her rights, we require an authority that will decide whether and to what extent these levels are correlated. This decision determines which rights are to be given or withdrawn. This issue is quite clear when considering legal rights, because there, rights get their validity in an explicit way. According to Joel Feinberg's terminology, which I previously adopted, rights, in general, are not only justified but also valid claims. This is a justification of a peculiar and narrow kind, making it something that takes place within a system of rules. Feinberg says that: "A man has a legal right when the official recognition of his claim (as valid) is called for by the governing rules".[179] This leads to the conclusion that the authority for recognizing a claim as a legal right, or validating it, is upheld by the legal system, or by someone appointed within the system. The rules that are recognized as legal, or are legislated by a legislature as the foundation of the legal system, define specifically all the components of a right, and the conditions and circumstances of its validity. The legislative authority empowers the judiciary, to carry out and enforce its legislation by a basic law, entrusting the laws to the judgment of the courts. Hence the judiciary is the authority that has the authorization to impose duties on parties, to declare what are a person's rights, and to compel the addressees to fulfill the demands that are claimed by these rights. It also has the authorization to withdraw a person's rights, whenever her possession of those rights is incompatible with the conditions, under which she was allegedly acknowledged to possess them.

However, my concern is with moral rights. When Feinberg discusses the validity of such rights, he mentions that his previous definition of legal rights "hardly applies to moral rights". He insists that a moral right is nothing other than a claim, whose validity may or may not be grounded on a different kind of a system of rules. According to Feinberg: "A man has a moral right when he has a claim the recognition of which is called for – not (necessarily) by legal rules, but by moral principles, or the principles of an enlightened conscience".[180] When we base moral rights on principles, the obligatory relations that they create are vaguer and more obscure. The definite identification of at least the addressees of legal rights does not explicitly exist in moral rights, and more or less the same applies to the other components of such rights. To understand the reason for this, we may apply Dworkin's distinction between rules and principles. Although he refers to the difference between legal rules and legal principles, his distinction clears up the main difference between moral and legal rights. According to Dworkin, there is a "logical distinction" between rules and principles. He contrasts rules and principles on two counts. The first regards their applicability. About this issue, he says:

> "Rules are applicable in an all-or-nothing fashion. If the facts a rule stipulates are given, then either the rule is valid, in which case the answer it supplies must be accepted, or it is not, in which case it contributes nothing to the decision...Of course, a rule may have an exception...However, an accurate statement of the rule would take the exception into account, and any that did not would be incomplete".[181]

Michael Bayles explains this statement by saying that when rules apply to a case, they determine the decision without any leeway for an alternative.[182] Principles, according to Bayles' understanding of Dworkin's concept, are rather different. They do not necessarily determine decisions even in the cases to which they apply.

This difference gives some idea about the ability to determine relations that are based on rules, in contrast to those which are based on principles. Relations which result from rules are sharply defined and specified, so that the status of each party involved is clearly understood, and the possibility of fulfilling their respective demands is clearly defined. This is also the implication of a second difference between principles and rules. This difference relates to the weight that principles have and, according to Dworkin, rules do not have. Dworkin says that the dimension of weight (or importance) is relevant only for principles. This means that when principles clash, the solution to their conflict must take into account the relative weight of the principles. He admits that there cannot be an exact measurement of this weight, and hence the judgment that one principle is more important than the other, can often be controversial. However, he insists that this dimension is an integral part of any principle, and it makes sense to ask how important or how weighty is this principle. Bayles' interpretation for this is that due to their having weight, principles can be added together and balanced. When several principles lead to one decision, and several others to the opposite, we can "add up" the weight of the principles of each side, and balance them in order to reach a decision.[183]

Rules do not have this dimension, and hence, according to Bayles, cannot be balanced. Dworkin mentions that sometimes we can speak of rules as being *functionally* important or unimportant. This means that one rule may be considered as more important than another rule, because it has a more important role in regulating behavior. Some rules of a specific activity can be more important for that activity, than other rules; but this importance cannot serve as a basis for balancing. We cannot say that one rule is more important than the other (within a system of rules), so that one supersedes the other by virtue of its greater weight, when those rules conflict with one another. Unlike the case of principles, when two rules are in conflict, one of them must be invalid. It is not the case that one has a greater weight, and hence overrides the other, but rather that the other has no validity in that particular case, and hence it does not apply.[184]

Dworkin's distinction helps us to understand the point I raised earlier: the identity of the framework that has the authority to withdraw moral rights. Considering the validity of moral rights as grounded on their being acknowledged by moral principles, or the principles of an enlightened conscience, requires that the content of both rights and principles will be justifiably specified. Unlike the case of a legal right, where the governing rules specify all the components of a certain right, in the case of moral rights it is more complicated, because we deal with principles. These principles can serve only as guidelines for our decisions about each component, including the weight of each right that is alleged to exist. When we empower any authority to withdraw someone's right, we must justify our decision, because this power has not been defined within the definition of the right, or within the system of rules (or principles) that creates the validity of this right. The acknowledgement of any moral claim as valid, may establish its general moral justification, but more must be done in order to recognize all the moral relations that this right establishes.

Among the components that need to be specified, are the identities of the addressees of the right, namely those whose duty it is to respond to the claim and to provide what is required for this right to be fulfilled, and the identity of those who have the power to withdraw this right, when its validity expires or when this right is suppressed by other moral considerations. The method by which we specify the identity of the former, directs us to the identity of the latter.

Many discussions regarding human rights identify their addressee with the state. Most of them also include an ethical or normative element in their concept of human rights. Carl Wellman, for example, defines human rights as:

> "...A cluster of ethical liberties, claims, powers and immunities that together constitute a system of ethical autonomy possessed by an individual as human being vis-a-vis the state".[185]

In this sense the state has to provide these rights to each and every person who claims them. We can even look at the state as the authority whose duty is to function as the guarantor of these rights, besides being their respondent.

In an analogy to human rights, we can say that the moral community is the guarantor for the realization of moral rights. In order to prove that this analogy is not arbitrary, and that it makes sense to see the community as the guarantor for this realization, I recall the status that was ascribed to the community in the previous chapter. There I insert a quotation from Golding, which more or less summarizes the position I maintain in that chapter. According to this position we cannot speak of rights as valid anterior to, or originating before, the community. Rights, in this view, are always exercised in relation to a community.[186] In the absence of a community, which functions as the social environment within which demands are called for, even rights-discourse has no foothold. The social acknowledgement of a claim as valid, and hence as a right, is the reason to see its respondent as being under a duty. The compelling power of the right results from this acknowledgement, and hence the fulfillment of the right by its respondent can be enforced. This means that the social acknowledgement functions not only as the foundation of the validity of rights, but also as the guarantee for its fulfillment. In order to fulfill this function, a well-ordered and well-established community includes the appropriate institutions that have the power to enforce rights as well as withdraw them. These institutions have the same functions as that of judges and the police in the legal system. Without authorizing certain institutions to assure the bestowing of rights and their withdrawal, the community cannot be regarded as functioning or even established.

The role that the community plays in establishing the validity of one's rights signifies the direction to which we must proceed, when identifying who has the authority to withdraw rights. Saying that the community's acknowledgement determines the validity of one's right, means that it is the community that determines the conditions and circumstances, under which one has a right. Besides the granting of rights and imposing of duties, the community, as the guarantor of all the rights within it, enforces their fulfillment, and uses sanctions against the respondents, whenever these rights are not fulfilled. This is an integral part of the community's function, as the framework within which rights can be exercised and capitalized. Being not only the conceptual, but also the practical environment that makes rights concrete (or "real" in Wellman's terminology), imposes upon the community the duty of guaranteeing these rights. This is to say that the community functions as a bailor, who has the power to enforce the duties upon the respondent, in order to assure the possessor's rights or the fulfillment of her interests. In this sense, the community can sometimes function as an arbiter between parties who are in conflict. The conflict can be between the possessor and the respondent (whenever the respondent is not the community itself), or, in a different kind of conflict, between different possessors whose rights are in opposition. In the first kind of conflict the community uses its authority to impose the duty upon the respondent who was acknowledged as such, by the acknowledgement of the possessor as having that specific right against that specific respondent. Of course, such a conflict can end in the community's decision that one does not possess this right any longer, and hence the respondent is released from being under a duty. The community can alter each of the components of one's right – for example, its weight or even the identity of its respondent (that is to say that A has a right to X against C, instead of against B) or the object of the right (that A has a right to Y instead of to X). These changes in the moral relations between the parties are all within the community's authority, as the logical substratum that lies in the background of the transactions of rights and duties. In each of these cases we can say that the community adjusts the moral relations, which are involved in the transactions of that specific right. The community adjusts the measure of rights that one actually possesses, to the extent to which the person is entitled to have them, under the new circumstances. Accordingly, it fits the correlative duty to which the respondent is bound, to the extent to which it is required by one's modified right.

The same happens with the second kind of conflict, those between different possessors of the same rights, or different possessors of different rights. Here it is more complicated, since more factors are involved; but the same considerations regarding each party's rights and duties apply. The community has to assess the extent to which each possessor fulfills the requirement of each component of her right, and accordingly decide the measure of her entitlement to possess this right. After assessing the possessor's entitlement to her own right, the community has to compare it to the right with which it conflicts. At this stage, the weight of one's right is compared to the weight of the conflicting right. When doing this, the community needs to use a new set of considerations that are not necessary in the former kind of conflict. Here the community is required to assess the extent of urgency that is to be assigned to the fulfillment of each right, and the extent to which it is to be fulfilled, when compared to the urgency of the conflicting right. Among these considerations, the community has to decide whether the fulfillment of one's acknowledged right can still be justified even when it hurts or strikes at the other's acknowledged right. This means that the community is required to reconsider the weight of one's right, under the new circumstances. This is, in fact, reconsideration of some of the justifying grounds of one's right, and a reassessment of one's moral status as the possessor of this right. The conclusions of this reconsideration determine whether one's right overrides the other's right, or both are to be partly fulfilled. However, these issues are discussed in detail in the following chapters. Here I want to show how the community, as the guarantor of the members' rights, functions in regulating and adjusting their conflicting rights.

The intervention of the community in the members' possession of rights is not only out of necessity to preserve the stability and functioning of the community, but is also part of its moral obligations towards its members. Being the guarantor of their rights obligates the community to intervene, whenever there is any incompatibility between what the members justifiably claim, and what they actually possess. This intervention requires authority in order to be efficient. And when we impose the obligation to protect and promote the members' rights upon the community, we must ascribe to (and confer upon) its acknowledged institutions, the authority to intervene in their rights. This enables the community to regulate and adjust the conflicts between claims. The authority includes the power to deny a person's rights, to prevent one from exercising one's rights, to abstain from giving a person rights (when the community is the respondent of these rights), etc.

3.4 THE JUSTIFYING GROUNDS FOR THE WITHDRAWAL OF RIGHTS

The last paragraphs led us, although indirectly, into the issue of the justification for the withdrawal of rights. Let me go back to the first kind of conflict that the community is supposed to regulate. In these cases, the community is required to settle a conflict between a possessor and a respondent of a right. When the community decides to release the respondent from his duty, the actual meaning of this decision is the denial of the possessor's right. This can happen in different situations, some of which can be understood as a withdrawal of one's right. In such situations, the community acknowledges one's right before the conflict, and a person is able to actualize her right until the situation changes and the community decides that she does not possess this right anymore. It does not matter whether the respondent is a person, an institution, or the community itself. In each of these cases, the community uses its authority to reassess a person's moral status, and hence her possession of rights, under the new circumstances.

The last remark is mostly relevant to the discussion of human and welfare rights, whether these rights are also acknowledged as legally binding or not. The community is considered the respondent of these rights. If these rights are acknowledged by the governing rules, and hence are recognized as legally binding, the direct and immediate respondent is the government, through its institutions (the welfare and legal institutions). This still does not release the community or the society from being the guarantor for the fulfillment of these rights, whenever the government abstains from its duty. However, in these cases the community is not the respondent but the guarantor. For reasons of convenience I shall explain my ideas regarding the community's withdrawal of one's rights, in the cases of non-legal human rights, where the community is considered as their respondent. When these rights are acknowledged as valid claims, the community actually admits that the possessor fulfills the conditions of possession, and also that the conditions of engagement do exist.

Let us look, for example, at one's right to freedom of expression. Under usual conditions, the community protects this right and promotes the exercising of it, by offering the appropriate forums or media for the expression of one's ideas and opinions. What should the community do when these opinions are not considered legitimate, according to the moral values of the community (for example, when a racist speaks against members of minority groups, and incites others to murder them)? If this is unbearable to the community, it is within its authority to deny the person permission to publish his racist opinions (although he can freely express his other opinions). Here the community withdraws the right to freedom of expression in this specific area, and this limitation of the right to freedom of expression (that forbids the incitement against minorities) applies equally to all the members of the community. For those who are unsatisfied with this conclusion, I also present this issue as a case that belongs to the second kind of conflict, where the possessor's right to freedom of expression, conflicts with the right of a member in a minority group not to be tortured or humiliated. In this point of view, the community must reassess a person's rights to freedom of expression under the new circumstances, vis-à-vis the rights of the member of the minority group, and decide whether the latter right overrides the former. If the community decides that these rights cannot coexist together, and that the latter right overrides the former, it must withdraw the former right. In any event, the consequences of both points of view in this case are the same, and the community withdraws the person's right, based on its moral judgment. What was considered as valid before (one's right to freedom of expression) is not valid anymore, and it is the community's duty to readjust and regulate one's moral status, and one's range of possessing rights.

This concept may be elucidated by comparing this to the case of one's legal right to have a driving license versus the right to exercise this privilege by legally driving a car. When a driver starts to suffer from poor eyesight, and her driving without glasses endangers herself and her surroundings, the authorities must force her to wear glasses when driving. In this act, the authorities (in this case the Ministry of Transport and the Licensing Office) withdraw or modify the driver's original right to drive, in accordance with the new conditions that arise. The same conclusion would be reached, if we regard this case as belonging to the second kind of conflict. We could say that one's right to drive without glasses, is in conflict with the rights of others to safety and security. When measuring the urgency of both sides' claims, we might conclude that the latter right overrides the former, and hence, justifies the withdrawal of one's right to drive without glasses. A court of law relates to this issue by asserting that one's right to drive without glasses is conditional, and when its possessor does not fulfill those conditions that validate her claim, she is not regarded as having this right anymore, and hence, its withdrawal is justified.

The function that the judiciary fulfills in allocating legal rights and duties (including the withdrawal of rights, and the release from duties) is fulfilled by the community itself insofar as moral rights are concerned, or human rights which are not as yet acknowledged as legally binding. Of course there are some differences, the most important of which is that legal rights are defined by the legislature, and implemented by the executive, while in moral rights, the community functions as both the legislator and the executive at the same time. However, with regards to the procedure of withdrawing rights, the similarity is quite evident. In both cases, the authority decides whether one is still entitled to have the same (moral or legal) status, and accordingly regulates the measure of rights to be retained.

However, there are certain differences between the community and the state which render the procedure as not completely analogous. The rules according to which rights are bestowed and withdrawn within the state, and the role of the judges and the police, as well as the sanctions that can be imposed by the legal system, are much clearer and more explicit in the state. The principles and guidelines that set the community in motion are not as sharp and clear (part of this results from the differences between rules and principles mentioned before), and the exact measure of bestowing and withdrawing rights is accordingly only approximate. However, we assume that a well-established community has its own mechanisms and institutions, which are capable of regulating the allocation of rights within it.

Hoping that the comparison above to legal rights indeed clarifies the procedure through which the community can justifiably withdraw rights, I return to another conflict, which is more complicated, but still, in my view, belongs to the first category of conflicts. I shall start to explain my position through another example. Supposing that everyone has a moral right to privacy, what should the community do in the case of a known HIV-positive carrier, who intentionally infects others? This can be seen as a conflict between the carrier's rights to privacy, and the rights of others to health, and protection of their physical integrity. Here, it seems quite obvious that the urgency of the latter right is much stronger than the former, and easily overrides it. This, at once, creates an obligation or imposes a duty upon the community, to warn its members regarding the carrier, and this strikes at his right to privacy. However, I prefer to deal with this example within the context of the first kind of conflict.

In the previous chapter, I defined an actual or moral agent (or a full-fledged member of the moral community) as a prospective agent, who does not intentionally harm, endanger or threaten the existence, integrity or the morality of the community. I mentioned Melden's idea, of demanding benevolence and good will from members of the moral community, and noted that I have lower standards for a person to be considered as a moral agent. I content myself with requiring only the abstention from doing the opposite, so that the lack of ill will or of wickedness, is sufficient for regarding a person as possessing moral agency. For me, an agent who fulfills his part of the social agreement (willingly or not), is considered as a moral agent, and entitled to possess the rights that are bestowed upon those who are acknowledged as having this status. In this context, I explained that to some extent, my notion of a moral agent can be reducible to the person's innocence, or absence of malice. In this sense, innocence can be used as a criterion for the assessment of the agent's morality, and hence can serve as a measure of the entitlement to possess rights. Now, imposing these requirements on the HIV carrier shows that since he is not innocent, he is not entitled to the full status of a moral agent, and hence is not entitled to possess the specific right of privacy. His mode of conducting his transactions within the community, debars him from being considered as a moral agent, and disqualifies him from possessing rights. The loss of his innocence removes part of his moral status, or his "moral standing" with regard to his right to privacy (even though he still possesses other rights such as property rights, etc.). What is relevant in this example, according to my view, is that the conditions of possession are not fulfilled, and this consideration is prior to the conflict with the rights of others. Here we avoided the need to consider the question of the conflict with the rights of others, because, in viewing this case as a conflict between the possessor of the right to privacy (the carrier), and the respondent of this right (the community), we straight away voided the person's right to privacy; so there is nothing left to conflict with the rights of the others. In Wellman's terminology, we can say that the carrier's alleged right becomes "unreal", under the new circumstances.

This is the way I prefer to deal with the question of the withdrawal of rights. I look at this question as directly connected to the matter of the possession of rights. In some sense, both possession and withdrawal of rights can be considered as lying on one lone continuum, along which rights are given and denied, conferred and forfeited, bestowed and withdrawn. When the community acknowledges one's right against others or against the community itself, it bestows upon the possessor a certain moral power to enforce her demand on the respondent, or on the community itself, in the case of the community itself being the respondent. When the claimant cannot exercise her right, or enforce her claims upon the respondent, it is the community's duty to enforce this right, and use its power whenever it is necessary, in order to support the possessor to achieve the fulfillment of her right. This is the comprehensive and real implication of the position, which argues that rights can be validated and implemented only within the community.

When saying that we cannot speak of rights apart from or originating before the community, we mean that it is the social acknowledgement, including the social guarantee and protection for the fulfillment of these rights, that makes them feasible, or "real". We also mean that it includes our acknowledgement of the community's authority, to use its power to sustain the possessor in achieving her demands. In any event, we mean that this power and authority are necessary in order to make sure that each member gets exactly what the community acknowledges as her due. Whenever the possessor gets less than what is acknowledged by the community as her due, it is the community's obligation to use all the necessary means, in order to complete the fulfillment of all the rights the agent should possess. The community has to make sure that she gets what she is entitled to, according to the community's acknowledgement of her claims as valid.

This is the way I understand the community's function regarding a person's use of rights that she is not entitled to possess. In my view, the measure of the person's possession of her rights is prescribed immediately with the community's acknowledgement of her claims as valid. The validity of the claims is limited by the community to the fulfillment of a certain set of conditions and circumstances (for example, conditions of possession, conditions of engagement, etc.), under which these rights are regarded as valid. Hence, it is the community's duty to make sure that she does not make excessive use of her rights, under the community's patronage or protection, whenever this use is incompatible with the community's authorization. When she uses or exercises her rights beyond the constraining conditions, or whenever her fulfillment of those conditions no longer applies, the community is required to prevent this misuse. This is, in other words, a demand for the withdrawal of some rights, or, in the relevant cases, a demand that the community should stop conferring these rights. In those cases, the withdrawal of rights is, in effect, interfering with a person's possession of rights, in a way that prevents her from using or possessing these rights.

For example, when the community decides that those, and only those, who are unemployed have a right to get a free meal each day, in one of the community's welfare institutions (and it does not matter whether this right was recognized as legal, or it is up to the community's good will), it means that one who starts working and getting a salary, is not entitled to have this free meal anymore. If the community does not make any exceptions to this free meal policy, then it is up to the community to prevent the newly employed person from eating in this institution. This may be regarded as inequitable, but the point is clear. The example regarding the HIV-positive carrier may seem much more justifiable, but refers to the same idea: that the community must regulate and adjust the exercising of rights, to the appropriate measure. Another example is when a community agrees to pay rent for its unemployed members. When someone finds a job and can pay the rent by herself, the community should stop paying her rent. Similarly, if the community supports a public accommodation for homeless people, and discovers the there is a person who enjoys this service but retains a house that he rents to someone else and keeps the money for himself, the community must stop this support to the person concerned.

This issue is clearer when considering the function of the community, in a case where there is a conflict between two individuals: a possessor and a respondent of a right, both of them living in the same community. Suppose A has been given the right to use B's parking lot, in return for washing and cleaning B's car twice a week. So long as both A and B fulfill their part of the agreement, the existence and function of the community remains dormant, and lies only in the background of this relation. The status of the community at this stage is to act as the guarantor of agreements or obligations within the community as a whole. Following Melden, we assume that such a foundation is possible, only subsequent to the existence of the normative and conceptual framework, within which there is a comprehensive consent between all parties to respect agreements. We said in the previous chapter, that rights and obligations exist "only where there is a community of understanding of the complex array of moral concepts, within which the concepts of rights and obligations have their place".[187] For Melden, a community which respects the conceptual framework is crucial, in order to provide an appropriate setting for the enjoyment and exercise of rights. When belonging to the same community, namely, voluntarily sharing the normative demands, and understanding the sense and meaning of the shared set of concepts, A and B can carry out moral transactions, that include rights and duties. In the situation I discuss, B fulfills her duty to provide a parking space for A's car, and enjoys a washed and clean car. No interference of the community is required for these transactions between A and B.

Let us explore this example, when there is a crisis in the relations between A and B. Suppose that B decides to lock her parking lot and prevent A from parking there. It seems obvious that A is released from her part of the agreement, because the respondent of her right has not fulfilled her duty. If she already managed to wash B's car twice this week, she has the right to keep on parking on B's parking lot, at least till the end of this week. If B refuses to enable A's parking, it is the community's obligation to intervene and force B to let A park, and to capitalize on her right. The same concept applies when A stops washing B's car, but keeps on using B's parking lot. The community must prevent A from making an excessive use of her right, which has expired when she stopped washing B's car. The community must protect B, whose obligation towards A was acknowledged before the crisis of her relations with A. If the community could enforce the fulfillment of her duty before, it is now reasonable for her to expect the community to intervene again, but this time in her favor.

However, the crisis can take other, complicated forms. Suppose A decides to wash B's car only once a week. It is clear that the original conditions that created A's original right against B are changed. This immediately raises the question about the implications of this change, on the new moral relations between A and B, and especially about A's former right against B. If both A and B arrive a new agreement under the new conditions, and announce that the former agreement is void, the community tacitly confirms this agreement and remains in its passive role, namely that of being the silent or dormant guarantor for the fulfillment of this new agreement. The community remains the basis for the existence of this agreement, and the guarantee for the solidity and applicability of its implications.

But what happens if they cannot reach a new agreement? B has a justification for her claim that the original agreement does not exist anymore. This releases her from being bound by a duty, and she is not obligated to fulfill any of A's demands, even though her car was washed once during the week. However, A can argue that the original agreement is partly fulfilled, so she should get part of her original right, let us say, parking in certain hours, or on certain days of the week (or alternately, a week in each fortnight). Each of the above claims has its point. Here the community, as the guarantor of A's former right, must function as an arbiter between the conflicting claims. It must reassess A's rights according to the new circumstances, and decide what (if any) rights she is still entitled to have. Part of this decision can take into account the urgency of A's right, and the loss that might be caused to both sides and to the community as a whole, as a result of any decision. Nevertheless, any decision reached by the community, binds the parties as members of the community. Just as A's former claim got its validity from the community's tacit acknowledgement, so the relations that result from the new decision are valid, because of their being acknowledged by the community. This decision, besides being an intervention in the moral relations between A and B, might end in the total withdrawal of A's former right, or in the establishment of new moral relations that may include a new (and maybe diminished) right for A against B. The readjustment and regulation of the moral relations between A and B can end in different results, according to a wide range of possible circumstances, within which this reassessment takes place. In any event, it is within the community's authority to withdraw or reduce someone's right, as part of its obligation towards its members to settle conflicts between their claims. The community might cancel the original agreement, and announce that no relations exist anymore between A and B. It may even impose a penalty on A, or force her to compensate B for the violation of the agreement. Another possible result can be the acknowledgement of A's violation of the agreement as unavoidable (suppose the city council prohibits washing a car more than once a week, if there is no water recycling apparatus, in order to reduce the community's water consumption), and hence confirm the existence of part of her former right, etc.

The interpretation of the last example, that views it as a conflict between two claims that are at least partly valid, brings us closer to what I called earlier: the second kind of conflict. In this kind of conflict, both claims have (at least) some justifying grounds. The last example cannot be a typical case for these examples, because A's right is doubtful, or at least uncertain. The question whether her claim has any validity, requires the community's decision, and only when this question is positively answered, can this case belong to the kind I now want to discuss. Here, the conflict is between two (or more) possessors of different rights, which cannot be entirely fulfilled together, or cannot be fulfilled together at all. In the latter case the fulfillment of one's right, precludes the fulfillment of the other's right, or even causes damage or harm to the other. One of the most typical cases of such a conflict is the case of abortion. I will not analyze this case in detail now, but I point out that it belongs to the kind of conflict I do discuss here, in order to clarify the role of the community in solving such conflicts.

In the case of abortion, the conflict is basically between the fetus' right to well-being, and the mother's right to freedom. It is clear that in ordinary conditions the community acknowledges both rights. However, a mother's decision to end her pregnancy through an abortion directly causes the death of the fetus, and hence the complete loss of its generic rights. There can be no way through which both rights can simultaneously be fulfilled. Having no one to protect the fetus' rights but the community (even though the fetus is not a member, but at most a future member), it is the community's obligation to consider its rights under the present conditions. Here, the community's role starts to become clear. The expectation that the community should consider the fetus' rights, is not based on the fact that this right is vis-a-vis the community (or similarly, not because the community is the respondent of this right). The conflict here, as in the former example, is between two different beings (and here we assume that the fetus has certain interests and a measure of a moral standing, otherwise there cannot be a conflict at all). We can raise doubts whether this is a conflict between two members of the community, because we do not consider the fetus as a member, and maybe not even a prospective agent. This is because the status of the fetus as an individual is not clear enough. I am not sure that defining the fetus as a future or prospective agent helps the clarification here, but I insist that the fetus' status is not the main issue in clarifying the community's role. The conflict here is between an actual member of the community, who is considered a moral agent, and a being whose moral standing is acknowledged by the community, for certain reasons and under certain conditions and circumstances. This acknowledgement expresses the way the community can ascribe a moral status to a human being, and when doing so, the community undertakes the obligations that result from this status. After all, the community epitomizes the shared moral principles of its members, and its morality reflects the common values and norms of the members. And it is the community that determines, according to shared values and moral principles, the actions within it and the moral status of its members. This is the meaning of a framework within which rights and obligations take place.

The mother's right is concrete because it has the guarantee of the community. In this situation the mother not only invokes the protection of the community, but also admits that this right is subordinated to the community's consideration. This entails the community's involvement in something that would seem to be the mother's private affair. The interference of the community is based here on its function as the background substratum of the mother's rights, and, in fact, everyone's rights. This authorizes the community to examine the limits and the conditions of anyone's rights, including the mother's right to freedom. Thus, the community regards the fetus' rights as one of the considerations that should be taken into account, when assessing the mother's rights. The community is the only authority that can uphold the fetus' claims, even though there is no claimant. The alleged biological father, in my opinion, has nothing to say about this issue, beyond his status as part of the community. The only relevant entities that have any moral status in this conflict are the mother, the community and the fetus. The fetus is endowed with a moral status (although it is not considered as autonomous in any possible way), as a result of the community's acknowledgement of the intrinsic value of its interests. In this sense, the community also intervenes in the interests of those who are not counted among its members, when these interests are connected in any form to the interests of members of the community.[188]

However, I discuss this specific conflict, regarding abortions, in detail later in this study, so for the time being, I set aside my views regarding this issue, and use it merely for clarifying my point. In this example I want to emphasize the status of the community, as the supreme authority regarding the allocation of obligations and rights. When considering the mother's rights, the community measures her moral status, as part of the same procedure that was described in the former kind of conflict. This means that every component of the mother's right is measured, and the moral status and hence the possession of rights, is set accordingly. The community does more or less the same with the fetus' right. It measures the extent to which the fetus fulfills the capacities that confer the moral status of a prospective agent. The result of this assessment determines the extent to which the community acknowledges its moral standing, and accordingly, its possession of rights. For both rights, the mother's and the fetus', the community defines the conditions of engagement, the scope and weight. The weight that these rights actually have is exactly what the community acknowledges, when validating the claims that are considered as rights. Hence, when the community decides that the mother's rights override those of the fetus', it is within the range of its authority. This decision means that the community gives more weight to the mother's rights, so it can override the fetus' rights. Although one of the implications of this decision is, in fact, an ultimate abolishment of the fetus' right to exist, the meaning of this is not a nonrecognition of its rights, but an acknowledgement of the mother's right as stronger, and hence can prevail against the fetus' rights.

The appeal to the community, as an arbiter in such a kind of conflict, results from the previous acceptance of its norms, values and conventions, by those who share them. The community, as the subject, or at least the representing institution of these common values, can genuinely examine the social or public aspects of each conflict, and from this point of view, solve these conflicts. If we appreciate and respect rights because of their social acknowledgement, we affirm the community's status as the guarantor of the exercising of rights. With such an ascription of moral authority, we regard the community as the court of appeal, when moral rights are in conflict. When we accept that it is the community's acknowledgement that confers our rights upon us, then our rights are subordinated to its decisions.

Another aspect of the fact that our rights are valid only within a social framework, is that changes in our moral status can result even when there is no change in ourselves, but only a change in our relations with the community, or even a change in the structure or circumstances of the community itself. Part of this community-dependence, reflects our former preference for regarding rights as valid claims and not as entitlements. Such a preference weakens the linkage between one's due – or what she is entitled to – and between what is actually imposed on the respondent, as the correlative duty of the possessor's right. In this preferred view, one's right is also limited to the boundaries of the addressee's ability to respond to this right. This can occur when the community acknowledges her right as valid, but at the same time the community recognizes that the correlative duty is something beyond the respondent's abilities to fulfill. However, the more significant aspect has its origins in the fact that according to this view, all rights are conditional. I have already mentioned the conditions of possession and engagement that affect one's range of possessing rights. In addition to these conditions, the most substantial constraining condition of one's right is its weight. When I presented this component of a right, I mentioned that it determines how significant is the right, when compared to other moral considerations.[189] I indicated this notion of weight as specifying the rank or importance of a given right, in relation to other norms. These norms can be rights of others, which sometimes have no connection to the possessor of the given right, but still affect her moral status and her possession of rights. Nevertheless, the weight of the right, like its other conditions, is determined by the community, through its acknowledgement of a claim as valid. Hence, the community allocates rights under certain conditions, only part of which pertain to the possessor. These are the conditions that I earlier called "subjective", i.e., those conditions that were found sufficient for one's being considered as a prospective agent. With regard to the other conditions, some of them are "social" or "communitarian", in the sense that they relate to the person's relations to other members of the community, and some of them pertain to the moral and social "environment", within which she transacts with others. When these conditions are changed, even without the possessor's involvement, her moral status and hence her possession of rights is accordingly changed.

Using the example of abortion, and, again, only for reasons of illustration, I want to clarify the last statement. Let us say that a woman became pregnant after reaching a mutual decision with her spouse, but soon after was abandoned by the spouse, who is the presumed father of the fetus. Hence, she decides that she does not want to bring up the child on her own, and she wants to terminate her pregnancy. Before the abandonment, the fetus had an acknowledged right to welfare and well-being. It did not have the ability to affect the decision of the presumed father to abandon the woman. It was not involved in this decision, and actually, had no connection to it (supposing that the man's decision had no connection to the pregnancy). The mother finally decides to have an abortion. This decision drastically changes the status of the fetus, including its moral status. The community's acknowledgement of the mother's right to abort, however we interpret it (whether we say that it overrides the fetus' right, or that the fetus ceased to have rights, etc.), changes the status of the fetus, and hence its possession of the former right. However, this change in the fetus' rights does not result from any act that was done by it, or from any change in the fetus. We can say that the change is in the weight (ranking or significance) of the fetus' rights, but this leaves the above statement as it is. The weight of a right is part of its definition, or at least, part of its validity. When the community defines a right, including its weight, it limits the exercising of this right to a certain set of conditions and circumstances, and any change that occurs in them changes the validity conditions of the right, and the ability to exercise this right. Even though the fetus was not associated with the mother's decision, its right was affected by it.

This consequence results from considering a right, as one of a complex array of normative terms and moral concepts, whose understanding creates the moral community, within which these terms have meaning, and they are capable of being used. In such a view, one's right is subjected to the whole aggregate of moral relations within the community, as the framework within which the members "are not only able but willing to join their lives with each other".[190] The assumption that members cannot have rights or obligations towards others unless they can join some segments of their lives with each other[191] (namely that they belong to the same moral community), turns the community and its members into the reference group of their moral considerations. With this understanding of the community, its members confirm not only the authority of the community to appropriate and allocate rights, but also the community's authority to adjust and regulate their moral relations, including their rights. The adjustment and regulation of their rights sometimes involves the withdrawal of members' rights, when the community finds this justifiable according to its moral considerations. These considerations are comprehensive, and include not only the possessors' interests, but also considerations like the community's interests, the compatibility of multiple claims with rights of others, etc.

In the former kind of conflict I showed how individual self-interests can conflict with the interests of other members (as in the example of the HIV-positive carrier), or with the interests of the community as a whole. In these conflicts, the community can cancel the possession of one's right, because of absence of fulfillment of the conditions of possession of the canceled rights. But in the kind of conflicts we deal with here, the community does not cancel the moral status or moral standing of the supposed claimant (the fetus cannot be considered as a claimant in the ordinary sense of this term, because he cannot carry out the act of claiming). The community proclaims here that the right (whose exercise may be acknowledged) is overridden by another right or by other moral considerations, even though the conditions of possession of this right still exist. To use Wellman's terminology, the community acknowledges both rights as "real", in all the cases in which they do not conflict with each other. What caused the change in the fetus' right was a change in the social circumstances or the environment, within which this right takes place, and within which a clash was created. We can roughly describe this change by saying that during the former conditions, circumstances and moral relations (let us say between its biological parents, the convergence between the mother's desires and the fetus' interests, etc.) the community found its claims justified, valid and applicable. However, under the new circumstances and moral relations, its right, even though it might be justified, is not applicable. This can be either because of a change in its weight, or because of a change in the conditions of engagement, or because the addressee is unable to respond. These changes do not pertain directly or indirectly to the fetus, but they do pertain to the complex array of moral relations, which remain in the background (and form the grounds) of its right.

The moral community, which is the common manifestation of this array of moral relations, is the framework within which the actual demands and implications of the shared values and principles take place. In addition, it is the substratum that enables these implications to exist and to be brought to fruition. By fulfilling this function, the community represents the public and social aspects of the transactions between its members. So long as there is no conflict between the constraints that the community imposes on these transactions, the community does not intervene with them. These limits are defined simultaneously with the acknowledgement of any moral relations within the community (including rights and obligations) as valid. The acknowledgement of these relations as valid includes their guarantee by the community, and an implicit commitment to their applicability. However, this commitment has a double role. On the one hand, it is a commitment to support those who are the beneficiaries of these relations (and when one of these relations is a moral right – the possessors of this right), to achieve their entitlements or whatever the community acknowledges as their due. This is the community's role when the actual transactions between the members of the community, are compatible with the constraints that were imposed on these relations. In the context of rights, this means that the exercising of the rights fulfills the conditions (of possession, of engagement, etc.) that validate them. On the other hand, whenever the exercising of rights (or other moral relations that received the guarantee of the community) is incompatible with its constraints (that is, with the conditions of possession or engagement, the weight or the range of their rights), the community's commitment is to prevent, or at least to adjust or regulate this unsuitable exercise.

Let us return to the example of abortion. The decision to enable the mother to have an abortion can be understood as supporting the mother to realize her freedom over her body, under the new circumstances that caused her to prefer to abort. Here, her right is found more urgent than that of the fetus and hence overrides it. To put this another way, we can say that the weight of the right of the fetus to welfare, is less than the weight of the mother's right to freedom. The community estimates the extent to which each side of the conflicting parties fulfills the requirements for agency and for moral agency, assesses the weight and urgency of each claim, and decides which one overrides the other.

The main difficulty in the above procedure lies in the exact quantification of those components. I discuss this in detail in the next section, but I want to clarify this difficulty in the example I deal with here. The opponents of my view, those who object to the legitimacy of abortions, can say that my description of the weight of the mother's right is misleading. They can say that the mother's right to the freedom of her body is limited to the situation where this right does not conflict with another's right to life. They might even raise a utilitarian argument, and say that the fact that the mother can have back her right to freedom soon after the delivery (by putting the baby up for adoption), while the fetus decisively and definitively loses its right to welfare with the abortion, inclines the decision in favor of the fetus' right. The fact that both rights are moral rather than legal, and hence based on principles rather than rules, is the main cause of this difficulty. This will be the next topic I deal with.

However, at this point I only wish to explain my method of reaching my decision, which is quite similar to Alan Gewirth's method when he deals with this issue. I assign the conditions of possession high priority, when assessing one's entitlement to one's moral status, and one's entitlement to possess rights. The extent to which the mother fulfills the subjective requirements of agency (the mental and perceptual capacities) is much higher than the extent to which the fetus fulfills these requirements. Therefore I assert that this affects the moral hierarchy between the mother's and the fetus' rights, and leads to the conclusion that the mother's right overrides the fetus' right. From a communitarian point of view, I present this conflict as a conflict between an actual (and full-fledged) member of the moral community, and a prospective or future member of this community. This explains the above hierarchy, and justifies it by saying that after assessing both rights, according to the fulfillment of the requirements that validate them, I find the mother's moral status much more resolute, powerful and convincing. The mother is considered as a full-fledged member of the moral community, while the fetus lacks some essential characteristics that are necessary for being considered as an agent. This is true even before considering the question whether we regard the fetus as an individual or ascribe autonomy to it. Since it is physically connected, totally dependent, and also absolutely inseparable from the mother's body, questions are raised regarding its individuality. In any event, I raise the issue of abortion at this stage of the theory just to illustrate my main argument, which I shall briefly summarize once more.

My central argument consists of regarding rights and obligations as moral relations, which take place only within the moral community. These rights get their validity only as a result of their acknowledgement by the community. In addition to acknowledging rights, the community determines the conditions and circumstances under which these rights are valid, and links the extent to which these conditions are fulfilled, to the extent of the possession of rights. Parts of these conditions are generic, but others are social or "communitarian". The former conditions relate to personal capacities, mainly mental (perceptual, cognitive and rational) that are necessary for getting "an entry ticket" to the moral community. That is to say, these conditions are the foundation for being considered as a prospective or mere agent, which is a preliminary stage before full membership in the moral community. The latter conditions (for full membership) relate to the agent's way of transacting with other members. The fulfillment of both kinds of conditions, makes one a full-fledged member of the community, and hence, possessing rights. When the community affirms the validity of claims, it confirms their status as rights, and their claimant as a possessor of rights. When specifying one's right, the community also specifies all the components of this right, including its weight, range and addressee. These are the limits of the right, and we can think of them as additional conditions that must exist for the exercising of this right. The community's function is not only to allocate rights and impose obligations, but also to guarantee the realization of both rights and duties. This requires that the community support the possessors in their attempts to capitalize on their rights, and force the addressees to fulfill their duties. The purpose of this interference is to adjust and regulate between the extent to which one is entitled to possess rights, and the extent to which one actually possesses them.

However, the interference of the community in the realizing of rights and duties can occur in different ways. Whenever the possessor is entitled to more rights than she actually possesses, the community uses its power in order to give this possessor her due. On the other hand, when the possessor makes excessive use of her rights, or uses them in a matter not commensurate with the conditions and limits to which these rights are subordinated, the community must prevent this excessive use, or withdraw the unjustified rights. When doing so, the community merely adjusts between the actual possession, and the member's entitlement to possess these rights.

Another kind of adjusting of one's rights is a gradual (or progressive) conferring of them. This can happen, for example, in children's rights. The extent to which we ascribe to them their moral status, or the extent to which we regard them as members of the moral community, increases in a way that corresponds with their maturity and their moral development. This is because we assume that during their growth, the extent to which children fulfill the necessary requirements for agency gradually develops. In any case, the guiding principle is the same: the community adjusts a person's measure of possessing a right, to the acknowledged measure of entitlement to this right, according to one's fulfillment of the requirements that validate the same right. This preserves the balance between one's due, and possession of one's moral status. The assumption is that there is a necessity for such a balance which, in certain cases, justifies the withdrawal of rights.

3.5 SOME CLARIFYING REMARKS

3.5.1 The Relevance of Dworkin's Distinction Between Rules and Principles

The above argument regarding the justifying grounds for the withdrawal of rights requires some clarifications and some constraints. The most relevant of them refers to Dworkin's distinction between rules and principles. When I recalled the differences between legal and moral rights, I recalled Feinberg's view regarding the official recognition of each kind of right. According to Feinberg, the official recognition of a legal right is called for by the governing rules, while for moral rights this recognition is determined by: "moral principles, or the principles of an enlightened conscience".[192] Dworkin makes a distinction between rules and principles and says that they differ in two main ways. The first distinction pertains to their applicability. Rules are applicable in an all-or-nothing fashion; that is, in cases to which they apply, they determine the decision without any leeway. On the other hand, principles do not necessarily determine decisions even in the cases to which they do apply.[193] The second distinction relates to the component of weight that principles contain, and, according to Dworkin, rules do not. Hence, when principles conflict, the resolution of the conflict must take into account the relative weight of each. Since rights are based on principles, then when rights conflict, the resolution of the conflict must take into account the relative weight of the rights. That is why it is significant to ascribe the relative-weight concept to principles.

However, even Dworkin himself realizes that it is impossible to quantify this weight exactly. Therefore it is very problematic to judge that one principle is more important than another, and such a rendering often leads to controversial decisions. Michael Bayles' suggestion for the ascription of weight to principles, tries to point to a solution to this problem, by saying that the characteristic of weight enables us to add principles together and to balance them. He says that when several principles lead to one decision, and several others to the opposite, we can "add up" the weight of the principles of each side, and balance them in order to reach a decision.[194]

However, a close look at Bayles' idea shows that the problem I raised remains unsolved. The two distinctions between rules and principles affect the decisions that are grounded on principles, in the same way. Doubts will always remain whether the weight we ascribe to any right (or other moral consideration), is the correct and appropriate weight, under the specific conditions and circumstances within which it was carried out. These doubts also relate to the applicability of the principle. In other words, there will always remain some measure of uncertainty regarding whether the principle we use, applies to the situation within which this principle is to be operated. When we derive moral relations, including the possession of rights, from principles, we import the uncertainty and doubt into the justifying grounds of these rights. When there is a doubt regarding the applicability of a certain principle to a specific case or situation, there is a corresponding doubt about the validity of the right that is based on this principle, and therefore, a sense of doubt regarding the entitlement to the moral status.

We confront this problem whenever we try to assess the moral status of children, in different ages and different levels of development. We encounter difficulties when we ascribe responsibility to them, and hence enable them to enjoy some rights and privileges. To explain these difficulties, I compare the case of moral rights, with the case of legal rights that are bestowed upon teenagers. The official recognition of legal rights is called for by rules, and hence we can decisively determine whether these rights are valid or not. Let us look, for example, at the legal right of children to vote. The law defines the exact age from which they possess this right, let us say 18. If they are younger than this age at the cutoff date, even by one day, they are not allowed to vote. The same is the case regarding their right to have a driving license. The age limitations are clear, explicit, and easy to apply. With legal rights that are conferred by legal principles, such as the right to freedom of speech in the United States, the decisions regarding their limits or applicability are less sharp and decisive than rights that are conferred by rules, such as the above-mentioned rights to vote or to have a driving license. This is part of the origin of the right to free speech, which is a legal principle, and hence involves borderline cases that lead to variable decisions. The same happens with children's moral rights. When we are unsure about rights that should be given to them under certain conditions, like their right to go out until late at night, we have hesitations even after we have decided one way or another. This is because there is no sharp demarcation that marks when a teenager is considered as responsible, or can he be trusted.[195] Some teenagers can be trusted earlier than others, and others can be accountable in certain domains, but cannot be relied on in the rest. The extent of their membership in the community is, itself, ambiguous. And the complete list of moral relations and liabilities that are obligated by this membership is only approximate and flexible.

These hesitations and doubts also exist when considering the moral rights of adults. Here, the main reason for the uncertainty is the second differentiation that Dworkin assigns, which pertains to the weight of a right. As mentioned previously, Dworkin only ascribes this characteristic to principles. So, according to Feinberg's distinction between moral and legal rights, only the latter can involve principles. This means that the decision whether a certain right outweighs another right, which is determined according to the measurement of the weight of each right, is itself something that cannot be accurate. When we have only an approximate estimation of each right (and this is something that Dworkin admits), the comparison of both rights is only a rough estimation. Even if we take a more definitive stance towards human rights than that of Feinberg (who considers human rights to be conferred by the moral rules of the positive moral code of the society), we still remain with only an approximate estimation of the weight of a moral right, since these rules are less sharp and decisive than legal rules.

The conclusion that one right is more important than the other, which is based on the comparative weights of both rights, depends on our assessment of this weight at a certain time and in a specific situation. Here, we encounter two difficulties. First, we cannot be sure that our present assessment of the weight of each right is accurate (as just mentioned). Second, our decision is relevant at this time and under these circumstances, and might be different in a different situation. This renders our decision relevant for a singular and unique conflict between rights, and requires us to repeat the procedure of assessing the weight of the same right, whenever it is in conflict with another right.

When we discuss the withdrawal of rights, we must take into account these two difficulties. We realize that there cannot be an exact and decisive decision that is based on principles. Our decision, that a person does not adequately fulfill the moral status requirements, will always be subject to doubt. The adjustment and regulation of a person's possession of rights should then be open to reconsideration. Just as we cannot precisely quantify a person's fulfillment of the conditions that bestow her rights, we also cannot quantify the exact measure that is required for adjusting or limiting these rights. Thus, we have to exercise caution regarding the withdrawal of rights, even though we are justified in doing so. This must not prevent us from withdrawing rights, but should remind us that our moral considerations have comprehensive implications, which we must relate to seriously, in order to reach morally justifiable decisions. We must take into account as many moral aspects of the issue as we can, and judge the case as fairly as possible. Accomplishing this task sometimes requires that we make tough and painful decisions, especially when they regard the withdrawal of basic rights and liberties. But in order to preserve the framework within which rights have any applicability, we must be unwavering both when conferring and guaranteeing rights, on the one hand, and when preventing their excessive or inappropriate use, on the other. If we are irresolute in our first mission (guaranteeing rights), we risk turning rights into a nullity, and undermining the ability to enjoy the benefits of possessing rights. If we are irresolute in our second mission (the withdrawal of rights), we risk bringing about the collapse of whole normative framework, within which the concepts of rights and obligations take place and have meaning. The long and painful struggle to internalize the significance of the possession of moral rights within the community will yield desirable outcomes, only if we are able to morally justify the use and exercise of rights. This means that we will avoid situations where the exercise of rights is incompatible with morality. When the use of rights is not compatible with the conditions that create its moral justification, we must prevent this use, sometimes by a temporary withdrawal of these rights, and sometimes by a permanent withdrawal.

3.5.2 The Limits Of The Withdrawal Of Rights

The background assumptions that rights are always conditional, and dependent on the possessor's fulfillment of certain requirements, links between the actual circumstances within which we assess the possession of rights, and the extent to which we acknowledge them as valid. However, these circumstances are constantly changing, and the ratio between one's entitlement to moral status and one's actual possession of rights changes accordingly. This change affects our judgment of a person's possession of rights, in a way that requires us to reassess her possession, whenever there is a relevant change in the above ratio or proportion. This issue exists in legal rights as well; for example, in the issue discussed earlier, regarding the teenager's right to vote or to drive. In these examples, the relevant variable dimension is age. As time goes on, the extent to which teenagers fulfill the age requirement (or limitation) constantly increases, until they reach the minimum age required by law. At this point, their legal status changes, and they are capable of possessing these rights. The same procedure takes place in other domains, such as the legal right to citizenship. In order to apply for citizenship, the immigrant must reside in the country a minimum period of time, and when this period passes, the immigrant's legal status changes, as well as the entitlement to possess the right of citizenship.

One common example in which we can follow the operation of this procedure with regard to moral rights, is children's rights. I already mentioned the uncertainty involved with the ascription of responsibility to teenagers and children. There, I raised this issue in the context of the inability to quantify the possessor's fulfillment of the required capacities for possessing certain rights. Here I raise the same issue in a different context: the effects of maturation. As children mature, they develop an understanding of the complex array of moral concepts and they learn to conform to the normative framework of the moral community. We refer to these changes as changes in the conditions of possession of rights, which allow us to make changes in the actual possession of rights.

However, this is the less complex part of the issue under discussion. The changes in the circumstances under which we measure one's moral status or one's possession of rights, can extend to a comprehensive array of considerations, with a multitude of variables that pertain to the moral status we examine. For example, we can change our assessment of welfare rights as the result of changes in the economic situation, which limit the ability of the community to support its needy members . This is a change in the addressee's ability to respond to what may be a morally justified claim, but no longer valid under the new circumstances. Suppose welfare recipients have a right to get two blankets per family, in the beginning of each autumn, from the social or welfare authority of the state or the county. One year a natural disaster destroys whole sections of the county, and leaves many people homeless and destitute. This change in the environmental conditions affects both the number of needy members (drastically increasing this number), and the authorities' ability to assist them (because it has to allocate resources to the restoration of these sections). We interpret this as a change in the addressee's ability to respond to the right of the needy members, sometimes even to the extent in which the community is released from its duty. The authorities can decide that they can afford only one blanket per family, or even none, because the budget is allotted to provide food and clothing to the members of the worst socio-economic group. If the community decides to provide only one blanket, it cancels the former right (of two blankets), and establishes, instead, a new right with a reduced scope. It also establishes a new right for those who became needy as a result of a sudden misfortune. In effect, then, some members lose part of their former right, and others acquire a new right, under circumstances of hardship, that brought them to fulfill the conditions of possession of this new right.

We can see that changes in the members' moral status in particular issues, depend not only on the fulfillment of certain conditions of possession. Their possession of certain rights results from comprehensive considerations that pertain to the common interests within the community. This is also true with regard to the extent and the content (or range) of their rights. The continuously changing conditions, and the dynamic social circumstances within the community, may change the decisions regarding the rights of members, according to the reassessment of the above considerations. However, this is also true when discussing the withdrawal of rights. The decision of the community to change a person's moral status or to withdraw a right, whether because of something that she did, or because of changes in the social circumstances within which she possesses her rights, are both subject to change. So, when we withdraw a member's right, because of the lack of symmetry between the conditions that entitle her to possess certain rights, and the actual fulfillment of them, we must take note of the changes in both the conditions and their actual fulfillment. Accordingly we should adjust and regulate the extent of this withdrawal, and the extent of the possession of this right. The main conclusion from the above argument is that not only the possession of rights, but also their withdrawal, is conditional. Both stipulations reflect the basic principle that rights themselves are always conditional. When we apply this concept to the withdrawal of rights, we realize that this procedure is subject to, and limited by, the extent to which the community finds it appropriate to the situation within which it operates. Limitations of measure, range and duration, which are an integral part of the possession of rights, have the same role and status in the case of the withdrawal of rights. Just as we bestow rights so long as certain conditions are fulfilled, we withdraw them when these conditions are not fulfilled.

In cases like punishment, when we withdraw a person's rights because of an injury or harm that she caused to the community or its members, we need to fit the severity of the punishment to the seriousness of the harm that was caused. In the previous chapter, I defined an immoral agent as one who intentionally hurts the community. Some of the rights of such an agent should be withdrawn, because her moral status has been reduced, and her fulfillment of the conditions of possession is accordingly reduced as well. This means, that the duration of the withdrawal of rights may be quantified in accordance with (or in proportion to), the seriousness of the harm that was caused. In the same way that we assess the weight of a person's right (that is, the power that is accorded to this right, in proportion to other considerations), so too do we assess the weight of that right, when deciding upon its withdrawal. We assess the weight of other moral considerations that justify the withdrawal of one's rights, when compared to the moral considerations that are involved with the possession of them. We need to make sure that the duration of the withdrawal is proportional to the harm, and the withdrawn rights will be re-possessed again, at the end of a fixed period of time.

What I have said about the *duration* of the withdrawal pertains as well to the *severity* of the withdrawal. Here I refer to the measure by which we withdraw one's rights. To explain this argument, let us go back to the example of the HIV-positive carrier. It may readily be agreed, that at least part of his right to privacy should be abolished, if he intentionally infects other people, without informing them about the dangers that are involved with having sexual intercourse with him. The community can (or must) reveal the fact that he is an HIV-positive carrier. This is something that strikes at his right to privacy, but can nevertheless be morally justified. He might even be imprisoned, and some of his liberty rights may be withdrawn. However, this is not to say that he also loses other rights, or even other parts of his right to privacy. The community cannot publicize his bank account or other private details, that are not relevant to the specific task of reducing the damage he can cause to the community. The withdrawal of rights should be relevant to the offence, or at least connected to it in one way or another. This idea has a correlative implication in legal rights, where it is more clear and applicable. Suppose someone was caught driving a car without having a driving license. The community might temporarily or permanently withdraw his right to acquire a license, but it should not withdraw his right to acquire a higher education (assuming that this was the only offense of which he was accused). The same proportionality should be preserved with regard to moral rights. The balance between a person's fulfillment of the conditions that bestow upon her certain rights, and the actual possession of these rights, entails that the withdrawal of the excessive rights will be adjusted to this balance. Hence both the duration and severity of the withdrawal of rights should fit the community's assessment of the offense that caused this withdrawal. Gewirth's Principle of Proportionality that was used for the assessment of a person's possession of rights, is used again for the assessment of the withdrawal of rights.

The demand for limiting the extent and duration of the withdrawal of rights becomes problematic, when a conflict between rights must result in a total and irreversible abolishment of one of the conflicting rights. This problem is even more acute for those issues in which one side of a conflict is likely to loses its rights, decisively and permanently. This includes issues like abortions or capital punishment that do not enable the decision maker, namely the community, to limit or restrain the withdrawal of the right under discussion. In the former case, when the community decides that the mother's right overrides the fetus' right, it, in fact, definitively and irrevocably abolishes the fetus' right. There is no way to determine the degrees for withdrawing this right. Nor is there a way to limit the duration of the withdrawal of this specific right. The whole question regarding the limitations of the withdrawal of rights, does not apply to this issue. The assumptions regarding the irreversibility of the act of abortion make the community's decision to allow it, ultimate and final. Still, this is not to say that the community should not allow abortion. It just means that abortion belongs to those cases where the above limitations do not apply.

I will not discuss it in detail here, but I want to say something about the complexity of the reason for the inapplicability of these limitations, to the case of abortion. We can view the reason for the denial of the fetus' right, as pertaining to the inability of the addressee to respond to the fetus' claim. The community cannot respond to this claim, because of its obligation to enable the mother to exercise and capitalize on her right to the freedom of her body. The community exists within a binary reality, where the two conflicting rights impose a forced choice between them. These rights, under the limits of this reality, are not capable of coexisting. The incapability of limiting the withdrawal of rights, results from the impossibility of responding to both rights within the reality, as we know it. Reality itself imposes the fact that the fetus' right cannot be partially or temporarily withdrawn. The possibility of partial or temporary withdrawal of the fetus' right falls beyond the range of the community's real possibilities. Hence, the community cannot be considered as the unique accountable source for the abolishment of the fetus' right. This is because at least part of the inability to prevent this is beyond its power. The irreversibility and finality that involved in abortion, are inevitable consequences of the desire to allow the mother's right to be exercised.

The other issue that was mentioned in the context of the inapplicability of the limitations of the withdrawal of rights is the case of capital punishment. In this case, the above insoluble problem does not exist. There is no binary conflict, whose solution automatically involves the abolishment of the right of one of the parties. When the community sentences a person to death, it does so despite the existence of other punishment options, such as incarceration. The irreversibility of capital punishment is not an inevitable or unavoidable consequence of the decision to punish the culprit. When the community allows this kind of punishment, it does so with awareness of the fact that this punishment cannot be limited in duration or intensity. Here the terminal withdrawal of the culprit's rights, results from a conscious decision and choice and not from a lack of alternatives. Again, this fact does not mean that the community should abandon or give up this choice, but it must take into account the fact that capital punishment is irreversible and terminal. Hence, such a decision requires that the community be much more unwavering and certain about the necessity of its decision. Since it alone is responsible for imposing capital punishment, which is irreversible, the community bears the entire responsibility for the fatal consequences of this act. This obligates the community to be completely resolute and absolutely sure about the execution, before deciding upon this.

These two examples are extreme cases of the withdrawal of rights, as there is no way to quantify the withdrawal by duration or severity. A comprehensive analysis of these examples is beyond the range of this chapter, and is instead presented in detail, later in this study. Here I bring them as counterpoint to the examples of the ordinary procedure of operating the withdrawal of rights. In most of the cases, the withdrawal of rights is limited in time and intensity, and must be correlated to its justifying grounds. The procedure, which is described there, is to match the extent to which rights are withdrawn, to the extent to which the community finds appropriate, in the circumstances under which this procedure takes place. When I examine this procedure in specific cases, I explain what considerations must be taken into account when deciding to withdraw rights in such cases. There, the issue of the limits of the withdrawal of rights will be very important. At this stage, it is sufficient to mention this issue and the fact that it is part of the procedure. Just as the possession of rights has limits and conditions, so too, the withdrawal of rights has limitations of its own. Just as the right's weight component is to be considered when discussing right possession, so too, the limitations of the right-withdrawal component must be reassessed, when discussing right withdrawal. This requires us to define, not only the conditions under which a right is valid, but also the conditions under which this right is subject to reassessment. The community's role is not only to make sure that the possessors will be able to enjoy their rights, or even to support them to capitalize on their rights, but also to prevent the inappropriate use of rights within the community. This sometimes means to withdraw rights. However, when this is carried out, it must be proportional to the justifying grounds of the withdrawal.

3.6 SUMMARY

This chapter invokes the conclusions of the first chapter regarding rights as valid claims. Their validity results from the acknowledgement of the community that a member's claims are valid, and hence that she possesses rights. This acknowledgement is predicated on the member's fulfillment of certain conditions that are defined by the community as bestowing the moral status of possessing these rights. The extent to which this member fulfills the above conditions, determines the extent to which she is entitled to her moral status, and hence, the extent to which she possesses these rights. This position (taken from the second chapter), links between membership in the moral community, and moral agency (and hence the possession of rights). This means that the extent to which any member fulfills the above conditions (and hence is entitled to possess rights), determines the extent to which she is considered as a member of the moral community. So long as the member's fulfillment of these conditions is appropriate to the community's requirement, she is entitled to possess her rights. However, if there is an incompatibility between the member's fulfillment of the required conditions, and her actual exercising of rights, some of her rights should be temporarily or permanently withdrawn.

The social function of rights, that is their role within the community, was defined in this study, following Rawls, as: "a final court of appeal for ordering the conflicting claims of moral persons".[196] Whenever there is a conflict between rights of different members, it should be resolved by the reassessment of the validity of each party's claim. This means that the community examines the extent to which each party is entitled to possess her rights under the new circumstances, and reaches its decision accordingly.

Here we can see that the possession of rights (and also their withdrawal) within a communitarian entity is determined not only by subjective circumstances, but also by social and communitarian circumstances. This means that changes in a member's moral status, and accordingly her possession of rights, can be caused not only by changes in her personality or conduct, but also by changes in the community itself, or in the moral relations within the community. In this chapter I pointed out that a full definition of a right, includes some conditions and components that should properly exist, when this right is acknowledged as valid. These are the conditions of possession, the conditions of engagement, the addressee, the weight and the range of the right. Each of these conditions must be satisfied, in order that this right is recognized as valid. This is to say that the validity of a right is conditional, and dependent on the existence and fulfillment of each of these components. The withdrawal of this right, then, can result from an inappropriate satisfaction of each of these conditions.

The authority that has the power to decide on the withdrawal of rights, and to implement this decision, is the community itself. This authority is also the community's obligation, since it is the guarantor for the members' rights. This obligation results from its essence as the manifestation of the members' will to join some segments of their lives to those of the other members. For this they establish a community to coordinate their mutual obligations and uphold their reciprocal commitments. By establishing the community, the members authorize a communal framework to determine their rights and duties, guarantee their applicability and enforce these rights when this is necessary. Thus, the community is not only the framework within which the concept of a right gets validity and becomes applicable, but also guarantees that the possessors of rights will be able to successfully exercise, that is, to capitalize on them. This imposes on the community the duty to intervene and use its authority whenever a possessor cannot exercise her rights, and support her so that she may enjoy what she is entitled to. On the other hand, the community must also intervene whenever a member exercises a right that she was not entitled to have under the specific circumstances. If she misuses her right, the community must prevent this abuse, by withdrawing at least the excessive part of her use.

Towards the end of this chapter, I mentioned a serious difficulty involved in discussing moral rights. This difficulty arises as a result of the assumption that legal rights get their validity from governing rules, while moral rights are valid as a result of being acknowledged as moral principles, or the principles of the enlightened conscience.[197] The distinction that Dworkin draws between rules and principles,[198] makes all the decisions that are based on principles, less certain and clear than those which are based on rules. The clarity relating to the applicability of legal rights is much greater than in the case of moral rights, and hence it is easier to reach decisions in the realm of legal rights, as opposed to moral rights. Another aspect of Dworkin's distinction is that only principles have weight, and hence we can measure the power that a right has, when compared with other moral considerations (not only with other moral rights). These two differences sometimes complicate the quantification of the members' entitlement to possess their rights. It is not easy to accurately and precisely quantify the exact measure to which a member fulfills the requirements that bestow rights upon her. We cannot precisely assess a person's moral agency, and accordingly, one's possession of rights. However, this is true also when considering the withdrawal of rights. When we decide that there is an imbalance between one's entitlement to possess a specific right, and between her actual possession of this right, we do so only on the basis of an approximate estimation. Our intention and attempt to adjust and regulate this, through a partial and limited withdrawal of this right, is done on the same approximate and inaccurate basis. This causes a measure of doubt regarding the required adjustment and regulation of the inappropriateness, which we want to correct. The consequence of this adjustment will always be accompanied by doubts, regarding the intensity and the duration of the withdrawal of this right. The desire to fit the actual possession of any right, to the exact measure of the fulfillment of the conditions that are acknowledged as validating it, cannot be completely satisfied, because of the inability to make it accurate. This leads us to limit the withdrawal of rights, both in time and intensity, to the extent that we assume as proportional, to the circumstances within which this is done. The cases where the withdrawal of rights cannot be moderated or limited, i.e., the cases where the withdrawal of rights is total and irreversible, require a comprehensive array of considerations in order to be resolved. In this chapter I just took note to the problems involved with such cases, but did not analyze their solutions. This will be discussed in detail, in the coming chapters.

In the next chapters I re-examine my argument regarding the justification for the withdrawal of rights. I deal with test cases in which I apply the guidelines for withdrawing rights that were presented in this chapter. Each case has its own specific considerations that should be taken into account, but the principles that we have suggested here, will be applied with particular modifications that are required in each specific case.

CHAPTER 4

PUNISHMENT

In this chapter I examine the most frequent act of withdrawing rights: Punishment. My intention is not to present a deep and detailed analysis of this matter, but instead, to discuss this issue within the framework of a rights-based theory. I show how the problems of both the justification of the institution of punishment (or in Rawlsian terms: "the practice"[199] that deals with the question why we use punishment at all), and of a particular form of punishment, can be seen as a justifiable withdrawal of rights. My intention is to discuss the act of punishment in the terms I used in the previous chapter, and to show that my approach deals with the conflicts that are raised as a result of inflicting punishment. It is, of course, first necessary to introduce the main theories regarding the justification of punishment, in order to see how my approach relates and refers to these theories. I deal with this, briefly and succinctly, in the first part of the coming chapter.

In the second section I survey my approach towards punishment, and demonstrate how my previous justification for the withdrawal of rights, is appropriate to this issue as well. I explain how the process that was specified in the previous chapter is compatible with the current concepts of punishment.

In the final part of this chapter I give a brief account of a specific case of punishment, namely Capital Punishment, and show how the withdrawal of rights functions in practice. I also attach an appendix that describes cases of non-legal withdrawal of rights that are not really punishments but express similar ideas, for example "outing", that can also be used as test cases for the theory of the withdrawal of rights. Here I try to uncover the complications involved, as the result of the attempt to apply guidelines and principles to concrete and actual problems. At the same time, these case studies may show how we can discuss such issues within rights-talk and offer responsible solutions, while being aware of their problematic character. This may explain the problems that I have mentioned in the previous chapter, regarding the uncertainty and the doubts that are always involved in the act of the withdrawal of rights.

4.1 GENERAL INTRODUCTION AND PRELIMINARY REMARKS

Generally, discussions of punishment can be divided into two principal approaches. The first can be regarded as "forward-looking" and represents a teleological view, according to which the institution of punishment is justified when it produces some benefit, aim or purpose at a future date. In this context, justifications for punishment stem from consequentialist or teleological ethics such as that of utilitarianism. In fact, in many discussions of the forward-looking approach, it is *identified* with the utilitarian approach. According to this approach, the harm that the punishment inflicts on the offender can be justified only if it yields some good or beneficent results.

The second approach can be regarded as "backward-looking". Here, the future consequences of punishment for a wrongdoing are irrelevant to the fact that this act should be punished. Punishment, according to this approach, is justified by the assumption that it is the intrinsically appropriate response to past wrongdoings.[200] There are many variations of this approach as well, but the main principle of all of them is that offenders should "pay back" for their wrongful deeds. Wrongdoers should pay for what they voluntarily and intentionally did. In the center of the backward-looking approach stands the retributive theory of punishment. In fact, the backward-looking approach is usually *identified* with retributivism.

Much has been said about these two ostensibly opposing approaches to punishment. The attempt to use either of them in order to justify both the practice of punishment and a particular form of punishment, has created insoluble problems for each approach. As S.I.Benn describes it, the situation became such that the strength of the retributivist's case rested on its answer to the utilitarian, and the strength of the utilitarian's case rested on its answer to the retributivist.[201] The unavoidable solution seemed to be that the justification of punishment should be a synthesis of both approaches. Basically, the justification of the practice as such rests on utilitarian considerations, whereas the justification for a certain form of punishment rests on a retributive basis.

However, before dealing with each of these approaches in detail, I want to present some elementary understandings of the term "punishment". They are necessary in order to clarify the issue discussed here, but the main reason is to examine to what extent my approach is appropriate or compatible with the common understandings about punishment. In the broadest sense of the term, it can be said that my view involves the lowering or diminishing of the moral status of offenders, and hence the lowering or diminishing of their entitlement to rights of freedom, property, money or other privileges. The diminishing of their moral status may strike at the range of their rights, or even abolish some of their rights. However, the harm that is caused by this deprivation of rights must be justified and limited, in order to be considered a real punishment and not a form of revenge or act of injustice. Hence, more specifications are required to clarify this term.

In one of the papers that has become a cornerstone of the discussion of punishment, Antony Flew offered a comprehensive analysis of the term, and this has become the foundation of some significant debates since then. Flew's analysis of the term clarifies not only the term itself, but also its implications. He indicates five elements that are integral parts of the meaning of "punishment":[202]

First, it must be a hardship or an unpleasantness to the victim (Flew distinguishes it from "pain", to avoid flogging or other physical torture that could mistakenly be regarded as punishment too, but Hart uses the term "pain").

Second, it must (at least be supposed to) be a reaction to an offense.

Third, it must (at least be supposed to) be inflicted on the offender (and Hart emphasizes: "for his offense").

Fourth, it must be the work of personal agencies (Hart formulates this element by saying that it must be intentionally administered by human beings other than the offender), while evils occurring to people by other causes, i.e., natural consequences of an action, may be called penalties but not punishment.

Fifth, it must be imposed (and administered) by virtue of some special authority, conferred by a system of rules, against which the offense has been committed.

In addition to these positive criteria of punishment, Flew suggests that punishment is not only confined to legal or moral offenses, but can also be used in connection with any system of rules or laws: those of states, schools, trade unions, associations, moral laws, etc.

These conditions appear, with some modifications, in most of the recent (and not-so-recent) discussions of punishment. Rawls' definition, for example, states more or less the same points, with some additions to support his view (which we can call "quasi utilitarian" or a combination of the two mentioned approaches to the justification of punishment).

Rawls' definition of the institution of punishment is as follows:

> "A person is said to suffer punishment whenever he is legally deprived of some of the normal rights of a citizen on the ground that he has violated a rule of a law, the violation having been established by trial according to the due process of law, provided that the deprivation is carried out by the recognized

> legal authorities of the state, that the rule of law clearly specifies both the offense and the attached penalty, that the courts construe statutes strictly, and that the statute was on the books prior to the time of the offense".[203]

Rawls' view about legal rights can easily be applied to moral or social punishment (when we recall Flew's remarks). However, Rawls regards this issue, more or less in the same manner as Hart, Flew, Benn and others, even though he derives all the components from Hobbes, who lived about three centuries earlier. This implies that there are some elementary components that must be considered in any serious discussion about punishment, regardless of the approach of justification used. Flew also suggests a formal structure of justification in such a discussion. He recommends that a justification has to be of A, rather than B, against C, and to or by reference to D. A is the thing justified, B the possible alternative(s), C the charge(s) against A, and D the person(s) or principle(s) to whom and/or by reference to which the justification is made.[204]

I employ this structure for a comprehensive understanding of the term and the required justification for it. Accordingly, I examine some of the most familiar attempts to justify punishment. I have mentioned before that one of the characteristics of these attempts is that the strength of each approach, comes mainly from the weakness of its rivals. This assumption focuses the analysis of each approach, mainly on the critical claims against it and the attempts to answer these critics. This is the manner in which I present the above-mentioned approaches.

4.2 THE FORWARD-LOOKING APPROACH TO PUNISHMENT

At the basis of most of the forward-looking approaches to punishment, stands the assumption (whose origin is identified with Jeremy Bentham) that any punishment is harmful, and is in itself evil. In other words, every kind of suffering is evil, and can be justified only if it prevents a greater suffering, or if it may yield some benefit or good. The expected utility that might justify the harm that is caused to the offender can be presented on different levels, three of which are the most familiar. The strongest support of the utilitarian approach (and I use this term as a general synonym for the different forward-looking approaches) comes from the assumption that its infliction reduces future offenses. This can be achieved through many possible ways. First of all, the incarceration of the offenders in itself reduces their future opportunities to commit crimes (at least during the incarceration). This is the crudest level of this reduction of future offenses. At the second level lies the assumption that after being punished, the offenders will be afraid to suffer another penalty, and will avoid recidivism. At the third and most significant level of punishment justification on a utilitarian basis, lies the assumption that the threatening and deterrent effects of punishment may reduce the temptations of other potential offenders to commit offenses.[205] The last two utilitarian expectations are based on the deterrent effect of punishment, and this is regarded by many theorists as the strongest utilitarian argument for punishment.[206]

A lot has been said about this approach towards justifying punishment. On the one hand, it presents a credible argument for the practice of punishment in that it is likely to bring about some social good and avoid future injustice and harm. However, when we consider possible outcomes of the utilitarian approach in general, and of the deterrent approach in particular, many problems and difficulties arise which give grounds for considerable apprehensions.

First, there is the fear that is considered the most familiar objection to any consequentialist theory: if deterrence really works, and certain punishment might (or will) reduce future harm, it may justify draconian punishments as a lesson for all to see, scapegoating innocents, or "making an example" of the guilty.[207] The attention paid to the effects of punishment, causes the utilitarian theories to somehow overlook the questions of innocence or guilt, as matters that belong to the past. For forward-looking approaches, such matters are beyond their interests or even irrelevant. The motto of this view, according to John Rawls, is "bygones are bygones", and hence "only future consequences are material to present decisions".[208] A similar but less extreme approach involves pretending to punish the innocent without really punishing him, in order to deter others from committing similar offenses.

Another concern is that punishment might be employed in *anticipation* of the offense, that is, punishing in order to prevent a possible offense.[209] Another criticism of the utilitarian approach rises from the concern that the considerations of deterrence may promote excessively severe punishment, disproportionately above and beyond the gravity of the offense.[210] This danger develops, when the only way to reduce the mentioned offense is by deterrence. It may lead to a situation where serious but easily detected offenses, might warrant lesser punishment than petty but hard-to-detect offenses,[211] because there are fewer chances to discover the offense, and hence the temptations of offending grow.

Of course, utilitarian theories have rejoinders to each of the above criticisms. The most familiar response, especially for the last criticism mentioned, is that the desire to reduce future crimes must be subjected to some "side constraints", that include, among others, the Principle of Proportionality between the gravity of the offense and the seriousness of the punishment. However, any attempt to formulate such constraints, ends, one way or another, in a retributive principle: the right of requital (*jus talionis).*[212] To the main criticism against them, namely the possibility of punishing the innocent, utilitarians have some standard replies. Almost no one is comfortable with the pure utilitarian calculation, saying that sometimes it is better to fabricate evidence and scapegoat an innocent person, in order to avoid greater harm and injury to the public. Instead, many utilitarian arguments stress that in the long run, the harm that results from "framing" or punishing the innocent, would be greater than the temporary and short-term benefits that might be achieved. These arguments state that a comprehensive understanding of the full range of aims that the penal system is supposed to serve (like gaining confidence in the legal system and the administration that organizes the social order), leads to conclusions that strictly prohibit punishing the innocent.[213]

However, even if true, such an argument misses the whole point that stands behind the objection to the punishment of the innocent. We condemn the punishment of the innocent not because of its inefficiency, or because we care about the stability of the social order. We find it unjust and unfair in the broader sense, and not merely as something that might produce some future benefit. We are also regretful when, for reasons of utility, a guilty culprit is not punished. However, this issue is less crucial than the former, because not punishing the guilty may be compatible with some feelings of compassion or mercy. Such feelings may function as an excuse or rationalization, or even as a partial answer to the discomfort, involved with the tendency to clemency towards the guilty culprit. Punishing the innocent, as a way of reducing future mischief through deterrence, collides with some of our most fundamental moral intuitions and beliefs. It conflicts with our moral sense of justice, our beliefs about compensation, desert, rewards and punishments. We find this act to be simply evil and wicked. These moral beliefs are shared by most of the utilitarian theorists, and they have relevance for some additional arguments regarding the meaning of the term "punishment", and of the practice of punishment. These arguments go beyond utilitarian considerations and refer to the nature of punishment, both as an institution and also as representing a form of social retaliation.

The rationale that stands behind the arguments of those who justify punishment on the basis of deterrence (or almost any consequentialist consideration), is that punishing the innocent contradicts the very logic of this institution. They maintain that whenever punishment is inflicted, it includes (at least) an implicit reference to an actual or supposed offense.[214] Antony Flew sums up this principle by saying that: "people (logically) cannot be punished for what they have not done". He maintains that a system that inflicts unpleasantness on scapegoats, even when they pretend to be offenders "could scarcely be called a system of punishment at all". For the most, such a system can use the term "punishment" metaphorically, or in a non-standard sense.[215] This approach is widely accepted. Baier expresses it more strictly, when he says that a system of inflicting hardship cannot be called "punishment", unless it satisfies some preconditions, whose most significant one does not permit sentencing and inflicting penalties on those who were found "not guilty". He insists that the aim of punishment as a system of inflicting hardship is to hurt **only** those who are guilty of an offense. Accordingly, the infliction of harm on the innocent (logically) cannot be called punishment.[216]

However, this is very close to the retributivist approach that is mentioned by Flew, and is ascribed to Bradley. According to Bradley, punishment is considered as such, only where it is deserved. We can justify repayment only from those who owe a debt, and not for any reason other than a debt. Punishing someone for any reason other than that which she deserves as a consequence of her wrongdoing, is a crying injustice and an abominable crime.[217] Here, we find two essential components of the concept of punishment. First, a harm inflicted when it is not deserved cannot be considered as punishment. Second, such an act cannot be justified, since it is unjust. And, again, as in the case of the utilitarian answer to the problem of proportionality between the seriousness of the offense and the severity of the punishment, the forward-looking approach requires some retributive grounds, in order to avoid gross immorality. At least some retributivist foundations seem to be necessary, to establish a reasonable and sensible justification for punishment. They may need the support of forward-looking or utilitarian considerations, in order to establish a complete justification for punishment, but the retributive explanation is unavoidable.

Before introducing the main principles of the backward-looking approaches (whose central conception is the retributive one), I briefly present two other forward-looking approaches, which do not deal with deterrence or ordinary social utility, but make use of a different motivation. These approaches have some corrective aims, and are sometimes conceived to be the same. The first is known as the "curative" or "rehabilitation" approach. The second is known as "reform". Let me summarize their main ideas, and the main criticisms against them.

4.2.1 The Curative Or Rehabilitation Approaches To Punishment

Among the many kinds of utilitarian arguments for justifying punishment, the curative and the reform ones are singular and worthy of mention. Very often, and not unintentionally, they are interchanged. Being both forward-looking and utilitarian approaches that have corrective aims, they are sometimes treated as if they were the same. The main reason for this is that their justifying grounds are supported by similar arguments, and they both are motivated by similar intentions. Even though my tendency is to regard them as belonging to the same category of justification for punishment (namely forward-looking, utilitarian and remedial or corrective), I briefly explain why some theorists divide them into two different approaches.

In the center of the "reform" approach to punishment, stands the desire to instigate a positive influence on the character of the offender. This approach posits that after the offender is punished she will realize the gravity of her offense, and that this will induce remorse and repentance that will change her character, or at least her behavior. The "curative" approach, in the eyes of those who distinguish between the two,[218] has a much more far-reaching (and possibly ambitious) aim. This approach wishes to change the whole system of punishment entirely. Its basic assumption is that committing a crime is only a symptom of the offender's psychological disorder or mental disturbance, and this requires appropriate treatment. This approach mandates that punishment be substituted by a therapeutic or other medical model of treatment. The reason I insert these two approaches in the same category is my supposition that the curative approach, like the reform approach, hopes to influence the offender's integration in society. This is probably the main goal of the reform approach. The desirable aim of the attempt to change the offender's heart (as this approach wishes to do) is to make her behavior more conventional, and cause her to follow the rules. In my opinion, the main difference between the two attempts is that the reform approach attempts to effect a direct change in the person's behavior, while the curative approach attempts to effect a psychological change that, in turn, affects her behavior. In any event, I wish to deal with punishment justification from the corrective point of view, and bring the standard support and criticism for this approach.

The principal motive of both the reform and the curative approaches (which is the main reason that many theorists assign them to the same category) is to reduce the social harm that is caused by crimes. This attitude regards the purpose of criminal law not as punishment, but as reducing social harm. Advocates of this approach are not as much interested in "punishing" the offenders, (which is causing additional harm to the offender), as in avoiding future harm that might be caused by these and other offenders. Hence, they are much more concerned with the underlying reasons and causes of the crime, than in the retributive aspects of punishment. Accordingly, they concentrate essentially on the social and psychological, rather than the moral and ethical aspects of the offender. At most, they are interested in the normative aspects of the offender's behavior, from the sociological rather than from the ethical point of view. This means that the relevant issue to them, is not the moral judgment of the act, but the extent to which this act follows societal standards.

For those who maintain this approach, crimes do not manifest a moral decision or judgment, but a failure to function appropriately within society. They assume that criminals have psychological or emotional difficulties in integrating with the community, and their offenses express the dissonance between them and societal norms. Punishing them for the difficulties they meet in integrating with their environment may be viewed in two ways. First, it might be found inappropriate to punish them because of the impoverished circumstances of their lives, which they have no ability to control or change. This is from a point of view that seeks justice.

The second approach, towards those whose offenses represent symptoms of incompatibility with social requirements, is the utilitarian calculation. The attempt to reduce further harm by restoring the offender's social conditions and circumstances, may fail by causing a present harm to the offenders. The adherents of the rehabilitation approach posit that dealing seriously with the causes of the crime may prevent future harm being caused by these offenders, and probably by others who are in the same social or emotional situation. Their main attention is directed to the causes that brought the offender to break the law, and they wish to change these causes during the period of incarceration. This attitude regards prisons as rehabilitation-orientated centers, whose concentration should be on the curative rather than the penal aspect. They believe that while an offender is confined to a prison or other detention center, a unique opportunity is created for equipping her with some socially desirable skills and attitudes.[219] The emphasis in such places should be on professional care – whether by social workers or by psychologists – and not on the penal functions of the jailers and wardens. The aim of such centers is to provide the prisoners with the means and abilities to become law-abiding and productive citizens when they leave jail. The means used should include psychological care, professional skills, communicative abilities, and other necessary conditions for full involvement, or "membership" in the community.

The rehabilitation approach has a different conception of the whole operation of the penal system. Since the role of incarceration is to rehabilitate the prisoners, and the time that this may take cannot be foreseen in advance, the period of incarceration cannot be determined beforehand. It can be limited in length, but with the possibility of a wide alteration in both directions, according to the progress of the rehabilitation-process. This is to say that instead of sentencing a lawbreaker to a fixed period in jail, let us say three years, one would be sent to jail for a period of between two to five years. The time the offender actually spends in jail is determined by parole boards, according to the extent to which the process of rehabilitation has succeeded. However, in our example, the offender would not be released prior to two years, or later than five years – the minimum and maximum time interval that was determined in the sentence.[220]

The starting point of the rehabilitation approach is usually that the deterrent function of punishment has proved to be a dismal failure. The threat of being caught and punished does not deter offenders from committing crimes, and incarceration usually does not deter the prisoner from recidivism. The theorists hold that when internal restraints (such as the lawbreaker's conscience or self-respect), as well as external restraints (such as public opinion and peer pressure), are ineffective, there is little chance that the fear of punishment will deter crimes. Furthermore, many of those who are imprisoned become even more firmly committed to their criminal way of life, and to continuing their feud with law enforcement officers.[221] They feel ostracized from society, and adopt the norms and lifestyles of those with whom they shared their cell in jail. When they finish their period of imprisonment, they re-join the criminal environment and commit more crimes, only to be caught again, sentenced and sent back to jail. The way out of this vicious cycle must be initiated by society. Society boasts power, authority and resources, and as such – society should create a therapeutic system, with a reform and rehabilitation process to transform offenders into useful and constructive members of the community.

4.2.2 The Rejection Of The Rehabilitation Approach

Generally speaking, criticism of the curative and reform theories stems from diverse considerations.[222] The first approach maintains that rehabilitation processes need not involve painful or unpleasant procedures. Those who establish such a justification on these grounds alone can support their claim by a purely utilitarian calculation. They can maintain that if a certain aim could be achieved through a non-painful process, then it would be preferable than causing additional pain to that which has already been caused. A possible answer to this criticism can be the claim, that insofar as the offender is compelled to undergo the rehabilitation process, we can regard this process as a punishment in the conventional sense. So long as she is deprived of her liberty and some of her basic rights, we can regard her as punished in the full sense. Her rehabilitation is an additional bonus that can reduce future offenses that she may commit. The offender cannot complain of the harm that is caused to her because of her offense, but should be grateful for the efforts to help her become a useful and productive member of the community, after her imprisonment. Another response to the above criticism is to claim that reform is not a punishment in the conventional sense, and it is, instead, an attempt to replace the institution of punishment by another practice that can be better justified by utilitarian considerations. This line of defense assumes that punishment cannot be justified on a utilitarian basis, and hence has to be replaced by another practice, that can be justified on utilitarian grounds.

The second respect in which the rehabilitation approach is regarded as odd (in the sense that some of its consequences diverge from the traditional idea of punishment), deals with the concept of treatment. The adherents of the curative approach assume that there is something wrong with the offender's mind, and what she needs is not only re-education but also mental indoctrination. This conclusion may sound plausible to utilitarians, but unbearable to retributivists, or even to adherents of many other moral doctrines that regard persons as moral entities. These latter theorists believe that the offender should develop an independent moral view, built by her own preferences and choices, which impose moral responsibility upon her. Shaping offenders' moral stance or even their moral personality by means of brainwashing, indoctrination, or tendentious moral education, impairs their status as moral agents, and makes their moral judgment very difficult to rely upon. The whole conceptual framework, within which we allow ourselves to punish such offenders, would be undermined. The essential core of our ascription of moral agency to members of the community, namely their being the self-originating sources of valid claims, will be, at least, modified, if not completely destroyed.

On a more specific level, objections to the rehabilitation approach as a workable alternative system to punishment arise from various directions. Some critics of this approach argue that we do not, as yet, know enough about the causes that bring someone to break the law.[223] Some of the basic assumptions about the criminal's character, or about the societal or environmental conditions that drive the offender to break the law, are sometimes totally inappropriate. Many white-collar offenses are committed by people who belong to the highest social class, who grew up in comfortable socioeconomic conditions, and are well integrated in society – except, of course, for the fact that they are thieves. There is nothing in their personality that would seem to be disturbed – apart from avarice or greed, which does not require psychological treatment or therapy.

Another criticism is raised against the idea of indeterminate sentencing. If a certain penalty is appropriate to a certain offense, why should the offender get a longer incarceration, with an option to reduce it if she reforms her character? This would cause justified resentment among prisoners and threaten the whole ideology of rehabilitation, in which indeterminate sentencing is one of the most important instruments.[224]

When we consider the practical objections to this approach, we find that most of them relate to the serious difficulties regarding the relevance of some of the basic assumptions. We do not yet have the ability to identify the characteristics of the "pathology" that drives one to criminal behavior. It is not at all obvious that social or environmental factors are the causes for such behavior. On the other hand, if they are the causes, what is the use of individual treatment, if the society and environment remain the same? This issue is summarized by the American Friends Social Committee, who says:

> "We do not, and probably cannot know the relative contribution of individual and social pathology to criminality; to the extent that social causation is relevant, the rational for individualization is undercut".[225]

Another difficulty rises from the fact that correctional treatment programs rest on speculations and assumptions unrelated to criminality. For the most part, these programs are taken from other disciplines that have some relevance to criminality, but lack the methodology that is the foundation of those disciplines. For example, these programs are not able to conduct comparisons of control groups with similar subjects that are not treated, do not isolate components and variables that are suspected to be the cause of crimes, and cannot even compile reliable criteria for determining success or failure.[226]

However, we can regard the above criticism as directed towards the implementation of the idea, not towards the justification or the moral and principal aspects of this idea. The principal objection to the rehabilitation approach, concentrates mostly on the idea that the traditional form of punishment, when inflicting unpleasant and unwelcome penalties on the offenders, treats them as responsible for their actions. Such an attitude towards offenders expresses an acknowledgement of their moral standing. By ascribing responsibility to them, we regard them as agents that can share some of our moral perceptions, and can join some segments of their life with ours. In other words, by punishing them we reconfirm the fact that they belong to our moral community, including the fact that they are entitled to enjoy the benefits and advantages, that are the results of this coexistence.

The curative approach, on the other hand, considers the committing of crimes as symptoms of illness, thus risking the erosion of the moral status of the offenders as agents. This may bring us to think that these offenders cannot join their life with ours, and we may not consider them as belonging to the same reference group, or, in the worst cases, to the same moral community. Hence, instead of treating them as fellow human beings, we may come to treat them in a paternalistic or humiliating manner.[227] This may not only pose a serious threat to some of the important safeguards of the ordinary penal system, but also to our concept of the human community. At the foundation of our moral beliefs, lies the ascription of responsibility to those with whom we interact and share our lifestyle. This is not only the core of our penal system, but is also the basis of what we consider to be morality. This is the main reason why curative approaches were rejected by many theorists of punishment, who came from the domain of ethics.

Some of the critics comment that the basic aim of the approach to reduce future offenses, concentrates only on those who have already broken the law.[228] Therefore, this approach neglects the lion's share of potential criminals: those who have committed crimes but have not been caught, as well as those who spring from crime-ridden disadvantaged backgrounds and are likely pursue a criminal way of life as well. The reduction of crime will not be achieved by dealing only with a small percentage of the potential criminals. There are a lot of difficulties implicit in any forward-looking approach, including the reform one, especially with regard to the success rate of rehabilitation programs. The principal difficulty that distinguishes the curative approach from the rest of the forward-looking approaches, is its obsessive concern with the past deeds and circumstances of the offenders. This makes the assumptions of both the causes of the crime and the effects of the treatment speculative, sometimes even groundless.[229] Like the rest of consequential theories, this approach is seriously threatened by the utilitarian calculation, which is unavoidable in view of the depressing statistics of recidivism. Both deterrent and curative approaches offer some rather lame explanations to defend their positions. Adherents of the former (deterrent approach) assert that recidivism cannot indicate the effects of punishment on those who did not commit crimes. After all, recidivism only reflects the statistics of those who were punished before, and commit a crime again. It is possible, they say, that there are many who refrain from breaking the law as a result of the fear of being punished, but that this number cannot be quantified. At most we can say that the deterrence did not work on those who have been punished already. This conclusion only partly undermines the whole doctrine.

Adherents of the curative approach have more difficulties in responding to this criticism, because the high level of recidivism shows that those who were punished do not change their ways, and are not rehabilitated. They may assert that this is a result of the present penal system, which in any event, they claim, should be reorganized. They may also assert (with some justification) that recidivism cannot serve as a reliable criterion for assessing the success of reform programs. This response is even shared by opponents of curative programs, who argue that we have no way of determining the real rate of recidivism because most of the crimes are undetected, and the official rate indicates only those cases in which offenders are caught and convicted. These cases are but a small portion of the phenomenon, and therefore, are not conclusive. This response is supposed to weaken the criticism that is directed towards the reform programs on the basis of high rates of recidivism.

Another rejoinder to the criticism also relates to the legitimacy of the use of the rates of recidivism. This argument says that it is inaccurate to evaluate reform programs according to such rates, because although the ideology of the treatment purports to look beyond the crime and onto the whole personality of the criminal, it measures the success of these programs against one single factor: the absence of reconviction for a criminal act.[230] In any case, the high rate of recidivism makes it difficult to justify these programs. In any event, the majority of theorists have attacked these programs both on the theoretical and practical levels so powerfully and determinedly, that the rehabilitation approach has deeply declined throughout the past decades.

In spite of the massive criticism garnered by the curative approach, a final word should be said in its favor. When offenses are committed by people who cannot be considered full members of the moral community, this approach gives us some guidelines in how to treat members of this group. The very same reasons that make this approach unsuitable for replacing the ordinary penal system, are useful in cases where conventional punishment is inappropriate, unacceptable or irrelevant. In such offenses as these, where the offenses are committed by people who are not responsible for their actions– offenses that result from compulsive behavior – our present concept of punishment is insufficient or inadequate. We do not regard such offenders as deserving of punishment, because we do not think that they had evil intentions when committing their crimes. In Gewirth's terminology, we consider their acts as lacking the generic features of actions, mostly the ability to choose. Hence, we cannot judge these acts as if they had been committed by a moral agent, because we believe that the agent lacked some of the capacities that are required in order to constitute moral agency, or in Melden's terminology, to become a full-fledged member of the moral community.

When we are unable to turn to the conventional penal system for those reasons, the curative approach can serve as a partial solution. On the one hand we do not want to punish those people, and yet on the other hand, we think that they cannot continue to live their lives without being controlled, or at least undergoing some treatment. Curative programs can solve the two problems that rise in such cases. The principal rationale to *reject* this approach as an alternative to punishment in cases of normal adult offenders, namely the risk of eroding the status of moral agency, might serve as a good reason to *accept* this approach in cases where we do not judge normal adults, or ordinary offenses. Even if this approach cannot replace the institution of punishment or the penal system, it might serve as a solution, in cases where conventional punishments are not suitable or applicable.

To sum up this issue I return to my interest in punishment. I want to review the ethical aspects and the justifying grounds for the withdrawal of rights. Punishment, as a significant instance of withdrawing rights, can be justified on the basis of moral presumptions about human beings, some of which might be weakened by accepting the assumptions on which the ideology of reform programs is based. Waiving the requirement to regard people as the self-originating source of their valid claims, or the requirement of responsibility, opposes some of my basic presumptions about moral agents, or those who have a moral standing.

The coming section deals with the dominant approach to punishment: the retributive one.

4.3 THE BACKWARD-LOOKING APPROACH TO PUNISHMENT

While the utilitarian or teleological approach is the core of the forward-looking approach towards punishment, the retributive approach is the core of the backward-looking approach. The forward-looking approach looks towards the future and anticipates some positive results to come out of the act of punishment, while the backward-looking approach looks at the past and accordingly decides that an offense that has been committed, deserves punishment. When investigating the ideas, contents and ideologies behind these attitudes, we find that they represent totally different concepts and beliefs about punishment. While the forward-looking approach justifies the act of punishment by the possible future benefits or social utility that this act may yield (mostly a reduction of crime through deterrence or rehabilitation of the offenders), the backward-looking theories lay the foundation for its justification, on the assumption that it is the intrinsically right response to wrongdoing. The fact that a moral wrongdoing has been carried out is sufficient reason to punish its executor.

Although there are many versions of backward-looking theories, we place them all under the *retributive theory* heading, which means that wrongdoers have to suffer for what they have voluntarily caused. In this sense, punishment is a sort of requital or repayment that is demanded from the offender, for the past wrongdoing that she committed. According to the retributive approach, she "has to pay her debt to society" for what she has done. The mere fact that she caused harm or offense is sufficient to justify the infliction of undesirable harm on her. If we insist upon identifying a moral principle upon which this approach rests, we might appeal to the *Lex Talionis*, the law of retaliation, as the core or the essence of this moral belief. However, even if so, we have to analyze our notion of retribution, in order to examine to what extent we can use this principle in particular, or the idea of retribution as a whole, as justifying grounds for punishment.

Lex Talionis, or the law of retaliation, views punishment within the context of repayment.[231] It is not clear why undergoing an unpleasant experience – whether incarceration, a fine or suspended prison sentence – is an appropriate or precise repayment; but it is quite apparent that its infliction on an offender, in order to make her pay for her offense, is justifiable on the basis of retribution. A similar version of retribution is that punishment is inflicted because it is deserved. The belief that a certain wrongdoing deserves requital or compensation, establishes the justification for punishing the person who carried it out.[232] A slightly different version of retribution, justifies the infliction of punishment on the fact that the one on whom it is imposed, has committed a crime. Such a Kantian view, regards punishment as a penalty, whose justification is the atonement for the knowing commission of an offense.

Other versions of retribution involve similar arguments for justifying punishment. We do not always agree that we can really call them retributive, but they represent more or less the same expectations for punishing offenders. The satisfaction theory, for example, maintains that there should be some kind of reciprocity, between the grievance of the victim of an offense and the satisfaction she gets from the suffering of the offender. The fair-play theory argues that not punishing an offender would be unfair to those who respect morality. The annulment theory argues that by punishing an offender, we annul the crime and restore the right, or "right the wrong".[233] However, the common denominator underlying retribution theories is that they presume that some balance must exist between what a person does to others, and the punishment that society doles out in return. Accordingly, when someone causes harm, she has to suffer for it.

This backward-looking approach, when it is carefully constrained, can circumvent most of the problems that we have encountered in the utilitarian approaches. The backward-looking approach dictates that punishment must be confined to the guilty, or as Flew indicates in the second and third characteristic of punishment, it must be inflicted on the offender alone. Here we cannot punish a scapegoat or an innocent victim in order to prevent future harm, or to achieve deterrence or any other kind of utility for the common good. Therefore, retribution cannot justify the fabrication of evidence against innocent people in order to "frame" suspects, when a swift conviction might avoid social harm. The second acute risk of the utilitarian approach is in dispensing a punishment which is disproportionate to the gravity of the offense. This danger is significantly reduced in the retributive approach, because we do not seek to deter would-be law breakers through "cruel and unusual" punishment.

Another constraint against excessive punishment results from the fact that the justification for the punishment is based on past wrongdoings. This links not only the offense and the penalty, but also the gravity of the offense and the seriousness or intensity of the punishment. The significance of the *Jus Talionis* – the right of requital – to the retributive approach, also links the severity of the punishment to the gravity of the offense. This principle correlates between the quality and the quantity of the punishment, and the wrongdoing that created the justification for it.[234] The danger of utilitarian theories, in which interests for reform or deterrence may lead to punishment in anticipation of the offense, also vanishes. This is due to the retrospective characteristic of the retributive theories. They look backwards when referring to an offense, and are unable to deal with an anticipated one. In other words, retributive theories overcome the main obstacles that result from concentrating on the future, or the future consequences and effects of punishment. The most crucial problem in the utilitarian outlook is the tendency to overlook the issues of guilt and innocence, as issues which belong to the past.[235] The blurring of these moral issues seems to impose a heavy shadow of dissatisfaction on the utilitarian approach as a justification for punishment. The retributive approach avoids these problems, and therefore, would seem to be superior to the utilitarian approach.

However, the retributive approach has its own problems. The principal one is that using it for justifying the institution of punishment turns it into a kind of revenge. When we look at specific cases of punishment, we can content ourselves with the metaphors of "balancing the moral equilibrium" that has been upset by the wrongdoing. But when we try to justify the institution itself, we cannot avoid the question: Why do we cause further suffering, by inflicting additional pain on the offenders? This must be judged bad, at the very least, when considered in isolation. The fact that one evil has been carried out cannot justify another one, or as Cottingham presents it: "two wrongs do not make a right". He reminds us of Bentham's position that all punishment is mischief, and is in itself evil.[236] If simple justice requires the infliction of harm on the offender, then justice might be no more than a delicate formulation of the demand for revenge or vendetta.

The version of J.D. Mabbott, one of the most determined adherents of retribution as the exclusive justification of punishment, might ameliorate this problem, but probably at the price of renouncing the basic sense of retribution: of repayment or redress. According to Mabbott, "the only justification for punishing any man is that he has broken the law".[237] His intent is to connect punishment with law-breaking and not with wrongdoing; but by doing this he abandons the fundamental assumption of retributive theories, that punishment is intended to balance or negate moral wrong. Antony Flew refers to Mabbott's concept of punishment, and says that his justification depends upon the very meaning of the word "punishment". By doing this, Mabbott does not offer a justification that is based on retributive ethical claims, but on a necessary truth drawn from the meaning of punishment that elucidates it.[238]

4.4 AN INTEGRATED JUSTIFICATION FOR PUNISHMENT

However, even Flew admits that Mabbott has identified a significant distinction, which explicates the sources of the dispute between the utilitarian and retributivist procedures of justification for punishment. He refers to Mabbott's distinction between systems and particular cases within those systems.[239] This distinction became a starting point for other theorists, who split the matter of justifying punishment into two different issues. The first one deals with the justifying grounds for the institution or the practice of punishment (as a system), and the second deals with the justifying grounds for specific cases of punishment.

There are different conclusions among theorists about the appropriate justification for each of these issues. Antony Flew, for example, thinks that the very nature of punishment is retributive, but that this applies to the justification as a system. He thinks that the retributive element of punishment refers only to the system of punishment as a whole, and not to individual cases of punishment.[240] However, there are others who think that the justification of certain cases should rely on retributive reasons, while the justification of the whole system remains utilitarian. S.I. Benn holds that the justification of punishment in general, must be thought of in terms of net advantages gained or mischief avoided. He also asserts that the first kind of advantage we expect from this institution is to secure societal conformity to rules, and this is gained primarily through deterrence. These are obvious utilitarian characteristics. However, when a particular verdict for a particular offender is in question, the first consideration is guilt (and not utility).[241] For Benn, the use of utilitarian considerations for every case of punishment would be to miss the point of punishment as an institution. In this matter he follows Bradley, who posits that inflicting a penalty for any reason other than that which is deserved by the wrong, is a crying injustice.[242] By employing the two modes of justification for the different aspects of punishment, Benn deflects some of the crucial criticism that is directed at each one of them, when it stands alone.

The synthesizing of the two approaches has become very frequent in recent theories.[243] These syntheses define the general aim of punishment in terms of one theory, and specify required constraints to avoid possible perversion and wrongs, on the other theory. Hart, for example, thinks that even though the general justifying aim of punishment is broadly utilitarian, we still can respect the requirements of "retribution in distribution", for justifying the specific cases of punishment. In his opinion:

> "It is perfectly consistent to assert *both* that the General Justifying Aim of the practice of punishment is its beneficial consequences *and* that the pursuit of this General Aim should be qualified or restricted out of deference to principles of Distribution which require that punishment should be only of an offender for an offense".[244]

A similar position is held by Rawls, when he distinguishes between two concepts of rules. This distinction is between a justification of a rule or practice, and a justification of a particular action falling under it.[245] Rawls maintains that: "utilitarian arguments are appropriate with regard to the question about the practice, while retributive arguments fit the application of particular rules to particular cases".[246] When we deal with a particular case of punishment, we justify it by looking back at the past. We see that the offender has committed a crime, was found guilty, and a penalty is inflicted on her for this. Here we adopt the viewpoint of the judge, which sounds like retribution. On the other hand, when we deal with the institution of punishment, we look forward, to the future, and adopt the viewpoint of the legislator, which sounds utilitarian. From this point of view, punishment, in the long run, will consequently further the interests of society. Rawls says:

> "Once the legislator decides to have laws and to assign penalties for their violation (as things are there must be both the law and the penalty) an institution is set up which involves a retributive conception of particular cases. It is part of the concept of the criminal law as a system of rules that the application and enforcement of these rules in particular cases should be justifiable by arguments of retributive character. The decision whether or not to use law rather than some other mechanism of social control, and the decision as to what laws to have and what penalties to assign, may be settled by utilitarian arguments; but if one decides to have laws then one has decided on something whose working in particular cases is retributive in form". [247]

Rawls' attempt to solve the crucial difficulties of both utilitarian and retributive justifications of punishment, by using both in two different perspectives, reflects the "integrative" trend of the current discussions regarding this issue. Anthony Ellis, who wrote (in 1995) a survey article entitled "Recent Work on Punishment", summarizes his review by saying that: "A theme running through most of the works I have mentioned is the desire to capture the center of both forward-looking and backward-looking theories of punishment".[248] He brings some examples of this trend, and his impression is that this is probably the best way to overcome the difficulties that rise from each approach when it is used on its own. Such an integrated approach ensures that even those who favor utilitarianism impose some side-constraints on punishment, which are motivated by retributive considerations. Among these constraints, there is an unequivocal demand that the sole grounds for punishment must be the offense committed, and there can be no license to justify the punishment of the innocent, or to justify collective punishment. This mode of justification also entails that the gravity of the offense must determine the severity of the punishment, or at least that they will be proportionate. This should prevent, among other things, draconian punishments. On the other hand, such an approach also entails, as part of the utilitarian justifying grounds of the practice of punishment, that punishment should act as a means to gain some utility (in avoiding future offenses, mostly through deterrence). This requires that punishment should not be marginal, in order to show that crime does not pay. S.I. Benn formulates this criterion by saying that: "the marginal increment of mischief inflicted should be preferable to the mischief avoided by fixing that penalty rather than one slightly lower".[249] This means that when we decide to reduce mischief by reducing the punishment, we should consider that we might squander the deterrent aims of punishment, and consequently increase future harm. The desire to reduce harm should also be measured with respect to the future implications of a reduced penalty. The decision for fixing the required penalty for each offense should result from weighing the avoided mischief against the gained advantage of the specific punishment, according to utilitarian calculations.

This method of justifying punishment provides a reasonable and even satisfactory answer to the two crucial questions about punishment, which are: *Why do we have this practice (or why we do punish at all),* and *why does the offender deserve to suffer?* However, there are two additional questions which should but cannot be answered, through this mode of justification. Even when we are sure that the practice of punishment is justified (by its utilitarian benefits), and that the culprit deserves to suffer for his offense (due to retributive considerations), we still have to answer the question: *Why is there a duty to punish him*? And even when there is a duty to punish him, there remains the question: *Why is it the state or the community's duty to inflict this punishment?*[250] In order to offer a reasonable answer to these questions, some theorists developed another approach, which in some ways reflects the revival of the retributive approach, yet also corresponds better to both communitarian as well as right-based theories. This brings us closer to my general view of rights, as well as my approach towards punishment as a kind of a withdrawal of rights. Following Cottingham, I shall call this approach "Fair-Play Retributivist", or "Rights-Retributivist".

4.5 THE "FAIR-PLAY RETRIBUTIVIST" OR "RIGHTS-RETRIBUTIVIST" APPROACH TOWARD PUNISHMENT

This approach is backward-looking, and its basic idea is that the offender is a "free-rider" who has taken advantage of benefits gained from social cooperation, but does not shoulder her share of the burdens that are imposed upon the others. By doing this she violates the rights of others, who obey the law. This gives her an unfair advantage over the others, and it is only fair that the others make her pay the price, by a reciprocal curtailing of her own rights.[251] Punishment, according to this view, annuls this unfair advantage, by balancing the benefits the offender gained from the law-obedience of the others whose rights were violated, against the harm she suffers by losing some of her rights. In other words, her unfair advantage is erased by the disadvantage she suffers.

This approach regards punishment in a manner quite similar to Murphy's interpretation of Kant, saying that punishment is: "a debt owed to the law-abiding members of one's community".[252] Duff and Garland interpret Murphy's approach as "positive retributivism". This means that punishment is not merely permissible, but is required by justice, because not punishing the offenders bestows them with an unfair advantage over the other law-abiding citizens. That is clearly an injustice towards the others.[253] However, all this is true only when people view themselves as belonging to the same moral community (in Melden's terminology), or to a system of social cooperation between free and equal persons, (in Rawlsian terminology). The idea that the obligation to obey the law is part of social cooperation is widely accepted, and it is part of the members' acknowledgement of their duties. One of the best formulations of this idea is expressed by Hart, who says:

> "When a number of persons conduct any joint enterprise according to rules and thus restrict their liberty, those who have submitted to these restrictions when required have a right to a similar submission from those who have benefited by their submission. The rules may provide that officials should have authority to enforce obedience and make further rules, and this will create a structure of legal rights and duties, but the moral obligation to obey the rules in such circumstances is *due to* the co-operating members of the society, and they have the correlative moral right to obedience".[254]

This brings us back to two former issues that can be connected together here. The first one was the main issue of the second chapter of this study: the considering of moral rights as existing within a moral community, or legal rights within the state, and the source of their validity as resulting from the acknowledgement of the social or legal framework. The foundation of rights and duties on the reciprocal commitment to the shared normative framework – or to the system of rules – creates the obligation of the members to obey, and the obligation of the social or political system to enforce the former obligation. This reciprocal commitment means that each member is bound by the common and shared rules, and obeys them, as part of his membership in the community. This provides the moral grounds for the member's obedience.

The second issue I explored is the main topic of the third chapter of this study. There I argued that the framework that confers rights, has to create a correlation between the extent to which the possessor has rights, and the extent to which she fulfills the conditions of possession and the conditions of engagement of these rights. This is the basic idea of society as the framework which functions as the guarantor or bailor of the members' rights. When there is an incompatibility between her rights and the fulfillment of her duties, the authorities have to rectify the situation. If a person possesses fewer rights than she deserves or a diminished measure of certain rights, she should be repaid with additional rights or with the missing sections of these rights, in order to maintain the required equilibrium. However, the demand for equilibrium is also activated when a person is not entitled to possess certain rights or certain parts of a right, since she does not fulfill the required conditions, or she does not deserve to possess them under certain circumstances. When this is so, the authorities have to withdraw the excessive rights or the excessive parts of the right from her. This imposes a duty on the social or legal framework to punish the offender and establish a new balance between her entitlement and her actual possession or rights. In this sense punishment is regarded as a deprivation or a withdrawal of rights.[255]

The basic idea of "balancing", that stands at the core of the "rights-retributivist" or "fair play retributivist" approach – in Cottingham's terms– or "just distribution theory" – in Ellis' terminology – reflects my theory of punishment within rights-talk. The fundamental principle of the retributive theory, that is, the demand for proportionate punishment – which means a reasonable balance between the severity of the punishment and the gravity of the offense – is carefully preserved here (Cottingham mentions it as an attractive feature of this approach[256]). Just as we can rank degrees of membership in the moral community, and determine different measures of possessing rights accordingly, we can also rank, with appropriate criteria, offenses in terms of their moral heinousness, or in the terms I used in the previous chapters: the measure of threat and hazard they pose to the moral community. This ranking enables us to set up penalties in order of severity, that will enable us to fit the severity of the penalty to the gravity of the offense (at least approximately). In terms of rights-talk we can say, that the measure of rights that should be withdrawn, is determined by the extent to which one's intentional conduct, caused harm or threat to the integrity and morality of the community. The most effective way of doing so is using Gewirth's Principle of Proportionality that was mentioned in the previous chapters.

Alan Gewirth states this clearly when he connects the criminal law with the PGC. He regards criminal law as instrumental to the PGC, and argues that the PGC requires an equal distribution of rights to well-being, between the agent and her recipients. When an agent inflicts harm on her recipients, the required equality is broken, and: "the punishment prescribed by the criminal law is justified as a way of restoring the equality by redressing the previously disturbed balance".[257] Here, Gewirth's attitude towards punishment expresses a backward-looking approach, which is very close to what Ellis calls "just distribution theory". The redressing of the balance requires that the penalties that are inflicted on wrongdoers be in proportion to the seriousness of their crimes. Gewirth considers this as an application of the Principle of Proportionality, although the content of penalties is not conferring rights, but removal of them. He views the treatment of both the offense and the punishment, in terms of calculation of rights; that is, when an agent commits a crime, she disturbs the equality between the rights she enjoys and those of the others, by removing a certain amount of rights from their side. Gewirth says that this amount is added to the offender's side. However, I do not think that this assumption is necessary. The required equality between the offender's rights and the others' rights is disturbed anyhow, while the offender enjoys the "illegal" benefit gained from the others' restraints on their conduct. This inequality should be restored by removing some of the offender's excessive rights, which are gained from the fact that the above-mentioned restraints were not respected by her. Gewirth also notes that the amount of rights that were withdrawn from the others, and that should be withdrawn from the offender, cannot be measured exactly. This "amount" is intended to enable us to quantify, both the impact of the crime on others' well-being, and the penalties that can be inflicted for this crime.[258]

In this matter I fully agree with Gewirth's concept of punishment, but I wish to emphasize this last issue. It is very difficult to measure or even assess one's possession of rights, and it is even harder to measure their withdrawal. First, sometimes one possesses rights without really exercising them. In this case, their withdrawal will not affect her, and will, in fact, be no punishment. Second, sometimes withdrawing one's rights may even improve one's welfare, and will, actually, be a reward (for example, the incarceration of a homeless person in Chicago or Minneapolis during the winter). These difficulties also occur when measuring the severity of offences.

For example, when one drives a car without a valid drivers license in order to bring a severely wounded person to the nearest hospital, she breaks the law to a lesser degree than one who drives to the theater without having a drivers license. These difficulties in measuring the possession of rights and their withdrawal, and in assessing the severity of each offence, require that these measures be carried out sensitively in response to all the relevant details.

One element of Gewirth's stance towards punishment hints at a communitarian approach, despite the fact that he does not usually support that method. When he summarizes his discussion of the matter, he says:

> "What requires rectification in this area is wrong, and punishment as inflicted by the state conveys the community's solemn public expression of disapproval. At the same time, the punishment serves to acknowledge that the criminal is a person who is responsible for his actions as a member of the moral community".[259]

Gewirth mentions the obligations the agent bears as a member of the community, and acknowledges the state's (and in fact the community's) authority to punish the offender, for not fulfilling the requirements that are implied by these obligations. Two complications arise here. First, if the community has the authority to punish by depriving an agent of some of his rights, it should also have the authority to allocate rights and duties within the community. This implies that rights are bestowed by the community only upon its members. Second, Gewirth maintains the correlation theory of rights (at least with regard to human rights, which he regards as claim rights), and therefore must admit that the rights lost by the law-abiding agents, are not vis-a-vis the offender, but rather the state or the community, and this is the source of the community's authority to punish.[260] Anyhow, this dispute had been discussed before, and I shall not go into it again here. My purpose here is to explain the concept of punishment from the perspective of a rights-based theory.

4.5.1 Punishment As A Withdrawal Of Rights

As mentioned before, right-based theories regard punishment as restoring a presumed balance between the rights of a certain individual, and the rights of the others in the community. These theories intend to rectify distortions and inequalities that are caused by the fact that offenders take unfair advantage of the constraints, which the law-abiding members impose upon themselves. This unfair advantage is translated into excessive rights on their behalf (for example, they enlarge their property rights by not paying taxes), or to diminishing the rights of the others (by stealing others' property, which reduces the property rights of the others). Punishing them by depriving them of some of their rights equalizes the inappropriate distribution of rights. The position I held in the previous chapters, regarding the possession and the withdrawal of rights, form the foundation of the present conception of punishment.

According to my view regarding the possession of rights, we can rank the membership in the moral community and determine different degrees of moral agency. Thus, we can determine different degrees for the possession of rights. The decision as to what extent one is entitled to possess rights is based upon two different criteria. The first regards the perceptual, cognitive and mental capabilities of the prospective agents. This criteria expresses the individual or subjective aspects of agency. Measuring the components of this criteria, those capacities that relate to the agent's understanding and her communication capabilities, tells us to what extent the prospective agent is competent to merit "an entry ticket" to the moral community. In other words, we assess the quality of responsibility of the prospective agent. This assessment determines the prospective agent's level of membership in the moral community, so long as her capabilities remain at the same level. Changes in these capacities will affect our estimation of her agency. Insofar as the prospective agent realizes her potential to the above capabilities, it is accordingly acknowledged that she is entitled to enter the moral community. If these capabilities are developed, and the extent to which the agent realizes this potential is increased (be it naturally, by maturation of a child to adult, or in any other way), the possible extent of membership in the moral community is correspondingly increased.

However, this process can also operate in the opposite direction. If, unfortunately, due to tragic circumstances, a person loses some of the above capabilities, the extent to which she can be acknowledged as a member of the moral community, is proportionally reduced. Such cases of partial possession of the subjective necessary requirements for full-fledged membership (cases of fetuses, children and mentally disabled or mentally retarded persons for example) are discussed in the next chapter. They are not considered as possessing all the rights that "normal adults" possess, and from the very beginning, there are some rights that they do not possess. Their rights are withdrawn only in the sense that they are deprived of them from the beginning, because they lack the required capabilities.

Nevertheless, in the case of punishment we deal with the second criteria. These criteria relate to the social aspect of moral agency, and to the degree of voluntariness and purposiveness of the agent's conduct within the community. This means that the possession of rights is also determined by the agent's behavior within the community. When she fulfills her obligations, she can possess the rights that she is entitled to have according to the first set of criterion. If she is a normal adult, she can be considered as a "full fledged" member of the community, and be entitled to enjoy all the acknowledged rights, that are conferred upon such agents. As a member she is considered as fully responsible for her actions, and is entitled to every advantage that can be achieved from social cooperation. On the other hand, as a responsible person (who is entitled to enjoy rights), she bears obligations and must impose some constraints on her conduct, in order to enable others to enjoy their own rights. The extent to which she fulfills her obligations determines her level of membership. When she reneges on some or part of her obligations, she reduces the level of her moral agency, which is determined by her fulfillment of her obligations as a member of the moral community. Accordingly, she loses some of her rights. At this stage, it is the community's duty to deprive her of some rights, in proportion to the harm or threat she imposed upon the integrity and morality of the community. Just as it was the community's duty to respond to some of the agent's rights, and to be the guarantor for the fulfillment of her other rights, it is now the community's duty to protect the others' rights, and to avoid the unjust inequality that results from the offense. The community's authority to allocate rights and duties among its members, entails that it should not allow unjustified possession and use of rights, and therefore, that it should inflict punishment (by withdrawing the excessive rights of the offender), in order to maintain the balance between the rights that the offender is entitled to possess, and those which she actually possesses. Just as the community has to enforce the possession of the justified rights of its members, so, too, it is obliged to prevent the misuse of these rights. This will protect the appropriate possession of rights by the law-abiding members.

Of course, the extent to which the offender is deprived of her rights should be determined according to the gravity of the offense for which these rights are withdrawn. Otherwise, there would be no balance between the rights one is entitled to have according to one's fulfillment of one's obligations within the community, and one's actual possession of rights. If we explain this according to Gewirth's metaphorical approach, we say that when the offender violates the others' rights by X units of well-being, and the same amount of units was added to her own well-being, she should pay this amount in return. This means that the same amount of well-being that was added to her side should be withdrawn from her, in order to rectify the inequality in possessing rights, which was caused by the offense. Using this metaphor of "units" to balancing rights by the withdrawing of part of them, means that this withdrawal should be proportionate to the damage that was inflicted on the morality or the integrity of the community. In my opinion, the withdrawal of rights should be implemented, only with regard to the excessive rights that one possesses, and that means that the offender should be deprived only of the rights she is not entitled to possess.

The quantification of these rights should be determined by the degree of threat and harm that was caused to the integrity and morality of the community, by the intentional actions of the offender. This amount expresses the measure to which the offender reneges on her obligations as a member of the community, and frees herself from the constraints on her conduct. Considering her rights as conditional to the social arrangements that bestow them, creates the direct linkage between her social transactions and the extent to which her rights are acknowledged by society. The more she reneges on her obligations, the fewer rights she is acknowledged to have, and hence, the more rights are to be withdrawn from her. Similarly, we can present this correlation in terms of an offender's level of moral agency or membership in the community. The more harm the offender causes, the lesser the degree of membership she is acknowledged to have. For this matter, the above justification of the "rights-distributive" or "fair play retributive" approach fits this conception of punishment, and is sufficient for justifying it.

This justification can serve as grounds for the practice or institution of punishment, as well as for certain forms of punishment. Its retributive foundations and its (fair and equal) distributive aims, explain why a certain offender deserves punishment: it is merely to balance the inequality between her entitlement and her actual possession of rights, and to rectify the unfair advantages that the offender has taken, in comparison with the other members of the community. Being a rights-based approach, it also explains why equality and fairness are necessary, or why we use punishment at all. I discussed this issue, of possession of rights, in previous chapters. I argued there, that without the intervention of the community in allocating rights and duties, and the enforcement of the respondents to fulfill their duties, the whole system of cooperation, which is based on mutual obligation of the parties, would collapse. This is a kind of utilitarian approach that can be understood in different ways, but not in terms of the ordinary utilitarian motivation. It does not have any deterrent intentions or aims, nor does it base itself on expectations for any future benefit. At the most, it aims to avoid future harm that might be caused by the collapse of the social scheme, and by the crumbling of the conceptual framework, within which rights have their meaning and validity. Avoiding the breakdown of the social scheme ensures the future benefits of the social framework, and in this sense we can regard the above position as utilitarian. However, this is the marginal use of the term "utilitarian" with regard to theories of punishment.

A similar approach is held by J.D. Mabbott, who insists that the infliction of punishment in a particular case should not be determined by the benefit that the criminal or society would gain from it. He illustrates his view by saying that: "In exactly the same way it is essential to a credit system that the repayment of a particular debt should not be determined by the good that particular payment will do."[261] In this sense, the benefit gained from punishing someone is not from external reasons, but from the preservation of the entire system of allocating rights and duties. If we examine it from Gewirth's point of view, we can say that consistency requires us to punish by depriving the offender of part of her rights, if we want to preserve the meaning and validity of our original claim to possess rights. According to my view, punishment as a deprivation of some of the offender's (or the immoral agent's) rights can be justified by the desire to enable moral agents to enjoy the rights to which they are entitled. Proportional punishment is mandated by that same desire, because we still regard the offender as a partial moral agent or member of the community, and as such she is entitled to have some rights, of which we do not want her to be unjustly deprived.

However, there is at least one issue where this formal presentation of the issue encounters some acute difficulties, and in which the implementation of the Principle of Proportionality is impossible. I refer to the issue of capital punishment. The inflicting of this punishment necessitates a total and ultimate deprivation of *all* of the offender's rights. This consequence cannot be seen as proportional to any harm, because it is terminal. One of its meanings is that we do not regard the offender as an agent, under any future conditions and circumstances. In communitarian terms, we disqualify her from membership in the community. This strikes at one of the essential agreements of communitarian theories, which states that even when being punished, the offender remains within the community. This is correlative to the assumption of agent-relative theories, where the offender has to be respected as an agent, even after being found guilty, since this is her basic right as a human being. These two problems, the impossibility of implementing the Principle of Proportionality, and the impossibility to regard the guilty – after being punished – as a member of the community or as an agent, require serious considerations for justifying capital punishment. In the next paragraphs, I discuss this issue, exploring whether we can justify this issue after all.

4.6 CAPITAL PUNISHMENT

Capital Punishment refers both to the terminal consequence of the death penalty, and to the fact that it is "a particular type, kind, or degree of punishment – one in which the punishment directly imposed or inflicted is death".[262] This means that the acknowledged characteristics of punishment, should be present when regarding a certain act of execution as capital punishment. This also entails that the justifying grounds for the practice or the institution of punishment, must include this type within its purview. It is obvious that the justification for a particular act of capital punishment should follow the principles according to which we usually punish. The discussion of this punishment in particular, must include the whole procedure of considering punishment as an appropriate response for an offense, with some additional considerations that express the uniqueness of capital punishment.

As in the discussion of ordinary punishment, the main controversy here is between the forward-looking and backward-looking approaches. The former approach views the most significant aim of capital punishment in the reducing of future offenses, whether by deterrence, or merely by permanently preventing the offender from committing additional crimes. The latter approach does not expect any social utility from the execution (or at least not directly), but insists that the past nefarious crime committed by the offender, requires such a punishment. However, unlike the comprehensive agreement about the social necessity and justification of the practice of punishment, which unites both forward-looking and backward-looking approaches, there is a serious dispute among theorists, about the necessity and the legitimacy of the practice of capital punishment. In this dispute, there are disagreements even within each of the above approaches, which divide the parties into supporters and detractors of this practice, regardless of their principal agreement about the justification of punishment as a whole. In the coming paragraphs I present the main arguments for and against capital punishment within the rival positions, and present my view about this matter. Each of the positions must be consistent according to its principal view about punishment, and adjust its specifications, constraints and limitations to the singularity of this issue.

4.6.1 The Forward-Looking Examination Of Capital Punishment

In the heart of the consequentialist discussion about capital punishment (on the basis of utilitarian measures), there rises the question whether execution is a more effective means for reducing future crimes, than its alternatives (e.g., life imprisonment). This question, in turn, leads to two additional questions. The first and the more obvious of the two, is the effect of such a punishment on the offender's capability of recidivism. This issue is among the very few questions that have a decisive answer. There is no doubt that the meaning of execution is an unequivocal incapacitation of the offender. The remaining question is whether the offender would have relapsed into recidivism if he had been released. This question cannot be answered, nor could an answer be of use in a specific decision regarding a particular execution, because it could can only give statistical likelihoods. It is true that we could measure the rate of recidivism of those who were imprisoned and released. However, those who favor capital punishment (the Retentionists) maintain that even a low rate of recidivism by convicted murderers is unbearable. The fact that an execution absolutely prevents any future offense from being committed by the convicted murderer, is a weighty consideration that supports the Retentionists' arguments.[263]

Since this kind of argument regarding possible future outcomes is complicated, speculative and usually unconvincing, the utilitarian objectors to capital punishment (the Abolitionists), tend to consider the arguments regarding the deterrent effects on other possible offenders. Even though there cannot be any concrete evidence, for or against the superior deterrence of capital punishment over its alternatives, this has become the most frequent argument used by utilitarian Retentionists, and utilitarian Abolitionists. The latter base their argument on statistical findings, that result from comparing murder rates in countries that inflict capital punishment, with those of socially similar countries that do not inflict such punishment. They also compare these rates within the same countries that used to have capital punishment and abolished it, or restored this punishment after a period of abolition. The findings do not show any superior deterrence that capital punishment has over alternative forms of punishment.[264]

Abolitionists say that the deterrent effect of capital punishment is not conspicuous, because most of the murderers committed their crime without premeditation. Victor Evjen, for example, argues that many of them committed the homicides impulsively and without forethought. These homicides were committed during quarrels, where the murderers were so overwhelmed and agitated, that they could not control themselves.[265] In such situations, under these conditions and circumstances, we do not really believe that deterrence would have worked, because no process of reasoning and considerations of discretion were in operation, when the crime was committed. A similar argument that opposes the deterrent argument, states that most criminals assume that they will not be caught. Considering this, they do not think much about the penalty that might be inflicted upon them, and, due to this fact, cannot be deterred.[266]

Another argument, which weakens the claim that the aim of execution is deterrence, has to do with the way executions are operated. If, in fact, capital punishment deters so effectively, it should be operated publicly and not discreetly.[267] Abolitionists claim that if we really want to achieve a full deterrent effect, we should execute the guilty in front of a crowd or on television, so it will discourage potential offenders. The fact that we go to great pains to conceal the actual execution, even when the execution is carried out by hanging or by firing squad, weakens the argument that the aim of execution is deterrence. Of course, Retentionists can answer on a utilitarian basis, that they want to withhold the trauma from innocent people, and by doing so they reduce unnecessary pain and suffering. However, this will cause them some difficulties, with regard to the consistency with which they use the utilitarian argument of deterrence.

One of the paramount disputes regarding the deterrent effects of capital punishment is its effects, not on the criminals, but on members of the society as a whole. One of the theories is that capital punishment increases the strength with which social values and sanctions are internalized within the citizens' minds. This may increase the degree, to which they resist external pressures that lead to the committing of crimes.[268] Even though this theory makes sense, it suffers from the same crucial difficulties that apply to all the arguments for and against capital punishment. I refer to the fact that we can never conceivably know whether, in fact, the death penalty (or as some radical Abolitionists call it, "judicial homicide") really has a deterrent effect, in what way, and to what extent. Hence we can never know whether retention of capital punishment will protect us, or if its abolition will endanger us.[269] These doubts and uncertainties are sufficient reasons for me to abandon this attempt to justify capital punishment, after I have presented this brief survey of the main arguments regarding the issue.

Nevertheless, there are arguments that use the above doubts and uncertainties regarding the question of deterrence, in order to support the death penalty. They use the minimax strategy, according to which, if our assumptions regarding the deterrence are incorrect, we should choose the policy that will minimize the possibility of loss of innocent life. George Schedler expounds this argument in the following way:

> "If we incorrectly assume that capital punishment deters and we retain it, we vainly execute convicted murderers (some of whom may be innocent). On the other hand, if we incorrectly assume it does not deter and we abolish it, then the uniquely deterrable group will kill an indefinite number of innocent people. It has been argued that the former alternative minimizes our losses, for the relative number of executed murderers (who may be innocent) will surely be smaller than the number of innocent victims. Thus, the rational alternative is to retain capital punishment".[270]

This argument admits that it is highly questionable whether capital punishment has a superior deterrent effect. However, it concludes that it should be retained nonetheless, because it "runs the risk of the loss of fewer innocent lives, than life imprisonment".[271] The tempting idea behind this argument is that greater value is given to the lives of the innocent victims of crimes, than to the lives of the convicted criminals. However, those who wish to reject this argument maintain that inflicting capital punishment, makes certain that someone will die (the convicted culprit), while on the other hand, by the abolition of capital punishment, there is only a remote possibility that some people might die (even though they may be innocent). Their assumption is that the certainty of one person's death, overpowers the doubt that some others might die. In addition, they mention the risk that among the convicted there might be innocent defendants, who will be unjustly executed. The excessive weight given to the lives of these innocent people, tips the scale against retention.[272]

The fact that so many theorists resort to arguments which are based on vague possibilities and uncertain premises, shows that solid evidential grounds are nonexistent. Since these arguments are unconvincing, it would behoove the utilitarian Retentionists to muster better arguments for justifying their claims.

Another utilitarian argument, which is sometimes raised in favor of capital punishment, is based on economical considerations. This argument assumes that rehabilitation is not possible for murderers. They might be imprisoned for the rest of their lives, or they might be released after a long incarceration and probably return to crime, and after that to prison. The cost of their upkeep in prison is very high, and it is imposed upon innocent taxpayers. This only adds more harm to the damage that has already been done by the culprit. By his execution, the additional damage can be prevented. The responses to this claim are divided into two different categories. The first is purely utilitarian, and based on cost estimations that assume that it would cost more to carry out the execution, considering the appeals and court actions that are usually involved in such a sentencing. The second is based on several value assumptions regarding human life. According to this line of thinking, a civilized and progressive society should not take into account financial considerations, when deciding on the loss of a human (even though culpable) life. This is, to some extent, a dehumanization of life, transforming it into salable or exchangeable merchandise. We can also translate this point into utilitarian terms. We can say that in the long run, this line of thought will have the disastrous consequence of causing us to weigh the lives of innocent people, as if they were exchangeable merchandise. However, it seems to me that the whole discussion regarding the costs of the upkeep of the culprits misses the point of the moral aspects of capital punishment. It transforms an argument concerning principles, into a matter of book keeping and shopkeepers' calculation. Hence I abandon the whole utilitarian method of justification, and move on to consider the backward-looking (and mainly retributive) attempts to justify the death penalty.

4.6.2 The Backward-Looking Examination Of Capital Punishment

Backward-looking Retentionists base their position on several presumptions that represent their principal view on punishment. They believe that retributive justice requires that crime deserves punishment. They also believe that the severity of the punishment should be proportional to the gravity of the crime. Hence, they believe that there are crimes that are so heinous, that the only appropriate response for them is capital punishment. This should adequately express society's wrath and indignation at the perpetration of such crimes. In a way, they literally interpret the law of retaliation, the *lex talionis.* They believe that for certain crimes, that are exceptionally vicious and heinous, the culprits simply "deserve" to die. They think that a lesser punishment would not "fit" the harm that was caused (or the gravity of these offenses), nor the severity of the other penalties that are inflicted for lesser crimes. Their obligation to proportionality between the crime and the punishment requires that crimes that are distinctively brutal, deserve penalties that are more severe than others. If, for example, we inflict life imprisonment on a murderer, we must then inflict a more severe punishment on a serial murderer or one who tortures his victims to death. Imposing the same penalty on the latter will nullify the difference between the two crimes, or our different attitude towards these crimes.

This last argument is somewhat of a moderation of *lex talionis.* It refers to what Reiman calls "proportional retributivism". [273] In other words, *lex talionis* is not to be understood in the biblical sense of "an eye for an eye, a tooth for a tooth". This biblical approach could not be applied to "the toothless assailant who knocks the victim's teeth" or, in a more serious restatement, to the penniless thief or the tax evader. Instead we regard *lex talionis* as a principle of measure or quantification of injury, and not a requirement to inflict the exact same harm on the offender as he inflicted on others. In short, this requires that the punishment fit the crime only in measure or extent, not in form. It does not mean that the retaliation should imitate the crime or should be modeled on the crime. It demands only that penalties should be ranked according to the severity of the crimes, for which they are inflicted. And when we judge crimes to be heinous, in which "paying them back" amounts to the most severe penalty, we can justly execute their perpetrators. This expresses society's aversion and loathing towards such crimes and criminals[274], and is not an act of revenge or vendetta.

When we discuss this issue from a retributive point of view, it means that we accept the fact that punishment is inflicted on the culprit for what he has done, and not because of what was done to the victim (which is an essential differentiation from a restitutional approach). This represents a principal position, which states that the conviction is not based solely on the harm caused to the victim, and that the procedure does not exist solely between the victim and the offender, but between *society* and the offender. If there is an aspect of revenge, it is a manifestation of the community's indignation towards these crimes. At the foundation of this view lays the assumption that the crime has injured society as a whole, by hurting its morality, stability or integrity.

The main criticism brought against the retributive arguments for capital punishment, is similar to the criticism that is brought against the retributive approach in general. It maintains that it is not necessary to cause additional injury in addition to the harm that has already been done, and that two wrongs do not make a right. On the question of capital punishment, Abolitionists like Victor H. Evjen, for example, maintain that: "the death penalty is a crude and primitive form of retributive justice".[275] They regard it as an act of hate and vengeance, and not of justice. They claim that the society's need for protection does not require it to avenge itself, and that capital punishment for the sake of revenge, is a repugnant act for a civilized society. In addition to the customary claim, that unnecessary and futile harm is not legitimate in a moral society, the act of execution itself is barbaric, brutal, sordid and savage. It is a manifestation of irreverence and disrespect towards human life and human dignity.

These kinds of arguments lean heavily on unproven hypotheses regarding the meaning of a civilized and progressive community. Evjen, for example, bases his argument on the assumption that the progress of civilization is measured by the reverence it accords to human life. In order to support this he brings Winston Churchill's view, regarding the criterion for a civilized society. According to Churchill, among the most unfailing tests of the civilization of a community, are the mood and temper of the public with regard to the treatment of crime and criminals.[276] From this Evjen concludes that harsh treatment towards criminals is not appropriate to a civilized society. Reiman follows Durkheim and maintains a similar approach, that punishment becomes less intense as societies become more advanced.[277] Hence abolition is appropriate for this concept of progress.

The arguments against the retributive justification for capital punishment are weakened by the fact that they are based on unproven hypotheses regarding civilization and society. Even Reiman admits that the content, direction or even the value of civilization, "are hotly contested issues". Van Den Haag's answer to Reiman's argument, regarding the inconsistency of capital punishment with the advancement of civilization, emphasizes the difficulties of such premises. They usually rely on arbitrary definitions of progress or civilization that usually create circular arguments.[278] I contemplate whether an suitable response to this kind of criticism against capital punishment would be, perhaps, to simply reject these definitions and formulate others. However, this is not appropriate because we want to examine the morality of the death penalty within a common conceptual framework. Therefore we must examine retributive arguments in light of the most persuasive arguments against capital punishment, those that refer to human rights and justice. In the coming section I present arguments which furnish more concrete arguments against the death penalty. Responding to or refuting them may elucidate the difficulties that are involved in inflicting this penalty. They raise questions regarding the injustice that might be caused as a result of such penalties, and some illustrations regarding the possession and forfeiture of rights.

4.6.3 Capital Punishment And Justice

Serious criticism against capital punishment results from the history of its actual implementation. Many Abolitionists demand the cancellation of judicial executions mainly because of the unequal, and hence the unjust implementation, of the death penalty. They maintain that the administration of the death penalty is biased against certain races, classes and minority groups, and that a moral society cannot tolerate such partiality. Part of this bias arises because the accused from higher social classes can hire better attorneys, who reduce the chances of being convicted as well as the penalties if they are convicted. This, in turn, decreases their chances of being sentenced to death. Another factor is their social status and connections, which influences judges to impose less severe penalties on them. For example, criminals from such backgrounds can bring expert testimonies from famous and influential persons, while criminals from oppressed or impoverished backgrounds often cannot even obtain adequate legal defense. In addition, those from underprivileged backgrounds suffer from social prejudice against their group, and are the most likely defendants to be convicted, and then executed. In the United States, African Americans, Hispanics, Native Americans, and other deprived groups are at a disadvantaged position in the courts, and have a greater chance of being executed. Thereupon, legally irrelevant factors such as the race or socio-economic status of the criminals or the victims, the location of the crime or trial, affect the severity of the penalty. This results in unequal punishments for similar crimes, which clearly contradicts the foundation of *lex talionis.*

Stephen Nathanson, one of the most renowned Abolitionists that use this argument, maintains that the inevitable discriminatory application of capital punishment, whether intentional or not, is grounds enough to cancel the death penalty as unjust. The fact that an African American who murders a white Protestant is much more likely to be sentenced to death, than a white Protestant who murders an African American, is sufficient reason to demand not to apply such a penalty as a whole. Nathanson finds it outrageous that the decisions regarding the severity of the punishment depend on factors that one cannot control. When the upshot of such decisions determines the life or death of the accused, they should not be affected by factors that have nothing to do with the nature of the crime. Nathanson maintains that racial prejudice is so deeply rooted in the American society, that juries and prosecutors cannot free themselves from its influence when meting out the severity of the punishment. So long as the influence of irrelevant factors is ineradicable, we cannot provide a just and impartial penal system. In such a situation there is a powerful reason for abolishing capital punishment.[279]

There are different responses to this argument. Those who reject it, claim that the law should be equal and color-blind, and applied impartially on all defendants, regardless of the race, color, social status and gender of the offenders, or of the victims. Retentionists argue that if there are offenders who deserve to be sentenced to death and be executed, the fact that only part of them will actually be executed, is not sufficient to abolish the whole procedure. An unfair or even unjust racial or social bias in the penal system is regrettable but tolerable in an imperfect legal system. Retentionists argue that if justice requires us to punish as many guilty offenders as possible, and to spare as many innocent persons as possible, it is better to mete out justice in *part* of the cases, than to treat *all* of the cases with equal injustice.[280] Van Den Haag, for example, says that unequal justice, where we punish some of the offenders according to their just deserts (even when some get away), is preferable to equal injustice where we let them all get away with murder. It is unjust not to punish the one who is guilty, and it is just to punish him; not the opposite. If there is something wrong with selective capital punishment, it is the fact that it may release some of those who deserve it, not the fact that it is inflicted on those who deserve it.[281]

Another answer to Nathanson's criticism regarding the discriminatory application of capital punishment can be found in a more general problem that is connected with the inequality of the penal system. All the above claims regarding the biased implementation of capital punishment are relevant to the whole framework of the penal system. The flaws revealed in the unequal infliction of the death penalty, exist at all levels of punishment. The influence of arbitrary factors on juries, prosecutors and judges, exists in the meting out of all sentences in the courtroom. In addition, the limited financial resources of members of the lower socioeconomic classes prevents them from hiring good attorneys, and this, in turn, critically affects the severity of the punishment and causes unequal penalties to be meted out for the same offenses. This is true for all sentences and for all crimes. Using this fact to demand the abolishment of capital punishment can justify the demand to abolish *all* other penalties, because they are also affected by factors that are irrelevant to the crime. This latter demand is, of course, outrageous, and undermines our entire legal system. It is true that the severity of a penalty depends on factors that one cannot control, which means that something is wrong with the whole system. However, the rejection of the entire legal system must be based on more fundamental grounds, and not only when it refers to a specific kind of penalty. We cannot ignore the discriminatory administration of imprisonment, on the one hand, and remonstrate only when capital punishment is involved. We can either demand that all punishments be abolished, or waive our demand for the abolishment of capital punishment. Discriminatory administration of penalties is either sufficient justifying grounds to cancel the penal system as a whole (because it is unbearable or unacceptable), or is insufficient for justifying any kind of penalty. Van Den Haag summarizes this argument by saying this:

> "Equal justice is best, but unattainable. Unequal justice is our lot in this world. It is the only justice we can ever have, for not all murderers can be apprehended or convicted, or sentenced equally in different courts. We should constantly try to bring every offender to justice. But meanwhile unequal justice is the only justice we have, and certainly better that equal injustice – giving no murderer the punishment his crime deserves".[282]

In any event, it seems clear that an argument that is based on the unequal administration of justice, cannot justify a basic demand for the abolishment of capital punishment, without undermining the justifying grounds for the practice of punishment as a whole. The only way to separate the linkage between the two justifications is to argue that the uniqueness of capital punishment makes this distinction relevant, because this matter demands special consideration. The main characteristic of this penalty is that it is absolutely and decisively terminal. The irreversibility of it, say the Abolitionists, may cause irreparable injustice in the case of a mistake. The legal system has never been infallible, and sometimes innocent people were convicted and punished for crimes that they never carried out. However, unlike imprisonment, an erroneous conviction that leads to execution is irremediable and irrevocable. This may raise the horrifying possibility of executing an innocent person, which cannot be repaired if the mistake is detected. The terrible injustice that might occur, as a consequence of a fault or an error in the legal procedure, imposes serious doubts on the legitimacy of capital punishment.

This kind of criticism declares that the imperfect enforcement of just laws has a critical significance on the decision to inflict the death penalty. The acute severity of capital punishment differs from the irreversibility of imprisonment. This argument states that even an erroneous incarceration is irreversible and irrevocable in the sense that an innocent person who has been punished can never erase or undo the years in prison and cannot ever return to the same situation which existed before he was wrongly convicted. Therefore, the claims regarding the serious dangers that are involved with the infliction of fatal penalties, must rest not only on the claim that capital punishment is irrevocable, but also that it leaves no possibility for redress. While we regret cases of unjust incarceration, nevertheless there are methods to compensate the victim, even if imperfect and partial, thus reducing the harm and injustice that was caused to the innocent victim. On the other hand, the death penalty nullifies all possibilities of compensating the victim, because after the execution he ceases to exist, and no one is left to be compensated.

However, this argument does not refer to the morality or the justifying grounds of capital punishment, but to the possibility of its mistaken administration. It says nothing about the appropriateness of the infliction of the death penalty on those who deserve it. If this is the case, then the principal justification for capital punishment in cases where it is deserved remains valid, and the criticism only concerns the matter of the certainty in such cases. This criticism might affect our view of the evidential foundations that are required for a conviction, but not our view of the legitimacy of the execution. We may demand a higher burden of proof from the prosecutors, when they demand capital punishment. However, when there is a sufficient measure of certainty or conclusive evidence, we can inflict this penalty with a reduced risk of executing the innocent. The above criticism requires a more cautious and careful consideration, when demanding capital punishment, and when inflicting it. But it does not support an argument for abolishing capital punishment, when it is deserved.

Before examining this issue from the relevant aspect for my study – namely from the rights-talk point of view – I want to mention a comprehensive agreement, regarding the core of the debate between Retentionists and Abolitionists. I refer to one of the most familiar charges that Retentionists impose upon Abolitionists (a charge that can also be imposed vice-versa). They charge their opponents of using "sham" arguments to support their view, or arguments that do not reflect their real reasons for opposing capital punishment. They believe that those who use arguments like discriminatory administration of the death penalty, would oppose it even if it were fairly and equally imposed.[283] Without addressing the imputed dishonesty that might be hinted at in this charge, I think that it points to a very complicated meta-ethical problem, which is beyond the range of this study. The question whether we hold a position, and then find the appropriate justification for it, or whether our opinions are determined by the convincing force of arguments, can be answered both positively and negatively. When considering the death penalty, it seems that the final stance a person takes is not so much affected by the impartial arguments of the issue, as it is shaped by the person's fundamental and basic beliefs. The person then tends to justify (if not rationalize) this stance through valid (or partially valid) arguments. Judith Jarvis Thomson aptly describes this difficulty by saying: "Is capital punishment permissible? To ask that question is to be asking what we should believe".[284] This is clear, since even the presumptions a person uses, that lead to her conclusions, are deeply affected by her preliminary moral beliefs, or even by her comprehensive worldview. The selection of the specific presumptions, results from a person's own perspective. Hence, it is not easy to convert Retentionists into Abolitionists (and vice versa), through arguments. At most, a person can demonstrate that her position regarding the death penalty is derived from her moral or political position, or at least how it fits coherently with it. This is what I try to do in the coming paragraphs.

4.6.4 Capital Punishment And Rights

The most determined objections to capital punishment come from human-rights activists, who claim that executions violate the basic and nonforfeitable right to life.[285] They think that this right can neither be annulled nor voided, nor can it be transferred to another (even though the possessor might think that her right can be waived or surrendered). They ascribe to human life an intrinsic value that establishes a unique worth to the right to life, which overrides the demands of *lex talionis,* even after the murderer had violated the same right of others.

This kind of argumentation is derived from the tradition of natural rights. Within this tradition one cannot use the claim that is standard for other kinds of punishment. Imprisonment, for example, definitely deprives a person of her liberty for a fixed amount of time, but we can still say that her rights to liberty are basically preserved. It is the same with fines that deprive a guilty person of part of her property; however, her property rights in general, are basically respected and intact. With these kinds of punishments, we still respect both the offenders' other rights, and the possibility of exercising and capitalizing on these rights in the future, if we decide that the offenders are entitled to repossess them. Such punishments, although striking at some basic and even natural rights, preserve the obligation of treating offenders according to their dignity as human beings. Punishing the offender still expresses a respect for her dignity and agency. It shows that we consider her as a moral agent, or as a member of the moral community, and treat her as such. However, we cannot use this argument for capital punishment. Once we deprive someone of their very life, we obviously cannot claim that are preserving their right to life. Here, there is nothing left after the execution that may be returned to the offender in the future. He can never repossess any of his rights. Forfeiting the offender's life cannot be distinguished from forfeiting his right to life, and the above justification for punishment does not apply here. Those who belong to the tradition of natural rights, insist that the right to life has to be respected, as the necessary condition for respecting any other right. This makes them argue that the right to life cannot be forfeited.

However, the priority they ascribe to the right to life over other rights does not necessarily entail that this right is nonforfeitable, unless we presuppose it. The fact that the right to life is a necessary condition that enables the possession of the rest of one's rights does not necessarily indicate that the possessor is entitled to have them. The claim that this right cannot be forfeited is not part of its being a natural right, but part of its supreme status. And the justification for this status is what we are looking for. We must admit that this requires a previous assumption regarding the nature of this right that establishes the grounds for the demand to abolish capital punishment.

Recalling Thomson's viewpoint regarding the question of the legitimacy of capital punishment, I wish to reiterate that the most we can sincerely hope to do, is to show how our innate views regarding the morality of capital punishment, coherently fits together with our moral and social views. This is what I shall try to show in the rest of this discussion.

In my discussion of punishment I said that I considered it as a redistribution of rights, according to the offender's entitlement. The extent to which a person should possess her rights should fit her level of agency, or her level of membership within the moral community. Correspondingly, the measure of the withdrawal of a person's rights should be in accordance with the way she failed to fulfill her obligations as a member of the community. When a person endangers the wholeness or the morality of the community, she loses part of her status as a moral agent, or reduces her moral status within the community. When she actually strikes at the integrity or the morality of the community, she must be punished for it by withdrawing some of her rights. The severity of her punishment should be appropriate to the gravity of the harm she caused.

In the ordinary form of punishment, we assume that the offender has until now been a full-fledged member of the community, and possessed all the rights that he should have had. As a full member we regarded him as a fully responsible agent, and his conduct is purposive, voluntary and exhibits self-control. This means that the first set of requirements or the subjective (or individual) requirements, were fully satisfied by the member before he committed a crime. Hence, the reassessment of his entitlement to possess rights after he carried out the offense, relates only to the second set of requirements, which deal with the member's conduct within the community. The measure of the withdrawal of his rights due to his offense, is determined by the scale of penalties that the community assigns to the various kinds of crimes. The community determines this scale according to the harm and threat to its own integrity and morality. The more danger and injury that one causes to the community (or its components), the more rights should be withdrawn from the offender, and for a longer time.

The above discussion regarding the criteria, according to which the severity of punishment should be determined, brings us now to deal with capital punishment. First, we must check whether this penalty is consistent with the present concept of possessing rights. The previous discussion regarded rights as valid claims, which means considering them as an outcome of social acknowledgement. Here I position myself outside the framework of the tradition of natural rights: since I regard all rights as conditional, I do not regard any right as absolute. In this way, I avoid the question whether there are nonforfeitable rights, and if so, which. The more complicated question is whether there are inalienable rights (in Feinberg's terminology), and this does not require an answer when discussing the matter of punishment, because we assume that the penalty is inflicted on an offender against her will and preferences. My view presumes that there are no such rights, and it is the possessor who waives or relinquishes her own rights, and in most cases it is possible to transfer these rights to another. The difference between waiving a right and transferring it is that waiving a right only releases the respondent from his correlative duty, while transferring a right means that the correlative duty still exists but towards a new possessor. Not always is the obligation toward the original possessor still valid, even when the original possessor wants to transfer it.[286]

However, punishment refers to *forfeiting* rights – not waiving or transferring them – because this does not require the possessor's consent. Once we view all rights as conditional, any right may be withdrawn if it is based on justifying grounds that are no longer valid, or if its conditions of possession are not fulfilled. In this sense, capital punishment is like any other penalty, except that instead of withdrawing the offender's rights to freedom or property, it is his right to life that is withdrawn. A significant difference between this penalty and the other punishments is that (except for life imprisonment) all other cases of withdrawing rights are limited in term (and even life imprisonment can be limited by the parole committees), while capital punishment is terminal and irrevocable. This makes it the most severe penalty, and requires some constraints on imposing it. In any case, its severity does not make it illegitimate, but limits its imposition only to the worst crimes – those that can be considered as proportionate to the most severe penalty. It means that its unique characteristics need careful consideration.

Capital punishment is the harshest penalty and, therefore, must be meted out only for the most brutal crimes against society. This means that such a penalty will not be used for minor offenses, as it used to be in the past (like pickpocketing, for example).[287] In addition, capital punishment should not be a *compulsory* penalty for those brutal crimes, but only an *optional* one. Its actual infliction would have to be considered with regard to additional circumstances and conditions involved in the specific crime. Furthermore, because it is a terminal penalty, and is irrevocable after it has been carried out, it must have some additional safety constraints. Such a constraint can be, for example, a requirement that the decision be made unanimously, and if one of the judges or jurors dissents – to refrain from it. Another constraint can be to ensure the right to appeal to a higher court, before the execution. These restraints intend to reduce the likelihood of executing innocent people.

However, even when we reduce the risk of punishing the innocent, we still need to formulate the guidelines according to which we accept the death penalty as legitimate, and the circumstances within which such a penalty should by considered. In more specific terms, we need to define the stage at which a person totally loses his moral agency, or when he arrives at a stage where he cannot be considered as a member of the moral community any more. In agent-relative terms, we need to identify the stage where we deny a person's rights to the generic features of action. In Raz's terms, we need to find the point where one's well-being ceases to be of an ultimate value. For the discussion here, we need to find the point where I deny a person's entitlement to keep on being a member of the community, or more specifically, the point when that person irrevocably renounces his obligations as a member of the community. This is the stage where the person becomes an immoral agent, in the sense that makes moral considerations of compassion or mercy irrelevant for his case. At this stage, the immoral person causes harm or injury that unbearably strikes at the morality and the integrity of the community. In other words, we need to find the stage where one strikes at the core or foundation of the social and moral life in a way that justifies his exclusion from the moral community, and his return to the community is considered inconceivable. That is the stage where the conventional penal system falls short.

Here I start mapping the domain where, according to my view, capital punishment is legitimate. Its retributive function requires that punishment should be imposed for an offense. That means that some of the offender's rights should be withdrawn, and the withdrawal of rights should be proportional to the gravity of the offense. For capital punishment to be adequate, we need to limit its applicability only to the gravest offenses, after we have exhausted the less severe punishments that deal with such crimes. This results from the fact that the withdrawal of rights in this case is operated against the most fundamental right that the offender actually possesses. Withdrawing the right to life means that the executed will not be able to possess any rights in the future, and that he is definitively excluded from the community. Hence, we must use this instrument only when there is no other way to leave the offender within the community (even as a life prisoner).

The above considerations lead us to the principle that I wish to suggest for inflicting capital punishment. I find that it is legitimate to inflict the death penalty on those who commit cruel and vicious crimes, while they are already serving a life imprisonment. Take, for example, a murderer who is sentenced to life imprisonment, and while serving his penalty in jail, murders his cellmate. Consider the fact that in many penal systems, life imprisonment is the most severe possible punishment, and inflicting it again on the culprit will actually be no punishment at all. Assuming that the murderer must be punished for his crime means that the option of additional incarceration will be a community's denial of its obligation to punish. This assumption is valid, of course, only when we agree that physical punishment has been excluded from our legitimate penal options, and we cannot, for example torture prisoners. The prohibition of corporal punishment became a convention among civilized societies and, as such, is no longer considered a relevant option. The only relevant right that the culprit still possesses and that the community can still withdraw, is his right to life. What we need to show is that this fact justifies the terminal withdrawal of any right from the offender. We also need to demonstrate why a specific crime is intolerable to the community.

When a murderer is sentenced for homicide, he is convicted for a grave crime, whose essential evil is depriving the victim of her most fundamental right, the right to life. When he committed the crime, he did not respect the humanity of the victim, he injured a significant component of morality, and caused harm not only to the morality of society, but also to its wholeness. This justifies punishing him according to the strict letter of the law. The gravity of his offense requires that most of his rights be withdrawn for a long period of time, or even forever. However, even after inflicting life imprisonment on him, his dignity and self-respect are preserved, and he must be treated with respect, due to our recognition of him as a human being. We are not allowed to torture or torment him, and we have to provide him with the elementary necessities for a decent existence, even in jail (not only food, clothing and a roof over his head, but also mental needs like books or mental care). The withdrawal of the rights to freedom and part of the rights to well-being does not include the denial of his subjectivity, or a total cancellation of his agency. It is a serious limitation of his membership in the community, but not an ultimate exclusion from it. Although the criminal is placed at the lowest level of the community, he is still considered, to some extent, a member. As such, he still possesses some basic rights, and the community is obliged to fulfill them. On the other hand, even as a prisoner, he has to respect the obligations that the community (which he, after all, still belongs to) imposes upon him. This results from his partial membership in the community.

Now, let us check the implications of his committing another crime. In addition to the cruel implications of the previous murder, this time the culprit endangers not only the morality and integrity of the community, but also the foundational conditions of the existence of any community. The culprit acted not only against the normative system, but also against the rules that enable the very existence of the common system. He has acted against the authority of the community to punish him, and against its duty to protect the imprisoned victim. By denying the authority of the community, the murderer, in fact, excludes himself from the community. He no longer acknowledges his obligations towards the community, and does not acknowledge the authority of the community to allocate rights and duties that apply to him. The community, on its side, denies his entitlement to membership within it and to possess the rights that are derived from it. When the offender is no longer a member, he is not entitled to have any moral status, and accordingly to possess any rights. The bilateral relations between a member and a community do not exist any more.

Is it really necessary to execute the murderer in such a case? Denying any relation between the community and the criminal may lead to the conclusion that the community has no authority to punish the criminal, because he is no longer a member in it. On the other hand, the fact that the criminal has no rights does not entail that it is the community's duty to *execute* him. However, this duty may be derived from the community's obligation to punish the offender, which was discussed earlier in this chapter. It is the community's obligation to adjust the person's actual possession of rights, to the measure he is entitled to have. This obligation is owed towards the other members who obey the rules. We can also present the argument from the "Fair-Play Retributivist" or "Rights-Retributivist" approach toward punishment. If the offender is not punished for his additional crime, it is unfair towards the other "law-abiding" prisoners, who possess the same amount of rights as the murderer does, even though they did not commit an additional crime. This would be another distortion of the required equality between prisoners. They should possess the same rights, after committing the same crimes. When one of them commits another crime, and nonetheless retains the same rights as they do, it is unfair. The distortion exists even when we consider the offender's own rights. When the offender is allowed to possess the same amount of rights prior to the additional offense as afterwards, it is tantamount to saying that society denies the existence of the additional crime. Therefore I conclude that the offender must be punished. Capital punishment is the only relevant option, and it should be inflicted on him.

At this point, Abolitionists can dispute this obligation by saying that executing the murderer means his exclusion from the community, and as an outsider he is not bound to the authority of the community. Hence, the community cannot interfere with his rights. This is not accurate. When the offender is sentenced, he is still considered as a member, and it is within the community's authority to decide to what extent he is considered as such. The community should allocate the prisoner's rights and duties in line with this decision. Nevertheless, exploring these side issues seems to miss the point. For me, the essential point regarding the community's duty to punish the offender in this case, is that this time it is an existential need. The additional crime committed by the life-prisoner, crucially undermines the foundational framework, which is a precondition of its ability to function as a community. Turning a blind eye towards it might shatter the substructure on which the society is based. In this sense we can say that the community's duty to preserve the framework, which enables it to exercise or even to recognize its members' rights, dictates that it must punish the murderer. Ignoring the additional crime, or even punishing the transgressor for his crime only moderately, may ruin the principle of proportionality, which determines the severity of punishment in every case. Hence, the response to such a crime should protect the foundations of the morality of the community, and its existence as a common framework as a whole. This is a moderate version of the claim that the community also has a right to self-defense, and when it is seriously endangered, it has to capitalize on this right. For those who deny the possession of such a right by the community, we can say that it is the community's obligation to preserve the possibility of the law-abiding members to possess rights. Repudiation of this duty will strike at their important interests of pursuing their own good. If there can be a conflict between this right and any of the criminal's rights, there is no doubt that this right should be fully protected by the community.

The community's duty to balance between the rights that a member actually possesses and her entitlement or merit to possess them, results from the community's obligations towards its other members, who bear the burden that is caused by the unjust possession of rights by the offender. When we consider that the community has to withdraw rights from the offender because he committed a second act of murder, and the only relevant right that is left to be withdrawn is his right to life, the community should do so. After committing the additional murder, the offender is not considered as one who is entitled to possess this right to life. Hence, in order to match his possession to his merit, this right should be withdrawn, which in this case can only mean the meting out of the death penalty.

This is the case in which I find capital punishment to be legitimate. When a life prisoner commits a harsh crime that justifies a grave penalty, the death penalty is the only punishment that fits the crime. This is mandated by my approach towards punishment, which demands the adjustment of possessing rights within the community. The possession of an excessive right by the offender causes injustice to the law-abiding members. When the only right left to withdraw is someone's right to life, because the offender is already sentenced to life imprisonment, a refrainment from withdrawing it, means refraining from punishing him. This is unfair, from the other members' point of view. In this specific case, the crime is a threat not only to the community, but also to its foundations, and hence it is regarded as an intolerable offense. Such an offense justifies an irreversible and irrevocable punishment. When there is no right left to withdraw and a withdrawal is still required, it is legitimate to execute the offender. The right to life, according to the position that considers all rights as conditional (as contrasted to absolute), has to be acknowledged by the community in order to be valid. When the community decides that the possession of this right by one of its members is not valid, this right is forfeitable. Our previous conception that denies the existence of any "natural" rights, and considers any right as resulting from social acknowledgement, enables us to withdraw any right that we find unjustifiably possessed. Considering punishment in general, and capital punishment it particular, as a readjustment of the possession of rights of the offenders, is a way to examine the legitimacy of the gravity of penalties, including the death penalty.

This is a backward-looking approach to punishment, but it is not detached from the utilitarian justification, even though it is only indirectly connected to it. The utility gained from punishment, is only the preservation of the framework of allocating rights and duties within the community. The justification of punishment is based on the mutual obligation that exists between the community and its members, who possess their rights as a result of their membership. The preservation of this reciprocity is the rationale behind the demand for punishing those who deny it.

4.7 SUMMARY

In this chapter I discussed the most frequent case of withdrawing rights: the case of punishment. At the beginning I mentioned two competing approaches to this matter: the forward- and backward-looking approaches. The former is characterized mainly as utilitarian, and more specifically, as deterrent or curative, while the latter is characterized mainly as retributive. To examine both approaches I make use of a concept of punishment, as formulated by Antony Flew, which could be accepted by all parties. This concept regards punishment as an unpleasant act towards an offender, inflicted on him for an offense, and intentionally administrated by an acknowledged authority.

When dealing with the forward-looking approach, I mentioned that its main premise is that imposing harm on the offender can only be justified by reducing or avoiding additional harm in the future. This might be achieved by the deterrent effect of punishment or by rehabilitation of the offender during his incarceration. I note the main problems of this approach, such as the danger of draconian punishment, or scapegoating the innocent, in order to reduce or avoid future harm. These problems lead to the conclusion that several side-constraints, some of which may be of a retributive form (like the demand for a proportionality principle such as *lex talionis*), have to be considered when deciding on punishment from a utilitarian point of view. The most important constraint is that only those who are guilty may be punished, and never the innocent. However, these constraints place the forward-looking approach very close to the backward-looking approach. At the next step I briefly sketch the curative or reform (or rehabilitation) approach towards punishment, and clarified the reasons for the massive objection to it. The most decisive objection was that such an approach might erode the moral responsibility we ascribe to people within the moral community. Considering the offenses they commit as a symptom of a disease will strike at their moral status as agents, and may require us to treat them as sick and limited or even incapable of agency.

The next step was a discussion of the backward-looking approach, in which the retributive principle plays the main part. The main idea of this approach is that punishment is a sort of requital or repayment that is demanded from the offender, for his past wrongdoings. The offender "has to pay" for what he has done. At the core of this approach lies the law of retaliation, or *Lex Talionis*. The adherents of this approach assume that the one who commits a crime "deserves" to be punished, because of the harm he has caused, or in other versions, because he broke a rule or broke the law. The immediate link between the crime and the offense, avoids many of the problems that we met in the forward-looking view, such as fabricating evidences against innocent people, etc. However, this concept has its own difficulties, when using it for justifying punishment. The essential problem is that such an argument does not justify the institution or the practice of punishment as a whole. It does not explain why we should cause additional harm in addition to that which has already been caused by the offender. Opponents of this view claim that there is no reason to inflict penalties and cause more afflictions, if nothing is gained from it. They look at it as mere revenge or vengeance in an institutional format, and claim that this is intolerable in a civilized society.

It seems that a better way to resolve the difficulties of both approaches, is to divide the issue into two separate matters. This attitude usually justifies the institution or practice of punishment in utilitarian terms, that is to say that the general aim of punishment is to reduce or avoid further mischief. However, in order to justify a particular case within this practice, we appeal to the retributive approach. This method of synthesizing the two approaches has become popular in recent theories, and I mention some of them earlier on in this chapter. However, in this case, although it gives a satisfactory answer to the crucial questions (such as why we punish the offender, and why does he deserve it), does not explain why there is a duty to punish him, and if there is, why is it the community's duty. To answer these questions I brought the "fair-play retributivist" or "right-retributivist" approach.

According to this approach, punishment is a sort of a debt owed to the law-abiding members of the community, within which the offender exists. The offender is considered as a "free rider", who inappropriately benefits from the others' respect for the law. He takes advantage of the social cooperation, without shouldering his share of the burdens that are imposed on the law-abiding members, and by doing so he violates their rights. This unfair advantage is balanced by a reciprocal curtailing of his rights. In other words, the unfair advantage that the offender gained, is erased by the disadvantage he suffers as a result of the punishment. The community is the framework within which the mutual obligation between its members takes place, and therefore, it has a central role in administering punishment. Since the community has the authority to allocate rights and duties among the members, it is also the community's duty to balance distortions and inequalities among its members. In other words, we can regard this action as an attempt to achieve a just distribution of rights and duties within the community, and it is the role of the authority which distributes rights and duties to make it fair, and in accordance with the requirements of justice. This brings us to my view of punishment, which I feel is a mechanism for readjusting the distribution of rights within the community. Thus I regard the matter of punishment as a case of the withdrawal of rights.

In my view, so long as the reasons that justify a person's possession of rights exist, she is entitled to possess these rights. These reasons include both the subjective or individual (mostly intellectual or cognitive) requirements for agency, and the communitarian requirements (mostly the concern with her conduct). The matter of punishment refers to those who answer the individual requirements for agency – and hence responsible for their actions – but deficient in fulfilling their obligations to the community. This positions the whole discussion at the communitarian level. When the agent's conduct does not fulfill the social requirements that entitle her to possess the moral status, and hence her rights, the proportion between the two should be readjusted by withdrawing some of the agent's rights. The more the offender reneges on her obligation, or accordingly, the more harm she causes, the fewer rights she is acknowledged to possess. Punishing her by depriving her of some rights rectifies the incompatibility between the measure of her moral agency and the measure of rights she possesses.

With this concept of punishment in mind, I examined the matter of capital punishment. The dispute between Abolitionists who want to cancel this kind of penalty, and Retentionists who wish to retain it, includes also the debate between the forward and the backward-looking approaches to punishment. Questions about the deterrent effect of this punishment, or its efficiency (or even if it is economical) were also raised in the current discussion. The severity and irreversible character of such a penalty adds some doubts as to its legitimacy within a civilized society, especially in light of the biased and discriminated administration of this penalty. I mentioned some of the arguments for and against the infliction of capital punishment, and some possible answers to these arguments.

The last section of the current discussion deals with capital punishment and rights. I explained that my view denies the existence of natural or absolute rights and assumes that every right is conditional and must be acknowledged by the community, in order to be valid. This includes the right to life. I said that even this right should be recognized by the community according to one's entitlement to possess it. When an offender commits an unbearable crime, he should be appropriately punished, by a proportional withdrawal of rights. I mentioned that such a grave penalty should be inflicted only for a serious crime, because we must preserve a reasonable balance between the gravity of the offense and the severity of its punishment. I argued that when such a crime is committed by an offender who already serves a life imprisonment, and the only right he possesses – and that can be withdrawn – is his right to life, he should be punished by death. Of course, some constraints should be used, for reducing the fear of executing the innocent (such as a demand for a unanimous decision by the juries or the judges, a right to appeal to a higher instance before the execution, etc.). However, I do not consider such a penalty to be morally illegitimate. That was the final conclusion of this chapter.

4.8 APPENDIX: NON-LEGAL WITHDRAWAL OF RIGHTS

So far, I have discussed the issue of the withdrawal of one's rights through punishment, mostly as a legal matter. A significant aspect of Antony Flew's criteria for punishment was only mentioned marginally, so I refer to it again here. Flew mentions that punishment should not be confined to legal or moral offenses, but might be connected with any system of rules or law, such as state, school, trades union, trade association, etc.[288] In my view, each of the institutions within which members possess rights that are bestowed upon them as a result of their membership in the institution, can also withdraw these rights whenever their conditions of possession are not sufficiently fulfilled by their possessors. This can be done by membership clubs, for example, who have the mandate to renounce any member who fails to fulfill his obligations (whether because he stopped paying the membership fee, or because he became unruly in the general assembly), or, on the macro scale, by society as a moral community. In this appendix I want to show how we can justify the withdrawal of a person's rights, without even going through the courts, as a response to his violating the welfare or rights of others. I choose to deal with the issue of withdrawing a person's right to privacy, in the matter that is known as "outing".

"Outing" is a phenomenon that was widespread in the late eighties and early nineties of the twentieth century. It was carried out by radical homosexual groups that exposed the identity of unproclaimed or closeted homosexuals, especially famous people, politicians and celebrities, in order to show the high distribution of homosexuality among the population. Another reason for this was to show that homosexuals are ordinary people who are represented among all levels of the population. They thought that the exposure or disclosure of the identity of popular figures would reduce prejudice, discrimination, oppression and homophobic persecutions against homosexuals. The original attempt was to promote positive images of the gay community.[289] However, in most cases it was done against the will of those who were exposed. Doing this was considered as a blatant violation of their right to privacy. In this appendix I try to explicate this issue, and examine the boundaries of its legitimacy, according to what I have formulated earlier about the withdrawal of rights.

This phenomenon arose due to the social (and in most cases, legal) reality of abusive treatment towards gay people, all over the world.[290] Even where homosexuality was legal, gay people paid a heavy price for disclosing their sexual orientation. They risked their careers, employment, family relations and sometimes even their lives. John Elwood argues that homosexuality is strongly condemned in most societies, and points out that a false allegation of homosexuality is considered a defamation in most states. He mentions the (US) Supreme Court's description of the society's treatment of gays. The court acknowledged that the revelation of their identity exposed them to "economic reprisal, loss of employment, threat of physical coercion, and other manifestations of public hostility".[291]

Through outing, members of gay rights groups tried to achieve some aims (and hence, justify their acts on a utilitarian basis). First, they wanted to expose the hypocrisy of closeted gay officials who promoted discriminatory policy against homosexuals. Second, they wanted to provide role models for youngsters that would encourage them to get into the mainstream of society.

Another important aim was to break down the stigma that surrounds homosexuals, by showing that this phenomenon is common, and crosses social and racial boundaries. Some of the advocates of outing did so as a remonstration against the indifference of the public towards the AIDS epidemic, while others did it as an act of frustration or despair.[292]

However, the disclosure of a person's sexual orientation causes some moral problems, some of which concern the withdrawal of rights. I do not want to deal with the legal problems that are caused by outing, but rather with the moral ones. From the legal point of view, two main problems may appear. First, there is the possible accusation of defamation, which at least in the case of public figures, can easily be rejected by showing that the disclosed person is indeed a homosexual (the US Supreme court noted that a public figure has to show that the publication is false, or that the publisher acted with reckless disregard for the truth[293]). The other possible accusation is that of the invasion of privacy. At least in the USA, the right to privacy is widely acknowledged since 1890, when Samuel Warren and Louis Brandeis wrote an article entitled "The Right To Privacy".[294] There, they actually laid the foundations for one's legal right "to be let alone". Leaving aside the question as to whether and under which circumstances such a legal right exists, I want to examine the moral problem concerning this issue. Some of the relevant arguments that are raised in the legal debate are used for the moral discussion as well, so I cite only these latter arguments. This also spares us the necessity of discussing the issue of defamation, which is principally a legal problem. I also choose to sidestep the discussion of whether the First Amendment overrides the individual's right to privacy, in cases where the media or the press are accused of slander or libel.

No doubt the disclosure of one's sexual orientation causes serious intrusion to the "private life, habits, acts, and relation of an individual".[295] Although it is quite redundant to explain why the moral right to privacy, at least in the context of sexual life, is acknowledged as a valid claim, I will support this assumption with some common arguments. This may help to show that such an assumption is not arbitrary or disconnected from our moral concept of a person. This right is comprehensively recognized as an essential part of one's autonomy.[296] When it concerns someone's sexual orientation, in addition to the psychological damage he may suffer as a result of the disclosure against his will, he may suffer serious economic and social harm. Those who deny the first argument that establishes the right to privacy as a basic right, have to admit this right as a derivative one, that is derived from one's right to welfare and well-being. The threat of losing one's job, friends, social status, etc., establishes one's right not to be disclosed.

Many discussions deal with the question whether one's sex life is a private issue. This question is of crucial importance for legal decisions regarding the invasion of privacy, but it is normally considered as one's private domain that should not be the concern of others. With some reservations this is widely accepted. For example, when a woman is pregnant or was raped, the fact that she was involved in sexual relations of some kind is not a totally "private fact", but is nonetheless one that good manners requires us to leave undiscussed. Those who object to this do not claim that one's sex life is a public matter, but that it depends on the context of the situation, within which sex is involved. However, for my discussion here, it is sufficient to say that one's right not to be injured by this exposure, overrides the future benefit that might be gained from such an exposure. So long as he possesses a right to well-being, he is entitled to keep his sexual orientation secret, in order to preserve this right.

This right is preserved even against the freedom of the press, because one's right not to suffer insult and discrimination (in a society where homosexuality is viciously condemned), overrides the public's right to information. Even though sex might be newsworthy, it does not justify the withdrawal of the individual's right to privacy. Some theorists (for example, Grant, Elwood, Pollack) believe that as far as outing concerns the disclosure of public figures, their right to privacy is limited as a result of their status. Public officials, for instance, might be suspected of hypocrisy or mistrustfulness if they "stay in the closet". Those theorists think that a public figure's life, including his sex life, is a public matter, and newsworthy. Hence, the disclosure is not an invasion of their privacy.

I think that the right of officials or celebrities to privacy exists even though they are recognized as public figures, and have more influence than others. So long as their sex life does not affect their public activities, they are entitled "to be let alone". The fact that they might be hurt by their outing creates a strict prohibition to violate their right to privacy, because this right protects their highly compelling interest to well-being. This interest should be protected even when it conflicts with the public interest in information, or the gay community's interests in having role models or in reducing discrimination. This is mainly because there is no reason to withdraw this right from innocent individuals. The conditions of possession of this right are fully fulfilled, and it is the same with the conditions of engagement, etc. So long as they respect others' rights and bear their share of the social obligations, they are entitled to possess the right to privacy.

However, what is the moral status of the disclosure of people like Arthur Finkelstein, who has been accused of being gay? He owns a public relations office and advertising agency, and manages the election campaigns of candidates to the US Congress and Senate. Some of them, mostly from the Republican Party or from the right wing of politics, used incitement and instigation against homosexuals in their election campaigns, as a significant component of their political program and platform. This was planned and promoted under Finkelstein's supervision. The specific issue is not important, but is used as an illustration. What is the validity of the right to privacy of a person who incites against homosexuals, or supports a homophobic policy, or pursues the deprivation of gays' rights? According to the former concept, such campaigns violate the rights of gays and try to achieve an unfair advantage from the oppression of the gay community. The disclosure of the sexual orientation of someone like Arthur Finkelstein might expose him to the same threats that gays suffer from, including the curtailment of their employment opportunities, limitation of their advancement possibilities or even physical intimidations.

When the community as a whole does not prevent the discrimination and the persecution against homosexuals, which is carried out or even assisted by certain persons, parts of the community can do this instead. This can be seen as the gay community's retaliation for the injury attempts that take advantage of the vulnerability of its members. This is based not on compensation, but on the need to balance the unjust advantage that is gained from the oppression of gays, with the disadvantage that is involved with being disclosed. When we reassess the measure of morality or immorality of the person who persecutes homosexuals, we find that after his incitement he is not entitled to possess the right to privacy, because he renounces his obligation to respect others' rights and dignity. The infringement of his excessive right to privacy adjusts the incompatibility between the measure in which he fulfills the social requirements for agency, and the measure in which he possesses rights. Of course, the Principle of Proportionality between the harm he caused or intended to cause and the social penalty that is imposed upon him must be kept. We should not withdraw his right to privacy in all aspects of life, and definitely not withdraw more basic rights from him. He is still regarded as a member of the community, and most of his rights (even most of his rights to privacy with regard to other aspects of his life) should be respected. However, his incitement should not be greeted without a response. His outing is therefore an appropriate one.

A similar debate took place concerning the right to privacy of HIV carriers. Here, being exposed as a carrier also means serious harm to career, social connections, social status, employment, etc. One's health condition does, for sure, belong to the private domain. A man's right to medical secrecy is acknowledged by the community, and should be strictly respected by all parties who are involved, or informed. So long as his intentional conduct does not endanger those who are in his immediate vicinity or those who are in touch with him, he is entitled to keep his secret. However, such a carrier must be aware of the danger he might impose upon his partners in sexual relations, and use the appropriate contraceptives to avoid infecting the partner. When he does not do so, the community or its institutions (health authorities or even the police) must expose his HIV carrier status by publishing it in the media, even if is fairly certain that he will not repeat his crime. This is because the carrier purposely caused harm to one of the community members, and hence, should be punished. This justification does not rely on a utilitarian basis, but on our attempt to adjust his measure of moral agency, to his measure of possessing rights.

The examples I mentioned in this appendix are used only as case studies of the proposed concept of a non-legal withdrawal of rights. I have not discussed them in detail, because they go much beyond the range of my original intentions. I just wanted to elucidate the option of analyzing controversial matters as disputes regarding the entitlement to possess rights, or as disagreements regarding the withdrawal of rights. I do not pretend to offer a fully reasoned argument, only to suggest a direction or a preliminary guideline to deal with such controversies. The rest is to be done by those who discuss them as specific topics (as I partly did in the discussion of capital punishment).

In the next chapter, I do not discuss an actual withdrawal of rights (that is, a withdrawing of rights from one who already possesses them), but a denial of rights from those who might possess them sometimes in their future. This is a sort of postponement of their possession of some rights, and sometimes even a permanent denial of them. In any case, I use the same principles that determine one's possession of rights, to discuss these cases as well. The subjects of the discussion are those who are not considered as full-fledged members of the community, or whose membership in the community is limited for some reason (like children, fetuses or mentally challenged people). I try to analyze the boundaries of their membership in the community, in order to draw the boundaries of their possession of rights.

CHAPTER 5

RIGHTS OF PARTIAL MEMBERS OF THE MORAL COMMUNITY

This chapter does not deal with the withdrawal of rights, but with their denial. In the previous chapter, I discussed the withdrawal of rights from those who already possess them, and lost the entitlement to keep on possessing these rights, after committing a crime. The possessors of these rights were considered full-fledged members of the moral community. They were considered as fully responsible for their actions, and fulfilled all the subjective requirements for agency. However, after reneging on their obligations as such (by committing an offense), they lose some of the rights that are conferred upon other members of the community, because they do not fulfill all the social requirements for agency. The motivation to punish them stems from the desire to find a balance between the measure of the possessors' entitlement to possess their rights, and the extent to which they actually do possess their rights. The reasons for depriving them of their rights do not concern their (mental) abilities, but relate to the way they purposively and voluntarily exercised these abilities.

This chapter goes one step backward, and deals with possible right-holders who lack some of the above abilities, and hence, are denied certain rights prima facie. They are not considered as full-fledged members of the community, for reasons that deal with their competence to be moral agents. The denial of some rights that should be possessed by full members, results from the same motivation to fit one's actual possession of rights, to the measure to which she fulfills the conditions of possession of these rights. When one does not fulfill some of the subjective (or individual) requirements for agency, one is not entitled to possess certain rights, until such time as one will fulfill those requirements. Unlike the previous chapter, here the question of guilt is not relevant to the possession of rights or to their denial. Instead, the relevant issue here is that we cannot regard them (the possessors) as fully responsible for their actions, due to their involuntary lack of certain mental capabilities. It is this deficiency of mental capacities that commensurately decreases their rights, because part of their autonomy, or in Rawlsian terms – their being the self-originating source of their valid claims – is not adequately developed.

In certain respects, we can regard the subjects of this chapter as potential right-holders or members of the moral community. Some of them will realize this potential and become full-fledged members, while others will never accomplish full moral agency, and hence will be permanently deprived of certain rights. In this chapter I discuss the matter of possessing rights by partial or potential members of the community, and divide the discussion into three main categories: Children, Fetuses and Mentally Retarded (or Mentally Challenged) persons. The common denominator is that they all have not acquired the status of a full-fledged member of the moral community, and hence are denied some rights. However, there are some essential differences that mandate a different discussion for each group. These differences lead to different restrictions that we impose on them, and different curtailment of their rights. In this chapter I try to characterize the legitimacy of the deprivation of their rights, and examine the justifiable boundaries of their rights, liberties and autonomy.

5.1 CHILDREN'S RIGHTS

The matter of children's rights is usually discussed from the libertarian point of view. This view concerns itself mostly with their rights to liberty, or more precisely, with their right to the non-interference by others, into their self-regarding behavior.[297] This right, which is acknowledged as obvious for normal adults, is extremely limited when ascribed to children. The usual justification for this is that children lack (or possess an insufficient measure of) the ability to make rational decisions, which usually serves as a necessary condition for independence.[298] Even though our ability to assess a person's rationality is, in general, quite limited, and the criteria according to which we measure this rationality are somewhat vague, we can reasonably say that children are usually supposed to be capable of being the self-originating source of their valid claims.

Without getting too involved in the dispute between Protectionists who support paternalist approaches toward children, and Liberationists who oppose them, I think I may reasonably assume that both sides agree that some rights should be denied to them, due to reasons of security and protection of children as well as considerations of consequences.[299] Even for those who hold a consequential point of view, the demand for the children's competence to possess rights is not based on an arbitrary connection to biological age. Instead, the same criteria for possessing rights are applied to adults and children alike. The utilitarian considerations that would have denied certain rights from adults who are not competent to possess them (for example, the denial of the right to possess a driving license by incompetent drivers, both for their own safety as well as the safety of other drivers and pedestrians), are relevant in the case of children's rights as well.

However, my view is bound to the consequential considerations only when they relevant for allocating rights, inasmuch as these considerations preserve the moral community, as a framework within which rights have meaning. My interest in the case of limiting children's rights, is concerned not so much with consequential considerations, but rather with children's competence to moral agency. We assume that they have not **yet** developed some cognitive capacities to make responsible decisions, or to be considered as autonomous. We believe that in the normal course of events, they will grow up, discard their diminished condition, and will attain full moral agency.[300] Till then they will be regarded as insufficiently fulfilling the first set of requirements for possessing rights (i.e. the subjective requirements), and hence entitled to possess some, but not all, of the rights of full-fledged members of their community.

This claim is widely accepted, and many participants in rights-talk justify the same idea but using different arguments. This is to say that they believe that children can be considered as moral agents, but only to some extent. In communitarian terms we can say that children are regarded as members of the community, but not full-fledged members. On the most general level, we can merely say that children have interests that justify and validate their claims, and make them possible right-holders. Others (MacCormick, for example) assert that children have needs, and hence deserve rights. Another option is offered by Samuel Stoljar who says that children have rights, not because of their claims and arguments as individuals, but because rights are *conferred* upon them, to safeguard them as potential members of the community. His justification is grounded on the need to replenish the human community. Children's rights, in this view, are "another aspect of how the community maintains its continuity".[301] However, such an approach can only justify the children's rights to well-being.[302] To possess other rights, children must fulfill some additional requirements, just as adults must.

Alan Gewirth, who assesses moral agency according to the possession of the generic features of action, makes an illuminating distinction between a prospective purposive agent, and a potential agent.[303] For full-fledged agency, according to Gewirth, one needs to have the ability to control one's behavior out of one's unforced choice, to have knowledge of the relevant circumstances beyond what meets the eye, and to reflect rationally on one's purposes.[304] Prospective agents have the proximate abilities for the generic features of action, even if they are not actually acting. As potential, but not yet full-fledged agents, children do not yet have a right to freedom which is respected by other agents. The Principle of Proportionality requires that they have generic rights to the degree of their attainment of agency, that is, to the degree they approach having the generic features of action. This principle allocates to them only the preparatory rights that enable them to develop the generic features of action, in order to become, during their maturation, full-fledged agents. This means that they have rights to a decent upbringing, education and protection that will foster their development of the generic features of action. Of course, as they grow up they should participate increasingly actively in decisions that affect their interests. However, their rights to freedom should not be fully respected, until they mature from potential to full-fledged agents, and this includes depriving them of some of the rights to freedom or non interference, that pertain to full-fledged agents.[305]

Carl Wellman's conception of moral agency explicates the difficulties involved with children's rights. Wellman argues that moral agency means that one is morally responsible for one's actions. That means that one is capable of acting in light of specifically moral reasons. This presupposes that one has the capacity to become aware of the relevant facts, to appreciate their moral relevance, to be motivated by them, "and to act in some broad nonmoral sense of doing something or other".[306] Wellman's argument presumes that "only an autonomous being could possess a right". According to his view, the exercise of a moral liberty involves voluntariness, so that one must have the capacity for purposive agency, in order to possess moral liberty. In addition, one needs to have the capacity for conceiving alternatives and choosing between them, as part of one's liberty. The fact that this liberty entails the absence of a contrary duty, means that one must understand not only the moral reasons to *take* action, but also the reasons for *refraining* from an action. Finally, a liberty right involves a claim for noninterference, and this requires the capacity to claim. This requires not only the performance of a claim, but having some conception of the grounds of such a claim.[307]

However, Wellman insists that moral agency is a necessary qualification for the capacity to possess moral rights. In this sense, infants (he uses this category to refer to children in about the first two years of their life), cannot be moral agents. He adds that this does not mean that there can be no children's rights. Children acquire moral agency as part of a gradual process as they mature.[308] Wellman specifies two other stages of childhood: young children (between infancy and adolescence) and adolescents (from puberty to maturity). They can be regarded as (at least) partial moral agents, and possess rights, not only because they acquire agency, but because they can, somewhat, be morally responsible for their actions. Wellman emphasizes that the growth of children's rights is "piecemeal, fragmentary, overlapping and complicated".[309]

I think it is unnecessary to enter here into a deeper discussion of the idea that children are deprived of certain rights, either because they lack some of the generic features of action (in Gewirth's terminology), or because they lack some abilities that establish moral responsibility for actions (in Wellman's). In the second chapter of this book I mentioned some requirements of potentiality, whose measure of fulfillment determines the actual measure of one's agency, and one's possession of rights. Among these requirements I mentioned Rawls' general criterion for autonomy, which is the potential to become a self-originating source of valid claims, which I considered as the most fundamental requirement for being recognized as a prospective agent. Generally speaking, I can say that the extent to which a child actually realizes and actualizes this potential, should be the extent to which she can be regarded as a moral agent. In this way the measuring of the entitlement to possess rights by children is not different from the same measurement of adults' rights. In both cases it is correlative with the fulfillment of certain requirements.

This attitude towards children's rights can also be connected with Golding's requirements for agency.[310] Among these requirements I mentioned the capacity to engage in voluntary activities; the capacity for having desires and interests; the capacity to consciously engage in purposive activities; the capacity for conscious response to demands; and the capacity to communicate demands. If we equate the realization of these capacities with expressing one's agency, then we can approximately assess the measure of a child's agency.

I am keenly aware of the complexity and vagueness of these criteria, and thus I only use them as general guidelines for conferring rights upon children. These criteria do provide a reasonable justification for denying some rights to those children who do not sufficiently fulfill the requirements. This impreciseness (of the criteria) is compatible with Melden's claim, that "there is no point at which a sharp line can be drawn, that would mark off non-promises from promises".[311] He expresses the idea that we can never know exactly to what extent a child can be considered a morally mature agent who understands the full array of moral concepts. Hence, the moral agency and the possession of rights by children will always be approximate and roughly estimated. In any event, the criteria I mentioned, can give some idea of the child's entitlement to possess rights, and of the rights that should be denied to her.

To illustrate this idea I want to mention the assumption held by proponents of children's liberation, according to which "any difference in treatment between children and adults must be justified by reference to some morally relevant difference between the members of the two classes".[312] My position is that since children are not full-fledged moral agents, and are only partial members of the community, there are sufficient grounds for differential treatment. For example, children have no right to non-interference and, therefore, can be compelled to attend school (at least with regard to elementary school). Here, the utilitarian constraints of libertarian arguments, demanding that the results of withholding children from equal rights as adults will not be destructive, are not necessary.[313] Nor is it necessary to heed the argument that their interests in acquiring necessary skills for decent well-being (like writing and reading, or some arithmetic abilities) override their interests in non-interference. We can simply argue that the demand for equal rights is only relevant when there is equal merit to possess these rights, and this is not the case with children's rights.

However, these considerations are also valid with regard to concrete rights, for example, the right to vote. Child Liberationists argue that refusing children the right to vote is an unjust disenfranchisement, and a violation of a fundamental principle of democracy.[314] They maintain that all those whose interests might be affected by government decisions – including children – are entitled to participate in the election of the government, and be represented in the legislative institutions. This argument is supposed to outflank the question whether the right to vote entails a certain competence, such as the capacity for making rational choices between alternatives. Instead of regarding this competence as the grounds on which adult citizens are accorded the vote, they appeal to the claim that democracy requires that those who are affected by the government's decisions, must have a voice in making these decisions. David Archard, for example, rightly thinks that this argument does not so much circumvent the necessity of competence, as emphasizes it. His argument goes as follows:

> "Someone is thought entitled to the vote because his interests are affected by policies which result directly or indirectly, from an exercise in voting. It is thereby assumed that in voting someone would and could act to protect and advance these interests. And that presupposes a capacity to recognize both what one's interests are and which policies, parties and persons, would best promote them. So even if children are affected by the laws passed and decisions made by government they would deserve the vote only if they are also competent to exercise it...The competence required of a voter is minimal rationality, an ability to distinguish between parties,

> candidates and policies in terms of interests, aims and goals which can be identified as worth promoting".[315]

Even though this is not exactly the same way I justify the withholding of the right to vote from children, it expresses the same idea. The right to vote (as other rights) is bestowed on an individual for having certain capabilities and capacities, whose essence is making a choice between alternatives on relevant grounds. So long as children lack a reasonable measure of responsibility, maturity, stability and decisiveness, they cannot validate their claims to vote. On the other hand, one can say that many adults also lack some of these requirements, and still maintain the right to vote. To this I respond with the same answer that I have already used in another context: two wrongs do not make a right. The claim that some adults lack these requirements may justify the withdrawal of this right from those adults; but it certainly does not justify according the right to vote to children.

This claim may, however, raise a problem, mainly with regard to legal rights. These rights usually have very formal and strict conditions for their validity. It is obvious that some teenagers below the official age that confer voting rights, are fully qualified and capable of making responsible choices, and possess all the mental and cognitive requirements for voting. Therefore, when we compare their entitlement to possess the right to vote to their actual possession of this right, we see that there is incongruity between what they deserve and what they really possess. We can try to circumvent this difficulty by pointing out that age is a requirement for other legal statuses (such as citizenship), and teenagers are simply not of legal age. This, however, merely illustrates the aspects of arbitrariness that are found in many formal rules. The same law also bestows voting privileges on some adults who are over the required age, even though they are not qualified to make reasonable choices. The inflexibility of legal rights makes their bestowing and withdrawing somewhat arbitrary, and sometimes even inappropriate and counter-intuitive. Sometimes we accept the justifying grounds for a certain law, and acknowledge that in specific cases its application causes some distortions and perversions.[316] This is because legal rights contain formal conditions and restrictions that must be fully fulfilled for validating these rights. We cannot bestow these rights until all the required conditions are satisfied, at least to the sufficient minimum level, and this includes age constraints. This is why, sometimes, children do not merit certain rights, even though they have the necessary capacities for possessing these rights, simply because they are underage.

However, when discussing moral rights, the required conditions for possessing rights, usually do not include arbitrary factors (such as a certain age), and refer to the possessors' ability to join some segments of their lives with those of other members of the moral community. And this ability, although it correlates significantly with age, can vary among different agents, according to their possession of the subjective requirements for agency. Hence, we can respect the right to noninterference of one specific child over another child, when the former is more morally or mentally mature than the latter, despite the differences in their ages. This cannot occur with the legal right to vote, because of its strict requirement of minimal age.

Most of the participants of rights-talk comprehensively accept the waiving of some children's rights, at least to some extent. This is usually because they either support the "Caretaker" approach or the utilitarian Liberationist viewpoint. The latter Liberationist approach believes that it is imperative to withhold some rights from children, in order to avoid future damage to their development or safety. The disputes (between the rights-talk participants) reappear when trying to draw the boundaries of the limitations that we should impose on children's rights and liberties. Complex questions relate to the extent to which we confer rights, and from which point do we deny children from possessing these rights.

Our assessment of a child's responsibility and trustworthiness is always somewhat tenuous and inexact. Sometimes we allow a child to decide an issue by himself, and this decision then leads to trouble and destruction. We can never be sure whether this error in judgment could have happened to an adult too, or was it premature on our part to let the child make this decision. The measure of rights children may possess is affected by the norms of society, the characteristics of those who may possess these rights, the content of these rights, and also the characteristics of their responders. The circumstances under which we decide on conferring rights upon children, have significant effects on the children's possession of rights. However, the framework within which these rights are bestowed, must be consistent with the principles according to which these rights are bestowed in general, and with the guidelines of conferring rights as a whole. We must exercise caution both when we confer rights upon children, as well as when we deny them elementary rights. This cautiousness is mandated not only with regard to liberty rights, but also with regard to welfare rights, such as the right to be cared for by their parents or by society. Sometimes we encounter a situation where we must force parents to carry out actions for the sake of the children's safety or security (for example, to immunize their children), even without getting the children's permission to do so. Here, we may ignore the children's rights to choose, because we do not assume that they are aware of their needs. In any event, we need to exercise caution here in the same way as when denying children's liberty rights.

In the previous chapter I discussed capital punishment, the most extreme withdrawal of rights from full-fledged members of the moral community. In the coming section I try to examine the most extreme denial of rights from partial or future members of the moral community. This also involves the right to life, and the issue is the denial of this right from a fetus or a human embryo. I examine whether and to what extent a fetus possesses rights, and under which conditions and circumstances these rights are valid. This enables us to determine, under which conditions an abortion may be morally justified.

5.2 FETUSES' RIGHTS: THE MORALITY OF ABORTION

The rights of the fetus to a decent, appropriate and safe development can be discussed at length, yielding some significant conclusions regarding our conception of the self, of human beings and moral agency. Although this can be very interesting for the study of withdrawing rights, I choose to limit my discussion only to the most controversial and disputable issue in the current debate regarding fetus' rights: the morality of abortion. This issue has become one of history's most fierce, notorious and acrimonious debates, both among the general public (including politicians) as well as ethical theorists. It has been discussed from numerous points of view. While the ongoing debate regarding capital punishment basically ensues between two principal attitudes (Abolitionists and Retentionists), the abortion debate spans a full range of positions: from an absolute Restrictive (Pro-Life) position, to an absolute Permissive (Pro-Choice) position. The majority of positions falls within the two extremes, and includes all the moderate versions.

For my discussion I use the term *abortion* in the same way as Nancy Davis does, for referring to: "the intentional termination of *in utero* fetal life after conception and before birth".[317] Although this term can refer also to spontaneous abortion, which is a premature termination of a pregnancy as a result of a miscarriage, I limit my use only to the intentional cases. In addition, for reasons of scope, I limit my discussion of this issue to its moral and ethical aspects, and not its legal ones (though I am aware of the reciprocal relations and interplay between the legal and moral aspects).

A conspicuous characteristic of the debates regarding abortion is the complication involved with the attempt to separate the arguments into clear or distinct ethical doctrines or disciplines. Arguments can contain at the same time, consequential, deontological and right-based considerations, which support or replace each other, in a way that one cannot separately present their components and aspects. Hence it is preferable to discuss positions or theorists, rather than trying to divide the arguments into utilitarian or right-based, as was possible in the previous discussions (like that of capital punishment).

The whole dilemma surrounding the question whether abortion is permissible, arises when one principally accepts the assumption that is clearly formulated by Alan Gewirth, which says:

> "Insofar as there is any biological possibility that the humans in question will attain the moral abilities of agency, they have rights to fostering of these abilities. Even when such attainment seems hopeless, they still have rights to be helped to attain as close an approximation of these abilities as possible".[318]

In the position I presented in chapter 2, according to which attaining agency requires us to have only a potential to achieve some mental and cognitive capacities, this problem is even more serious. This is because an intentional abortion terminates the fetus' generic rights to attain any of the abilities for agency, and in fact, totally cancels its existence as a human being. In the coming paragraphs I present some of the main arguments regarding the morality of abortion, and try to clarify the sources of the debate between the opposing positions.

5.2.1 The Restrictive Position

By a Restrictive view I refer to the position that holds, "that abortion is morally defensible only when (though not necessarily always when) the continuation of the pregnancy poses a threat to the woman's life".[319] Among various possible Restrictive arguments, I take for granted that at least one is conclusive, and accepted by any adherent of any position, including extreme Permissivists. I refer to the comprehensive acknowledgement that a community cannot force a woman to abort, against her will or desire. In such cases the restriction is absolute and unequivocal. This prohibition even applies to cases when the woman's life is in danger, or when there is a threat that the child born will be deficient, and also where the woman's personality or welfare are in doubt (because of psychological or economic problems). The rationale behind this prohibition will be better understood towards the end of the current discussion. However, the core of the prohibition is the desire to ensure the mother's authority to decide whether she allows interference in her pregnancy. No pressure, whether under the cloak of concern for her health or safety, or the fetus' future, should be imposed on a woman, to abort her fetus. The pregnant woman can consult with medical or social professionals, but should not be manipulated by them, in order to save money or resources to the community. If the community is so much concerned about the fetus' health or development, it has to express its opinion and advise the mother, but not to force her, in one way or another, to accept its position. The arguments regarding the fetus' interests are relevant at this stage, but can be conclusive only after birth, and then they may even justify the removing of the child from the custody of the mother, and transferring her to foster parents. Nevertheless, claims that can become conclusive with regard to a live infant, cannot cancel the exclusive right of a woman, to decide on the continuation of her pregnancy. When this exclusiveness is respected with regard to the restriction of abortion, it has some significant implications regarding the woman's exclusive authority to stop her pregnancy.

The above point seems so obvious that it is not mentioned in most of the discussions about abortion, probably for reasons of redundancy. The main dispute takes place around the opposite case, where a woman does not want to maintain her pregnancy, and Restrictivists argue that she **has** to. I thought it appropriate to remove any doubts about this marginal and undiscussed issue, of not forcing a woman to terminate her pregnancy. In my opinion, I believe that this is the lone case where the Restrictive argument is correct. Now I start with the most resolute Restrictive argument: the argument that bases the objection to abortion, on the assumption that it means deliberately killing an innocent person.

The basic assumption of Restrictivists is that human life begins at conception, and a fetus is considered a person from the moment that chromosomes of the sperm and the ovum are united. Terminating this life is "a murder or homicide or an assault on the sanctity of human life".[320] Ronald Dworkin clarifies this stance, by noting that the above assumption may express two different ideas. The first claims that fetuses are live human beings and therefore, creatures with interests of their own (including the interest of remaining alive), with the right to protect these interests and not to be killed. Abortion is wrong because it violates this right, just as killing is wrong because it violates a person's right not to be killed. Dworkin calls this "the *derivative* objection to abortion". This is because this objection is derived from universal interests that are common to all human beings, including fetuses. The government, as the authority who bears a derivative responsibility to protect these interests, through their acknowledgement of rights, should prohibit or regulate abortions.

The second idea expounded by Restrictivists is that human life has an intrinsic and innate value, and hence is sacred. This sacredness begins at once with biological life, even before the fetus exhibits movement, sensation or interests. According to this idea, abortion is wrong because it disregards and insults the sacredness of human life, at any stage or form. Dworkin calls this "the *detached* objection to abortion", because it does not depend on any particular set of interests or rights of the fetus. According to this view, the government must prohibit or regulate abortion, because of its detached responsibility to protect the intrinsic sacred value of life.

These are the principal and most crucial issues that Permissivists have to relate to. There are some other Restrictive arguments, of lesser importance, which I mention but deal with them only briefly. One of these is the claim that was relevant until some decades ago, according to which an abortion imposes a danger on the woman's life, because it involves an intrusion into her body (vagina and womb). In addition, this can increase the woman's likelihood of having a miscarriage in a future pregnancy. It is not difficult to respond to this argument, because modern medical skills and facilities ensure fairly safe abortions at almost any stage of pregnancy. This argument can even be used against Restrictivists, because the only dangerous abortions are those which are performed by unskilled or unqualified personnel, in unsuitable locations. Prohibiting abortions increases these cases and endangers the woman's health or even life. Another aspect of possible harm to the pregnant woman may be psychological damage. However, the psychological harm that can be caused to the woman (mainly that of guilt feelings) is possibly outweighed by the harm that might be caused because of the same feelings of guilt, when giving birth to an unwanted child.

Another argument that Restrictivists use, is related to the two main arguments. This refers to what is called "The Domino Effect". Restrictivists assert that legalizing abortion can dehumanize society and initiate a process of making human life worthless, which might even result in massive killing and brutality. They maintain that abortion is a fragile and vulnerable starting point for the Domino Effect, because the termination of human life is not visible and blatant as it is in an ordinary murder. When we show disregard for any form of human life, we can end with a complete disregard for human life in other contexts.[321] However, this argument is not supported by any convincing evidence. Sometimes, Hitler's policies are brought as an example of the Domino Effect, but this example is slightly bizarre with regards to the issue of abortion. Also, there are many countries that have legalized abortion but still outlaw other practices such as capital punishment and euthanasia.

The last Restrictivist argument I want to mention is the claim that a woman who seeks abortion, is refusing to take responsibility for her (sexual) actions.[322] This claim has two points. The first point says that the widespread accessibility of contraceptives, imposes the entire responsibility of avoiding unwanted pregnancies on the woman. If she fails to bear this responsibility of avoiding an unwanted pregnancy, she must complete her pregnancy as payment or penalty for her indiscretion, injudiciousness or carelessness. The second point is that she ought to avoid heterosexual intercourse unless she is prepared to accept any of the possible results, including the obligation to complete a resultant pregnancy, if it occurs. However, such an attitude of attributing blame requires some clarifications. Imposing the whole responsibility for pregnancy exclusively on the woman ignores a very significant part of sexual intercourse. The attempt to punish the woman for her pregnancy, while her partner could have easily avoided the same pregnancy by using a contraceptive of his own, seems quite unfair and inappropriate. Besides, it makes sense to assume that "being responsible" includes the authority to decide on terminating pregnancy, and not only to decide on completing the full term.

Regarding the second point of the above charge: accepting the idea that women should be celibate, unless they are ready to bear any possible consequence of sexual intercourse, denies to them a thing that is considered as intensely pleasurable. This requires some serious consideration in order to be valid, and not only from a consequential point of view. In any concept of facing the consequences, there must be some proportionality between the penalty and the guilt. Carelessness or negligence in using contraceptives, does not seem sufficient to inflict so serious punishment as giving birth to an unwanted child, and nurturing the child for many years. For this we need a more serious charge, and the only possible one is the first restrictive argument that was mentioned. There must be extremely weighty considerations that involve human life or human rights to justify such self-sacrifice from a woman , because the interdiction of abortion violates some fundamental and elementary rights of the pregnant woman. Hence, the most tempestuous and furious debates turn around these questions. When presenting approaches that allow abortion in some or most cases, I will clarify both the issues at stake, and the possible answers that are given to them, in order to justify abortion. The coming paragraphs deal with Moderate approaches. These approaches claim that abortion is not inherently wrong, and under certain circumstances (usually connected with the stage of pregnancy), it is legitimate and justifiable.

5.2.2 The Moderate Position

Moderates regard abortion as legitimate in some cases (under certain conditions, restrictions and circumstances), and illegitimate in others. This approach is divided into many different sorts of justifications for abortion. Some Moderates determine the legitimacy of abortion according to the stage of the pregnancy. Others determine it according to the future prospects of the potential child (health, welfare status or age of the parents, etc.). Still others assess the justification of abortion in light of the possible effects it might have on the mother's health, her family or surroundings. Another approach is to determine the morality of an abortion according to an assessment of the mother's responsibility for the pregnancy, or according to the reasons for her desire to abort.[323]

However, most of the discussions within this approach center on the question whether and when the fetus becomes a viable human being, and then take a stand about the morality of abortion, at different stages of development of the fetus. The main thrust of these attempts is to mark a stage in which they can ascribe personhood to the fetus, and from then on to regard it as a moral entity (whether an agent or merely a human being). As such, it is entitled to have rights, or at least to be protected by the community. Terminating its continued existence after this stage is morally wrong.

Absolute Restrictivists, on the other hand, assert that a fetus is, in most morally relevant respects, a fully developed person, right from conception. They usually use two lines of justification. One is based on genetic and teleological assumptions, according to which the whole genetic makeup of the fetus is established, when the chromosomes from the father's sperm and the mother's ovum are united. At that point the fetus acquires its unique genetic traits that characterize it as the same individual it will be in the future. In essence, the person before birth is not different from what she will be when developed, and hence is entitled to the same respect as an adult. The second line of justification is based on the assumption, that there is no morally relevant difference between a newly born infant and an adult, with regard to their personhood, or at least to their right to protection. In addition, Restrictivists claim that there is no significant difference between this infant and a fully developed fetus that has not yet been born. On the other hand, they cannot mark any point during pregnancy, to which they can point as so significant as to regard a fetus as a person from then on. They regard pregnancy as an equable and linear continuity of human development, and hence, from the very beginning, the fetus is to be regarded as a person.[324] This approach regards personhood as mainly a biological or human structural matter, and prohibits abortion at any stage of the biological development of the fetus.

Those who consider personhood a more complicated matter that involves some mental, psychological or sensational capacities, tend to position the onset of personhood at later stages. Accordingly, they permit abortion up to these stages, and expound their concept of personality to justify this. In this part I briefly present such positions, and at the same time, try to respond to some of the arguments that are raised by adherents of the Restrictive approach.

Probably the most famous Moderate position was declared by the US Supreme Court Decision in *Roe v Wade.* This decision expresses an approach that connects the legitimacy of abortion to the stage of abortion.

> 'To Summarize and to repeat:
>
> 1. A state criminal abortion statute of the current Texas type, that excepts from criminality only a *life-saving* procedure on behalf of the mother, without regard to pregnancy state and without recognition of the other interests involved, is violative of the Due Process Clause of the Fourteenth Amendment.
>
> (a) For the stage prior to approximately the end of the first trimester, the abortion decision and its effectuation must be left to the medical judgment of the pregnant woman's attending physician.
>
> (b) For the stage subsequent to approximately the end of the first trimester, the State, in promoting its interest in the health of the mother, may, if it chooses, regulate the abortion procedure in ways that are reasonably related to maternal health.
>
> (c) For the stage subsequent to viability, the state in promoting its interests in the potentiality of human life, may, if it chooses, regulate, and even proscribe abortion, except where it is necessary, in appropriate medical judgment, for the preservation of the life or health of the mother".[325]

This decision regards viability – the stage in which the fetus is potentially able to live outside the mother's womb, albeit with artificial aid – as the critical stage for abortion to be permissible. This stage is placed between the 26th and 28th week of pregnancy (sometimes even earlier, up to the 24th week). This is the "compelling" point with regard to the state's interests in potential life, because from there on, the fetus presumably has the capacity of meaningful life outside the mother's womb.

Even though the Supreme Court considers the "compelling" point with regard to the mother's health, at the end of the first trimester of pregnancy, it acknowledges the state's regulations protecting fetal life, as justified only after viability. Before that, the state is justified in proscribing abortion only under considerations of the mother's health.

However, viability as a criterion for personhood is only one option to define the fetus's possession of the right to life. There are other points that can be reasonably used for this purpose. Another option is raised by Richard Werner, who maintains that the relevant criterion for being a fully-fledged member of the moral community is being a sentient human being. Accordingly, he regards abortion of a nonsentient fetus as permissible. After sentiency – that is, somewhere between the eighth and tenth week of pregnancy – it cannot be justified.[326]

Werner's position refers to the issue of personhood in a more complicated way. Like Michael Tooley and Mary Ann Warren, he distinguishes between a "human being" – which means a bona fide member of the biological species of *Homo Sapiens* – and a "person". By a "person" he refers to a fully-fledged member of the human community, who has the capacity of developing the concept of the self, who has memories, language, etc. A fetus is a human being from the moment of conception (according to the argument that development proceeds in a straight line from conception to adulthood). However, when dealing with the moral issues regarding abortion, we need to relate to the relevant criterion for membership in the community, which is, according to Werner, being a sentient human being. He justifies his position, by saying that a creature's life cannot be good or bad, better or worse, unless this creature is capable of experiencing pleasure, satisfaction, pain or anguish. Without these capabilities, any appeal to the quality of its future experiences is irrelevant, since it is not capable of having experiences consonant with helping or harming. Hence, there is no moral obligation to a nonsentient being (i.e. one that will never become sentient), and such a creature cannot possess any moral right.[327] Werner concludes that sentiency is a necessary condition for having rights. Therefore he holds that abortion during the first eight to ten weeks of pregnancy is never wrong, because it has no moral effect on the unborn. After this period, when there are no considerations of unavoidable death or self-defense, abortion cannot be justified. In his view, there are some exceptions where these considerations would justify abortion even after the tenth week. Some examples are: when the continuation of pregnancy endangers the mother's life, or when the pregnancy is a result of rape and the continuance of the pregnancy might have severe psychological effects, or when the mother is a young girl.[328] In any event, Werner's approach still uses the concept of personhood as an all-or-nothing matter. The distinction between a "human being" and a "person" enables us to draw a line between a nonsentient fetus – which does not possess rights – and a sentient fetus – which has a moral status.

Many other options to define the onset of personhood have been raised by different Moderates. They choose certain points in fetal development as morally significant, and not merely part of the continual process of the fetus' growth. Some of them point to the end of the embryonic stage (when all the organ systems are developed into a complete organism), as a morally significant stage that establishes personhood. Others consider the completion of the neurological development (like Werner, who think that the beginning of sentience is critical for moral judgment), as the onset of personhood. Accordingly, killing a fetus after the first trimester will terminate a stream of experiences (some of which may be pleasurable), and this is morally wrong. We can also follow the US Supreme Court's position and define viability (the stage at which the fetus could survive on its own outside the mother's womb), as the morally relevant point that can establish personhood.[329]

Each of the above positions leads to a different conclusion about the permissible timing of abortion. The identifying of the fetus' moral standing with its personhood seems tempting to Moderates, who think that there can be a demarcation between a mere human being and a person. However, this is not exactly true. Many theorists claim that it is impossible to pinpoint a single criterion that captures the concept of a person, and which draws a sharp line between an unborn fetus who is a person, and one who is only a human being.[330]

Moreover, many theorists believe that the stance a person takes regarding abortion is not so much affected by the impartial arguments of the issue, as it is shaped by the person's fundamental and basic beliefs. The person then tends to justify (if not rationalize) this stance through valid (or partially valid) arguments. (This opinion was cited in references to beliefs regarding capital punishment as well.) In other words, those who oppose abortions propose that fetuses fulfill the conditions for personhood, while those who support abortions, counter with conditions that fetuses lack in personhood.[331] Our concept of a person includes so many factors: biological, psychological, rational, social and legal, that this issue can be widely manipulated. This leads theorists to think that "our concept of a person is not sharp or decisive enough to bear the weight of a solution to the abortion controversy".[332] In addition, the same arguments that are used to protect the fetus' rights can be turned around to support the opposite stance, by changing the concept of a person into a communitarian matter. On the communitarian level we can measure personality according to the ability to communicate, to act autonomously, to be aware of one's own existence, etc.[333] This would disqualify any fetus from personhood, and allow abortion at any stage of pregnancy.

Another aspect that presumably might sustain the Moderate approach is the moral status of the fetus. If we can roughly summarize that Restrictivists claim that a fetus is equal to a fully developed adult human being, and Permissivists claim that a fetus is only a discrete human organ and hence can not possess moral rights, Moderates take an intermediate position. This position gives up the "all-or-nothing" course, and regards the fetus as a "relatively unique moral category in which its status is close to but not identical with that of a typical adult".[334] According to Richard Wasserstrom, who maintains this position, though a fetus is different from an adult in respect of its not being autonomous, self-conscious or sentient, a fetus' distinctiveness is uniquely expressed in its capacity to become (in the usual case) a fully developed adult. A human fetus is the only entity that can acquire the moral capabilities of an adult. The moral value of a fetus rests on its potential for becoming a human adult.

Wasserstrom's attitude supports the Moderates position, in its ascription of a special moral status to a fetus. This means that the fetus can be considered as an agent in certain senses.[335] The problem here is to translate the moral status that results from potentiality, into actual possession of rights. In this matter, the work of Joel Feinberg is of great value, even though in the end we must abandon the track of fetal personhood, and move into rights-talk and duty-based terms. Feinberg agrees that fetuses are not people in the ordinary commonsense meaning of this term. However, he thinks that they are not moral persons either, because they lack the actual possession of the characteristics for personhood, even though they have the potentiality to acquire them. The problem with this assertion is that infants and young children also lack the actual possession of the required characteristics. However, Feinberg is not really concerned about this problem, since there are powerful reasons against infanticide that apply even if infants are not moral persons, so that this difficulty is serious only in theory.[336] When Feinberg examines the morality of abortion, he assumes that a fetus is a moral person whose rights ought to be honored, since he wants to investigate this issue as a conflict between genuine claims. This assumption seems to be unfounded even for him, since he considers the Actual Possession criterion the most reasonable criterion for moral personhood. Before presenting his analysis of a possible conflict between the mother's rights and those of the fetus, I want to dwell upon the difference between having the potential for moral action, and moral action itself, with regard to the possession of rights.

Carl Wellman refers to the concept of potentiality as a means to measure the moral status of the fetus, in somewhat different way than Feinberg does. Wellman holds that only moral agents (normal adults, children and mentally limited persons – to the extent that they possess agency) are possible possessors of rights. This hypothesis implies that human fetuses cannot be right-holders, since, surely, no fetus actually possesses moral agency.[337] Wellman distinguishes between agency – the capacity for action – and the capacity for acquiring agency – which is the capacity for acquiring the capacity for action. Wellman maintains that although the fetus has agency in the broad sense (growing, moving about in the womb and developing organs), it does not possess moral agency. This kind of agency is the relevant one for our discussion. It includes "the capacities for becoming acquainted with the relevant facts, for recognizing their moral relevance, or for being motivated by them".[338] What the fetus possesses is the capacity or potential to acquire these capacities, and hence to acquire moral agency. However, Wellman thinks that this capacity does not qualify the fetus to possess rights.

For him, moral rights involve action, and only those who have the capacity for action, are entitled to possess them. And since the capacity to acquire moral agency is still not moral agency itself, the possession of this capacity is not sufficient for qualifying a fetus as possessing moral rights. Wellman insists that the possession of rights means having a special sort of position under moral norms. This expression characterizes the way in which certain moral reasons apply to the possessor of these rights. Any set of reasons sufficient to confer a right must include (at least) liberty-conferring and power-conferring reasons. For any creature, which is totally incapable of acting on such reasons, these reasons have no relevance. Hence, the capacity for action is necessary for the possession of any moral right, and a creature, which lacks this capacity, is not capable of possessing rights.[339]

Wellman's analysis directs us to a solution of the previous question raised by Feinberg – whether a fetus is a moral person or not – by considering the actual-possession criterion that he suggests for personhood. Nevertheless, when discussing Feinberg's view within the framework of the Moderate approach to abortion, we even notice some Moderate aspects in his analysis, which also includes some noticeable Restrictivist elements. Feinberg examines the matter of abortion as if it were a conflict between the fetus' right to life, and some possible rights of the mother. Even though he denies that the mother's property rights[340] or her right to self-defense can justify abortion (since he believes that the mother will suffer a lesser harm than the fetus as a result of the abortion)[341], he adds an exception to his position. Feinberg acknowledges the mother's right to self-defense as justifying abortion in cases where there is a genuine *threat* to the mother's well-being, and that threat is to her very life. In these cases the Moderate tone is quite minor. But there is a more characteristic Moderate reasoning, in his discussion of the link between voluntariness and responsibility in the context of pregnancy.

Feinberg refers to the issue of the mother's responsibility for her pregnancy, and agrees that the mother's duty to continue the pregnancy depends (at least in part) on her responsibility for being pregnant in the first place. He thinks that her duty is determined according to the extent to which the pregnancy results from her own voluntary actions. He bases his view on the principle that imposes a duty on X to rescue or support Y (even a stranger, and even in cases that involves risking one's life), to the degree that X, through his own voluntary actions or omissions, is responsible for Y's difficult plight. In order to explicate this principle, Feinberg uses a few examples that are taken from Sissela Bok. According to the first example, a late-arriving bystander at the seaside has no duty to risk his life in order to save a drowning swimmer. However, if the swimmer is in danger only because the bystander erroneously informed him that there is no danger, then he has a duty to make some efforts at rescue (although not suicidal), even though these efforts might be dangerous. But if the swimmer is in danger only because the bystander had pushed him out of a boat, the bystander has an obligation to attempt to rescue the swimmer at any cost, since his own voluntary actions initiated the swimmer's plight.[342]

Feinberg now attempts to deal with the mother's duties in abortion, by taking into account the degree to which the woman is responsible for her situation. In other words, he maintains that the mother's duty to complete her pregnancy is much stronger in cases where her pregnancy was fully voluntary, than in cases where the pregnancy was totally involuntary. He ranks possible causes for pregnancy, and accordingly determines the responsibility that the mother bears. The spectrum he offers is as follows:

> "1. Pregnancy caused by rape (totally involuntary).
>
> 2. Pregnancy caused by contraceptive failure, where the fault is entirely that of the manufacturer or pharmaceutical company.
>
> 3. Pregnancy caused by contraceptive failure within the advertised one percent margin of error (no one's fault).
>
> 4. Pregnancy caused by the negligence of the woman (or the man, or both). They are careless in the use of the contraceptive or else fail to use it at all, being unaware of a large risk that they *ought* to have been aware of.

> 5. Pregnancy caused by the recklessness of the woman (or the man, or both). They think of the risk but get swept along by passion and consciously disregard it.
>
> 6. Pregnancy caused by intercourse between partners who are genuinely indifferent at the time whether or not pregnancy results.
>
> 7. Pregnancy caused by the deliberate decision of the parties to produce it (completely voluntary)".[343]

According to the previous principle regarding the ranking of responsibility according to the mother's voluntariness, Feinberg finds that in cases 5, 6, and 7, there is no justification for the mother to cease her bodily support for the fetus. This is because her pregnancy results from her voluntary actions. In case 4, even wholly or partially involuntary, the actions of the parents were faulty, and the pregnancy resulted from this fault (or negligence). Accordingly, their degree of responsibility for the pregnancy is substantial, since they should be more careful or knowledgeable. Feinberg maintains that in failing to exercise due care, they were doing something else, to a certain degree, voluntarily. This leads him to conclude that in cases 4, 5, 6, and 7, the parents are responsible for the pregnancy, and hence have a duty not to kill the fetus, or permit its death.[344]

However, cases 2 and 3 are much more complicated. In cases 1 and 2, the mother is not responsible, and she has no obligation to continue her pregnancy.[345] The negligence of the manufacturer of the contraceptive in case 2 can be considered as the main cause of pregnancy, and the woman cannot be held responsible for the pregnancy, or as bearing a duty to continue it. Case 3 is a difficult one for Feinberg. The parents did take strong precautions against pregnancy. Nevertheless, they knew that there is a small chance that the woman might become pregnant, and still chose to run the risk. The result is that the woman is pregnant against her will. From the fetus' point of view, even though the mother took a small risk, the fetus did not take any, and is not responsible at all, while the mother bears minimal responsibility. On the other hand, we can say, like in case 2, that the mother is no more responsible for the pregnancy than the fetus, because she took all the precautions that she could reasonably be expected to take. Feinberg regards this case as a borderline case. Our judgment of it depends on our consideration of the small risk of pregnancy, within the advertised margin of error, as a reasonable risk for the woman to run in the circumstances. But this appraisal itself is a disguised moral judgment that is very difficult to make. If we find it reasonable, then the woman is relieved of any responsibility for the pregnancy, just as she is in cases 1 and 2, and the fetus' right to life does not impose a duty on her part, to make an extreme sacrifice.[346]

To sum up Feinberg's current analysis, we can say that he denies that the mother's property rights on her body can support a moral weight that will be sufficient for justifying the termination of the fetus's life. When he examines the mother's right to self-defense, he says that it is applicable only in cases where the mother's life is in danger. Her right to bodily autonomy is more concrete than in the previous two cases, because it permits the woman to deprive the fetus of her "life support system". But this can serve only to justify cases where the pregnancy was caused by rape, or a contraceptive failure caused by a negligence of another party, when the mother seems to be in no way responsible for the pregnancy. This view is considered Moderate, because it allows abortion in certain cases, according to the criterion of responsibility of the mother, just as other views use the criterion of the development of the fetus, etc. However, let me emphasize that this whole analysis is based on the assumption that a fetus is a moral person, which is an assumption that has not yet been proved. Feinberg himself does not relate to this assumption, so we cannot really ascribe the analysis above to Feinberg's stance regarding the issue. However, it suggests a way of dealing with this issue as a conflict between rights, an idea that I will try to propose later in this chapter.

The next section deals with the Permissivist approach, and continues the discussion regarding the question whether a fetus is a moral person. I present views that determine such criteria for personhood that fetuses do not possess, and hence cannot be considered as moral persons. But I am aware of the claim made by Jane English, that theorists first decide if they are for or against abortion, and only then choose the qualifications for personhood of the fetus, that fit their a priori theory. Therefore, I also offer a different hypothesis of justification. I will show that just as Feinberg's discussion results in a Moderate position, when assuming that this question regarding the moral status of the fetus has a positive answer, there are other views that end in a Permissivist position, assuming the same status for the fetus. This shows that we can justify a Permissive position, even when ascribing the status of a person to a fetus. In my opinion, abortion is a conflict between rights, and has to be solved according to the entitlement of each side of the conflict to possess its or her rights.

5.2.3 The Permissivist Position

Permissivists hold that abortion is permissible whenever the pregnant woman so desires. They may justify it on the basis of the woman's reproductive rights, including her right to decide whether her pregnancy will be carried out or terminated. Other Permissivists base it on the mother's right to self-determination or on her personal autonomy. Some base their argument on the difference or hierarchy, between the moral status of the woman and that of the fetus. Some Permissivists even deny that a fetus has any moral personhood. Those who do not regard it as a person, say that the question of personhood relates to communitarian capacities such as the ability to communicate, to respond, etc. Their denial of the personhood of a fetus, even when admitting that it is a human creature, make abortion permissible, because of the absence of the fetus' moral status. This absence disqualifies the fetus from possessing rights, and in some versions weakens the claim that abortion strikes at the sanctity of human life. I briefly present such a position and examine its capacity for justifying abortion.

One of the most familiar Permissivists who use the argument that a fetus is not a person, is that of Mary Anne Warren. Her principal position is that since the fetus is not a person, it is not the sort of entity to which it is proper to ascribe moral rights. She believes that full and equal moral rights are conferred within the moral community, and in order to identify who is entitled to possess such rights, we have to know what kind of creature is capable of being a member in this community. Warren denies the presupposition that genetic humanity is sufficient for being morally human, and says that someone genetically human can only be considered as having the potential for becoming human in the moral sense.[347] For her, a moral community – the relevant moral framework for possessing rights – consists only of *people* rather than only of *human beings*. In order to distinguish a person from a mere human being, she suggests some characteristics which she assumes are most central to the concept of personhood, or what she regards as "humanity in the moral sense".

> "(1) consciousness (of objects and events external and/or internal to the being), and in particular the capacity to feel pain;
>
> (2) reasoning (the developed capacity to solve new and relatively complex problems);
>
> (3) self-motivated activity (activity which is relatively independent of either genetic or direct external control);
>
> (4) the capacity to communicate, by whatever means, massages of an indefinite variety of types, that is, not just

> with an indefinite number of possible contents, but on indefinitely many possible topics;
>
> (5) the presence of self-concepts, and self-awareness, either individual or racial, or both".[348]

Regarding these capacities as the primary criteria of personhood makes it clear that genetic humanity is neither necessary nor sufficient for moral humanity. Warren insists that there are human beings who are not people (and some people who are not human beings). She brings some examples of cases where human beings are not considered as persons. Among these she mentions a man or woman whose consciousness has been permanently obliterated but who remains alive, as an impaired human being with no appreciable mental capacity. These kinds of human beings are not considered as persons, even though they were persons before. Fetuses are also human beings, which are not yet persons, and therefore, cannot have moral rights. She thinks that ascribing moral rights to such entities as fetuses is just as absurd as ascribing to them moral obligations and responsibilities.[349]

The above analysis leads Warren to conclude that in the *relevant* respects, a fetus (even a fully developed one) is less personlike than the average mature mammal. And if its right to life is based on its resemblance to a person, it does not have a moral right to life more than a newborn guppy, and a right of that magnitude cannot override the mother's right to obtain an abortion at any stage of her pregnancy.[350] Warren, who basically regards the capacity for moral reciprocity as essential for personhood,[351] denies the fetus' right to moral equality, and hence assumes that the mother's right to abort will always override the fetus' rights.

Another line of justifying the Permissivist approach deals with the claim that a fetus, as a human being, has the potentiality to become a person, and hence, entitled to possess rights. I have already cited Carl Wellman's discussion of this issue. Here I want to clarify to this line of thought, and illuminate its relevance to the Permissivist position. Michael Tooley holds a position similar to Warren's, with regard to the distinction between a human being and a person. For him the term "person" is purely a moral concept, free of any descriptive content. The basic property that he suggests for being capable of possessing rights, and in particular the right to life, is not genetic. One can possess rights "only if he possesses the concept of the self as a continuing subject of experiences and other mental states, and believes that he is himself such a continuing entity".[352] An entity that lacks the consciousness of itself as a continuity of mental states cannot possess any right, even the right to life.

Tooley examines the claim that one who has the potential of possessing the required characteristic for possessing rights (the self-consciousness requirement in his theory) is entitled to possess rights. This entitlement is based on the assumption that one will come to have this property, in the normal course of one's development. One way to attack that this claim is used by Wellman, is to insist that only the actual possession of that property can qualify one to possess rights, and not merely the potential of having that property in the future. Feinberg's concept of the actual possession criterion is based on the same principle of distinguishing between the actual possession of a property, and having the potential for possessing it. This is mainly because the rights in question are demanded now and not in the future, while the property that bestows them will be possessed only in the future. Hence, at present, there is no entitlement to possess the right.

However, Tooley confronts the potentiality claim in a slightly different way. He suggests an imaginary example, according to which he presumes the injection of a chemical into a kitten, which would cause it to acquire the mental abilities of a human adult sometime in the future. Tooley thinks that there would be nothing wrong with killing this kitten, or interfering with the process of its development, just as it was not wrong to interfere with its development before the injection. Similarly, it would not be wrong to interfere with the development of a human being who has the same potentiality. This is because the only difference between these two cases is that in the case of the human being, the potential must have been present from the very beginning of the organism's development, and in the kitten's case the potential appeared only after the injection. This difference in the starting point of the potential is regarded by Tooley as morally irrelevant.[353] The potential for possessing rights is not sufficient for the actual possession, in both cases.

A more simple way to explain the objection to the argument that confers rights upon human beings, as a result of their potential of becoming persons in the future, can come from some examples. There is no doubt that a seventeen-year-old girl has the potential of becoming eighteen, and to acquire the right to vote at this age (in those countries where this is the prescribed age). But this does not mean that her "potentiality" entitles her the right to vote at seventeen. The same is the case with membership rights of a club, for example. When someone is only a candidate to join the club, she has the potential of becoming a member, but she cannot vote for the club's presidency, because this right is conferred only upon members. In a more radical way we can say that each locally born citizen of the USA has the potential of becoming the president, but until she actually becomes a president, she has no authority to perform any presidential act. These examples show that having the potential to acquire a certain moral status, does not entitle one to enjoy the benefits that are given as a result of this status. Accordingly, the potential to become a person does not give a human being the right to the status of a person, and does not enable the human being that possesses the above potential, to possess rights.

The perplexity and complexity involved in the attempt to judge the morality of abortion according to the fetus' personhood, brought theorists to the conclusion that this line of discussion cannot resolve the disagreements between the disputing parties. Theorists came to believe that disagreements about the nature of personhood, and about the methods by which it can be discovered or conferred, are irresolvable, thus making the whole discussion futile and pointless.[354] I have already mentioned Jane English's criticism, who claims that the properties required for personhood are purposely selected by Permissivists or Restrictivists, for their own purposes.[355] She thinks that using our disputable, unclear and vague concepts of a person to solve the problem of abortion "is to clarify *obscurum per obscurius*".[356] To illustrate the perplexing nature of this issue, we recall Joan Callahan's objection to the Restrictive claim that human life begins at conception. She argues that human life begins long before conception, since the sperm and ovum are alive, and these are not different kind of creatures, but are human living gametes.[357] It is impossible to render a convincing argument for or against abortion, when the whole issue of "personhood" of the fetus is not resolved.

Besides the difficulties involved with achieving an accepted or putative concept of personhood, there are other objections to the use of this concept for resolving the dispute about abortion. One of them says that personhood is a plausible criterion, for the *inclusion* of its possessors within the circle of moral subjects. This means that any moral theory that denies equal moral status to persons must be rejected. However, the use of this criterion for the *exclusion* of human beings (such as infants or mentally retarded individuals), who do not fulfill the mental and social requirements for personhood, seems to be less plausible. Another argument against this use of the concept is that there is a tendency among dominant groups to rationalize the oppression of other groups, by claiming that the members of the oppressed groups are not persons, because of some alleged mental or social deficiencies.[358]

These claims and the above difficulties lead many people to change their strategy, and examine the morality of abortion in the light of the unique relations between the fetus and the pregnant woman, mainly the total dependence of the fetus upon the woman's body. They prefer to assume that a fetus is a person, and entitled to possess certain rights, including the right to life, under certain conditions and circumstances. However, these conditions and circumstances are tightly bound to the relations between the mother's health, welfare, freedom, autonomy, reproduction rights, etc., and the fetus' rights. The pregnant woman and the fetus are not like two tenants in a small house that has been rented to both, as Judith Jarvis Thomson picturesquely describes these relations, but the mother *owns* the house.[359] This is a fundamental fact about pregnancy. It validates the mother's right to defend her life and protect her interests, against threats that the fetus, even though an innocent creature, imposes on them. It also negates the claim that a third party cannot choose between the rights of the woman and those of the fetus. Thomson compares it to a situation where one found a coat, and used it to keep his body warm. At the same time there is another person who also needs the coat to avoid his freezing. However, the only relevant difference between them is that the second one owns the coat. Can we say that a third party cannot choose between the conflicting claims? Both need the use of the coat, but its owner's claims have priority over those of the person who does not own the coat. When applying this idea to the matter of abortion, Thomson insists that: "if a human being has any just, prior claim to anything at all, he has a just prior claim to his own body".[360] A third party may refuse to intervene in the disagreement, both in the case of the coat and the case of abortion, saying that it is none of his business or that he leaves it to the treatment of the authorities, who are responsible for securing people's rights. But he cannot say that he cannot choose between the conflicting rights. For the most he can say, that he does not want or have to choose or interfere. However, no one argues for his duty to do so, but only that he can, if he wishes to.

The matter of the third party's right to perform abortions has been widely discussed. Jane English thinks that when both parties are innocent (not responsible for their actions), we need to consider other factors, in order to justify the doctor's right to interfere. Her example is that of a senior citizen who does not want to be hurt by a crazed attacker (who is dangerous but not responsible for his actions). So, he hires a bodyguard to accompany him. If he is attacked, it is clear that the bodyguard, as his agent, has a right to kill the attacker, in order to save the senior citizen from a beating. The citizen's rights to self-defense are transferred to his agent. Similarly, we regard the doctor as the pregnant woman's agent, in carrying out a defense she is physically incapable of accomplishing by herself.[361] This still does not impose a duty on any doctor to perform an abortion if he prefers not to do so, but as the woman's doctor, he definitely has a right to. Of course, if his intervention is required to rescue the woman's life, he has no choice. Otherwise, he will be responsible for her death (which will almost automatically terminate the fetus' life too). However, this can illuminate the doctor's duty in a different way. If we acknowledge the mother's right to abort (which we still need to demonstrate), and assume that there is a possibility of a self-induced abortion – where the woman performs the abortion by herself, without medical aid, and without sterilized equipment – we realize that it will put her in serious danger. And if reducing that danger requires us to place the matter in the hands of a doctor, we might think that it is the doctor's obligation, to concern himself with the possible risk to this woman. This cannot, of itself, oblige a particular doctor to perform the abortion, but if there is no one else who is capable of doing it, we can regard him as being duty-bound to save the woman from danger. We can also derive the doctor's duty from an earlier assumption I used (taken from Henry Shue), which was that: "if everyone has a right to y, and the enjoyment of x is necessary for the enjoyment of y, than everyone has a right to x".[362] We can regard everything that is necessary for accomplishing a safe abortion, as part of the woman's right to abort, and this includes her right to have it with the doctor's help. This right imposes a duty on society to provide doctors who agree to perform abortions, and society might assert its authority against doctors who refuse, just as it does when a doctor refuses to perform some other necessary operations. However, our concern is not regarding the doctor's duty, but the doctor's **right** to intervene, and to be able to derive this, we still need to show that the pregnant woman has a right to have an abortion, if she prefers to.

For this we go back to Thomson's landmark article (which caused Jane English to use the term "Pre-Thomson literature"[363]), and to the unique relation between the pregnant woman and the fetus. Thomson insists that: "having a right to life does not guarantee having either a right to be given the use of, or a right to be allowed continued use of another person's body – even if one needs it for life itself".[364] Her principal attitude to the right to life is that this right does not consist of the right not to be killed, but in the right not to be killed unjustly. The pregnant woman who performs an abortion, does not violate the fetus' right to life, because she does not treat it unjustly when denying it the use of her body. It would be nice and generous of her to let the fetus use her body, even though she does not want to do so. Her refusal might even be self-centered, callous, indecent, but in no way unjust.[365] What Thomson emphasizes is that when she argues for the permissibility of abortion, she does not argue for the right to secure the death of the fetus. Many times, especially in early stages of pregnancy, the fetus cannot survive outside the mother's body, and abortion means unavoidable death of the fetus. However this is not what she means by justifying abortion.[366]

Jane English extends Thomson's idea, saying that though the fetus is innocent, its presence imposes an implied threat to the woman's well-being, her life prospects and her physical or mental health. This gives her a right to free herself of this implied threat. It is unfortunate that the only way to release the woman from her pregnancy entails the death of the fetus. However, it is still her right to defend herself from that implied threat. So this right is limited only to the freeing herself of the fetus, and not to the demanding of its death. She illustrates this by saying that if, after birth, the presence of the infant or the need to support it, imposes a grave threat on the mother's welfare, well-being, sanity or life prospects, she can avoid these problems by simply putting the baby up for adoption. However, such a solution during pregnancy is not available to her, because of the unique dependence of the fetus upon the woman's body. Her option to defend herself by less drastic means than killing the infant occurs only after birth (through giving up the baby to adoption), and this is what makes birth so crucial to the relations between the mother and the offspring. This leads English to conclude that the self-defense argument can be used to justify abortion, without necessarily justifying infanticide.[367]

The assumption that birth is a crucial point for the discussion of abortion is accepted by many Permissivists, who acknowledge the unique relations between the pregnant woman and the fetus. Mary Anne Warren mentions that the major reason for treating birth as the threshold of moral equality is that only at this stage can the infant be granted basic equal rights, without violating anyone else's basic rights. The authorities can assume responsibility for him, even find him a good home (in many countries), and enable him to have decent conditions for growth. The infant's development can be managed without imposing an excessive hardship upon women and families, who do not want them. However, this cannot happen in the case of a fetus, because treating it equally, would involve an unequal treatment of the pregnant woman.[368] This might impose a heavy burden upon her, and hence deprive the woman of her right to be treated as equal, for the sake of the fetus' equality. In short, the link between mother and fetus can be severed only after birth.

This brings us closer to the view I want to defend in this section. The question regarding whose right will be denied (the mother or the fetus), requires some background information regarding the way rights function as "a final court of appeal for ordering the conflicting claims of moral persons".[369] I suggest dealing with the morality of abortion by using the same method I use in the case of conflicts between rights in other contexts. Of course, the uniqueness of the specific issue, determines the unique mode of operating the principles, according to which we solve the conflicts between claims. However, the preliminary guidelines remain the same. In the coming section I present my outlook of this matter, from a right-based point of view.

5.3 ABORTION AS A CONFLICT BETWEEN RIGHTS

Before dealing with my suggested approach in resolving the problem of abortion, I emphasize the uniqueness of the case of abortion, as a conflict between opposing rights. What makes this case so unique is first, the total dependence of the fetus on the woman's body, which cannot be compared to any other kind of relationship. The second significant fact is that abortion usually terminates the fetus' life, unless it is carried out at a very late stage of pregnancy (when the fetus is fully developed). This kind of conflict, between the mother's and fetus' rights, cannot be resolved with a compromise, until a very advanced stage of pregnancy. Exercising the rights of one side of the conflict (the fetus') threatens the rights of the other, and capitalizing one's rights (the mother's), abolishes the exercising of the other's. This does not happen after birth. These two fundamental facts have to be considered in any discussion of abortion, whether from a right-based perspective, or from any other.

However, from the right-based point of view, this conflict can be considered in light of the moral status of the conflicting parties. In this sense, we do not appeal to the question of harm that is caused to each side, or to the extent to which each party is innocent or bears responsibility for the situation. The right-based approach takes the lenient and mitigatory assumption that a fetus can possess rights to some extent (the rigorous and extreme assumption that the fetus cannot possess any rights would nullify the conflict since a conflict can occur only between right-holders). When considering abortion as a conflict between possessors of rights, the right-based approach examines to what extent each of the conflicting parties is considered as a moral agent (in an agent-relative approach), or as a member of the moral community (in a communitarian approach). Accordingly, we decide whose rights override the other's.

This is the way Alan Gewirth deals with this matter. He believes that there are degrees or stages in the process of becoming a prospective purposive agent. In order to be an agent, one must have the practical abilities of the generic features of action. This includes the ability to understand the situation, evaluate the circumstances and make an unforced choice. Human beings possess these abilities to greatly varied degrees. And since being a prospective purposive agent is the quality that determines whether one has the generic rights for action, members of certain groups (such as children or mentally retarded persons) possess the requisite abilities in varying degrees as well. This is a direct implication of the Principle of Proportionality.[370] With regard to children, this principle determines that their lesser practical abilities, justifies their having fewer rights, because of the bearing of their abilities on their own fulfillment of their purposes.

In the case of a human fetus, we must consider the fact that abortion involves its death, and consequently the complete loss of its generic rights. If there were no conflict between the fetus's rights and the mother's, the fetus' rights to well-being would be guaranteed to the required degree for developing its potentiality for growth towards purpose-fulfillment[371] , even though the fetus has no right to freedom. However, since the right of the fetus to well-being conflicts with the mother's generic rights, Gewirth insists that the latter should take priority. He says that the relation between possessing rights and the generic abilities for action, which is determined by the Principle of Proportionality, should be preserved even in the cases of the rights of a fetus. The preservation of the above formula means that when someone is less than a full-fledged prospective agent, her generic rights should be proportional to the degree she approaches having the generic abilities that constitute agency. The fetus, except in a remotely potential form, lacks these abilities, just as it is lacking any purposes of even the most rudimentary sort. This results from the lack of any physically separate existence, and the lack of memory or consciousness. Hence, its generic rights, in comparison with the mother's rights, are assessed to be minimal.[372] This brings Gewirth to conclude that the mother's rights override the fetus' rights, as a conclusion of the Principle of Proportionality. He thinks that abortion is justified, since:

> "The mother, as a purposive agent, already has the generic practical abilities and the purposes to which these are directed, and their being lost, endangered, or attacked for the sake of the fetus would involve that the generic rights of someone who has them in full would be drastically subordinated to a minimal possessor of these rights".[373]

Gewirth concludes with a Moderate position that tends to the Permissivist approach. He mentions the weight that should be given to the extent to which the mother's rights are threatened by the continuation of the pregnancy, and to the fetus' prospects for fulfilling its right to well-being. These latter prospects (of the fetus) are meager when the mother's physical, psychological or social circumstances, render her unable or unwilling to give her baby the necessary nurturing care. This threatens both the mother's rights to freedom and well-being, and the fetus' right to well-being. In such cases, "it is vitally important that the concern for the fetus' right to life be matched by the concern for its right to adequate nutrition and other components of well-being".[374] The considerations of dismal prospects for the fetus, can support the justification of abortion even in cases of a late abortion.

Within the agent-relative theory we can extend Gewirth's view, and say that the mother's rights should override the fetus' right, since she fulfills a lot more requirements that qualify a person for moral agency. This can be deduced from the Principle of Proportionality, since the difference between the mother's fulfillment of the generic abilities of action, and that of the fetus, is decisive.

However, when dealing with this matter from a communitarian point of view, we must reconstruct the way we rank membership in the community, and the way we assess and evaluate the validity of any right within the community. In the second chapter of this study, I invoked the agent-relative approach as the foundation of the construction that creates the moral community. This approach is used for determining who can obtain "an entry ticket" to the moral community, and for the assessment of the extent of one's membership in the community. This extent or degree is determined by the measure to which the subjective requirements for agency, are fulfilled by the alleged member of the community. The moral status within the community is dependent on the above measure and, accordingly, so too is the possession of rights. This is, of course, under the assumption that we are discussing an innocent member, that is, one who did not intentionally renege on his moral obligation as a member, or one who is not an immoral agent. In the first part of this chapter, in the course of my discussion of children's rights, I used agent relative considerations for determining children's entitlement to possess certain rights, and in fact, to assess and evaluate the validity of their claims for these rights.

I have emphasized that there are no absolute rights; all rights are conditional. I mentioned (in chapter 3) James W. Nickel's division of the components of a fully specified right.[375] Among these components I mentioned the *conditions of possession, conditions of engagement, weight, addressees* and *scope.* When one or more of these components are not or cannot be substantiated, the right-claim may fail. This analysis may help in finding solutions to conflicts between rights, and I will show how it can be used for the current discussion. As to the right of the fetus, I will refer to its right to life and to well-being. This is the *scope* of the right in Nickel's terminology.

The first component, namely the *Conditions of Possession,* was discussed in the previous paragraphs, and showed that the mother is in a clearly superior position compared to the fetus. This is because the mother fulfills the subjective requirements for agency, especially those with respect to the cognitive and communicative capacities, to a far greater extent than the fetus. This places her higher than the fetus in the ranking of moral agency, in the grading of membership in the moral community and accordingly in the possession of rights within it. This conclusion, which is based on the Principle of Proportionality, significantly affects also the third component, namely the *weight* of the right. This component determines how strong or weighty is the right, in competition with other considerations. Since the second component – the Conditions of Engagement – indicates that the fetus' right to life applies in the discussed situation, we need to check whether the considerations of the mother's rights outweighs the fetus' rights. We assess her rights to freedom, welfare and well-being, her autonomy and her right to self-determination, self-esteem and self-respect, her reproduction rights, all of which challenge the fetus' right to life. The higher moral status of the mother than that of the fetus, gives more weight to her rights, and overrides the fetus' rights. The fact that the mother possesses a higher measure of the capacities for agency than the fetus, gives her priority in cases where there cannot be a compromise between the opposing claims.

If we focus on the fourth component, we can see the difficulties involved with this conflict. The fetus' rights are human rights under all criteria. Hence their *addressee,* according to communitarian approaches, is the moral community, which is the authority that bears obligations and normative burdens because of the fetus' rights. However, the mother's rights are also considered as human rights, whose addressee is the moral community. This puts the moral community in a situation where any attempt to respond to the fetus' rights will violate the mother's. At this stage we can regard the community as unable to grant the fetus' rights, because of its obligations towards the mother's rights. This situation of forced choice binds the community to its most compelling obligation, which is to the mother's rights. The stronger obligation results from the higher moral status of the woman, when compared to that of the fetus. When there is no way to comply with both claims, the community has to decide for the rights of its actual member, rather than those of a possible, potential or future one.

However, this leads to a conclusion similar to Thomson's, saying that the right to abortion does not include the right to kill the fetus. If there is a chance to save the infant's life after performing the abortion, the community must do so. This results from the fact that in such cases, the community can comply with both conflicting rights, namely the mother's rights to freedom, well-being, autonomy, etc., and *at the same time* to respect the infant's right to life. Such cases do not belong to the forced choice category, and hence the argument that the community, as an addressee, cannot comply with the fetus' claim, is not valid. The conclusion of the above argument is that abortion is permissible at any stage of pregnancy, since the mother's rights override the fetus' (and hence the fetus' rights are outweighed by them). However, if there is a chance to save the fetus after being aborted, when she is considered as an infant, the community must fulfill its obligations towards her, without violating the mother's rights. This obliges the community to make all possible efforts to realize the infant's rights too.

5.4 DOES ABORTION STRIKE AT THE SANCTITY OR VALUE OF LIFE?

In the beginning of this section I mentioned two possible arguments against abortion. The first was the one that Dworkin calls "the *derivative* objection to abortion". In this argument, the objection to abortion is derived from the interests that it assumes are possessed by every human being, including a fetus. This objection is based on the assumption that fetuses are creatures with interests of their own (including the interest of remaining alive), and hence they have the right (like any human being) to protect and promote these interests, and not to be killed. According to this objection, abortion is wrong because it violates this right, just as killing is wrong because it violates a person's right not to be killed. Hence, the government, as the authority who bears a derivative responsibility to protect these interests through their acknowledgement as rights, should prohibit or regulate abortions.[376] The previous discussion regarding the matter of abortion from a right-based point of view, and in particular, according to the analysis of the components of the fetus' rights, when compared to the mother's rights, gives a reasonable answer to this kind of objection to abortion.

The second argument against abortion was the one that Dworkin calls: "the *detached* objection to abortion". Here, the objection to abortion does not depend on any particular set of interests or rights. This objection assumes that human life has an intrinsic and innate value, and hence life is sacred, and that this sacredness begins at once with biological life, even before the fetus has any movement, sensation or interests. Hence, abortion is wrong because it disregards and insults the sacredness of human life at any stage of pregnancy. According to this view, the government has to prohibit or regulate abortion, because of its detached responsibility to protect the intrinsic value of life.[377] In order to render abortion as permissible, this objection still has to be refuted, even though such an objection comes from domains that are far beyond rights-talk. Rights-talk principally belongs to what Dworkin calls: "secular convictions about morality, fairness and justice". Such convictions address themselves to the attempts to solve or adjust competing interests of people. Beliefs about the intrinsic value of human life belong to the much deeper existential questions, whether and why human interests have an intrinsic value, that leads us to believe that they are sacred and should be treated with reverence.[378]

Dworkin clarifies this issue by distinguishing between three kinds of imports that we ascribe to objects. They can be *instrumentally* important, when their value depends on their usefulness to people, who are helped by them to get what they want or need. They can also have *subjective* value, when they are valuable only to those people who desire them, and no value at all to other people. When we speak of something that has *intrinsic* value, we mean, according to Dworkin, that its value is independent of people's needs, preferences or desires. It is important in itself, regardless of its relations to external factors.[379]

Among objects with intrinsic value, Dworkin distinguishes between those which are incrementally valuable, i.e. we always want more of them no matter how much we already have (for example, knowledge), and those which we value once they already exist. Human life belongs to this second kind, which Dworkin calls "the sacred" or "inviolable".[380] Human life acquires its sanctity as a result of being a product of two processes of creation, the first being the process of natural creation, and the second being the human creative force, which is deliberate. That is why even individual human life is sacred, because it is also part of both natural and human creative forces. In this sense, any human creature, including a fetus, is a triumph of natural (evolutionary) creation, and of human deliberate creation. As such, the life of the fetus, as human, commands respect and demands protection, because of the complex creative investment it represents, both natural and human.[381]

Dworkin describes the disputes between extreme Restrictivists and Permissivists as resulting from the different weight that each side ascribes to the natural and the human investments, that together create the sanctity of life. Extreme Restrictivists (especially religious Roman Catholics) maintain that only the natural investment counts, in deciding whether abortion destroys human life, while their opponents count only the human investment as significant. However, Dworkin mentions that very few people take such extreme positions. Most people take the more moderate positions. The more they regard human life as created by personal choice, training, commitment and decision (rather than divine or natural factors), the more they believe that abortion is permissible. From this point of view, Permissivists think that: "it may be more frustrating of life's miracle when an adult's ambitions, talents, training, and expectations are wasted because of an unforeseen and unwanted pregnancy that when a fetus dies before any significant investment of that kind has been made".[382] Secular Permissivists think that sometimes abortion is even necessary for true respect of the intrinsic value of human life that is created by the human creative investment, including acts and decisions, through which people shape their own life.[383]

Dworkin's mode of examining the sacred value of life, touches upon the crucial question: whether abortion strikes at the sanctity of life. We do not ascribe to human life an intrinsic value merely because it belongs to a live organism. Being biologically alive is not a sufficient reason for being considered as sacred. We think that human life is sacred because of some capabilities and characteristics that do not exist in other species. We ascribe an intrinsic value to persons' abilities of purposiveness, voluntariness, free choice, autonomy, and because of their dignity, integrity self-respect and self-esteem. The prohibition of abortion displays disregard for the woman's procreative autonomy, which is part of her human dignity. This dignity entitles her to the moral right (and the moral responsibility), to make her own choices regarding the fundamental questions about the meaning and value of her own life, and the right to answer these questions according to her own conscience and convictions.[384] Our recognition of a woman's procreative autonomy, requires us to respect her decisions not only when she decides whether to conceive or not, but also when she decides whether to bear the fetus or not. When we consider the effects of abortion on the sacred value of life, we need to find out the reasons for that sanctity, and to check whether we give the appropriate respect to these reasons, with regard to the pregnant woman. If we respect human life for its freedom, we should not deny this freedom to the pregnant woman, who is a developed human being. Respecting her freedom is definitely compatible with the sacred value of life, because freedom is part of the roots of the sanctity of life. Reverence for human life means respecting the human values that make this life so unique and sacred. In this sense, we do not desecrate the intrinsic value of life, but preserve its components in the mother's life. Respecting the mother's freedom and choice, means giving an intrinsic value to her humanity, which consists of her freedom. Hence, abortion is not regarded as a denial of the sanctity of life, but an act of respect to human freedom and autonomy, which makes human life sacred.

The next section deals with a third category of partial members of the moral community: Mentally Retarded people. Their rights will be discussed along the lines of my previous discussions of the rights of children and fetuses.

5.5 RIGHTS OF MENTALLY RETARDED PERSONS

The withdrawal of mentally retarded people's rights, relates to the subjective requirements of agency, that is, to their competence of being awarded an "entry ticket" to the moral community. Unlike the discussion about fetus' rights, there is no doubt or question regarding the personhood of mentally retarded people, and their acknowledgement as persons is obvious. Hence, the discussion about their rights refers only to the extent to which they are entitled to possess certain rights, and not to the question of their being persons and not merely human beings. This makes the questions regarding their rights more similar to those of children's rights than those of fetuses'.

However, while children are potentially purposive prospective agents, mentally retarded persons can only partially attain the requisite abilities for agency.[385] Their abilities to control their behavior, to have knowledge of the relevant circumstances beyond what meets the eye, and to reflect rationally on their purposes, will always be limited. Thus, according to the Principle of Proportionality, the extent to which they are entitled to have the generic rights depends on the extent to which they possess the requisite abilities. This results from the relation between the generic abilities for action, and the purposes which the agent wants to fulfill.[386]

It was mentioned earlier with regard to children, that as potential moral agents they have all the rights that are preparatory for their taking on the generic rights pertaining to full-fledged agency.[387] This includes mainly a proper upbringing, education, a development of their decision-making skills, etc. I quoted Gewirth with reference to such cases, as saying:

> "Insofar as there is any biological possibility that the human in question will attain the moral abilities of agency, they have rights to fostering of these abilities. Even when such attainment seems hopeless, they still have rights to be helped to attain as close an approximation of these abilities as possible".[388]

This is meant to ensure some of the generic rights of mentally retarded persons (whom Gewirth calls "mentally deficient").

However, it is quite clear that the reliance on the Principle of Proportionality entails that some of their generic rights (especially those which concern freedom) will be limited. Their possession of certain rights is not only symbolically expressed, when Carl Wellman classifies them as "possible right-holders", together with normal adults and children (in this order). Their distinction from "alleged right-holders" (among whom he mentions fetuses, the dead, corporations, teams, collections, classes and peoples), results from their actual possession of agency (at least to some extent).[389] That means that to some extent, they are considered as morally responsible for their actions, or that they have some measure of the capacity to act in the light of specifically moral reasons.[390] However, their possession of moral agency is limited, and can be impaired in various ways, and in each way to varying degrees. When Carl Wellman interprets Gewirth's argument that moral rights should be proportional to the possessors' moral agency, he suggests three dimensions: They can possess *fewer* rights; narrower, contracted, rights; or only *partial* rights in comparison with those of normal adults. In addition, there are rights that they may not be able to possess at all.

With regard to the first dimension on which the capacity to possess moral rights, varies with the kind and degree of moral agency of an individual, namely the range of moral rights such an individual can have, Wellman notes that there are so many different and heterogeneous kinds of cognitive limitations, that any simple classification of the rights they might possess or lack, will be insufficient. Some of them can be denied liberty-rights or claim-rights, and the distinction between the different kinds of rights, will not be helpful for deciding which rights mentally retarded persons are entitled to possess, and which are to be denied to them.

With regard to the second dimension, i.e. the scope of the defining content of any right, Wellman says that sometimes mentally retarded persons have the same kind of rights that normal adults possess, but in a narrower range. He illustrates this by saying that someone suffering from a moderate degree of Down's Syndrome has a claim-right to be educated, but the education he has a moral claim to, is considerably less than that to which a normal adult (or even a normal child) has a right to have. The same is true with regard to the rights to freedom of movement of senile persons. They may be capable of moving within their house or neighborhood, but not of moving long distances. A similar case is that of the kleptomaniac's rights to move freely in department stores. It is not the case that his liberty rights are overridden by the vendor's property rights, but that he cannot be said to possess moral control over his movements in such an environment, where he cannot be motivated by the morally relevant facts.

The third dimension concerns the complexity of the rights. This aspect means that a mentally retarded person may be capable of possessing only a portion of the full right that is possessed by a normal adult. We recognize, for example, an adolescent's right to be protected by his parents against serious harm. This includes the moral power to claim for protection when it is not forthcoming, and the moral power to waive such protection when it is not necessary. When this adolescent is mentally retarded, we may recognize his right to claim for protection against harm, but not his power to waive it. So, he has only a portion of the right we ascribe to a normal adolescent.[391]

As a matter of fact, Wellman basically accepts Gewirth's suggestion that the moral rights of mentally retarded persons should be in proportion to their agency. This is also my view. However, there are so many different ways of assessing and evaluating one's agency, that we have to consider each case separately, and regard each right differently between different people. In the coming paragraphs I try to discuss the complexity of this issue, in a little more specific way.

5.5.1 The Freedom Rights Of Mentally Retarded Persons

The most vulnerable domains of mentally retarded person's rights are their rights to non-interference and their rights to freedom. While most of their welfare rights are widely acknowledged as necessary for their survival, and hence valid according to all criteria for conferring rights, their freedom is always subjected to limitations and queries. The basic welfare rights that are necessary for survival are based on the principle, borrowed earlier from Gewirth, that insofar as there is any possibility of attaining moral agency, even to some extent, they have rights to foster their moral abilities. What Gewirth emphasizes is that even if this attainment seems hopeless, they still have rights to be helped to attain as close an approximation as possible of the abilities to attain moral agency.[392] So, we do not have to worry about the acknowledgement of their welfare rights, since they fulfill the minimal subjective requirement for agency, and hence are entitled to the minimal basic rights.

However, their possession of freedom rights is a more complicated issue. Considering that their abilities of being aware of morally relevant facts, and their abilities of being the self-originating source of their valid claims, are partial and limited, the extent to which they are considered as responsible for their actions, is accordingly limited. In Gewirth's terminology we can say that the two generic features of action, purposiveness and voluntariness, are only partially ascribed to mentally retarded persons. With regard to their voluntary behavior, we assume that their control over their behavior does not entirely result from their unforced choice. When considering the purposive aspect of their behavior, we assume that this is not sufficiently directed to achieve certain results and goals. This means that their actions are not carefully directed towards a certain and well-defined purpose, and not always do they use the most effective means to achieve this purpose. In other words, we do not assume that their action is completely free and intentional. This reduces the extent to which they are regarded as prospective-purposive agents, and according to the Principle of Proportionality, they are entitled to possess fewer rights than normal adults.

To illustrate this concept, I turn to the issue of their right to consent to medical treatment. This issue could be discussed with equal relevance to the rights of children, because in both cases we raise some doubts and uncertainties regarding their autonomy, or their ability to make rational choices. With regard to ordinary or physical medical care (and not to their involuntary commitment to mental institutions), we can deal with both children and mentally retarded people in a similar way. In matters of public health we can always take the paternalistic position and force them, for example, to take vaccinations, by using the excuse of the public interest in avoiding epidemics. We do not expect them to respect the public interest, because we do not assume that they fully understand the implications of not being immunized, and we cannot ascribe to them the responsibility for the results of their failure to do so. The public interest can justify the denial of their preferences or will, and the absence of their consent to being immunized. Sometimes, such a justification can even serve for overriding the rights of normal adults to consent to medical treatment, when their refusal may threaten the health of the community.

But what about treatment that cannot be justified by the public interests, but only by the patient's welfare, well-being or quality of life? Can we still force treatment on mentally retarded persons on behalf of their best interests, against their will, or even just without their consent?

Let us begin with cases where a specific treatment is dangerous, and involves risk to the patient's life. In such cases, the consent of normal adults is required whenever possible. In my opinion, this is not so obvious in the case of mentally retarded persons. When such a treatment is necessary only for improving the quality of life, or even for reducing pain and suffering, the consent of the mentally retarded persons is required for this treatment. This is because we respect their personhood and agency, at least to the point that their decisions refer to their well-being or the quality of their lives. Just as we respect a normal adult's decision to keep suffering rather than risk their life, or to abstain from a treatment that improves their condition, we should respect the mentally retarded person's preference, and not deprive him of his rights to decide about the quality of his future life. So long as it does not involve a danger to the patient's life, we cannot use the excuse that he does not have any real insight into the nature of his illness, and consequently is unable to appreciate what can be done for the relief of his suffering.[393] We must relate to the mentally retarded as persons or individuals, which means that we accept their preferences even when these are not compatible with ours, just as we respect the decisions of other normal adults. In addition, we cannot risk the patient's life against his will or even without his consent. We know that normal adults also sometimes refuse to have certain treatments that involve risks or physical pain, even when these adults are fully aware of all the consequences of their decisions. We can assume that even if the mentally retarded person would understand all the relevant considerations, he might also decide not to have that treatment. This is true even when the treatment is necessary to prevent a crippling or even a long-term serious illness, just as it is in the case of normal adults. The rationale of this position is that we assume that is of ultimate value that every person (even a mentally retarded one) has the right and authority to decide on his or her quality of life. We must not interfere with this decision, since it is this person himself who will suffer the consequences of that decision, for better or for worse. If *we* make the decision for someone, *we* become responsible for the suffering and pain that he will undergo.

However, this may not be true when such a treatment is crucial for saving the mentally retarded person's life. We said earlier, regarding the quotation from Gewirth, that if there is any possibility that a human being will attain the moral abilities of agency, he has rights to the fostering of these abilities. In cases when such attainment seems hopeless, he still has rights to be helped to attain as close an approximation of these abilities as possible. If we let such a patient die, we have failed in our correlative duty to help him attain the moral abilities of agency by destroying the necessary conditions for him to aspire to agency – that his, his life. In this case, we might force him to accept the required medical care that may save his life. We believe that his right to make his own decisions, is outweighed by other considerations, such as the community's duty to protect the lives of its members.

The above case seems reasonable and acceptable to most people, even those whose principal concern are the rights of mentally retarded persons. The more complicated cases are those where treatment is not intended to save the patient's *life*, but instead, to significantly improve the patient's *quality* of life, or substantially reduce his pains or disabilities. Here we cannot use the argument that to deny the treatment would risk his life. On the other hand, a minor deprivation of his rights may help him to improve his quality of life and hence, perhaps attain the requisite abilities of agency (in cases where such attainment does not seem hopeless). Even when the results of such a treatment may be only a temporary relief of the patient's pain, and the patient – without any apparent reason – is afraid to undergo it, we have to determine whether there is a duty to force him to undergo such compulsory treatment. When we examine the same case with normal adults, there is no doubt that we must respect their choice, even if it does not make any sense to us. Does the fact that we deal with a mentally retarded patient, give us the authority to deny his right to consent, on behalf of his interests? My opinion is that the mentally retarded person's right to consent to medical treatment, remains valid in all cases (except where such treatment is necessary for survival). Generally, we should not take a paternalistic stance and say that their health interests override their autonomy – although this is exactly what we do with underage children. This is because in the case of children, we take the paternalistic position only temporarily, until the children become mature and full-fledged members of the moral community. At the end of their maturation, they become responsible for their choices and their future. Mentally retarded persons, on the other hand, may never become completely independent, and therefore we should only interfere with their choices when their behavior becomes a danger to any member of the community including themselves. We must entrust the opportunity to affect their future into their hands, as much as is possible. Of course there are levels of mental disabilities, and sometimes a severely mentally retarded person can hardly make any choice at all, so we might have to treat him as a child. Nevertheless, whenever he expresses any sign of dissatisfaction or refuses medical treatment, we should respect his preferences as much as possible.

When Tom Campbell and Chris Heginbotham suggest some non-discriminatory paternalistic rules for interventions restricting liberty, they require that the individual whose liberty might be restricted, would fall into one of the following two categories:

> "1. non competent, that is unable to make decisions on his own behalf due to a general lack of understanding of the nature or significance of his actions or inactions in relation to his own well-being; and
>
> 2. needs care or assistance of a type which normally requires the consent of the individual; and
>
> 3. such care and attention is in his best interest;
>
> *or*
>
> 1. at substantial risk of serious physical harm, or enduring suffering; because
>
> 2. either he is unable to appreciate the nature and degree of the harm or suffering in question, or holds a manifestly false

> belief or beliefs on account of which he is unwilling to adopt or accept measures which would avoid or alleviate them; and
> 3. he can be protected of such harm or suffering by the proposed intervention; and
> 4. the proposed intervention is not more intrusive than is necessary to protect him from the harm or suffering".[394]

Campbell and Heginbotham think that the first alternative permits "weak paternalism", that is, substituted consent in the cases of people who cannot give their consent because of incapacity. According to their view, this is relatively unproblematic.[395] The second alternative involves "strong paternalism". In this case we override someone's expressed refusal – someone who has only partial understanding of the situation – to accept the compulsory treatment or service. In this alternative, Campbell and Heginbotham tend to limit intervention only to extreme situations, in which the consequences of non-intervention are very grave. Another condition which justifies intervention, is that the mentally retarded person refuses treatment because of reasons that "are evidently based on incontrovertibly false premises".[396]

I have some difficulties in accepting this view, because we sometimes see that even those whom we consider "competent" or "able to make decisions on their own behalf", refuse the same treatments, and apparently act against their best interests. Even the first alternative, the "weak paternalism" that substitutes consent when there is no expressed objection, may sometimes distort the patient's preference. After all, consent is a positive act that means taking a position towards something. We may misinterpret the situation if we take for granted that the patient would have consented if he were aware of the risks and dangers involved. In my opinion, the only factor that should justify a paternalistic approach is the risk of death. Under all other circumstances, we should be as careful to obtain the consent of mentally retarded persons, as we are with the consent of normal adults to medical treatment.

In order to show how complicated is the discussion about the rights of mentally retarded persons, I devote the rest of this chapter to one of the most controversial and painful issues in rights-talk. This refers to the parental rights of mentally retarded people. I elucidate my approach to this thorny issue even though it is clear to me that there are no magic solutions or conclusions that could satisfy everyone equally.

5.5.2 The Parental Rights Of Mentally Retarded Persons

One of the difficult questions which raises intense emotional reactions is whether mentally retarded people have the right to bear children. This question involves children, the status of parenthood, the responsibility of the community for the safety and welfare of its members, the power of the authorities to control internal family relations, and other thorny issues; therefore it is highly doubtful that we can reach the perfect solution. No matter what conclusions we reach, there will always remain doubts as to whether the conclusions are sufficiently humane, fair, just or optimal. I prefer to deal with only two aspects of this complicated question.

The single issue above actually includes at least two separate issues, that should be distinguished and discussed separately. Even though they both concern reproduction rights, they apply to different aspects of these rights, and require different considerations for answering them. The first is the question whether mentally retarded people have the right to procreate, in the sense of being allowed to produce babies. In the case of women, this question can be further sub-divided into two questions: whether they have the right to become pregnant (i.e. to retain their fertility), and whether they are to be allowed to complete their pregnancy. I prefer to deal with these two questions together, and to include each of them under the more general title "the right to become pregnant". Another question is whether mentally retarded people who have children, should be allowed to care for them with some limitations, or whether they must give them up for adoption to other parents, or to educational institutions in which the children can grow up safely. This question also encompasses additional issues, such as the authority's obligation to guide such parents, the measure of autonomy that such parents should retain (issues which are controversial even when discussing normal parents). Here too, I refer to these additional issues as part of a single principal question, and not separately.

I start with the first question. Arguing that mentally retarded people have no right to reproduction, demands that we either prohibit them from having sexual intercourse or sterilize them. Both acts are considered inhuman, since they deny the mentally retarded people their bodily integrity and their freedom of choice. These are fundamental elements of being an individual, and to deny them is tantamount to denying their personhood. Prohibiting something that is considered pleasureful and recreative to someone, or mutilating them, does not only strike at their bodily integrity, it also denies part of their self-respect, self-esteem and even self-determination. Such an intrusion cannot be tolerable. We employed a similar argument in our discussion of abortions, namely that the reproductive rights of people consist not only of the right to have children but also the right to abstain from pregnancy. We apply this to our present context by asserting that: just as it is prohibited to *force* people to reproduce, so it is prohibited to *prevent* them from reproducing.[397] We can cast light on this issue by comparing compulsory sterilization (and occasionally castration), to coercing a pregnant woman to abort. Both cases involve an offensive invasive interference in a person's procreation rights, and strike at the basic liberties that all human beings share.

There is broad acknowledgement that the state has a duty not to interfere with the freedom to reproduce, and that it should not interfere with choices about reproduction.[398] Sheila McLean identifies the core of the right to reproduce in two interrelated ways. First, she maintains that the person's capacities to reproduce are subject to her exercise, and may not be interfered with. Second, it is the woman who may choose whether or not to exercise her existing capacities.[399]

We must have some very significant reasons in order to justify the withdrawal of such a basic liberty as the right to reproduce. It is not enough to argue that the common welfare or the interests of the society as a whole, overrides the rights of mentally retarded individuals to reproduce. Just as we refuse to force people to reproduce in the interests of expanding society, so we reject the fear of overpopulation from serving as justifying grounds for the withdrawal of the rights to reproduction. We evaluate people's rights to reproduction, at least those which directly refer to their basic liberties, as much more important than any interest of the community.

When we say that a woman has a right to reproduction, and that she is free to choose whether or not to exercise this right, it is the community's duty to provide her with all the necessities for exercising this right. This includes fertility treatments, when necessary, or even artificial insemination, or in-vitro fertilization. However, there can arise some situations where the community is unable to provide these expensive treatments; for example, financial constraints, even when referring to fertility problems of normal adults. However, any compulsory interference is strictly illegitimate. When the community cannot respond to the claims of all its members, to exercise the rights to reproduction (because of financial constraints, or not having enough sperm donations), it has to decide who will receive the treatment, and who will be denied treatment. Of course, the most egalitarian and equal path might be to deny treatment to *all* the members, but this is the worst approach of using limited resources.

In a situation where resources are insufficient to satisfy all needs, we can apply the criterion of the measure or extent of membership in the moral community. The community can assess the level to which each of the applicants fulfills the requirements of membership in the community, and accordingly decide who gets the treatment. Only in such cases, can the community decide to grant preference to the rights of normal adults, over those of mentally retarded people, because the former possess a higher level of membership in the community. We justify denying the latter's rights by saying that the addressee (the community) is unable to respond to their valid claims. In such a situation, though it might seem cruel, the community has the right to favor claims of one person (normal adult) over the claims of another (mentally retarded adult).

It is morally defensible to withdraw the reproduction rights of mentally retarded persons only from a consideration of the interests of other individuals (in this case, the reproduction claims of other persons), and not from considerations of the common good or the public interest. This leads me to conclude that sterilization or castration of mentally retarded people should be strictly prohibited as immoral, because there cannot be any justification for striking at a person's rights to bodily integrity. This cannot be any other person's direct or indirect interest. The same prohibition is relevant for the other alternatives of denying mentally retarded persons the ability to reproduce, even with (almost) the same justification. Under no circumstances can we prohibit mentally retarded people from having sexual intercourse. No one's interest can override their right to enjoy sex (with the consent of both partners), just as is true for normal adults. In addition, I cannot see any moral way to force mentally retarded people to use contraceptives, because respecting their freedom – as part of their agency – binds us to respect their choice of not using contraceptives. I conclude that mentally retarded people can conceive or procreate, just like any normal adult, because I cannot find any moral justification for preventing mentally retarded people from exercising these rights. Preventing them could only be justified, if exercising their rights to procreate would clash with someone else's rights, and this cannot happen: it happens only in the positive sense of the community's duty to assist women to become pregnant, and having to decide who gets priority in this assistance.

The second issue deals with the rights of mentally retarded people to bring up their children (or even to adopt and bring up other people's children), and this is a much more complex issue that is connected to a completely different set of considerations. This is because we deal now with a new entity: the babies that are born to mentally retarded people. As I explained in the context of the discussion on abortion, fetuses have a lower moral status than their mothers, and as such, less weight is accorded to their claims and interests. This, however, drastically changes after birth, when fetuses become infants whose personhood is not under doubt, and hence, whose interests should be strictly respected. When these interests conflict with their (mentally retarded) parents' rights, there is a crucial conflict that involves serious moral dilemmas.

When we discuss whether mentally retarded people have the right to bring them up their own children, the only relevant considerations are those which involve their own interests and the interests of other individuals, not the community's or certain institutions' interests. Hence, answering this question should concentrate on the conflict between the rights of parents to keep their child, and the interests of the child. The most relevant interests are those which Joel Feinberg identifies as "*C Rights*". These rights are characteristic of children and usually originate from the child's dependence upon others for the basic necessities of life: food, shelter and protection. However, besides these dependency rights, children have also special rights that they will be able to exercise only in the future, but have to be maintained for the children's future autonomy. Feinberg calls them "rights in trust", and sums them up as the single "right to an open future".[400] I interpret this as the right to "healthy well-rounded growth into full maturity as citizens, with all that this implies in a democracy".[401] This is to say that a child has the right to be well-protected, well-educated, physically and mentally nurtured, and to acquire all the cognitive and mental abilities that are necessary for maturation.

When discussing the child's right to an open future, Feinberg notes that:

> "The existence of such a right...sets limits to the ways in which parents may rear their own children, and even imposes duties on the state, in its role as *parens patriae*, to enforce those limits".[402]

Among parental duties, Feinberg deals in detail with the parents' obligation to rear their child in such a way that promotes her self-fulfillment. Accordingly, they have to give her opportunities to develop her talents, to discover, through various experiences, what exactly those talents are, etc. They should steer the child towards the type of career that complements her personality or temperament, rather than a career that will force her to change her temperament.[403] In sum, they should provide her all the necessities for becoming a happy, productive moral citizen, who is well involved and integrated into her community.

Respecting the rights of children vis-a-vis their parents means that the community is responsible for seeing to it that parents provide their children with all the necessities for them to achieve growth and maturity. Feinberg asserts that the community has a duty to force parents to provide the above requirements for the fulfillment of the children's rights to an open future.

Such intervention is necessary to guarantee the rights of children, who are partial members, so that by the time they become full-fledged members, they are fully equipped with all the qualifications and abilities that are required for enjoying the common good, and bearing the burdens that are imposed on the shoulders of members.

A major part of children's rights to an open future is satisfied by their parents' efforts in their own homes (for example, linguistic competence). In cases where the parents are incapable of providing these skills, it is the community's duty to intervene, in order to protect the children's rights. This does not necessarily mean taking the children away from their parents – an act which would brutally strike at the parental rights of the parents, and can be justified only in very extreme cases, where the child's safety or security is in danger. It does, however, mean that the community has to provide all the necessities for the children's decent development and growth, which may include economic aid and necessary guidance to the parents, in order to enable them to fulfill the children's rights. Only in cases where even the community's assistance cannot help parents rear their children appropriately (for example, when the mentally retarded parents are extremely low-functioning), can the community remove the children from the parents. This would include those cases in which leaving the children with their parents would endanger their future, whether the danger is of a physical, cognitive or psychological character.

Therefore, the only justification for such interference can be the children's interests and nothing else. Intervention is justified when the community evaluates the children's rights as overriding the parent's rights, and there is no way to effect a compromise between the conflicting claims. In other words, the parents' rights should be fully respected, unless they strike at the children's rights. In cases where the parents' rights *can* be respected without violating those of the children (even at a high financial cost to the community), the community has to enable the capitalization of these parental rights.

I will clarify this idea by comparing parental rights to other rights of mentally retarded persons. If, for example, a mentally retarded person can learn to read and write (a basic right of even partial members of the community, including children), but only at significant financial cost to the community, then the community must pay this price to enable the person to capitalize on his right. In this sense, this person's parental rights are not different. They must be respected even at high costs. Similarly, in our previous discussion regarding abortions, we said that if there is a way to respect both the mother's and the fetus' rights (for example, aborting the fetus in a very advanced stage of pregnancy, when the fetus can survive outside the mother's body), we have to choose this alternative. The same idea is implemented here. If we can leave the child with her parents (thus respecting their parental rights), and guarantee the child's right to an open future (by appropriate guidance to her parents), we must prefer this option. However, when there is a forced-choice situation we must prefer the child's rights, just as in the standard cases of abortion, we prefer the mother's rights to the fetus. That is because the child can develop into a full-fledged agent, while her parents (who are mentally retarded) will never reach this status. We usually assume that the accumulated harm that will be caused to the child if she grows up with her mentally retarded parents, will be *less* than the harm that will be caused to her parents, if the child is be taken away from them to a foster home or adoptive parents.

I do not pretend to be able to clearly define those situations where the child's right to an open future is guaranteed, or to evaluate when parents are competent enough to bring up their children. All I want to show is that right-based considerations can provide guidelines for resolving such conflicts, with the assistance of experts who provide the relevant information about the parents' competence for parenthood, and the educational requirements of the children. In any event, we must consider the interests of all the individuals who are involved in such conflicts, and decide according to our judgment of the weight to be given to each interest. In this context, we have to remember that even mentally retarded persons are members in the community, even though they are not fully-fledged members. As such, their rights should be respected as much as possible, even at great cost to the community. The withdrawal of their rights can be justified only when the fulfillment of these rights strikes at others' interests, and there is no other way to respect the interests of both sides.

5.6 SUMMARY

In this chapter I discussed the primary cases of the denial of rights. These are the cases in which rights are denied to particular persons who have the potential of being members of the community. Unlike the previous chapter, where the withdrawal of rights from certain members results from the non-fulfillment of their obligations as members of the community, in the cases discussed in this chapter the possible members are not involved in any immoral activity. In this sense they are considered innocent, and as having no evil intentions. This should entitle them, under normal conditions, full membership in the community. Accordingly, they should enjoy the rights that are conferred upon other members.

However, their "entry ticket" to the community, that is the fulfillment of the subjective requirements for agency (or the generic features of action: voluntariness and purposiveness), is only partly valid. They do not possess the mental, cognitive and rational capacities that are required for full-fledged agency, in sufficient quantity. Hence, they are denied some rights, permanently or temporarily, in order to adjust their actual possession of rights to their entitlement, or to their level of membership in the community.

The first issue that was examined was children's rights. Their welfare and socialization rights are fully acknowledged. The essence of these rights was termed by Joel Feinberg as "the right to an open future". Since we ascribe to children only limited responsibility and limited choice, we therefore limit some of their liberty rights and their rights to noninterference. However, these rights are only temporarily denied. As children mature they gradually acquire more and more rights and liberties, according to their development, and their fulfillment of the required capacities for agency. The end of this process is maturation, when they are acknowledged as full-fledged members of the community, and enjoy all the rights that are bestowed upon moral agents.

The second issue is that of the rights of fetuses, and particularly in the context of the morality of abortion. This issue is examined on two different levels. One of them is not directly involved with the possession of rights, but with the sanctity of human life. Hence it was not discussed in detail. The main objection on this level was based on the claim that abortion strikes at the sacred value of human life, because the fetus is considered to be a human being. The answer to this argument is based on Dworkin's analysis of the origins of the sacred or intrinsic value of life. According to Dworkin, this sacredness results from both natural and human investments in human life, that together make it sacred. The human investments in human life include values such as liberty and self-determination. These values should also be respected as part of the pregnant woman's life, and hence, we have to respect her freedom, her rights to bodily integrity and to self-determination, which are components of the sanctity of every human being's life. When we ascribe more weight to the human investments in human life than to the natural ones, we can justify abortion as showing respect to the sacred components of the woman's life.

The second level was to examine the matter of abortion as a conflict between the mother's rights and the fetus' right to life. Those who oppose abortions (extreme Restrictivists or Pro-Lifers) argue that a fetus, as a human being, is a person from the moment of conception, and hence has the right to life. Abortion violates this right by terminating this life, and hence is morally prohibited. Besides extreme Restrictivists, there are those who ascribe personhood to a fetus only at later stages of pregnancy, and allow abortion before these stages (whether it is when the fetus becomes sentient or viable, etc.). Those who hold such positions were called Moderates. The third group consists of those who permit abortion at any stage of pregnancy, and these are called Permissivists (or Pro Choicers). Some Permissivists argue that a fetus does not possess rights, because it cannot be considered as a person before birth. Others argue that even if the fetus does possess rights, the mother's rights override those of the fetus, and hence, abortion is legitimate. I support this position, saying that since both the rights of mother and fetus cannot be respected simultaneously, I prefer to respect the mother's rights, because she possesses a higher moral status in the community, and hence her claims get more weight than those of the fetus. However, I just noted that the right to abort does not directly legitimate the killing of the fetus, and its death is only an inevitable and unavoidable result of abortion. So, if there is a way to save the fetus's life after the abortion (in the case of a very late abortion), the community has to respect this right. The most important issue which is acknowledged by *all* the parties of this debate, is that abortion should never be forced on a woman against her will, even when her life is in danger. Her ultimate control over her body and life must never be taken away from her.

The third issue discussed in this chapter is the rights of mentally retarded persons. The discussion about their liberty rights "borrowed" some assumptions from the case of children's rights, because in both cases, we ascribe to them only limited responsibility and autonomy (or dominion in Wellman's terminology). Accordingly, we deny them some of their liberty rights. However, there is a principal difference between children and mentally retarded persons, which has significant effects on our consideration of their rights. This difference concerns the duration of our denial of rights from members of these groups. While children's rights are temporarily denied, the rights of mentally retarded persons are usually permanently denied. This difference obliges us to be much more careful with the denial of the rights of mentally retarded persons, because such a denial is usually permanent.

In order to show how complicated and painful this issue is, I presented two troubling problems, which involve the rights of mentally retarded persons. The first was their right to consent to medical treatment. In this context I argued that their rights should be respected almost at the same level as those of normal adults, and when they refuse their consent, we are not allowed to force treatment upon them. The only cases that do not require their consent are those treatments which are necessary for saving their lives. This is because the community is responsible for assuring the necessary condition for their agency, that is their life. This results from the community's duty to enable their agency, in order to enable them to exercise any right in the future.

The second question that was discussed regarding this matter is whether mentally retarded persons have reproduction rights. This question is subdivided into two different questions. The first is the question whether they have the right to procreate, in the sense of giving birth to babies. The answer to this question was absolutely positive, and this means that any attempt to deny them of having sexual intercourse is evil. The same is with any attempt to sterilize or to castrate them, or even to force them to use contraceptives. Respecting their reproduction rights, which are part of their rights to self-determination, entails that the community should not interfere with their decisions. I insist that any denial of their reproduction rights can be justified only when these rights conflict with the rights of other individuals.

The additional question was whether mentally retarded people who have children, have the right to bring them up by themselves. The answer here is more complicated, because a new factor appears: the rights of the infants after birth. As future members of the moral community, they possess certain rights, to acquire the necessary capabilities and qualifications for being productive and involved members in the community. Most of these abilities are developed at the children's homes, and imparting them is part of the parental obligations that their parents bear. When their parents are incapable of fulfilling the children's rights, it is the community's duty to assist them to bear these obligations. By doing so, the community both helps the parents to exercise their parental rights, and protects the children's interests.

However, when assistance of the community cannot guarantee the children's healthy physical, mental and psychological development, the community has to consider taking children away from their parents. This should be used only as a last resort, because it brutally strikes at the parents' rights, and should be carried out only in forced-choice situations, where there is no way to simultaneously respect both the parents' and the children's rights. In any event, the justification for taking children away from their parents can be based only on children's rights, and not on any other grounds. When there is a opportunity to respect both the mentally retarded parents' rights as well as the children's rights, this option should decisively be chosen. We have to respect the mentally retarded person's rights, to the highest level we can, so long as this respect does not strike at the rights of other individuals. When there is a conflict between their parental rights and the rights of others, we must resolve this conflict fairly, and according to the principles that serve in any conflict between rights. These principles require the assessing of the moral status of each possessor, the weight of her rights and the capabilities of her exercising her rights. We should never immediately sacrifice the mentally retarded persons' rights, before we consider the moral aspects of the decision.

CONCLUSIONS

Like most discussions within the tradition of rights-talk, this study is motivated by the desire to promote the idea that rights are moral assets that people should acquire in the course of their membership within their social and political framework. The goal of this study is to enable as many people as possible to enjoy as many rights as possible to the highest degree, and to minimize the possibility of unjustified violation of their rights.

However, while most participants in rights-talk concentrate on the safety and protection constraints required for a successful exercising of rights, the present study has inquired into the circumstances under which people's rights lose their validity. I believe that if we want to prevent the erosion of the role of rights within society and to encourage their obligatory status, we must prevent their misuse, or their unjustified or excessive use. We must maintain stringent watch on the fulfillment of the conditions of possession of rights, in order to strengthen the ability of those who justifiably possess rights, to enjoy them, and to reinforce the obligation of the community to prevent unjustified possession of rights by its members.

In any event, in order to define how rights can lose their validity, we must first sketch our concept of rights and our conceptual framework, within which rights acquire their validity. This framework defines the relations between the different moral concepts that create our concept of a right, as well as its moral and obligatory status. It also defines the relations between all the components of a right, such as the possessor, the respondent, and the community.

In general, this study shares the widely held position that rights exist within a normative system, which establishes their validity, scope and power. The concept of rights that is preferred is the one which Joel Feinberg calls "valid claims", and stresses the fact that rights are justified within a system of rules. Another characteristic of this concept is that the possession of rights includes the possession of all the necessary requirements for capitalizing on them, as integral parts of the possession of those rights.

This communitarian approach towards rights is central to both the possession and the withdrawal of rights within the community. According to my view, there are two sets of requirements a person needs to fulfill in order to possess rights. One is "subjective", and relates to the person's perceptual, cognitive and metal abilities. The fulfillment of these requirements entitles the person to an "entry ticket" to the moral community, in which this person can possess rights. The second set of requirements is "communitarian" and relates to the person's fulfillment of his obligations as a member of the community, by following the shared normative conventions, principles and rules that define the moral community, which acknowledges the person's interests and claims as rights. The fulfillment of the second set requires mutuality and reciprocity between the members in all their transactions within the common social framework. The exact measure of the actual possession of rights by a particular member, is proportional to the extent to which this member fulfills the two sets of requirements.

The community, in this view, functions as a guarantor of its members' rights. Since we want the actual measure of a member's possession of rights to be conditional and proportionate to the actual fulfillment of the above requirements, we need the community to regulate and adjust this measure. Whenever there is an incompatibility between a member's entitlement to have a certain measure of rights, and the actual measure of possession, we expect the community to rectify this by matching the correct measure of rights to the member's entitlement. Thus, when a member possesses fewer rights than she deserves, the community must bestow upon her the missing rights. On the other hand, when she possesses more rights than she is entitled to possess, the community must take away the excessive rights from her. This lays the foundations for my view of the withdrawal of rights.

In this study I argue that it is the acknowledgement of the moral community that authorizes the validity of a person's claims, and hence their consideration as rights. This acknowledgement is conditional on the fulfillment of certain requirements, and the extent to which these requirements are fulfilled determines the extent to which the person is allowed to possess rights. When the community decides that one or some of these requirements are not sufficiently fulfilled, the possessor's entitlement to keep his rights is reduced, and the range, scope or power of these rights may be reduced or canceled accordingly. In such cases, it is the community's obligation to withdraw the excessive part of the exercising of these rights, or even to completely withdraw particular rights.

The assessment of a member's entitlement to possess certain rights according to the fulfillment of certain conditions, can be used also for settling conflicts between different rights or different possessors. When the community needs to resolve such conflicts, it examines the extent to which each party is entitled to possess its rights under the new circumstances, and reaches its decision accordingly. In this sense, the community uses rights as "a final court of appeal for ordering the conflicting claims of moral persons" just as John Rawls defines rights.

In any event, the community has a crucial role in ordering the rights and obligations of its members. Thus, the community is not only the framework within which the concept of a right gets validity and becomes applicable, but also guarantees that the possessors of rights will be able to successfully exercise or capitalize on them. This imposes on the community the duty to intervene and use its authority, whenever a possessor is unable to exercise her rights, and help her to enjoy what she is entitled to. On the other hand, the community must also intervene whenever a member exercises a right that she was not entitled to have under the specific circumstances. If she misuses her right, the community must prevent this abuse by withdrawing at least the excessive part of her use.

Among many different matters that were raised in this study, I wish to recall two of the principal issues that were discussed.

A. The first is the topic that has been my main interest, which is the question of the withdrawal of rights. I believe that the concept of rights has been comprehensively accepted not only in contemporary literature, but also in most modern societies. Here I fully agree with Alan Gewirth, who thinks that we, in contemporary times, are capable of judging moral actions and practices in terms of their consideration of the rights of individuals.[404] The significance of possessing rights in contemporary societies plays a central role when making moral, social and political decisions. Thus, the main goal of both theorists and human-rights activists should be to ensure that people are aware of their rights and are able to exercise them. In order to achieve this aim, our efforts should focus on two complementary procedures, both of which are motivated by the same desire to enable people to realize and make use of their rights to the highest possible degree. The first procedure should be to determine and define the contents, range, grounds of validity, duration, limits and boundaries of those interests that we think should be acknowledged as rights. The second procedure should be the determination of the guarantees and safeties that are required to protect the rights that are specified in the first procedure.

This study has devoted itself largely to the first of the above procedures. It skips the stage of justifying the necessity of rights for contemporary society, assuming that the role and significance of their possession are widely accepted. However, it is crucial that we determine the extent, range, limits and boundaries of the possession of rights, in order to protect and secure these rights from invasive attempts. We must also define the conditions under which the rights are valid, as well as when the rights expire, in order to refer to them when ordering conflicting claims of moral persons[405]. The first set of conditions defines the appropriate possession of rights, namely the identity of the possessors, the conditions of possession and engagement, the range, the identity of addressee, etc. The second set defines the conditions and circumstances where rights do not apply, and should not be exercised. The main focus of this study has been the investigation of those cases where rights should *not* be possessed or should be denied to their possessors. I think that the desire to guarantee that people who are entitled to enjoy certain rights will be able to exercise them, is directly tied to the appropriate use of these rights. The denial of certain rights to those who are not entitled to possess them, increases the ability of the others to enjoy their rights, and attaches additional significance and value to the possession of rights. If we will be strict and stringent about the appropriate use of rights, and withdraw those rights that are unjustifiably possessed or exercised, this will force us to be equally determined with regard to the fulfillment of the justified use of rights. A serious and sincere approach towards rights obliges us to be determined and decisive when we allocate rights and duties within the community. This should apply both to the possession of rights as well as to their withdrawal. Repudiating this obligation will erode and weaken the moral status of a possessor of rights, and may decrease the possibility of her enjoying rights within the community. Hence, I ascribe an equal significance to the possession of rights by those who justifiably possess them, and to the withdrawal of rights from those who are not entitled to possess or exercise these rights. Even though the literature deals mainly with the possession of rights, I think that their withdrawal should receive the same amount of attention and appreciation. This study is my modest contribution to this line of thought.

B. The second issue I want to evoke in the conclusion of the present study, is the significance and the function of the moral community for the solidity and applicability of rights within itself. The concept of a person in modern life is almost inseparable from that person's social interactions, and sometimes is even established by the person's social transactions. This concept of personhood refers to people's understanding of themselves as belonging to the same reference group, or the same social framework or moral community. Almost every action carried out by an agent is directed towards other members of the community, affects their lives, and often involves their responses or reactions. Hence, a significant aspect of the identity of persons is created by their social and communal relations and connections. In addition to this, the main part of their individual rights is claimed against the community. Some of these rights are considered by Gewirth as necessary conditions for agency; for example, the rights to well-being, or some elementary welfare rights. If we really mean that every agent has a right to basic needs (such as health treatment or education) and to some measure of freedom, we must presume that a correlative duty is imposed on the community, to recognize and grant these rights. Without the backing of the community, many agents would not be able to enjoy their basic rights or even to take part in any kind of social interaction. . Imposing the duty to provide members with all the means to exercise their rights, including all the guarantees that are required for the fulfillment of these rights, ensures the durability of members' rights, and their capability of exercising these rights. However, sometimes there are cases where protecting a given person's rights, requires that the community withdraw the rights of other persons, who unjustifiably possess more rights than they are entitled. Not infrequently, the rights of a given person unavoidably conflict with the rights of the others, and it is the community that has to decide which rights take precedence over the others, or which rights are invalid. There are also cases where two conflicting rights are partly (or even fully) valid, but cannot be fulfilled simultaneously, and the community has to decide which one overrides the other. In all these cases the community must have the authority to change the moral status of the possessors, and to regulate and adjust the distribution of rights and duties within the community. This will guarantee the appropriate use of rights and the correct fulfillment of duties.

Reduction of the community's role in allocating rights and duties, will strike at the mutuality and reciprocity between its members, and will significantly reduce their welfare, quality of life, security and freedom. I think that even for the interests of the individuals themselves, it is better to define an individual's interests within an acknowledged social framework, which protects these interests and guarantees their fulfillment. Even when we wish to emphasize the rights of individuals, we are inevitably forced to be concerned with the solidarity and fraternity between people. Thus we must encourage the communal tendencies of human life, and the common aspects of social interaction. Over-emphasizing the individualistic aspects of human life will lead to estrangement and alienation between people, while emphasizing their shared and common destiny will lead to unity and harmony. Thus, the preferred approach to human rights is the understanding of a moral person as a member of the moral community. I hope that this study will make its modest contribution to the understanding of people as cooperating in the same moral community, rather than merely coexisting in the same living space.

Since this study is another link in the long-lasting tradition of rights-talk, I want to make a final comment on the significance of its continuity. The intensity of modern life and society very often sweeps away the interests of individuals, and sacrifices them for the sake of modernization or progress. Questions regarding certain elementary necessities of individuals, or conflicts between opposing interests, may face the risk of being subjected to considerations of social utility. And the risk of the social utility outlook is that the solutions of conflicts may lose their human dimension. The interests of individuals may be trampled on by the desire for progress and advancement. If we are sincere in our desire to protect the interests of the weak, needy or vulnerable persons in our society, we must organize the social framework on the basis of a just distribution of rights and duties. The function of rights-talk should be the continuing reassessment of the balance between people's *entitlement* to rights, and their actual *possession* of rights. This may help to provide the appropriate justification for allocating rights in society, and to make their distribution more just and appropriate to our moral and social overview. Hence, the development of rights-talk should concentrate on finding solutions to thorny issues, as well as elaborating people's consciousness of their own and others' human rights. The philosophical clarification and development of rights-talk, can, I hope, be regarded as a contribution to the general struggle for human rights. In this way, what might be otherwise regarded as something merely theoretical can come to be respected as a participation in something which is very practical, and which seems to me to be of great significance in the improvement of the human condition.

REFERENCES

Aiken Henry David. "Rights, Human And Otherwise". In: *The Monist*. Vol. 52. No. 4. October 1986. pp. 502-520.

Alexy Robert. "Rights, Legal Reasoning And Rational Discourse". In: *Ratio Jurris*. Vol. 5. NO. 2. July 1992. pp. 143-152.

Archard David. *Children. Rights And Childhood.* Routledge. London. 1993.

Audi Robert. *The C ambridge Dictionary Of Philosophy.* Cambridge University Press. Cambridge. 1995.

Baier K. "Is Punishment Retributive?". In: *Analysis*. Vol. 16. No. 2. December 1955. pp. 25-32.

Baird Robert M. & Rosenbaum Stuart E. (eds.). *Philosophy Of Punishment.* Prometheus Books. Buffalo, New York. 1988.

Baird Robert M. & Rosenbaum Stuart E. (eds.). *The Ethics Of Abortion.* Prometheus Books. Buffalo, New York. 1989.

Baker Judith. *Group Rights.* University Of Toronto Press. Toronto. 1994.

Bankowski Zenon And MacCormick Neil, (eds.). *Enlightenment, Rights And Revolution.* Aberdeen University Press. 1989.

Barzun Jacques. "In Favor Of Capital Punishment". In: Rachels James. (ed.) *Moral Problems. A Collection Of Philosophical Essays.* Third Edition. Harper & Row. New York. 1979. pp. 353-364.

Bayles Michael. "Hart VS. Dworkin". In: *Law And Philosophy*. No. 10. 1991. pp. 349-381.

Becker Lawrence C. And Becker Charlotte B.(eds). *Encyclopedia Of Ethics*. St. James Press. London. 1992.

Bedau Hugo Adam. "Capital Punishment". In: Becker Lawrence C. And Becker Charlotte B. (eds). *Encyclopedia Of Ethics*. St. James Press. London. 1992. pp. 122-125.

Benjamin Marlene. "Moral Theory And Human Rights: Sheffler On Structure And Content". In: *Dialogue*. XXXI. No. 2. Spring/Printemps 1992. pp. 273-293.

Benn S.I. "An Approach To The Justification Of Punishment". In: *Philosophy*. Vol. 33. No. 127. October 1958. pp. 325-341.

Benn Stanley I. "Rights". In: Eduards Paul. (ed). *Encyclopedia Of Philosophy.* New York. 1967. Vol. 7. pp. 191-195.

Benn Stanley I. "Human Rights—For Whom And For What?" In: Kamenka Eugene And Tay Erh-Soon Alice (eds.) *Human rights*. Eduard Arnold. London. 1978. pp. 59-73.

Berlin Isaiah. *Four Essays On Liberty*. Oxford University Press. Oxford. 1969.

Berns Walter. "The Morality Of Anger". In: Baird Robert M. & Rosenbaum Stuart E. (eds). *Philosophy Of Punishment.* Prometheus Books. Buffalo, New York. 1988. pp. 85-93.

Blackstone W.T. "Equality And Human Rights". In : *The Monist.* Vol. 52. No. 4. October 1968. pp. 616-639.

Blackstone W.T. "Human Rights And Human Dignity". In: *The Philosophical Forum.* Vol. 3. 1971. pp. 3-37.

Brandt Richard B. *A Theory Of The Good And The Right.* Clarendon Press. Oxford. 1979.

Brandt Richard B. *Morality, Utilitarianism And Rights*. Cambridge University Press. Cambridge. 1992.

Bricke John. (Ed.). *Freedom & Morality*. University Of Kansas Humanistic Studies. Lawrence. 1976.

Brown Stuart M. Jr. Inalienable Rights. In: *The Philosophical Review*. Volume LXIV. Number 2. April 1955. pp. 192-211.

Callahan Joan C. "The Fetus And Fundamental Rights". In: Baird Robert M. & Rosenbaum Stuart E. (eds.). *The Ethics Of Abortion*. Prometheus Books. Buffalo, New York. 1989. pp. 115-129.

Campbell Tom. *The Left And Rights*. Routledge & Kegan Paul. London 1983.

Campbell Tom, Goldberg David, Mclean Sheila, Mullen Tom. (eds). *Human Rights: From Rhetoric To Reality*. Basil Blackwell. Oxford. 1986.

Campbell Tom. "The Rights Of The Mentally Ill". in: Campbell Tom, Goldberg David, Mclean Sheila, Mullen Tom. (eds). *Human Rights: From Rhetoric To Reality*. Basil Blackwell. Oxford. 1986. pp. 123-147.

Campbell Tom, "The Rights Of The Mentally Ill". In: Campbell Tom, Goldberg David, Mclean Sheila, Mullen Tom. (eds.). *Human Rights: From Rhetoric To Reality*. Basil Blackwell. Oxford. 1986.

Campbell Tom & Heginbotham Chris (eds.). *Mental Illness: Prejudice, Discrimination And The Law*. Dartmouth. Aldershot, England. 1991.

Cavadino Michael. *Mental Health Law In Context*. Dartmouth. Aldershot, England. 1989.

Conway David A. "Capital Punishment And Deterrence: Some Considerations In Dialogue Form". In: Simmons John A., Cohen Marshall, Cohen Joshua, Beitz Charles R. (eds.). *Punishment*. A Philosophy & Public Affairs Reader. Princeton University Press. Princeton, New Jersey. 1995. pp. 261-273.

Cottingham John. "Punishment". In: Becker Lawrence C. And Becker Charlotte B. (eds). *Encyclopedia Of Ethics*. St. James Press. London. 1992. pp. 1053-1055.

Cottingham John. "Varieties Of Retribution". In: Duff Antony. (ed.). *Punishment*. Dartmouth. Aldershot, Hants. 1993. pp. 75-83.

Cranston Maurice. *What Are Human Rights?* The Bodley Head. London 1973.

Crawford James. (ed.) *The Rights Of People*. Clarendon Press. Oxford. 1988.

Cronin Kieran. *Rights And Christian Ethics*. Cambridge University Press. Cambridge. 1992.

Dagger Richard. "Playing Fair with Punishment". In: *Ethics*. Volume 103. Number 3. April 1993. pp. 473-488.

Davis Nancy (Ann). "Abortion And Self Defense". In: *Philosophy And Public Affairs*. Volume 13. Number 3. Summer 1984. pp.175-207.

Davis Nancy (Ann). "Abortion" In: Becker Lawrence C. And Becker Charlotte B. (eds). *Encyclopedia Of Ethics*. St. James Press. London. 1992. pp. 2-6.

Davis Nancy (Ann). "The Abortion Debate: The Search for Common Ground, Part 1." In: *Ethics*. Volume 103. Number 3. April 1993. pp. 516-539.

Davis Nancy (Ann). "The Abortion Debate: The Search for Common Ground, Part 2." In: *Ethics*. Volume 103. Number 4. July 1993. pp.731-778..

Davis Michael. "How To Make The Punishment Fit The Crime". In: Duff Antony. (ed.). *Punishment*. Dartmouth. Aldershot, Hants. 1993. pp. 315-341.

Davis Michael. "Harm And Retribution". In: Simmons John A., Cohen Marshall, Cohen Joshua, Beitz Charles R. (eds.). *Punishment*. A Philosophy & Public Affairs Reader. Princeton University Press. Princeton, New Jersey. 1995. pp. 188-218.

Devlin Lord Patric. "Morals And The Criminal Law". In: Wasserstrom Richard A. *Today's Moral Problems*. Second Edition. Macmillan. New York. 1979. pp.416-429.

Donnelly Jack. *Universal Human Rights In Theory And Practice.* Cornell University Press. Ithaca, New-York. 1989.

Downie R.S. "The Justification Of Punishment". In: Rachels James. (ed.) *Moral Problems. A Collection Of Philosophical Essays.* Third Edition. Harper & Row. New York. 1979. pp. 321-331.

Duff Antony. (ed.). *Punishment.* Dartmouth. Aldershot, Hants. 1993.

Duff Antony, & GarlAnd David. (eds.). *A Reader On Punishment.* Oxford University Press. Oxford. 1994.

Dworkin Ronald. *Taking Rights Seriously.* Harvard University Press. Cambridge, Massachusetts. 1977.

Dworkin Ronald. *A Matter Of Principle.* Clarendon Press. Oxford. 1986.

Dworkin Ronald. "Rights As Trumps". In Waldron Jeremy. (ed). *Theories Of Rights.* Oxford University Press. Oxford. 1986

Dworkin Ronald. *Life's Dominion.* Harper Collins Publishers. 1993.

Eidenmuller Horst. "Rights, Systems Of Rights, And Unger's System Of Rights. Part 1." In: *Law And Philosophy.* No. 10. 1991. pp. 1-28.

Ellis Anthony. "Rights And The Criminal Law". In: *Analysis.* Vol. 54. No. 2. (New Series No. 242). April 1994. pp.77-83.

Ellis Anthony. "Recent Work On Punishment". In: *The Philosophical Quarterly.* Vol. 45. No. 179. April 1995. pp. 225-233.

Elwood John P. "Outing, Privacy And The First Amendment". In: *The Yale Law Journal.* Vol. 102. No. 3. December 1992. pp. 747-776.

English Jane. "Abortion And The Concept Of A Person". In: Baird Robert M. & Rosenbaum Stuart E. (eds.). *The Ethics Of Abortion.* Prometheus Books. Buffalo, New York. 1989. pp. 83-92.

Ermanski Robert A. "A Right To Privacy For Gay People Under International Human Rights Law". In: *Boston College International And Comparative Law Review.* Vol. XV. No. 1. Winter 1992. pp. 141-164.

Evjen Victor H. "Against Capital Punishment". In: Rachels James. (ed.) *Moral Problems. A Collection Of Philosophical Essays.* Third Edition. Harper & Row. New York. 1979. pp. 346-352.7

Farson Richard. *Birthrights.* Macmillan Publishing. New York. 1974.

Fawcett J.E.S. "The International Protection Of Human Rights". In: Raphael David Daiches. (ed.). *Political Theory And The Rights Of Man.* Macmillan Press. London. 1967.

Feinberg Joel. "Wasserstrom On Human Rights". *The Journal Of Philosophy.* Vol. LXI. No. 20. October 1964. pp. 641-645.

Feinberg Joel. "Duties, Rights, And Claims". In: *American Philosophical Quarterly.* Volume 3, Number 2, April 1966. pp. 137-144.

Feinberg Joel. "The nature And Value Of Rights". In: *Journal Of Value Inquiry.* Vol. 4. 1970. pp. 243-257.

Feinberg Joel. *Social Philosophy.* Prentice-Hall. Englewood Cliffs. New Jersey. 1973.

Feinberg Joel. "Legal Paternalism". In: Wasserstrom Richard A. *Today's Moral Problems.* Second Edition. Macmillan. New York. 1979. pp. 434-451.

Feinberg Joel. *Rights, Justice, And The Bounds Of Liberty.* Princeton University Press. Princeton, New Jersey. 1980.

Feinberg Joel. *Freedom & Fulfillment.* Princeton University Press. Princeton, New Jersey. 1992.

Feinberg Joel. "The Expressive Function Of Punishment". In: Duff Antony, & GarlAnd David. (eds.). *A Reader On Punishment.* Oxford University Press. Oxford. 1994. pp. 71-91.

Flew Antony. "The Justification Of Punishment". In: *Philosophy*. Vol. 29. No. 3. October 1954. pp. 291-307.

Frankena William K. "Natural And Inalienable Rights". In: In: *The Philosophical Review*. Volume LXIV. Number 2. April 1955. pp. 212-232.

Freid Charles. "Privacy: A Rational Context". In: Wasserstrom Richard A. *Today's Moral Problems*. Second Edition. Macmillan. New York. 1979. pp. 365-377.

Gensler Harry J. "An Appeal For Consistency". In: Baird Robert M. & Rosenbaum Stuart E. (eds.). *The Ethics Of Abortion*. Prometheus Books. Buffalo, New York. 1989. pp. 93-107.

Gert Bernard. "Transplants And Trolleys". In: *Philosophy And Phenomenological Research*. vol. LII. No. 1. March 1993. pp. 173-179.

Gewirth Alan. "Categorical Consistency In Ethics". In: *Philosophical Quarterly*. Vol. 17. 1967. pp. 289-299.

Gewirth Alan. "The Normative Structure Of Action". In: *The Review Of Metaphysics*. Vol. 25. 1971. pp. 238-261.

Gewirth Alan. "Moral Rationality" In: Bricke John. (Ed.). *Freedom & Morality*. University Of Kansas Humanistic Studies. Lawrence. 1976. Pp. 113-150.

Gewirth Alan. *Reason And Morality*. The University Of Chicago Press. Chicago. 1978.

Gewirth Alan. "The Epistemology Of Human Rights". In: Kamenka Eugene And Tay Erh-Soon Alice (eds.) *Human rights*. Eduard Arnold. London. 1978. pp. 1-24.

Gewirth Alan. "A Reply To Danto". In: In: Kamenka Eugene And Tay Erh-Soon Alice (eds.) *Human rights*. Eduard Arnold. London. 1978. pp. 31-34.

Gewirth Alan "Human Rights And The Prevention Of Cancer". In: *American Philosophical Quarterly*. Volume 17. Number 2. April 1980. pp. 117-125.

Gewirth Alan *Human Rights*. The University Of Chicago Press. Chicago. 1982.

Gewirth Alan. "Rights And Virtues". In: *The Review Of Metaphysics*. Vol. 38. No. 4. June 1985. pp. 739-762.

Gewirth Alan. "Are There Any Absolute Rights?" In : Waldron Jeremy.(ed). *Theories Of Rights*. Oxford University Press. Oxford. 1986. pp. 91-109.

Gewirth Alan. "Human Rights And Conceptions Of The Self". In: *Philosophia*. Volume 18. No. 2. 1988.

Gewirth Alan. "Ethical Universalism And Particularism". In: *The Journal Of Philosophy*. Vol. 85. No. 6. June 1988. pp. 283-302.

Gewirth Alan. "Rights". In: Becker Lawrence C. And Becker Charlotte B. (eds). *Encyclopedia Of Ethics*. St. James Press. London. 1992. pp. 1103-1109.

Gewirth Alan *The Community Of Rights*. The University Of Chicago Press. Chicago. 1996.

Goldberg Steven. "Does Capital Punishment Deter?". In: Wasserstrom Richard A. *Today's Moral Problems*. Second Edition. Macmillan. New York. 1979. pp. 538-552.

Golding Martin P. "Towards A Theory Of Human Rights". In : *The Monist*. Vol. 52. No. 4. October 1986. pp. 521-549.

Goldman Alan H. "Toward A New Theory Of Punishment". In: Duff Antony. (ed.). *Punishment*. Dartmouth. Aldershot, Hants. 1993. pp.177-196.

Goldman Alan H. "The Paradox Of Punishment". In: Simmons John A., Cohen Marshall, Cohen Joshua, Beitz Charles R. (eds.). *Punishment*. A Philosophy & Public Affairs Reader. Princeton University Press. Princeton, New Jersey. 1995. pp. 30-46.

Goodin Robert E. & Pettit Philip. (eds). *A Companion To Contemporary Political Philosophy*. Basil Blackwell. Cambridge, Massachusetts. 1993.

Grant Jon E. "Outing And The Freedom Of The Press: Sexual Orientation's Challenge To The Supreme Court's Categorical Jurisprudence". In: *Cornell Law Review*. Vol. 77. No. 1. November 1991. pp. 103-141.

Halpin Andrew. "More Comments On Rights And Claims". *Law And Philosophy*. Vol. 10. 1991. pp. 271-310.
Hampton Jean. "The Moral Education Theory Of Punishment". In: *Philosophy And Public Affairs*. Volume 13. Number 3. Summer 1984. pp. 208-238.
Hare R.M. "Abortion And The Golden Rule". In: Rachels James. (ed.) *Moral Problems. A Collection Of Philosophical Essays*. Third Edition. Harper & Row. New York. 1979. pp. 151-173.
Harman Gilbert. "Stringency Of Right And 'ought'". In: *Philosophy And Phenomenological Research*. Vol. LII. No. 1. March 1993. pp. 181-185.
Hart Herbert L.A. *Punishment And Responsibility. Essays In The Philosophy Of Law*. Oxford University Press. New York And Oxford. 1968.
Hart Herbert L.A. "Immorality And Treason". In: Wasserstrom Richard A. *Today's Moral Problems*. Second Edition. Macmillan. New York. 1979. pp. 429-434.
Hart Herbert .L.A. "Are There Any Natural Rights? In : Waldron Jeremy. (ed). *Theories Of Rights*. Oxford University Press. Oxford. 1986. pp. 77-90.
Hart Herbert .L.A. "Prolegomenon To The Principles Of Punishment". In: Baird Robert M. & Rosenbaum Stuart E. (eds). *Philosophy Of Punishment*. Prometheus Books. Buffalo, New York. 1988. pp. 15-21.
Hartshorne Charles. "Concerning Abortion: An Attempt At A Rational View". In: Baird Robert M. & Rosenbaum Stuart E. (eds.). *The Ethics Of Abortion*. Prometheus Books. Buffalo, New York. 1989. pp. 109-114.
Heginbotham Chris. *The Rights Of Mentally Ill People*. The Minority Rights Group. Report No. 74. May 1987. London.
Hohfeld Wesley Newcomb. *Fundamental Legal Conceptions As Applied Judicial Reasoning*. Yale University Press. New Haven. 1919.
Houlgate Laurence D. "Children And Ethical Theory". In: Becker Lawrence C. And Becker Charlotte B.(eds). *Encyclopedia Of Ethics*. St. James Press. London. 1992. pp. 136-139.
Jecker Nancy S. "Are Filial Duties Unfounded". In: *American Philosophical Quarterly*. Volume 26. Number 1. January 1989. pp. 73-80.
Jordan Jeff. "Why Negative Rights Only?" In: *The Southern Journal Of Philosophy*. Vol. XXIX. No. 2. Summer 1991. pp. 245-255.
Kamenka Eugene And Tay Erh-Soon Alice (eds.) *Human rights*. Eduard Arnold. London. 1978.
Kamenka Eugene. "Human Rights, Peoples' Rights." In: Crawford James.(ed.) *The Rights Of People*. Clarendon Press. Oxford. 1988. pp. 127-139.
Kaufman Arnold S. "A Sketch Of A Liberal Theory Of Fundamental Human Rights". In : *The Monist*. Vol. 52. No. 4. October 1986. pp. 595-615.
Koller Peter. "A Conception Of Moral Rights And Its Application To Property And Welfare Rights". In: *ratio Jurris*. Vol. 5. No. 2. July 1992. pp. 153-171.
LaFollete Hugh. *Ethics In Practice*. Blackwell. Cambridge. Massachusetts. 1997.
Laslet P. & Fishkin J. (eds). *Philosophy, Politics And Society: Fifth Series*. Basil Blackwell. Oxford. 1979.
Lyons David. "Rights, Claimants And Beneficiaries". In: *American Philosophical Quarterly*. Vol. 6. 1969. pp. 173-185.
Lyons David. "The Correlativity Of Rights And Duties". In: *Nous*. Vol. 4. 1970. pp. 45-55.
Lyons David. "Human Rights And The General Welfare". In: *Philosophy And Public Affairs"*. Vol. 6. pp. 173-185.
Lyons David. "Moral Aspects Of Legal Theory". In: *Midwest Studies In Philosophy*. Volume VII. 1982. pp. 223-254.

Lyons David. "Utility And Rights". In: Waldron Jeremy. (ed). *Theories Of Rights*. Oxford University Press. Oxford. 1986.

Mabbott J.D. "Punishment". In: Baird Robert M. & Rosenbaum Stuart E. (eds). *Philosophy Of Punishment*. Prometheus Books. Buffalo, New York. 1988. pp. 23-35.

MacCormick Neil. "Rights Claims And Remedies". In: *Law And Philosophy*. No. 1. 1982. pp. 337-357.

MacCormick Neil. "Legal Reasning And Practical Reason". In: *Midwest Studies In Philosophy*. Volume VII. 1982. pp. 271-286.

MacDonald Margaret. "Natural Rights". In: Waldron Jeremy. (ed). *Theories Of Rights*. Oxford University Press. Oxford. 1986

Machan Tibor R. *Individuals And Their Rights*. Open Court. La Salle, Illinois. 1989.

Machan Tibor R. "Some Recent Work In Human Rights Theory". In: *American Philosophical Quarterly*. Volume 17. Number 2. April 1980. pp. 103-115.

MacIntyre Alasdair C. *After Virtue*. Duckworth. London. 1981.

Mack Eric. "Natural And Contractual Rights". In: *Ethics*. Vol. 87. 1977. pp. 145-153.

Mack Eric. "Personal Integrity, Practical Recognition, And Rights." In: *The Monist*. Vol. 76. No. 1. 1993. pp. 101-118.

Mack Eric. "Of Transplants And Trolleys". In: *Philosophy And Phenomenological Research*. Vol. LII. No. 1. March 1993. pp. 163-167.

Mack Eric. "Sighting Rights". In: *Ethics*. Volume 103. Number 4. July 1993. pp. 779-791.

Mackie J.L. "Can There Be A Rights Based Moral Theory?". In: Waldron Jeremy. (ed). *Theories Of Rights*. Oxford University Press. Oxford. 1986

Martin Rex And Nickel James W. "Recent Work In The Concept Of Rights". In *American Philosophical Quarterly*. Volume 17. Number 3. July 1980. pp. 165-180.

Martin Rex. "On The Theory Of Legal Rights As Valid Claims". In: *Midwest Studies In Philosophy*. Volume VII. 1982. pp. 175-195.

Martin Rex. *A System Of Rights*. Clarendon Press. Oxford. 1993.

Mayo Bernard. "What Are Human Rights?". In: Raphael D.D. (ed.). *Political Theory And The Rights Of Man*. Macmillan. London. 1967. pp. 68-80.

McCloskey H.J. "Rights". *The Philosophical Quarterly*. Vol. 15. No. 59. April 1965. pp. 115-127.

MacCloskey H.J. "The Right To Life". In: *Mind*. Vol. 84. 1975. pp. 403-425.

McLean Sheila. "Right To Reproduce". In: Campbell Tom, Goldberg David, Mclean Sheila, Mullen Tom. (eds.). *Human Rights: From Rhetoric To Reality*. Basil Blackwell. Oxford. 1986. pp. 99-122.

McNaughton David, &, Rawling Piers. "Deontology And Agency". In: *The Monist*. Vol. 76. No. 1. January 1993. pp. 81-100.

Melden A.I. *Rights And Right Conduct*. Basil Blackwell. Oxford. 1959.

Melden A.I. *Free Action*. Routledge & Kegan Paul. London. 1961.

Melden A.I. "The Play Of Rights". *The Monist"*. Vol. 56. No. 4. October 1972. pp. 479-502.

Melden A.I. *Rights And Persons*. University Of California Press. Berkeley And Los Angeles. 1977.

Miller David. *Social Justice*. Clarendon press. Oxford. 1976.

Miller Fred D. Paul Ellen Frankel, Paul Jeffrey (eds.). *Human Rights*. Basil Blackwell. Oxford. 1984.

Milne A.J.M. *Human Rights And Human Diversity*. Macmillan Press. London. 1986.

Morris Herbert. "Persons And Punishment". In : *The Monist*. Vol. 52. No. 4. October 1986. pp. 475-501.

Morris Herbert. "A Paternalistic Theory Of Punishment". In: Duff Antony. (ed.). *Punishment*. Dartmouth. Aldershot, Hants. 1993. pp. 133-141.

Murphy Jeffrie G. "Marxism And Retribution". In: Wasserstrom Richard A. *Today's Moral Problems.* Second Edition. Macmillan. New York. 1979. pp. 491-512.

Nathanson Stephen. "Does It matter if The Death Penalty is Arbitrarily Administered?". In: Simmons John A., Cohen Marshall, Cohen Joshua, Beitz Charles R. (eds.). *Punishment.* A Philosophy & Public Affairs Reader. Princeton University Press. Princeton, New Jersey. 1995. pp. 308-323.

Neumann Michael. "Needs No Rights". *Canadian Journal Of Philosophy.* Volume 22, Number 3, September 1992, pp. 353-364.

Nickel James W. "Are Human Rights Utopian?". In: *Philosophy And Public Affairs.* Vol. 11 No. 3. Summer 1982. pp. 246-264.

Nickel James W. *Making Sense Of Human Rights.* University Of California Press. Berkeley, California. 1987.

Nickel James W. "Human Rights". In: Becker Lawrence C. And Becker Charlotte B.(eds). *Encyclopedia Of Ethics.* St. James Press. London. 1992. pp. 561-565.

Nielsen Kai. "Skepticism And Human Rights". In : *The Monist.* Vol. 52. No. 4. October 1986. pp. 573-594.

Nino Carlos Santiago. *The Ethics Of Human Rights.* Clarendon Press. Oxford. 1991.

Nino Carlos Santiago. "A Consensual Theory Of Punishment". In: Simmons John A., Cohen Marshall, Cohen Joshua, Beitz Charles R. (eds.). *Punishment.* A Philosophy & Public Affairs Reader. Princeton University Press. Princeton, New Jersey. 1995. pp. 94-111.

Nozick Robert. *Anarchy, State, And Utopia.* Basic Books. New York. 1974.

Orucu Esin. "The Core Of Rights And Freedoms: The Limit Of Limits". in:Campbell Tom, Goldberg David, Mclean Sheila, Mullen Tom. (eds). *Human Rights: From Rhetoric To Reality.* Basil Blackwell. Oxford. 1986. pp. 37-59.

Paynter Roger A. "Life In The Tragic Dimension: A Sermon On Abortion". In: Baird Robert M. & Rosenbaum Stuart E. (eds.). *The Ethics Of Abortion.* Prometheus Books. Buffalo, New York. 1989. pp. 143-150.

Plant Raymond. *Modern Political Thought.* Basil Blackwell. Oxford. 1991.

Petchesky Rosalind Pollack. *Abortion And Woman's Choice.* Verso. 1986.

Pojman Louis P. "Are Human Rights Based On Equal Worth?" *Philosophy And Phenomenological Research.* Vol. LII, No. 3, September 1992. pp. 605-622.

Pollack David H. "Forced Out Of The Closet: Sexual Orientation And The Legal Dilemma Of Outing". In: *University Of Miami Law Review.* Vol. 46. No. 3. January 1992. pp. 711-750.

Postema Gerald J. "In Defense Of 'French Nonsense'. Fundamental Rights In Constitutional Jurisprudence" In : Bankowski Zenon And MacCormick Neil, (eds.). *Enlightenment, Rights And Revolution.* Aberdeen University Press. 1989. pp. 107-133.

Primoratz Igor. "Punishment As Language". In: Duff Antony. (ed.). *Punishment.* Dartmouth. Aldershot, Hants. 1993. pp. 55-73.

Purdy Laura M. In Their Best Interest? The Case Against Equal Rights To Children. Cornell University Press. Ithaca, New York. 1992.

Quinn Warren. "Abortion: Identity And Loss". in: *Philosophy And Public Affairs.* Volume 13. Number 1. Winter. 1984. pp. 24-54.

Rachels James. (ed.) *Moral Problems. A Collection Of Philosophical Essays.* Third Edition. Harper & Row. New York. 1979.

Rainbolt George W. "Rights As Normative Constraints On Others". In: *Philosophy And Phenomenological Research.* Vol. LII. No. 1. March 1993. pp. 93-111.

Raphael David Daiches. (ed.). *Political Theory And The Rights Of Man.* Macmillan Press. London. 1967.

Raphael David Daiches. "Human Rights, Old And New". In: Raphael D.D. (ed.). *Political Theory And The Rights Of Man.* Macmillan Press. London. 1967. pp. 54-67.

Rawls John. *Theory Of Justice*. Oxford University Press. Oxford. 1971.
Rawls John. "A Well-Ordered Society". In: Laslet P. & Fishkin J. (eds). *Philosophy, Politics And Society: Fifth Series.* Basil Blackwell. Oxford. 1979. pp. 6-20.
Rawls John. "Two Concepts Of Rules". In: Wasserstrom Richard A. *Today's Moral Problems*. Second Edition. Macmillan. New York. 1979. pp.452-460.
Rawls John. "Kantian Constructivism In Moral Theory". In: *The Journal Of Philosophy*. Vol. LLXXVII. No. 9. September 1980. pp. 515-577.
Rawls John. "Justice As Fairness: Political not Metaphysical". In: *Philosophy And Public Affairs*. Vol. 14. No. 3. Summer 1985. pp. 223-251.
Rawls John. "Two Concepts Of Rules". In: Baird Robert M. & Rosenbaum Stuart E. (eds). *Philosophy Of Punishment.* Prometheus Books. Buffalo, New York. 1988. pp. 37-45.
Raz Joseph. "On The Nature Of Rights". In: *mind*. Vol. XCIII. No. 2. April 1984. pp. 194-214.
Raz Joseph. "Right-Based Moralities". In: Waldron Jeremy. (ed). *Theories Of Rights*. Oxford University Press. Oxford. 1986. pp. 182-200.
Raz Joseph. *The Morality Of Freedom*. Oxford University Press. Oxford. 1986. (a)
Raz Joseph. "Rights And Individual Well-being". In: *Ratio Jurris*. Vol. 5. No. 2. July 1992. pp. 127-142.
Raz Joseph. Ethics In The Public Domain. Essays In The Morality Of Law And Politics. Clarendon Press. Oxford. 1994.
Reagan Leslie J. *When Abortion Was A Crime*. University Of California Press. Berkeley And Los Angeles. California. 1977.
Reiman Jeffrey H. "Privacy, Intimacy And Personhood". In: Wasserstrom Richard A. *Today's Moral Problems*. Second Edition. Macmillan. New York. 1979. pp.377-392.
Reiman Jeffrey H. "Justice, Civilization And The Death Penalty: Answering van den Haag". In: Simmons John A., Cohen Marshall, Cohen Joshua, Beitz Charles R. (eds.). *Punishment.* A Philosophy & Public Affairs Reader. Princeton University Press. Princeton, New Jersey. 1995. pp. 274-307.
Richards B.A. "Inalienable Rights: Recent Criticism And Old Doctrine". In: *Philosophy And Phenomenological Research.* Vol. 29. 1968-9. pp. 391-404.
"Roe v. *Wade* Supreme Court Decision". in: Baird Robert M. & Rosenbaum Stuart E. (eds.). *The Ethics Of Abortion.* Prometheus Books. Buffalo, New York. 1989. pp. 13-22.
Rosenbaum, Alan, S. *The Philosophy Of Human Rights*. Aldwych Press. London. 1980
Ross, Jacob Joshua. *The Virtues Of The Family*. The Free Press. New York. 1994.
Ross, Steven L. "Abortion And The Death Of The Fetus". in:: *Philosophy And Public Affairs*. Vol. 11 No. 3. Summer 1982. pp. 232-245.
Ross William David. *The Right And The Good.* Clarendon Press. Oxford. 1930.
Ross William David. *Foundations Of Ethics*. Clarendon Press. Oxford. 1939.
Sandel Michael J. *Liberalism And The Limit Of justice.* Cambridge University Press. Cambridge. 1982.
Scanlon T.M. "Rights, Goal And Fairness". In: Waldron Jeremy. (ed). *Theories Of Rights*. Oxford University Press. Oxford. 1986
Scarf Maggie. "The Fetus As Guinea Pig. In: Rachels James. (ed.) *Moral Problems. A Collection Of Philosophical Essays.* Third Edition. Harper & Row. New York. 1979. pp. 174-192.
Schedler George. "Capital Punishment And Its Deterrent Effect". In: Wasserstrom Richard A. *Today's Moral Problems*. Second Edition. Macmillan. New York. 1979. pp. 552-560.
Schoeman Ferdinand. "Rights Of Children, Rights Of Parents, And The Moral Basis Of The Family". In: *Ethics*. 91. No. 1. October 1980. pp. 6-19.

Schonfeld Martin. "Who Or What Has Moral Standing?". In : *American Philosophical Quarterly*. Vol. 29. No. 4. October 1992. pp. 353-362.
Schrag Francis. "The Child In The Moral Order". In: *Philosophy*. Vol. 52. 1977. pp. 167-177.
Sen Amartya. "Rights And Agency". In: *Philosophy And Public Affairs*. Vol. 11 No. 1. Winter 1982. pp. 3-39.
Sheleff Leon. *Generations Apart*. McGraw-Hill. New York. 1981.
Sher George. "Ancient Wrongs And Modern Rights". In: *Philosophy And Public Affairs*. Volume 10. Number 1. Winter 1981. pp. 3-17.
Sher George. "Subsidized Abortion: Moral Rights And Moral Compromise". In: *Philosophy And Public Affairs*. Volume 10. Number 4. Fall 1981. pp. 361-372.
Shue Henry. *Basic Rights*. Princeton University Press. Princeton. 1980.
Simmons John A., Cohen Marshall, Cohen Joshua, Beitz Charles R. (eds.). *Punishment.* A Philosophy & Public Affairs Reader. Princeton University Press. Princeton, New Jersey. 1995.
Singer Peter. "Fetal Research". In: Rachels James. (ed.) *Moral Problems. A Collection Of Philosophical Essays*. Third Edition. Harper & Row. New York. 1979. pp. 197-203.
Singer Peter. (ed.). *A Companion To Ethics*. Basil Blackwell. Oxford. 1991.
Singer Peter. (ed.). *Ethics*. Oxford University Press. Oxford. 1994.
Smilansky Saul. "The Time To Punish". In: *Analysis*. Vol. 54. No. 1. (New Series No. 241). January 1994. pp. 50-53.
Smith Tara. "On Deriving Rights To Good From Rights To Freedom". *Law And Philosophy*. Vol. 11. 1992. pp. 217-234.
Stewart Robert M., "Agent-Relativity, Reason And Value". In: *The Monist.* Vol. 76. No. 1. January 1993. pp. 66-80.
Stoljar Samuel. "White On Rights And Claims". In: *Law And Philosophy*. Vol. 4. 1985. pp. 101- 114.
Stoljar Samuel. *An Analysis Of Rights*. Macmillan Press. London. 1984.
Tamir Yael. *Liberal Nationalism.* Princeton University Press. Princeton, New Jersey. 1993.
Ten C.L. "Crime And Punishment". In: Singer Peter. (ed.). *A Companion To Ethics*. Basil Blackwell. Oxford. 1991. pp.366-372.
Thiroux Jacques. *Ethics Theory And Practice*. (Fifth Edition). Prentice Hall. Englewood Cliffs. New Jersey. 1995.
Thomson Judith Jarvis. "Self Defense And Rights". In: *The Lindley Lecture"*. University Of Kansas. 1976.
Thomson Judith Jarvis. "A Defense Of Abortion". In: Wasserstrom Richard A. *Today's Moral Problems*. Second Edition. Macmillan. New York. 1979. pp. 19-34.
Thomson Judith Jarvis. *The Realm Of Rights*. Harvard University Press. Cambridge, Massachusetts. 1990.
Thomson Judith Jarvis. "Precis Of The Realm Of Rights. In: *Philosophy And Phenomenological Research*. vol. LII. No. 1. March 1993. pp. 159-162.
Thomson Judith Jarvis. "Reply To Commentators" In: *Philosophy And Phenomenological Research*. Vol. LII. No. 1. March 1993. pp. 187-194.
Tomasi John. "Individual Rights And Community Virtues". In: *Ethics*. Vol. 101. April 1991. pp. 521-536.
Tooley Michael. "Abortion And Infanticide". In: Baird Robert M. & Rosenbaum Stuart E. (eds.). *The Ethics Of Abortion*. Prometheus Books. Buffalo, New York. 1989. pp.45-60.
Tribe Laurence H. *Abortion. The Clash Of Absolutes*. W.W. Norton Company. New York. 1990.

Van Den Haag Ernest. "Refuting Reiman And Nathanson". In: Simmons John A., Cohen Marshall, Cohen Joshua, Beitz Charles R. (eds.). *Punishment.* A Philosophy & Public Affairs Reader. Princeton University Press. Princeton, New Jersey. 1995.

Vlastos Gregory. "Justice And Equality". In: Waldron Jeremy. (ed). *Theories Of Rights.* Oxford University Press. Oxford. 1986

Waldron Jeremy. (ed). *Theories Of Rights.* Oxford University Press. Oxford. 1986.

Waldron Jeremy. "Rights". In: Miller David. (ed.). *The Blackwell Encyclopedia Of Political Thought".* Basil Blackwell. Oxford. 1987. pp. 443-446.

Waldron Jeremy. "Rights In Conflict". In: *Ethics.* Vol. 99. No. 3. April 1989. pp. 503-519.

Waldron Jeremy. "Rights". In : Goodin Robert E. & Pettit Philip. (eds). *A Companion To Contemporary Political Philosophy.* Basil Blackwell. Cambridge, Massachusetts. 1993. pp. 575-585.

Waldron Jeremy. *Liberal Rights.* Cambridge University Press. 1993.

Warren Mary Anne. "On The Moral And Legal Status Of Abortion". In: Wasserstrom Richard A. *Today's Moral Problems.* Second Edition. Macmillan. New York. 1979. pp. 35-51.

Warren Mary Anne. "Abortion". In: Singer Peter. (ed.). *A Companion To Ethics.* Basil Blackwell. Oxford. 1991. pp.303-314.

Wasserstrom Richard A. "Rights, Human Rights And Racial Discrimination". *The Journal Of Philosophy.* Vol. LXI. No. 20. October 1964. pp. 628-641.

Wasserstrom Richard A. *Today's Moral Problems.* Second Edition. Macmillan. New York. 1979.

Wasserstrom Richard A. "Privacy". In: Wasserstrom Richard A. *Today's Moral Problems.* Second Edition. Macmillan. New York. 1979. pp. 392-408.

Wasserstrom Richard A. "The Status Of The Fetus". In: Rachels James. (ed.) *Moral Problems. A Collection Of Philosophical Essays.* Third Edition. Harper & Row. New York. 1979. pp. 118-129.

Wasserstrom Richard A. "Capital Punishment As Punishment: Some Theoretical Issues And Objections". In: *Midwest Studies In Philosophy.* Volume VII. 1982. pp. 473-502.

Wasserstrom Richard A. "Punishment v. Rehabilitation". In: Baird Robert M. & Rosenbaum Stuart E. (eds.). *Philosophy Of Punishment.* Prometheus Books. Buffalo, New York. 1988. pp. 57-65.

Wellman Carl. "Upholding Legal Rights". In: *Ethics.* Vol. 86. 1975. pp. 49-60.

Wellman Carl. "A New Conception Of Human Rights". In: Kamenka Eugene And Tay Erh-Soon Alice (eds.) *Human rights.* Eduard Arnold. London. 1978.

Wellman Carl. *A Theory Of Rights.* Rowman & Allanheld. Totowa NJ. 1985.

. "Right, Concept Of". In: Becker Lawrence C. And Becker Charlotte B. (eds). *Encyclopedia Of Ethics.* St. James Press. London. 1992. pp. 1100-1103.

Wellman Carl. *Real Rights.* Oxford University Press. New York. 1995.

Wellman Carl. *An Approach to Rights.* Kluwer Academic Publishers. Dordrecht. 1997.

Werner Richard. "Abortion: The Ontological And Moral Status Of The Unborn". In: Wasserstrom Richard A. *Today's Moral Problems.* Second Edition. Macmillan. New York. 1979. pp. 51-73.

White Alan R. "Rights And Claims". In: *Law And Philosophy.* No. 1. 1982. pp. 315-336.

White Alan R. *Rights.* Clarendon Press. Oxford. 1984.

Wick Ronald F. "Out Of The Closet And Into The Headlines: "Outing" And The Private Facts Tort". In: *The Georgetown Law Journal.* Vol. 80. No. 1. December 1991. pp. 413-433.

Wootton Barbara. "The Problem Of The Mentally Abnormal Offender". In: Wasserstrom Richard A. *Today's Moral Problems.* Second Edition. Macmillan. New York. 1979. pp. 460-471.

Zaitchik Alan. "Viability And The Morality Of Abortion". In: *Philosophy And Public Affairs.* Volume 10. Number 1. Winter 1981. pp. 18-26.

INDEX

NOTES

[1] On the difference between right-based and duty-based theories, see, for example, Dworkin 1977. p. 172.

[2] Such a view is held, among others, by Raz, in Raz 1986, p. 180. Nozick's view is in Nozick 1974. p. 29.

[3] See Rawls, 1971, p. 135.

[4] This is Raz' position regarding the question who is capable of having rights. Raz 1986a. p.166.

[5] About the concept of the realm of rights, see Thomson 1990. p. 2.

[6] See Feinberg 1980. p. 154.

[7] Shue 1980. p.32,

[8] Gewirth 1996. p. 5.

[9] Gewirth 1985. p. 746.

[10] About these debates, see Ross 1994, pp. 38-43.

[11] See Ross 1994. p. 41. He refers to Feinberg 1970. pp. 256-257.

[12] See Postema 1989, pp. 109-110.

[13] Thomson 1990, p. 3.

[14] Ibid.

[15] Dworkin 1986, p. 370.

[16] Robert Alexy says that rights are special kind of norms. Alexy 1992, p. 144.

[17] Thomson 1990, p. 2. There Thomson insists that the fact of having a right has moral consequences, and this is the reason for the moral status. I think that the moral status that is created by having the right leads (only when the right is capitalized or at least exercised) to consequences. The moral demands from others to act as the right orders exist immanently in the content of the right.

[18] See Melden, 1977, p.79. Melden, like Thomson, thinks that the conception of a right is to be understood "only in the scheme of related concepts in which it has its place".

[19] This is Jeremy Waldron's presentation. Waldron 1986, p.14-5.

[20] See Hart, 1986, p.83, 88. He uses the same meanings of "lexical" as Rawls does.

[21] Rawls 1971, p.135.

[22] See Martin 1993, p.29.

[23] Shue 1980, p.32.

[24] Machan 1989, p.2 (the emphasis is in the text).

[25] This version is taken from MacCormick 1982, p.337, but the whole literature is replete with such arguments. For example Raz 1984, Thomson 1990, Melden 1977, Alexy 1992, p.145, Rainbolt 1993, p.94 -- there he says that claims (which he identifies with rights) exist within a rule system and almost the same attitude exists in Koller 1992, p.153.

[26] Raz 1986, p.166, defines an individual as one who is capable of having rights when his well-being is of ultimate value.

[27] MacCormick 1982, p. 338.

[28] Raz refers to this in his article from 1992, saying that this primacy is because corporations are individuals "by extenuation, on sufferance only" (p.127).

[29] See McCormick 1982, p.338. There he gives this characterization of rights.

[30] McCormick notes another characteristic, saying that not everything that is good for any individual is his by right. I will deal with the specific content of right later, and explain why this characteristic is redundant.
[31] Hohfeld 1919, p.38 & p. 60.
[32] This version is taken from Gewirth 1978, p.65 (and almost the same formulation is found in Gewirth 1982, p.2), but has some other sources in which the same structure is in use (see Feinberg 1980, p.154, Rosenbaum 1980, p.26-28, etc.). I choose Gewirth because I will refer to his analysis.
[33] Here and in the next paragraph I will use the two versions that Gewirth used, in: 1982, pp. 2-3, and 1978, p.65.
[34] Hohfeld 1919, p. 38.
[35] Raz 1986, p.166.
[36] This quotation is from Feinberg 1980, p.149, where he does not refer directly to moral systems. But I will use his position, for my own purpose, only for the ethical and political applications of rights. This enables me to hold the duties that are correlative to rights as moral but not formal duties.
[37] Feinberg 1980, p.149. The next paragraphs are a brief clarification of his position.
[38] Feinberg 1980, p.151 (the emphasis is in the text).
[39] Feinberg 1980, p.154.
[40] Kamenka 1988, p.127.
[41] See for example Stoljar 1984, pp. 1-2.
[42] See for example Milne 1986, p.102. On page 89 he asserts that law, morality and custom are the sources of rights. Those three entail rules or principles.
[43] For primary distinction between rules and principles, see Dworkin 1977, pp. 24-27.
[44] MacCormick 1982, p.337 (the emphasis is mine).
[45] Peter Koller clearly represents this position in Koller 1992, p.154.
[46] Rainbolt 1993, p. 97. This position is very close to Robert Nozick view of rights as "side constraints upon the actions to be done". Nozick 1974, p.29, even though Rainbolt mentions that his use of the term "constraints" is different from Nozick's use.
[47] Rainbolt 1993, p.98.
[48] Nickel, 1982 p.248-249.
[49] These are Tara Smith's definitions, and I use them as they are to explain her main position.
[50] I use here Melden's terminology, taken from Melden 1977, p.79, but the point is widely agreed within the rights talk.
[51] Martin 1993 p. 27.
[52] Martin 1993 p. 59-60.
[53] About the distinction between "right-based" and "duty-based" theories, see Dworkin 1977, p.172 and further.
[54] Waldron 1986, p.15. Emphasis in the source..
[55] Rawls 1971, p.135.
[56] D.D. Raphael 1967, p.58.
[57] Gewirth (1988, p.135-6) divides them to three hierarchical kinds of goods: basic goods, which are the essential preconditions of action (physical integrity, food, clothing, shelter et cetera); nonsubtructive goods, which are the abilities and conditions needed for maintaining undiminished one's level of purpose-fulfillment; additive goods which are the abilities and conditions needed for increasing one's level of purpose-fulfillment. All these kinds entail having someone to claim against for having them fulfilled.
[58] Hart 1986, p.83. emphasis in the text.
[59] Gewirth 1986, p.92.

[60] Wellman 1995, p.245. He quotes Feinberg 1980, p.225, saying that: "An absolute right...is a right that would remain in one's possession, fully effective as a ground of other people's duties to one, in all possible circumstances...There are no circumstances in which it is "subject to legitimate limitation" or in which the correlated duties of others... are suspended. "

[61] This attitude is detailed in Ross 1930, p.17-29. Wellman deals with it in Wellman 1995, pp. 244-251.

[62] See Ross 1930, p.20. One objection that Wellman mentions is Melden 1972, pp. 483-484.

[63] I use here the explication and interpretation of Carl Wellman, since his terminology seems fitting for the current discussion. His discussion is in: Wellman 1995, p.250.

[64] The example is taken from Aristotle's *Nichomachean Ethics*, 1110a9-14. Wellman's reference to it is in Wellman 1995, p.256.

[65] See Wellman 1995,p.261.

[66] See chapter 1. The analysis is taken from Gewirth 1982 p.2-3, and 1978 p.65.

[67] Raz 1986a p.166.

[68] Feinberg 1980 p. 154.

[69] Kamenka 1988 p. 127.

[70] See Rawls 1985 p.228. There he uses this phrase to refer "the shared fund of implicitly recognized basic ideas and principles".

[71] See Blackstone 1968 p.639.

[72] Blackstone ,whose concern is human rights, summarizes these features as rationality or purposeful abilities. He thinks that if these characteristics are regarded as descriptive, they cannot establish any right on the part of their possessors just because they suit to these features. However, if these features are regarded as normative concepts with the notion of rights built into them, the justification of possessing rights turns out to be circular. p.624. To partly extricate ourselves from this we need another aspect besides the mental and biological features. I will suggest one towards the end of this chapter.

[73] Blackstone 1968 p.624.

[74] Blackstone 1968 p.625.

[75] For a comprehensive debate regarding this idea, see Feinberg 1980 pp. 18-20.

[76] See Rawls 1985 p. 242-4.

[77] See Gewirth 1978 p.27.

[78] Gewirth 1978 p.31.

[79] Gewirth 1978 pp. 48-63.

[80] For reasons of brevity I use the concise version of this argument, taken from: Gewirth 1988. pp. 135-139. It is sufficient for presenting the main conception, that will be inspected later.

[81] With the exception of several explications, I have brought the complete argument, which is valid according to the conventional usage of the terms he uses, and according to his conception of the correlativity of claim rights and strict 'oughts'.

[82] Gewirth notes that one cannot claim for generic rights simply on the basis of a more restrictive property (like being American or white male). This is so, because everyone must hold, that he has generic rights as an agent. If one does not do so he would be in the position of accepting that he normatively need not have what he normatively must have (i.e. freedom and well-being that are the necessary conditions of any action). The conclusion of this is that there cannot be any restrictive property rather than the most general characterization, of simply being a prospective purposive agent, that can function as a necessary and sufficient justifying condition for having generic rights. Gewirth 1988. pp. 137-138.

[83] Gewirth 1988 p.138.

[84] Gewirth 1978 p.63.

[85] Gewirth 1996. p. 4. See also p. 5.

[86]Gewirth says: "The right in question are human rights, rights that are had by every human being simply insofar as he or she is human. But when the rights involves claims to the protection of human interests, they also require of each of each person that she act with due regard for other persons' interests just as their own. For, as human rights, they are not only had by all humans; they are also rights against all humans. In other words, each human being is both the subject or right-holder and the respondent or duty-bearer." Gewirth 1996, p. 6.

[87] See, for example, Gewirth 1978, p. 72, and in reply to

[88] See Raz 1984 p. 204.

[89] This view is widely held, so I choose Milne 1986 p. 102-3, as an example here.

[90] M.P.Golding maintains that a community is not only a prior condition for having rights, but a necessary condition for making rights-talk possible. He argues that we cannot speak of rights existing anterior to or outside of a community. See Golding 1968. p.529.

[91]Melden 1977 p.53.

[92]Melden 1977. p.68.

[93]Melden 1977. p.79-81.

[94]Melden 1977. p.134.

[95]Melden 1977. p.144.

[96]Melden 1977. p.144.

[97]Melden 1977. p.162.

[98]Milne 1986. p.42.

[99]Melden 1977. p.186.

[100]Melden 1977. p.187.

[101]Melden 1977. p.192.

[102]Melden 1977. p.192-4.

[103] Milne 1986. p.36. For him, to be a member of the community, is *inter alia* to be a moral agent.

[104] Milne 1986. p.36.

[105] Melden 1977. pp. 202-206. The following paragraphs summarize the approach that he introduces there.

[106] Melden 1977. p.205, and also p.232.

[107] This idea is similar to Rawls' idea of ordering the two principles of rights, the first of which has a "lexical" priority upon the other. See Rawls 1971.p.43.

[108] Wellman 1995. p.78.

[109] Gewirth 1982 p.2.

[110] Rawls 1985 p. 233.

[111] Feinberg 1980 p.160.

[112] Wellman 1995 p.106.

[113] Wellman 1995. p.107.

[114] Rawls 1980. p.525. The principles mentioned are determined by the participants of the social scheme as a manifestation of their autonomy. The significance of this point will be emphasized later.

[115] Rawls 1980.p.543.

[116] Gewirth 1988. p.139.

[117] Gewirth 1988. p.139.

[118] Gewirth 1988. p.140.

[119] Gewirth 1977 p.121. I summarize his conception here and in the article mentioned as Gewirth 1988. The relevant pages there are mostly 140-141.

[120] Gewirth 1988 p.140.

[121] Here I follow several philosophers, mentioned by W.T.Blackstone in Blackstone 1968. p. 624.

[122] Golding 1968. pp. 522-526.

[123] Golding 1968 p.522.

[124] I refer to Melden 1986. pp. 202-206. Section 2.5.3. in this chapter.

[125] Especially the reference to Milne 1986, p.36, p,42, and in the presentation of the acquiring of agency in Melden's theory.

[126] Blackstone 1968. p. 629.

[127] Golding 1968. pp. 627-628.

[128] Golding 1968. pp. 529-530.

[129] See Gewirth 1982, p.2.

[130] Melden 1977. p.145.

[131] Melden 1977. p. 145. The emphasis is in the text.

[132] Gewirth 1977 p.121. I discussed it in section 2.6.2.

[133] Feinberg 1980 p.160. See section 2.6. of this chapter.

[134] Golding 1968. p.540. His use of this notion is in a different context, and for him those who have less than full membership are, for example, slaves. For me, this is not necessarily connected with status.

[135] This is the same way that Gewirth treats this issue, with almost the same terminology. See Gewirth 1988 p.140.

[136] Gewirth 1988 p.140.

[137] Joel Feinberg refers to this question and raises options of reasons to identify rights with valid claims, like "theoretically illuminating", or "strategically useful". I think there is a more essential set of reasons, the most important of them being the desire to assure and secure the exercising and capitalizing of rights. See Feinberg 1966. p.137.

[138] Gewirth holds the same position regarding right-claims. He also thinks that the relation between the justifying ground (the fulfillment of a certain description) and the possession of rights must be that of sufficient condition and not only necessary condition. See Gewirth 1978. p.104.

[139] The detailing and explanation of this term are in Dworkin 1977. p. ix.

[140] Rawls 1971. p.135.

[141] Horst Eidenmuller insists that each system of rights should fulfill two minimum requirements: Legitimacy and Functionality. The former requirement entails that the system should offer some sort of background justification, that tells us why we should prefer this system to other systems. The second requirement has three aspects. The first is an absence of internal contradiction, at least on the level of definitive positions. The second is that this system will be practicable in the broad and general sense. That means, that it should work, to some effective degree. The third is that the system will be as simple to administer as possible. See Eidenmuller 1991.p.3

[142] The question whether mentally disabled persons have the right to parenthood is very complicated and controversial. This question has at least two different aspects, each of which requires a separate discussion. The first is whether they have the right to give birth (or to procreate). The second is whether they have the right to bring up their biological children. The more general question, whether they have the right to have children, has another distressing aspect: whether they have the right to adopt children. This is, again, a different question that requires a separate discussion. Anyway, all these questions are to be

examined within rights-talk, after we have justified the reasons for choosing the particular theory within which we try to answer these questions.

[143]This position is detailed in Gewirth 1977. pp. 296-7. The quotation is from p.297.

[144]This is almost an exact quotation from Gewirth 1977. p.140.

[145]Gewirth 1977.p.142.

[146]Gewirth 1977.p.142.

[147]A.J.M. Milne expresses this clearly by saying that: to be a member of the community is *inter alia* to be a moral agent. Milne 1986. p.36. A similar position we can find in Melden 1977. p.162, 187, 192.

[148]Melden 1977. p.162.

[149]See Milne 1986. p.42.

[150]Milne 1986. p.39. The context there is slightly different, but he tries to justify the precedence of the community's interests over each agent's interests.

[151]Judith Jarvis Thomson argues that the source of our having claims consists of two features. The first is that we are subject to the moral law, and the second is that we have inherently individual interests. Thomson 1990. p. 222. Milne's idea disregards the second aspect of our having claims. Even though my view is different from Thomson's, I agree that this point requires more weight than it gets in Milne's position.

[152]Further details regarding modality and stringency of rights are to be found in Gewirth 1977. p.65.

[153]See Rawls 1985. p.227. Even though Rawls mentions that this is only a contrast of style, and historically inaccurate, he uses this distinction to fix his ideas. For me the relevant issue is that both traditions desire to realize and actualize rights, and hence deal with their achievement and not with their withdrawal.

[154]This is the status and function that Rawls ascribe to rights. Rawls 1971. p.135.

[155]Gewirth 1986. p.92.

[156]Feinberg mentions this in Feinberg 1980. pp. 229-231. He quotes from Thomson 1976. The emphasis is mine.

[157]Feinberg thinks that a full theory of the nature of rights would explain how they can be preserved, waived, renounced, transferred, sold; surrendered, forfeited, prescribed (cf. "imprescriptible"); annulled or made void, withdrawn, canceled; overruled, overridden, outbalanced, invaded, infringed, violated; recognized, enforced, vindicated, respected; possessed, enjoyed, exercised, stood upon, acted on, abused; acquired, inherited, purchased. Some of these categories are defined in terms of the uses to which they may or may not be put. Feinberg selects those terms that are functional for his discussion, and explains their meanings, according to his interpretation. I use his discussion in order to clarify the semantic domain of my subject. See Feinberg 1980. p.239.

[158]Feinberg 1980. p.239-240.

[159]Feinberg 1980. p.242-246.

[160]Wellman 1995. p.242-243.

[161]Thomson 1990. p.348.

[162]There is a thesis saying that **only** right-holders can make themselves cease to have rights. Thomson calls this "the libertarian thesis". I do not examine this thesis here, but only mention some of the ways that even according to this thesis, are legitimate cases of ceasing to have rights.

[163]Thomson 1990. p.361.

[164]See Hohfeld 1919. p.39.

[165]Rawls 1971. p.135.

[166]See Nickel 1982. pp. 248-249

[167]In ordinary language, we could call this component the "power" that the right has. However, this term is a recognized Hohfeldian relation, that has a specific meaning. So we need to content ourselves with saying that the weight of a right is its "force", or, better speak of its "durability potential".

[168] Nickel 1982. p. 249.

[169] Nickel 1982. p. 249.

[170]The position I took in the first chapter, that insists that possessing a right includes the possession of all the necessary conditions for its exercise, might lead to the conclusion that in this case, the specific right does not really exist, or in Wellman's terminology, it is an "unreal" right..

[171]By using this term I mean that rights also include the justifying grounds for their withdrawal, when the justifying grounds for their existence collapse.

[172]This is also Melden's view. See Melden 1972. p.497.

[173]See Hart 1986.

[174]In Brown 1955.

[175]Frankena 1955. p.221.

[176]For example: Feinberg 1980. pp. 221-251. Frankena 1955. pp. 212-232. Richards 1968. pp. 391-404.

[177]The only case that might give rise to this question may be the issue of capital punishment. When I will discuss this issue, I will present some criticism against the assumptions of some rights as inalienable.

[178]A similar attitude is to be found in Martin & Nickel. 1980. p.173.

[179]Feinberg 1980. p.154.

[180]Feinberg 1980. p.154.

[181]Dworkin 1977. p.24-25.

[182]Bayles 1991. p.351.

[183]This issue is discussed in Dworkin 1977. pp. 26-27, and Bayles 1991 pp. 351-352. I use Dworkin's words and Bayles interpretation of them as complementary statements that clarify Dworkin's view.

[184]Dworkin himself recognizes that it is not always clear from the form of a standard whether it is a rule or a principle. In many cases the distinction is difficult to make, and this issue may itself be a focus of controversy. Sometimes a rule and a principle have the same role, and the only difference between them seems to be a matter of form, rather than of substance. However, the difference between them, is that a rule clarifies its "conditions of possession", "conditions of engagement" "addressee", etc.(if I am permitted to use Nickel's terminology in this discussion) in a more specified way than a principle.

[185]Wellman 1978. p.56. A similar position regarding the addressee of human rights is held by Bernard Mayo, in Mayo 1967. p.77.

[186]Here I refer to Golding 1968. p.529.

[187]Here I refer to Melden 1977 p.144, from where this quotation is taken.

[188]This is where animals' rights can exist in communitarian theories of rights. Animals are not considered as members of the community, but members do have interests in animals, and on behalf of these interests, we have to avoid the torturing of animals. Their rights arise from the interests of members who care about animals, and any harm that is caused to animals hurts the members' feelings. However, there is an essential difference between the grounds of animals' rights and fetus's rights. The difference is that the right of the fetus is based on its having a potential of becoming a member of the moral community, while animals do not have any potential for possessing the perceptual mental and cognitive abilities which are required for being an agent.

[189]Here I use James W. Nickel's definition and explication of this term. It is taken from Nickel 1982 pp. 248-9.

[190]This quotation is taken from Melden 1977. p.162.

[191]This is, more or less, Melden's view, In Melden 1977. p145

[192]See Feinberg 1980. p.154.

[193]This distinction is in Dworkin 1977. p.24-25. The way I present it here is taken from Bayles 1991. p.351.

[194]This issue is discussed in Dworkin 1977. pp. 26-27, and Bayles 1991 pp. 351-352.

[195]The same idea regarding the absence of any point at which a sharp line can be drawn that would mark off non-promises from promises of children, is to be found in Melden 1977 p.203.

[196]Rawls 1971. p.135.

[197]This position was taken from Joel Feinberg in :1980, p. 154.

[198]In Dworkin 1977, p. 24-25.

[199] See Rawls 1988. p. 37.

[200] This description, with some modifications is taken from Cottingham 1992. p. 1053.

[201] Benn 1958. p. 326.

[202] These elements are specified in Flew 1954. pp. 293-295. They became commonly accepted and were used as the basis for most of the known and prominent discussions. Among these see Benn 1958. pp. 325-326. Hart 1968. p. 17. etc.

[203] Rawls 1988. p. 41.

[204] Flew 1954. p. 295.

[205] See Cottingham 1992. p. 1053-4.

[206] See for example, Benn 1958. p. 330.

[207] This criticism is taken from Duff and Garland p. 7, but is to be found in similar formulations in almost every discussion regarding the consequentialist approach to punishment. For example Rachels 1979. p. 315.

[208] Rawls 1988. p. 38.

[209] This and other possibilities are mentioned in Benn 1958. p. 331.

[210] This criticism is raised in Ten 1991. p. 367.

[211] This is what Benn mentions in Benn 1958. p. 335.

[212] See Benn's brilliant analysis of the criteria that must be satisfied in justifying the degree of punishment attached to different classes of offense. Benn 1958, pp. 335-339.

[213] See for example Duff and Garland 1994. p. 7. Ten 1991. p. 367. etc.

[214] This view is presented by most of the theorists that mention this kind of justification. I used here Cottingham's in Cottingham 1992. p. 1054.

[215] Flew 1954. pp. 293-4.

[216] Baier 1955. p. 27. The emphasis is mine. This is almost the only issue where Baier agrees with Flew, so we may regard this point as something conceded by all parties who deal with the meaning of punishment. The very same wording is used in Benn 1958. p. 331.

[217] Flew cites Bradley's words in Flew 1954. p. 299.

[218] See, for example, Cottingham 1992, p.1054.

[219] See Downie 1979, p.329.

[220] Many of the above claims regarding the rehabilitation approach are to be found in Rachels 1979, p. 315-317.

[221] See Menninger 1988, p.47-48. Karl Menninger, a noted psychiatrist, who is one of the most well-known adherents of the therapeutic attitude, believes that ordinary penology has to be changed. He argues that the principle upon which the penal system is based, namely the pain-pleasure principle, does not satisfactorily describe the way in which people

conduct themselves or behave. This is not the way people respond to punishment either. We need to find the way in which the incentives and motivations of those who obey the law would be shared by the offenders, so that they will stop committing offenses.

[222] The coming claims are expansions of Downie's presentation in Downie 1979, pp. 329-320.

[223] For Example, the report of the American Friends Service Committee -- the Quakers, in: Rachels 1979, pp. 332-345.

[224] See Rachels 1979, pp. 317-318.

[225] Rachels 1979, p. 339.

[226] These and many other difficulties are discussed in detail in Rachels 1979, pp. 338-345.

[227] John Cottingham raises another problem, that might be acute on the practical level. He warns that the curative approach may involve "open-ended" incarceration, as a result of the policy of indeterminate confinement. See Cottingham 1992. p. 1054.

[228] Such a criticism occurs in Wasserstrom 1988.

[229] This kind of objection is the main content of the report of the American Friends Service Committee. They express this by saying that: "the content of the correctional treatment programs rests largely on speculation..." See Rachels 1979, p. 341.

[230] These are some of the objections of the authors of the report of the American Friends Service Committee. See Rachels 1979, pp. 342-343.

[231] John Cottingham notes the Latin source of this notion: *re+tribuo*, which is *to pay back.* Even though he admits that etymology is no arbiter in philosophy, he is inclined to suggest that the notion of repayment encapsulates the basic or fundamental sense of retribution. He distinguishes the repayment version of retribution from atonement. The relevant difference for him is that atonement is voluntarily undertaken, while punishment is exacted. See Cottingham 1993. p. 75.

[232] Cottingham quotes M.P. Golding and Ted Honderich who hold such a concept of retribution. He notes that there are some differences between this view and the one of repayment, which warrant the distinction between the two, although in a close look they appear to be quite similar. See Cottingham 1993. p. 76.

[233] These and some other retributive theories are detailed in Cottingham 1993. pp. 78-83.

[234] See S.I. Benn's discussion regarding the degree of punishment attached to different cases of offense. Benn 1958. pp. 335-339.

[235] See Rachels 1979. p. 315.

[236] Cottingham 1992. p. 1053.

[237] Mabbott 1988. p. 28.

[238] Flew 1954. p. 299.

[239] See Flew 1954. p. 302. He interprets Mabbott's position as expressed in Mabbott 1988. p. 31, and 28. Mabbott's article was originally published in *Mind* 48. April 1939, but the references are from its reprint, in 1988.

[240] This is Baier's interpretation to what Flew explains in Flew 1954, p. 299-300. See Baier 1954 p. 27-28. I think this is an interpretation that Flew accepts without any hesitation. Baier himself thinks that punishment, whether a system or a single case is of its nature retributive.

[241] Benn 1958. p. 341.

[242] Benn 1958. p. 334. The reference to Bradley is in p. 332.

[243] See Ellis 1995. p. 225.

[244] Hart 1988. p. 19. The emphasis are in the origin.

[245] See Rawls 1988. p. 37.

[246] Rawls 1988. p. 38.

[247] Rawls 1988. p. 39.

[248] Ellis 1995. p. 232.

[249] Benn 1954. p. 338.

[250] See Ellis' queries regarding these questions, when they are traced towards what he calls "The Intrinsic Desert Theory".

[251] This is Cottingham's presentation of the main idea of this approach, when he emphasizes this trend as a "right-retributivist" approach.

[252] Murphy 1979. p. 501.

[253] Duff and Garland 1994. p. 13.

[254] Hart 1986, p. 85.

[255] Rawls elaborates the Hobbesian conception of punishment, and defines the institution of punishment as follows: "a person is said to suffer punishment whenever he is legally deprived of some of the normal rights of a citizen on the ground that he has violated a rule of law, the violation having been established by trial according to the due process of law, provided that the deprivation is carried out by the recognized legal authorities of the state, that the rule of law clearly specified both the offense and the attached penalty, that the court construed statutes strictly, and the statute was on the books prior to the time of the offense". Rawls 1988. p. 41. In this definition he refers to a deprivation of legal rights, that is legal punishment. Leaving aside the specific components, this definition reflects the conception that regards punishment as a deprivation of rights. I think that within the rights-talk point of view, or from a right-based theories' point of view, this is the appropriate way to look at both the institution or practice of punishment, and certain acts within this practice. From this point of view, this is a justified act of withdrawing rights from someone who has already possessed them, but lost the justification of doing so.

[256] Cottingham 1992. p. 1053.

[257] Gewirth 1978. p. 297. A similar approach to punishment is expressed in Gewirth 1982. p. 236.

[258] Gewirth 1978. p. 297.

[259] Gewirth 1978. p. 299.

[260] This position is supported by Judith Jarvis Thomson, who justifies the government's privilege to punish, by arguing that the offender, by committing a crime, forfeited his claim against the government. She insists that this justification can only succeed with a background that supplies a justification for the adoption of the penal code itself. Thomson 1990. p. 365-366. From a communitarian approach towards rights, we assume that the right that a citizen has against the community exists only during his being acknowledged a (full fledged) member. Hence, it is the community's duty to withdraw it when it is unjustifiably held. Thomson admits this when she examines the appropriateness of the government's punishment of offenders.

[261] Mabbott 1988. p. 31.

[262] Richard Wasserstrom insists that this is the appropriate way to examine this issue. See Wasserstrom 1982. p.474.

[263] Such an argument exists in Bedau 1992. p. 123.

[264] See Ten 1991. p. 370. A similar argument is held in Evjen 1979. pp. 347-348.

[265] Evjen 1979. pp. 348.

[266] Steven Goldberg mentions this kind of argument in Goldberg 1979. p.539.

[267] An argument of this kind is to be found in Thiroux 1995. p. 217.

[268] This possibility is raised in Goldberg 1979. pp.

[269] Ernest Van Den Haag who is a retentionist, mentions that even Reiman, an abolitionist, admits the latter claim, and says that if abolition would endanger us, then death penalty should be retained. However, Reiman does not believe that abolition will involve any risk.

Van Den Haag himself adds that Reiman may be right. That means that he himself is not sure about the deterrence effects of capital punishment, and may agree that abolition would not increase crime. See Van Den Haag 1995. p. 329. He refers to Reiman 1995. A clear presentation of the difficulties that are involved in answering the question whether deterrence works or not, on whom and to what extent, is to be found in Schedler 1979. p. 553-557.

[270] Schedler 1979. p. 557-558.

[271] This is Schedler's interpretation of this kind of argument. See Schedler 1979. p. 552.

[272] See for example Ten 1991. pp. 370-371.

[273] Reiman 1995. p. 279. Reiman regards this principle as completing *the golden rule*. This rule mandates "Do unto others as you would have others do unto you" while the *lex talionis* counsels "Do unto others as they have done unto you". These two principles express the inspiration of equality of persons. Hence they can justify punishment, both on the basis of the Hegelian desire "to annul the crime", and the Kantian argument that a rational being who acts in a certain way towards others, implicitly authorizes the others to act similarly towards him See Reiman 1995 pp. 280-284. According to both ways of justifications of punishment in general, we can justify capital punishment on the basis of *lex talionis*, at least in cases of murder.

[274] Walter Berns holds a similar position when justifying capital punishment on retributive grounds. He founds his justification on the legitimacy and communal necessity of anger.

[275] Evjen 1979. p. 351.

[276] Evjen 1979. p. 351.

[277] Reiman 1995. p. 296.

[278] Van Den Haag 1995. p. 329.

[279] Nathanson 1995. pp. 318-319.

[280] This is Nathanson's interpretation to Van Den Haag's arguments, in Nathanson 1995. p. 310. Nathanson explains this argument in terms that are taken from Feinberg 1980, pp. 265-266. Feinberg argues there that in all cases, justice consists of giving a person his due. However, in some cases, one's due is determined independently to that of other people, while in other cases a person's due is determined only by reference to his relations to other persons. The former cases refer to what he calls *noncomparative justice,* while the later refer to *comparative justice.* The Retentionists' argument regards the justice of a particular punishment as if it were a noncomparative matter.

[281] Van Den Haag 1995. p. 333.

[282] Van Den Haag 1995. p. 333.

[283] See, for example, Nathanson's complaints about Van Den Haag's charges against him. Nathanson 1995. p. 321-322.

[284] Thomson 1990. p. 23.

[285] Here it is relevant to recall Feinberg's distinction between nonforfeitable and inalienable rights. The former is a right "that a person can not lose through his own blundering or wrongdoing". The latter is a right "that a person can not give away or dispense with through his own deliberate choice". Feinberg 1980. p. 240.

[286] Welfare rights are the clearest example for rights that cannot be transferred, because they are bestowed for certain reasons that refer only to the individual who possesses them, and to her needs. For example, if an invalid has a right to buy a vehicle or has a right to subsidized public transportation she can waive it, but she cannot transfer this right to another. The same is with people who have rights to public housing, and decide not to exercise these rights. They cannot oblige the authorities to provide accommodation to someone else, simply because they did not themselves capitalize their right.

[287] In England, in the beginning of the nineteenth century, there were over 225 separate offenses, some of which we consider now as trivial (like pickpocketing), punishable by death. See Rachels 1979. p. 318.

[288] Flew 1954, p. 295.

[289] See Pollack 1992. p. 715.

[290] In Ermanski 1992, this abuse is described as a global problem. In some states, homosexuality is considered as a crime that deserves capital punishment. Ermanski mentions Iran, Columbia, Peru and Argentina, where gay activists were under a death threat. He notes that even the local parliament of the Isle Of Man, "has refused to repeal a local statute banning homosexual sodomy, despite pressure from the parliament of Westminster". See Ermanski 1991. p. 141.

[291] Elwood 1992. pp. 765-766. He mentions NAACP v. Alabama, 357 U.S. 449, 462-62 (1958).

[292] See, for example, Grant 1991, p. 104.

[293] According to Grant 1991, p. 105.

[294] Brandeis Louis & Warren Samuel. "The Right To Privacy". in *Harvard Law Review*. No. 4. 1890. p. 193. This reference is taken from Wick 1991. p. 416. footnote no. 18.

[295] These are the domains that Brandeis & Warren define as private, and hence should be respected and immunized against invasion. See Grant 1991. p. 117.

[296] In Pollack 1992. p. 712, there is a list of those who argue this. However, it is quite understandable that one's autonomy includes his freedom to live the way he chooses, so long as it does not strike at the others' rights. Other's interference, even when it is of a passive kind, is invasive.

[297] See Haulgate 1991. p. 138.

[298] See Schrag 1977. p.170. Quoting Warnock, Schrag mentions the conventional stance that regards one as rational when one is able to achieve some understanding of the situation in which one is placed, to envisage alternative courses of action in such situations, to grasp and weigh considerations for and against those alternatives, and to act accordingly. Unless he possesses these abilities, a person is not able to act in his own best interests, and hence needs a paternalistic protection.

[299] Laura Purdy present the libertarian argument for children's equal rights as containing two parts. The first argues that justice requires granting children equal rights. The second is a demand that the consequences of doing so will not be catastrophic. See Purdy 1992 p. 15, and also p. 87.

[300] See Archard's presentation of the "caretaker thesis", in Archard 1993. p. 53.

[301] Stoljar 1984. p. 120. The emphasis is in the origin.

[302] A.J.M. Milne clearly expresses this idea by saying: "If a community is to survive, it can not afford to neglect the well-being of the next generation. It is in its interest that this well-being should be adequately provided for: for instance, by organizing and maintaining education, by arranging for the care of orphans and protecting children from abuse by adults". Milne 1986. p. 54.

[303] Gewirth 1978. p. 141.

[304] Gewirth 1978. p. 120.

[305] This is a summary of Gewirth's position about children's capability of moral agency, in Gewirth 1978. p. 141.

[306] Wellman 1995. p. 113.

[307] Wellman 1997. p. 28.

[308] Wellman 1995. p. 125. The sub categories of childhood are on p. 113. Wellman vigorously rejects Joel Feinberg's suggestion to regard infants as right-holders even though they

cannot make claims, since their interests can be represented by adults. The idea that right-holders can be represented by others is suggested in Feinberg 1980. Chapters 9, 10.

309 Wellman 1997. p. 139.

310 Taken from Golding 1968. pp. 522-526.

311 Melden 1977. p. 203.

312 That is Laura Purdy's presentation of the position of those to whom she objects. She mentions Aharon Aviram who argues that the fact that such a difference has been taken for granted by writers on education and society at large, caused a failure in providing the necessary justification for subjecting children to compulsory schooling. See Purdy 1992. p. 150.

313 Laura Purdy mentions this demand in several places (for example, in Purdy 1992, p. 87), as one of the two fundamental components of the libertarian argument that it is unjust to withhold equal rights from children. She says that the demand that bestowing equal rights to children will not lead to disastrous consequences is an integral part of the libertarian argument from justice.

314 Archard 1993. p. 70.

315 Archard 1993. p. 71-72.

316 Such a perversion can rise when examining one's rights to inherit, when a person kills his parents, and claims for inheriting their property as their acknowledged legal legatee.

317 Davis 1992 p.2.

318 Gewirth 1988. p. 140. Gewirth mentions this issue with regard to biological humans who are incapable of any kind of action, or infants who suffer from disabling diseases. However, the problem remains the same (if not aggravated) when discussing the rights of a fetus to generic rights, because the biological possibility of attaining the moral abilities of agency is relatively high, although in many respects, a fetus is placed in a lower degree of agency.

319 I use Nancy Davis' definition, taken from Davis 1984. p. 176. I will not refer to the most extreme position that prohibits abortion even when it endangers the woman's life, because I think that such a position comes from a different conceptual framework: mostly a religious one, which does not have sufficient commonly accepted denominators that enable most people to even argue with.

320 This quote and the two possible interpretations of the above assumption is taken from Dworkin 1993. p. 11.

321 See Thiroux 1995. p.280. The answer to this argument is on p. 287-288.

322 See, for example, Warren 1991. p. 304.

323 See Davis 1992. p. 3.

324 Richard Wasserstrom presents such a position in his survey of the most frequent positions. See Wasserstrom 1979. pp. 118-119.

325 This quotation is taken from Baird & Rosenbaum 1989. p. 20.

326 Werner 1979. p. 52.

327 Werner 1979. p. 64. He also argues that this criterion is a sufficient condition for membership of the community, in order to avoid cases in which human creatures that lack the more sophisticated criteria (such as self consciousness) will not be considered as members of the community. However, for my purposes the previous argument is more relevant, because it excludes dead human beings from possessing rights, on the one hand, and human sperm or unfertilized ovum on the other.

328 Werner 1979. p. 73.

329 See Davis 1991. p. 5.

330 For example: English 1989. p. 83.

[331] English 1989. p. 84.
[332] English 1989. p. 86.
[333] These capacities and others are to be found at Wasserstrom 1979. p. 119-120.
[334] This is the position that is held by Richard Wasserstrom, in Wasserstrom 1979. p. 119-120.
[335] Wasserstrom's interest in the matter of the moral status of a fetus is for the sake of the foundation of guidelines for experimentation *ex Utero* and *in Utero.*
[336] Feinberg 1992. p. 57.
[337] Wellman 1995. p. 137.
[338] Wellman 1995. p. 138.
[339] Wellman 1995. p. 140.
[340] Feinberg 1992. p. 60.
[341] Feinberg 1992. p. 62.
[342] Feinberg 1992. p. 68. These examples were taken by him from Sissela Bok's article: "Ethical Problems Of Abortion". In: *Hastings Center Studies.* 2. 1974. p. 35.
[343] Feinberg 1992. p. 68-69.
[344] Feinberg 1992. p. 69.
[345] Feinberg mentions that there is a very small chance of being pregnant when using contraceptive pills, and the only way to absolutely avoid pregnancy is by abstaining from sex altogether. However, demanding this is similar to demanding that the raped girl should have remained in a locked building, patrolled around the clock by armed guards, without never getting out. He thinks that when a person takes all the precautions that can *reasonably* be expected against a certain outcome, he cannot be fairly described as responsible for this outcome if it occurs despite his efforts. Feinberg 1992. p. 69-70.
[346] Feinberg 1992. p. 70.
[347] Warren 1989. p. 75.
[348] Warren 1989. p. 77-78.
[349] Warren 1989. p. 79.
[350] Warren 1989. p. 80.
[351] Warren 1991. p. 311.
[352] Tooley 1989. p. 49.
[353] Tooley 1989. p. 56-57.
[354] See Davis 1992. p. 5.
[355] English 1989. p. 84.
[356] English 1989. p. 86.
[357] Callahan 1989. p. 117.
[358] These two claims are taken from Warren 1991. p. 26.
[359] Thomson 1979. p. 24.
[360] Thomson 1979. p. 25.
[361] English 1989. p. 87.
[362] Shue 1980, p.32.
[363] See her expression in English 1989. p. 87.
[364] Thomson 1979. p. 27.
[365] This is an interpretation, but very near to Thomson's view in Thomson 1979. p. 30.
[366] Thomson 1979. p. 34.
[367] English 1989. p. 88-89.
[368] Warren 1991. p. 312.
[369] This is Rawls' concept of rights, and it reflects the way I use the term here. See Rawls 1971. p. 135.
[370] Gewirth 1978. p. 122.

[371] Gewirth 1978. p. 142.
[372] Gewirth 1978. p. 142.
[373] Gewirth 1978. p. 143. Of course, being consistent with the Principle of Proportionality, Gewirth maintains that the justification of abortion, and hence the abrogating the fetus's generic rights may vary in degree. He notes, for example, that a six month fetus has the right to well-being to a greater degree than does a three month fetus. This is because it approaches having the generic practical abilities and the corresponding purposes or desires, to a greater degree. So the there is correspondingly less justification for abortion, the greater the approach to maturation. The justification of abortion is also affected by the nature of the conflict and the circumstances of the pregnancy (when it results from a rape, or violence, etc.).
[374] Gewirth 1978. p. 144.
[375] Taken from Nickel 1982. p. 248-249.
[376] This is Dworkin presentation of the "derivative objection to abortion". See Dworkin 1993. p. 11.
[377] See Dworkin 1993. p. 11.
[378] Dworkin 1993. p. 156.
[379] Dworkin 1993. p. 71.
[380] Dworkin 1993. p. 73.
[381] Dworkin 1993. p. 82-84.
[382] Dworkin 1993. p. 93.
[383] Dworkin 1993. p. 157.
[384] See Dworkin 1993. p. 167.
[385] See Gewirth 1978. p. 120.
[386] Gewirth 1978. p. 122. See also p. 141.
[387] Gewirth 1978. p. 141.
[388] Gewirth 1988. p. 140. Gewirth mentions this issue with regard to biological humans who are incapable of any kind of action, or infants who suffer from disabling diseases. However, the problem remains the same (if not aggravated) when discussing the rights of a fetus to generic rights, because the biological possibility of attaining the moral abilities of agency is relatively high, although in many respects, fetus is placed in a lower degree of agency.
[389] Wellman 1995, p. 126. The reasoning for this distinction is mentioned in Wellman 1995. p. 137.
[390] See Wellman 1995, p. 113. He specifies the above capacity as the capacity to become aware of relevant facts, to appreciate their moral relevance, to be motivated by them, and to act in some broad nonmoral sense of doing something or other.
[391] Wellman 1995, pp. 129-131.
[392] Gewirth 1988. p. 140.
[393] Tom Campbell raises this as a possible excuse of those who hold the paternalistic position towards mentally ill persons. See Campbell 1986. p. 142.
[394] Campbell and Heginbotham 1991. p.124.
[395] For the distinction between weak and strong paternalism, see Campbell and Heginbotham 1991. p.84
[396] Campbell and Heginbotham 1991. p.124. They mention a further category of what they call "short term emergency intervention" that might be permitted, in order to enable the assessment of apparently risky situations, or to give the individual who is in danger of serious harm the opportunity to appreciate the gravity of his situation. My position towards this category is similar to that of the two former alternatives.

[397] See McLean 1986. p. 101.
[398] McLean 1986. p. 115.
[399] McLean 1986. p. 118.
[400] Feinberg 1992 pp. 66-67.
[401] This is a quotation that Feinberg brings from the US Supreme Court decision in 1944, in *Prince v. Massachusetts.* See Feinberg 1992. p. 80.
[402] Feinberg 1992. p. 89.
[403] Feinberg 1992. p. 96.
[404] For this interpretation of Gewirth's position, see Ross 1994. p. 38.
[405] Here I adopt Rawls' view, as specified in Rawls 1971. p. 135.

SYNTHESE LIBRARY

1. J. M. Bochénski, *A Precis of Mathematical Logic.* Translated from French and German by O. Bird. 1959 ISBN 90-277-0073-7
2. P. Guiraud, *Problèmes et méthodes de la statistique linguistique.* 1959 ISBN 90-277-0025-7
3. H. Freudenthal (ed.), *The Concept and the Role of the Model in Mathematics and Natural and Social Sciences.* 1961 ISBN 90-277-0017-6
4. E. W. Beth, *Formal Methods.* An Introduction to Symbolic Logic and to the Study of Effective Operations in Arithmetic and Logic. 1962 ISBN 90-277-0069-9
5. B. H. Kazemier and D. Vuysje (eds.), *Logic and Language.* Studies dedicated to Professor Rudolf Carnap on the Occasion of His 70th Birthday. 1962 ISBN 90-277-0019-2
6. M. W. Wartofsky (ed.), *Proceedings of the Boston Colloquium for the Philosophy of Science, 1961–1962.* [Boston Studies in the Philosophy of Science, Vol. I] 1963 ISBN 90-277-0021-4
7. A. A. Zinov'ev, *Philosophical Problems of Many-valued Logic.* A revised edition, edited and translated (from Russian) by G. Küng and D.D. Comey. 1963 ISBN 90-277-0091-5
8. G. Gurvitch, *The Spectrum of Social Time.* Translated from French and edited by M. Korenbaum and P. Bosserman. 1964 ISBN 90-277-0006-0
9. P. Lorenzen, *Formal Logic.* Translated from German by F.J. Crosson. 1965 ISBN 90-277-0080-X
10. R. S. Cohen and M. W. Wartofsky (eds.), *Proceedings of the Boston Colloquium for the Philosophy of Science, 1962–1964.* In Honor of Philipp Frank. [Boston Studies in the Philosophy of Science, Vol. II] 1965 ISBN 90-277-9004-0
11. E. W. Beth, *Mathematical Thought.* An Introduction to the Philosophy of Mathematics. 1965 ISBN 90-277-0070-2
12. E. W. Beth and J. Piaget, *Mathematical Epistemology and Psychology.* Translated from French by W. Mays. 1966 ISBN 90-277-0071-0
13. G. Küng, *Ontology and the Logistic Analysis of Language.* An Enquiry into the Contemporary Views on Universals. Revised ed., translated from German. 1967 ISBN 90-277-0028-1
14. R. S. Cohen and M. W. Wartofsky (eds.), *Proceedings of the Boston Colloquium for the Philosophy of Sciences, 1964–1966.* In Memory of Norwood Russell Hanson. [Boston Studies in the Philosophy of Science, Vol. III] 1967 ISBN 90-277-0013-3
15. C. D. Broad, *Induction, Probability, and Causation.* Selected Papers. 1968 ISBN 90-277-0012-5
16. G. Patzig, *Aristotle's Theory of the Syllogism.* A Logical-philosophical Study of *Book A* of the *Prior Analytics.* Translated from German by J. Barnes. 1968 ISBN 90-277-0030-3
17. N. Rescher, *Topics in Philosophical Logic.* 1968 ISBN 90-277-0084-2
18. R. S. Cohen and M. W. Wartofsky (eds.), *Proceedings of the Boston Colloquium for the Philosophy of Science, 1966–1968, Part I.* [Boston Studies in the Philosophy of Science, Vol. IV] 1969 ISBN 90-277-0014-1
19. R. S. Cohen and M. W. Wartofsky (eds.), *Proceedings of the Boston Colloquium for the Philosophy of Science, 1966–1968, Part II.* [Boston Studies in the Philosophy of Science, Vol. V] 1969 ISBN 90-277-0015-X
20. J. W. Davis, D. J. Hockney and W. K. Wilson (eds.), *Philosophical Logic.* 1969 ISBN 90-277-0075-3
21. D. Davidson and J. Hintikka (eds.), *Words and Objections.* Essays on the Work of W. V. Quine. 1969, rev. ed. 1975 ISBN 90-277-0074-5; Pb 90-277-0602-6
22. P. Suppes, *Studies in the Methodology and Foundations of Science. Selected Papers from 1951 to 1969.* 1969 ISBN 90-277-0020-6
23. J. Hintikka, *Models for Modalities.* Selected Essays. 1969 ISBN 90-277-0078-8; Pb 90-277-0598-4

24. N. Rescher *et al.* (eds.), *Essays in Honor of Carl G. Hempel.* A Tribute on the Occasion of His 65th Birthday. 1969 ISBN 90-277-0085-0
25. P. V. Tavanec (ed.), *Problems of the Logic of Scientific Knowledge.* Translated from Russian. 1970 ISBN 90-277-0087-7
26. M. Swain (ed.), *Induction, Acceptance, and Rational Belief.* 1970 ISBN 90-277-0086-9
27. R. S. Cohen and R. J. Seeger (eds.), *Ernst Mach: Physicist and Philosopher.* [Boston Studies in the Philosophy of Science, Vol. VI]. 1970 ISBN 90-277-0016-8
28. J. Hintikka and P. Suppes, *Information and Inference.* 1970 ISBN 90-277-0155-5
29. K. Lambert, *Philosophical Problems in Logic.* Some Recent Developments. 1970 ISBN 90-277-0079-6
30. R. A. Eberle, *Nominalistic Systems.* 1970 ISBN 90-277-0161-X
31. P. Weingartner and G. Zecha (eds.), *Induction, Physics, and Ethics.* 1970 ISBN 90-277-0158-X
32. E. W. Beth, *Aspects of Modern Logic.* Translated from Dutch. 1970 ISBN 90-277-0173-3
33. R. Hilpinen (ed.), *Deontic Logic.* Introductory and Systematic Readings. 1971 *See also* No. 152. ISBN Pb (1981 rev.) 90-277-1302-2
34. J.-L. Krivine, *Introduction to Axiomatic Set Theory.* Translated from French. 1971 ISBN 90-277-0169-5; Pb 90-277-0411-2
35. J. D. Sneed, *The Logical Structure of Mathematical Physics.* 2nd rev. ed., 1979 ISBN 90-277-1056-2; Pb 90-277-1059-7
36. C. R. Kordig, *The Justification of Scientific Change.* 1971 ISBN 90-277-0181-4; Pb 90-277-0475-9
37. M. Čapek, *Bergson and Modern Physics.* A Reinterpretation and Re-evaluation. [Boston Studies in the Philosophy of Science, Vol. VII] 1971 ISBN 90-277-0186-5
38. N. R. Hanson, *What I Do Not Believe, and Other Essays.* Ed. by S. Toulmin and H. Woolf. 1971 ISBN 90-277-0191-1
39. R. C. Buck and R. S. Cohen (eds.), *PSA 1970.* Proceedings of the Second Biennial Meeting of the Philosophy of Science Association, Boston, Fall 1970. In Memory of Rudolf Carnap. [Boston Studies in the Philosophy of Science, Vol. VIII] 1971 ISBN 90-277-0187-3; Pb 90-277-0309-4
40. D. Davidson and G. Harman (eds.), *Semantics of Natural Language.* 1972 ISBN 90-277-0304-3; Pb 90-277-0310-8
41. Y. Bar-Hillel (ed.), *Pragmatics of Natural Languages.* 1971 ISBN 90-277-0194-6; Pb 90-277-0599-2
42. S. Stenlund, *Combinators, γ Terms and Proof Theory.* 1972 ISBN 90-277-0305-1
43. M. Strauss, *Modern Physics and Its Philosophy.* Selected Paper in the Logic, History, and Philosophy of Science. 1972 ISBN 90-277-0230-6
44. M. Bunge, *Method, Model and Matter.* 1973 ISBN 90-277-0252-7
45. M. Bunge, *Philosophy of Physics.* 1973 ISBN 90-277-0253-5
46. A. A. Zinov'ev, *Foundations of the Logical Theory of Scientific Knowledge (Complex Logic).* Revised and enlarged English edition with an appendix by G. A. Smirnov, E. A. Sidorenka, A. M. Fedina and L. A. Bobrova. [Boston Studies in the Philosophy of Science, Vol. IX] 1973 ISBN 90-277-0193-8; Pb 90-277-0324-8
47. L. Tondl, *Scientific Procedures.* A Contribution concerning the Methodological Problems of Scientific Concepts and Scientific Explanation. Translated from Czech by D. Short. Edited by R.S. Cohen and M.W. Wartofsky. [Boston Studies in the Philosophy of Science, Vol. X] 1973 ISBN 90-277-0147-4; Pb 90-277-0323-X
48. N. R. Hanson, *Constellations and Conjectures.* 1973 ISBN 90-277-0192-X

49. K. J. J. Hintikka, J. M. E. Moravcsik and P. Suppes (eds.), *Approaches to Natural Language.* 1973 ISBN 90-277-0220-9; Pb 90-277-0233-0
50. M. Bunge (ed.), *Exact Philosophy.* Problems, Tools and Goals. 1973 ISBN 90-277-0251-9
51. R. J. Bogdan and I. Niiniluoto (eds.), *Logic, Language and Probability.* 1973 ISBN 90-277-0312-4
52. G. Pearce and P. Maynard (eds.), *Conceptual Change.* 1973 ISBN 90-277-0287-X; Pb 90-277-0339-6
53. I. Niiniluoto and R. Tuomela, *Theoretical Concepts and Hypothetico-inductive Inference.* 1973 ISBN 90-277-0343-4
54. R. Fraissé, *Course of Mathematical Logic* – Volume 1: *Relation and Logical Formula.* Translated from French. 1973 ISBN 90-277-0268-3; Pb 90-277-0403-1 (For *Volume 2* see under No. 69).
55. A. Grünbaum, *Philosophical Problems of Space and Time.* Edited by R.S. Cohen and M.W. Wartofsky. 2nd enlarged ed. [Boston Studies in the Philosophy of Science, Vol. XII] 1973 ISBN 90-277-0357-4; Pb 90-277-0358-2
56. P. Suppes (ed.), *Space, Time and Geometry.* 1973 ISBN 90-277-0386-8; Pb 90-277-0442-2
57. H. Kelsen, *Essays in Legal and Moral Philosophy.* Selected and introduced by O. Weinberger. Translated from German by P. Heath. 1973 ISBN 90-277-0388-4
58. R. J. Seeger and R. S. Cohen (eds.), *Philosophical Foundations of Science.* [Boston Studies in the Philosophy of Science, Vol. XI] 1974 ISBN 90-277-0390-6; Pb 90-277-0376-0
59. R. S. Cohen and M. W. Wartofsky (eds.), *Logical and Epistemological Studies in Contemporary Physics.* [Boston Studies in the Philosophy of Science, Vol. XIII] 1973 ISBN 90-277-0391-4; Pb 90-277-0377-9
60. R. S. Cohen and M. W. Wartofsky (eds.), *Methodological and Historical Essays in the Natural and Social Sciences. Proceedings of the Boston Colloquium for the Philosophy of Science, 1969–1972.* [Boston Studies in the Philosophy of Science, Vol. XIV] 1974 ISBN 90-277-0392-2; Pb 90-277-0378-7
61. R. S. Cohen, J. J. Stachel and M. W. Wartofsky (eds.), *For Dirk Struik. Scientific, Historical and Political Essays.* [Boston Studies in the Philosophy of Science, Vol. XV] 1974 ISBN 90-277-0393-0; Pb 90-277-0379-5
62. K. Ajdukiewicz, *Pragmatic Logic.* Translated from Polish by O. Wojtasiewicz. 1974 ISBN 90-277-0326-4
63. S. Stenlund (ed.), *Logical Theory and Semantic Analysis.* Essays dedicated to Stig Kanger on His 50th Birthday. 1974 ISBN 90-277-0438-4
64. K. F. Schaffner and R. S. Cohen (eds.), *PSA 1972. Proceedings of the Third Biennial Meeting of the Philosophy of Science Association.* [Boston Studies in the Philosophy of Science, Vol. XX] 1974 ISBN 90-277-0408-2; Pb 90-277-0409-0
65. H. E. Kyburg, Jr., *The Logical Foundations of Statistical Inference.* 1974 ISBN 90-277-0330-2; Pb 90-277-0430-9
66. M. Grene, *The Understanding of Nature.* Essays in the Philosophy of Biology. [Boston Studies in the Philosophy of Science, Vol. XXIII] 1974 ISBN 90-277-0462-7; Pb 90-277-0463-5
67. J. M. Broekman, *Structuralism: Moscow, Prague, Paris.* Translated from German. 1974 ISBN 90-277-0478-3
68. N. Geschwind, *Selected Papers on Language and the Brain.* [Boston Studies in the Philosophy of Science, Vol. XVI] 1974 ISBN 90-277-0262-4; Pb 90-277-0263-2
69. R. Fraissé, *Course of Mathematical Logic* – Volume 2: *Model Theory.* Translated from French. 1974 ISBN 90-277-0269-1; Pb 90-277-0510-0 (For *Volume 1* see under No. 54)

70. A. Grzegorczyk, *An Outline of Mathematical Logic.* Fundamental Results and Notions explained with all Details. Translated from Polish. 1974 ISBN 90-277-0359-0; Pb 90-277-0447-3
71. F. von Kutschera, *Philosophy of Language.* 1975 ISBN 90-277-0591-7
72. J. Manninen and R. Tuomela (eds.), *Essays on Explanation and Understanding.* Studies in the Foundations of Humanities and Social Sciences. 1976 ISBN 90-277-0592-5
73. J. Hintikka (ed.), *Rudolf Carnap, Logical Empiricist.* Materials and Perspectives. 1975 ISBN 90-277-0583-6
74. M. Čapek (ed.), *The Concepts of Space and Time.* Their Structure and Their Development. [Boston Studies in the Philosophy of Science, Vol. XXII] 1976 ISBN 90-277-0355-8; Pb 90-277-0375-2
75. J. Hintikka and U. Remes, *The Method of Analysis.* Its Geometrical Origin and Its General Significance. [Boston Studies in the Philosophy of Science, Vol. XXV] 1974 ISBN 90-277-0532-1; Pb 90-277-0543-7
76. J. E. Murdoch and E. D. Sylla (eds.), *The Cultural Context of Medieval Learning.* [Boston Studies in the Philosophy of Science, Vol. XXVI] 1975 ISBN 90-277-0560-7; Pb 90-277-0587-9
77. S. Amsterdamski, *Between Experience and Metaphysics.* Philosophical Problems of the Evolution of Science. [Boston Studies in the Philosophy of Science, Vol. XXXV] 1975 ISBN 90-277-0568-2; Pb 90-277-0580-1
78. P. Suppes (ed.), *Logic and Probability in Quantum Mechanics.* 1976 ISBN 90-277-0570-4; Pb 90-277-1200-X
79. H. von Helmholtz: *Epistemological Writings. The Paul Hertz / Moritz Schlick Centenary Edition of 1921 with Notes and Commentary by the Editors.* Newly translated from German by M. F. Lowe. Edited, with an Introduction and Bibliography, by R. S. Cohen and Y. Elkana. [Boston Studies in the Philosophy of Science, Vol. XXXVII] 1975 ISBN 90-277-0290-X; Pb 90-277-0582-8
80. J. Agassi, *Science in Flux.* [Boston Studies in the Philosophy of Science, Vol. XXVIII] 1975 ISBN 90-277-0584-4; Pb 90-277-0612-2
81. S. G. Harding (ed.), *Can Theories Be Refuted?* Essays on the Duhem-Quine Thesis. 1976 ISBN 90-277-0629-8; Pb 90-277-0630-1
82. S. Nowak, *Methodology of Sociological Research.* General Problems. 1977 ISBN 90-277-0486-4
83. J. Piaget, J.-B. Grize, A. Szeminśska and V. Bang, *Epistemology and Psychology of Functions.* Translated from French. 1977 ISBN 90-277-0804-5
84. M. Grene and E. Mendelsohn (eds.), *Topics in the Philosophy of Biology.* [Boston Studies in the Philosophy of Science, Vol. XXVII] 1976 ISBN 90-277-0595-X; Pb 90-277-0596-8
85. E. Fischbein, *The Intuitive Sources of Probabilistic Thinking in Children.* 1975 ISBN 90-277-0626-3; Pb 90-277-1190-9
86. E. W. Adams, *The Logic of Conditionals.* An Application of Probability to Deductive Logic. 1975 ISBN 90-277-0631-X
87. M. Przełęcki and R. Wójcicki (eds.), *Twenty-Five Years of Logical Methodology in Poland.* Translated from Polish. 1976 ISBN 90-277-0601-8
88. J. Topolski, *The Methodology of History.* Translated from Polish by O. Wojtasiewicz. 1976 ISBN 90-277-0550-X
89. A. Kasher (ed.), *Language in Focus: Foundations, Methods and Systems.* Essays dedicated to Yehoshua Bar-Hillel. [Boston Studies in the Philosophy of Science, Vol. XLIII] 1976 ISBN 90-277-0644-1; Pb 90-277-0645-X

90. J. Hintikka, *The Intentions of Intentionality and Other New Models for Modalities.* 1975 ISBN 90-277-0633-6; Pb 90-277-0634-4
91. W. Stegmüller, *Collected Papers on Epistemology, Philosophy of Science and History of Philosophy.* 2 Volumes. 1977 Set ISBN 90-277-0767-7
92. D. M. Gabbay, *Investigations in Modal and Tense Logics with Applications to Problems in Philosophy and Linguistics.* 1976 ISBN 90-277-0656-5
93. R. J. Bogdan, *Local Induction.* 1976 ISBN 90-277-0649-2
94. S. Nowak, *Understanding and Prediction.* Essays in the Methodology of Social and Behavioral Theories. 1976 ISBN 90-277-0558-5; Pb 90-277-1199-2
95. P. Mittelstaedt, *Philosophical Problems of Modern Physics.* [Boston Studies in the Philosophy of Science, Vol. XVIII] 1976 ISBN 90-277-0285-3; Pb 90-277-0506-2
96. G. Holton and W. A. Blanpied (eds.), *Science and Its Public: The Changing Relationship.* [Boston Studies in the Philosophy of Science, Vol. XXXIII] 1976 ISBN 90-277-0657-3; Pb 90-277-0658-1
97. M. Brand and D. Walton (eds.), *Action Theory.* 1976 ISBN 90-277-0671-9
98. P. Gochet, *Outline of a Nominalist Theory of Propositions.* An Essay in the Theory of Meaning and in the Philosophy of Logic. 1980 ISBN 90-277-1031-7
99. R. S. Cohen, P. K. Feyerabend, and M. W. Wartofsky (eds.), *Essays in Memory of Imre Lakatos.* [Boston Studies in the Philosophy of Science, Vol. XXXIX] 1976 ISBN 90-277-0654-9; Pb 90-277-0655-7
100. R. S. Cohen and J. J. Stachel (eds.), *Selected Papers of Léon Rosenfield.* [Boston Studies in the Philosophy of Science, Vol. XXI] 1979 ISBN 90-277-0651-4; Pb 90-277-0652-2
101. R. S. Cohen, C. A. Hooker, A. C. Michalos and J. W. van Evra (eds.), *PSA 1974. Proceedings of the 1974 Biennial Meeting of the Philosophy of Science Association.* [Boston Studies in the Philosophy of Science, Vol. XXXII] 1976 ISBN 90-277-0647-6; Pb 90-277-0648-4
102. Y. Fried and J. Agassi, *Paranoia.* A Study in Diagnosis. [Boston Studies in the Philosophy of Science, Vol. L] 1976 ISBN 90-277-0704-9; Pb 90-277-0705-7
103. M. Przełęcki, K. Szaniawski and R. Wójcicki (eds.), *Formal Methods in the Methodology of Empirical Sciences.* 1976 ISBN 90-277-0698-0
104. J. M. Vickers, *Belief and Probability.* 1976 ISBN 90-277-0744-8
105. K. H. Wolff, *Surrender and Catch.* Experience and Inquiry Today. [Boston Studies in the Philosophy of Science, Vol. LI] 1976 ISBN 90-277-0758-8; Pb 90-277-0765-0
106. K. Kosík, *Dialectics of the Concrete.* A Study on Problems of Man and World. [Boston Studies in the Philosophy of Science, Vol. LII] 1976 ISBN 90-277-0761-8; Pb 90-277-0764-2
107. N. Goodman, *The Structure of Appearance.* 3rd ed. with an Introduction by G. Hellman. [Boston Studies in the Philosophy of Science, Vol. LIII] 1977 ISBN 90-277-0773-1; Pb 90-277-0774-X
108. K. Ajdukiewicz, *The Scientific World-Perspective and Other Essays, 1931-1963.* Translated from Polish. Edited and with an Introduction by J. Giedymin. 1978 ISBN 90-277-0527-5
109. R. L. Causey, *Unity of Science.* 1977 ISBN 90-277-0779-0
110. R. E. Grandy, *Advanced Logic for Applications.* 1977 ISBN 90-277-0781-2
111. R. P. McArthur, *Tense Logic.* 1976 ISBN 90-277-0697-2
112. L. Lindahl, *Position and Change.* A Study in Law and Logic. Translated from Swedish by P. Needham. 1977 ISBN 90-277-0787-1
113. R. Tuomela, *Dispositions.* 1978 ISBN 90-277-0810-X
114. H. A. Simon, *Models of Discovery and Other Topics in the Methods of Science.* [Boston Studies in the Philosophy of Science, Vol. LIV] 1977 ISBN 90-277-0812-6; Pb 90-277-0858-4

115. R. D. Rosenkrantz, *Inference, Method and Decision.* Towards a Bayesian Philosophy of Science. 1977 ISBN 90-277-0817-7; Pb 90-277-0818-5
116. R. Tuomela, *Human Action and Its Explanation.* A Study on the Philosophical Foundations of Psychology. 1977 ISBN 90-277-0824-X
117. M. Lazerowitz, *The Language of Philosophy.* Freud and Wittgenstein. [Boston Studies in the Philosophy of Science, Vol. LV] 1977 ISBN 90-277-0826-6; Pb 90-277-0862-2
118. Not published 119. J. Pelc (ed.), *Semiotics in Poland, 1894–1969.* Translated from Polish. 1979 ISBN 90-277-0811-8
120. I. Pörn, *Action Theory and Social Science.* Some Formal Models. 1977 ISBN 90-277-0846-0
121. J. Margolis, *Persons and Mind.* The Prospects of Nonreductive Materialism. [Boston Studies in the Philosophy of Science, Vol. LVII] 1977 ISBN 90-277-0854-1; Pb 90-277-0863-0
122. J. Hintikka, I. Niiniluoto, and E. Saarinen (eds.), *Essays on Mathematical and Philosophical Logic.* 1979 ISBN 90-277-0879-7
123. T. A. F. Kuipers, *Studies in Inductive Probability and Rational Expectation.* 1978 ISBN 90-277-0882-7
124. E. Saarinen, R. Hilpinen, I. Niiniluoto and M. P. Hintikka (eds.), *Essays in Honour of Jaakko Hintikka on the Occasion of His 50th Birthday.* 1979 ISBN 90-277-0916-5
125. G. Radnitzky and G. Andersson (eds.), *Progress and Rationality in Science.* [Boston Studies in the Philosophy of Science, Vol. LVIII] 1978 ISBN 90-277-0921-1; Pb 90-277-0922-X
126. P. Mittelstaedt, *Quantum Logic.* 1978 ISBN 90-277-0925-4
127. K. A. Bowen, *Model Theory for Modal Logic.* Kripke Models for Modal Predicate Calculi. 1979 ISBN 90-277-0929-7
128. H. A. Bursen, *Dismantling the Memory Machine.* A Philosophical Investigation of Machine Theories of Memory. 1978 ISBN 90-277-0933-5
129. M. W. Wartofsky, *Models.* Representation and the Scientific Understanding. [Boston Studies in the Philosophy of Science, Vol. XLVIII] 1979 ISBN 90-277-0736-7; Pb 90-277-0947-5
130. D. Ihde, *Technics and Praxis.* A Philosophy of Technology. [Boston Studies in the Philosophy of Science, Vol. XXIV] 1979 ISBN 90-277-0953-X; Pb 90-277-0954-8
131. J. J. Wiatr (ed.), *Polish Essays in the Methodology of the Social Sciences.* [Boston Studies in the Philosophy of Science, Vol. XXIX] 1979 ISBN 90-277-0723-5; Pb 90-277-0956-4
132. W. C. Salmon (ed.), *Hans Reichenbach: Logical Empiricist.* 1979 ISBN 90-277-0958-0
133. P. Bieri, R.-P. Horstmann and L. Krüger (eds.), *Transcendental Arguments in Science.* Essays in Epistemology. 1979 ISBN 90-277-0963-7; Pb 90-277-0964-5
134. M. Marković and G. Petrović (eds.), *Praxis.* Yugoslav Essays in the Philosophy and Methodology of the Social Sciences. [Boston Studies in the Philosophy of Science, Vol. XXXVI] 1979 ISBN 90-277-0727-8; Pb 90-277-0968-8
135. R. Wójcicki, *Topics in the Formal Methodology of Empirical Sciences.* Translated from Polish. 1979 ISBN 90-277-1004-X
136. G. Radnitzky and G. Andersson (eds.), *The Structure and Development of Science.* [Boston Studies in the Philosophy of Science, Vol. LIX] 1979 ISBN 90-277-0994-7; Pb 90-277-0995-5
137. J. C. Webb, *Mechanism, Mentalism and Metamathematics.* An Essay on Finitism. 1980 ISBN 90-277-1046-5
138. D. F. Gustafson and B. L. Tapscott (eds.), *Body, Mind and Method.* Essays in Honor of Virgil C. Aldrich. 1979 ISBN 90-277-1013-9
139. L. Nowak, *The Structure of Idealization.* Towards a Systematic Interpretation of the Marxian Idea of Science. 1980 ISBN 90-277-1014-7

140. C. Perelman, *The New Rhetoric and the Humanities.* Essays on Rhetoric and Its Applications. Translated from French and German. With an Introduction by H. Zyskind. 1979 ISBN 90-277-1018-X; Pb 90-277-1019-8
141. W. Rabinowicz, *Universalizability.* A Study in Morals and Metaphysics. 1979 ISBN 90-277-1020-2
142. C. Perelman, *Justice, Law and Argument.* Essays on Moral and Legal Reasoning. Translated from French and German. With an Introduction by H.J. Berman. 1980 ISBN 90-277-1089-9; Pb 90-277-1090-2
143. S. Kanger and S. Öhman (eds.), *Philosophy and Grammar.* Papers on the Occasion of the Quincentennial of Uppsala University. 1981 ISBN 90-277-1091-0
144. T. Pawlowski, *Concept Formation in the Humanities and the Social Sciences.* 1980 ISBN 90-277-1096-1
145. J. Hintikka, D. Gruender and E. Agazzi (eds.), *Theory Change, Ancient Axiomatics and Galileo's Methodology.* Proceedings of the 1978 Pisa Conference on the History and Philosophy of Science, Volume I. 1981 ISBN 90-277-1126-7
146. J. Hintikka, D. Gruender and E. Agazzi (eds.), *Probabilistic Thinking, Thermodynamics, and the Interaction of the History and Philosophy of Science.* Proceedings of the 1978 Pisa Conference on the History and Philosophy of Science, Volume II. 1981 ISBN 90-277-1127-5
147. U. Mönnich (ed.), *Aspects of Philosophical Logic.* Some Logical Forays into Central Notions of Linguistics and Philosophy. 1981 ISBN 90-277-1201-8
148. D. M. Gabbay, *Semantical Investigations in Heyting's Intuitionistic Logic.* 1981 ISBN 90-277-1202-6
149. E. Agazzi (ed.), *Modern Logic – A Survey.* Historical, Philosophical, and Mathematical Aspects of Modern Logic and Its Applications. 1981 ISBN 90-277-1137-2
150. A. F. Parker-Rhodes, *The Theory of Indistinguishables.* A Search for Explanatory Principles below the Level of Physics. 1981 ISBN 90-277-1214-X
151. J. C. Pitt, *Pictures, Images, and Conceptual Change.* An Analysis of Wilfrid Sellars' Philosophy of Science. 1981 ISBN 90-277-1276-X; Pb 90-277-1277-8
152. R. Hilpinen (ed.), *New Studies in Deontic Logic.* Norms, Actions, and the Foundations of Ethics. 1981 ISBN 90-277-1278-6; Pb 90-277-1346-4
153. C. Dilworth, *Scientific Progress.* A Study Concerning the Nature of the Relation between Successive Scientific Theories. 3rd rev. ed., 1994 ISBN 0-7923-2487-0; Pb 0-7923-2488-9
154. D. Woodruff Smith and R. McIntyre, *Husserl and Intentionality.* A Study of Mind, Meaning, and Language. 1982 ISBN 90-277-1392-8; Pb 90-277-1730-3
155. R. J. Nelson, *The Logic of Mind.* 2nd. ed., 1989 ISBN 90-277-2819-4; Pb 90-277-2822-4
156. J. F. A. K. van Benthem, *The Logic of Time.* A Model-Theoretic Investigation into the Varieties of Temporal Ontology, and Temporal Discourse. 1983; 2nd ed., 1991 ISBN 0-7923-1081-0
157. R. Swinburne (ed.), *Space, Time and Causality.* 1983 ISBN 90-277-1437-1
158. E. T. Jaynes, *Papers on Probability, Statistics and Statistical Physics.* Ed. by R. D. Rozenkrantz. 1983 ISBN 90-277-1448-7; Pb (1989) 0-7923-0213-3
159. T. Chapman, *Time: A Philosophical Analysis.* 1982 ISBN 90-277-1465-7
160. E. N. Zalta, *Abstract Objects.* An Introduction to Axiomatic Metaphysics. 1983 ISBN 90-277-1474-6
161. S. Harding and M. B. Hintikka (eds.), *Discovering Reality.* Feminist Perspectives on Epistemology, Metaphysics, Methodology, and Philosophy of Science. 1983 ISBN 90-277-1496-7; Pb 90-277-1538-6
162. M. A. Stewart (ed.), *Law, Morality and Rights.* 1983 ISBN 90-277-1519-X

163. D. Mayr and G. Süssmann (eds.), *Space, Time, and Mechanics.* Basic Structures of a Physical Theory. 1983 ISBN 90-277-1525-4
164. D. Gabbay and F. Guenthner (eds.), *Handbook of Philosophical Logic.* Vol. I: Elements of Classical Logic. 1983 ISBN 90-277-1542-4
165. D. Gabbay and F. Guenthner (eds.), *Handbook of Philosophical Logic.* Vol. II: Extensions of Classical Logic. 1984 ISBN 90-277-1604-8
166. D. Gabbay and F. Guenthner (eds.), *Handbook of Philosophical Logic.* Vol. III: Alternative to Classical Logic. 1986 ISBN 90-277-1605-6
167. D. Gabbay and F. Guenthner (eds.), *Handbook of Philosophical Logic.* Vol. IV: Topics in the Philosophy of Language. 1989 ISBN 90-277-1606-4
168. A. J. I. Jones, *Communication and Meaning.* An Essay in Applied Modal Logic. 1983 ISBN 90-277-1543-2
169. M. Fitting, *Proof Methods for Modal and Intuitionistic Logics.* 1983 ISBN 90-277-1573-4
170. J. Margolis, *Culture and Cultural Entities.* Toward a New Unity of Science. 1984 ISBN 90-277-1574-2
171. R. Tuomela, *A Theory of Social Action.* 1984 ISBN 90-277-1703-6
172. J. J. E. Gracia, E. Rabossi, E. Villanueva and M. Dascal (eds.), *Philosophical Analysis in Latin America.* 1984 ISBN 90-277-1749-4
173. P. Ziff, *Epistemic Analysis.* A Coherence Theory of Knowledge. 1984 ISBN 90-277-1751-7
174. P. Ziff, *Antiaesthetics.* An Appreciation of the Cow with the Subtile Nose. 1984 ISBN 90-277-1773-7
175. W. Balzer, D. A. Pearce, and H.-J. Schmidt (eds.), *Reduction in Science.* Structure, Examples, Philosophical Problems. 1984 ISBN 90-277-1811-3
176. A. Peczenik, L. Lindahl and B. van Roermund (eds.), *Theory of Legal Science.* Proceedings of the Conference on Legal Theory and Philosophy of Science (Lund, Sweden, December 1983). 1984 ISBN 90-277-1834-2
177. I. Niiniluoto, *Is Science Progressive?* 1984 ISBN 90-277-1835-0
178. B. K. Matilal and J. L. Shaw (eds.), *Analytical Philosophy in Comparative Perspective.* Exploratory Essays in Current Theories and Classical Indian Theories of Meaning and Reference. 1985 ISBN 90-277-1870-9
179. P. Kroes, *Time: Its Structure and Role in Physical Theories.* 1985 ISBN 90-277-1894-6
180. J. H. Fetzer, *Sociobiology and Epistemology.* 1985 ISBN 90-277-2005-3; Pb 90-277-2006-1
181. L. Haaparanta and J. Hintikka (eds.), *Frege Synthesized.* Essays on the Philosophical and Foundational Work of Gottlob Frege. 1986 ISBN 90-277-2126-2
182. M. Detlefsen, *Hilbert's Program.* An Essay on Mathematical Instrumentalism. 1986 ISBN 90-277-2151-3
183. J. L. Golden and J. J. Pilotta (eds.), *Practical Reasoning in Human Affairs.* Studies in Honor of Chaim Perelman. 1986 ISBN 90-277-2255-2
184. H. Zandvoort, *Models of Scientific Development and the Case of Nuclear Magnetic Resonance.* 1986 ISBN 90-277-2351-6
185. I. Niiniluoto, *Truthlikeness.* 1987 ISBN 90-277-2354-0
186. W. Balzer, C. U. Moulines and J. D. Sneed, *An Architectonic for Science.* The Structuralist Program. 1987 ISBN 90-277-2403-2
187. D. Pearce, *Roads to Commensurability.* 1987 ISBN 90-277-2414-8
188. L. M. Vaina (ed.), *Matters of Intelligence.* Conceptual Structures in Cognitive Neuroscience. 1987 ISBN 90-277-2460-1

189. H. Siegel, *Relativism Refuted.* A Critique of Contemporary Epistemological Relativism. 1987 ISBN 90-277-2469-5
190. W. Callebaut and R. Pinxten, *Evolutionary Epistemology.* A Multiparadigm Program, with a Complete Evolutionary Epistemology Bibliograph. 1987 ISBN 90-277-2582-9
191. J. Kmita, *Problems in Historical Epistemology.* 1988 ISBN 90-277-2199-8
192. J. H. Fetzer (ed.), *Probability and Causality.* Essays in Honor of Wesley C. Salmon, with an Annotated Bibliography. 1988 ISBN 90-277-2607-8; Pb 1-5560-8052-2
193. A. Donovan, L. Laudan and R. Laudan (eds.), *Scrutinizing Science.* Empirical Studies of Scientific Change. 1988 ISBN 90-277-2608-6
194. H.R. Otto and J.A. Tuedio (eds.), *Perspectives on Mind.* 1988 ISBN 90-277-2640-X
195. D. Batens and J.P. van Bendegem (eds.), *Theory and Experiment.* Recent Insights and New Perspectives on Their Relation. 1988 ISBN 90-277-2645-0
196. J. Österberg, *Self and Others.* A Study of Ethical Egoism. 1988 ISBN 90-277-2648-5
197. D.H. Helman (ed.), *Analogical Reasoning.* Perspectives of Artificial Intelligence, Cognitive Science, and Philosophy. 1988 ISBN 90-277-2711-2
198. J. Woleński, *Logic and Philosophy in the Lvov-Warsaw School.* 1989 ISBN 90-277-2749-X
199. R. Wójcicki, *Theory of Logical Calculi.* Basic Theory of Consequence Operations. 1988 ISBN 90-277-2785-6
200. J. Hintikka and M.B. Hintikka, *The Logic of Epistemology and the Epistemology of Logic.* Selected Essays. 1989 ISBN 0-7923-0040-8; Pb 0-7923-0041-6
201. E. Agazzi (ed.), *Probability in the Sciences.* 1988 ISBN 90-277-2808-9
202. M. Meyer (ed.), *From Metaphysics to Rhetoric.* 1989 ISBN 90-277-2814-3
203. R.L. Tieszen, *Mathematical Intuition.* Phenomenology and Mathematical Knowledge. 1989 ISBN 0-7923-0131-5
204. A. Melnick, *Space, Time, and Thought in Kant.* 1989 ISBN 0-7923-0135-8
205. D.W. Smith, *The Circle of Acquaintance.* Perception, Consciousness, and Empathy. 1989 ISBN 0-7923-0252-4
206. M.H. Salmon (ed.), *The Philosophy of Logical Mechanism.* Essays in Honor of Arthur W. Burks. With his Responses, and with a Bibliography of Burk's Work. 1990 ISBN 0-7923-0325-3
207. M. Kusch, *Language as Calculus vs. Language as Universal Medium.* A Study in Husserl, Heidegger, and Gadamer. 1989 ISBN 0-7923-0333-4
208. T.C. Meyering, *Historical Roots of Cognitive Science.* The Rise of a Cognitive Theory of Perception from Antiquity to the Nineteenth Century. 1989 ISBN 0-7923-0349-0
209. P. Kosso, *Observability and Observation in Physical Science.* 1989 ISBN 0-7923-0389-X
210. J. Kmita, *Essays on the Theory of Scientific Cognition.* 1990 ISBN 0-7923-0441-1
211. W. Sieg (ed.), *Acting and Reflecting.* The Interdisciplinary Turn in Philosophy. 1990 ISBN 0-7923-0512-4
212. J. Karpiński, *Causality in Sociological Research.* 1990 ISBN 0-7923-0546-9
213. H.A. Lewis (ed.), *Peter Geach: Philosophical Encounters.* 1991 ISBN 0-7923-0823-9
214. M. Ter Hark, *Beyond the Inner and the Outer.* Wittgenstein's Philosophy of Psychology. 1990 ISBN 0-7923-0850-6
215. M. Gosselin, *Nominalism and Contemporary Nominalism.* Ontological and Epistemological Implications of the Work of W.V.O. Quine and of N. Goodman. 1990 ISBN 0-7923-0904-9
216. J.H. Fetzer, D. Shatz and G. Schlesinger (eds.), *Definitions and Definability.* Philosophical Perspectives. 1991 ISBN 0-7923-1046-2
217. E. Agazzi and A. Cordero (eds.), *Philosophy and the Origin and Evolution of the Universe.* 1991 ISBN 0-7923-1322-4

218. M. Kusch, *Foucault's Strata and Fields.* An Investigation into Archaeological and Genealogical Science Studies. 1991 ISBN 0-7923-1462-X
219. C.J. Posy, *Kant's Philosophy of Mathematics.* Modern Essays. 1992 ISBN 0-7923-1495-6
220. G. Van de Vijver, *New Perspectives on Cybernetics.* Self-Organization, Autonomy and Connectionism. 1992 ISBN 0-7923-1519-7
221. J.C. Nyíri, *Tradition and Individuality.* Essays. 1992 ISBN 0-7923-1566-9
222. R. Howell, *Kant's Transcendental Deduction.* An Analysis of Main Themes in His Critical Philosophy. 1992 ISBN 0-7923-1571-5
223. A. García de la Sienra, *The Logical Foundations of the Marxian Theory of Value.* 1992 ISBN 0-7923-1778-5
224. D.S. Shwayder, *Statement and Referent.* An Inquiry into the Foundations of Our Conceptual Order. 1992 ISBN 0-7923-1803-X
225. M. Rosen, *Problems of the Hegelian Dialectic.* Dialectic Reconstructed as a Logic of Human Reality. 1993 ISBN 0-7923-2047-6
226. P. Suppes, *Models and Methods in the Philosophy of Science: Selected Essays.* 1993 ISBN 0-7923-2211-8
227. R. M. Dancy (ed.), *Kant and Critique: New Essays in Honor of W. H. Werkmeister.* 1993 ISBN 0-7923-2244-4
228. J. Woleński (ed.), *Philosophical Logic in Poland.* 1993 ISBN 0-7923-2293-2
229. M. De Rijke (ed.), *Diamonds and Defaults.* Studies in Pure and Applied Intensional Logic. 1993 ISBN 0-7923-2342-4
230. B.K. Matilal and A. Chakrabarti (eds.), *Knowing from Words.* Western and Indian Philosophical Analysis of Understanding and Testimony. 1994 ISBN 0-7923-2345-9
231. S.A. Kleiner, *The Logic of Discovery.* A Theory of the Rationality of Scientific Research. 1993 ISBN 0-7923-2371-8
232. R. Festa, *Optimum Inductive Methods.* A Study in Inductive Probability, Bayesian Statistics, and Verisimilitude. 1993 ISBN 0-7923-2460-9
233. P. Humphreys (ed.), *Patrick Suppes: Scientific Philosopher.* Vol. 1: Probability and Probabilistic Causality. 1994 ISBN 0-7923-2552-4
234. P. Humphreys (ed.), *Patrick Suppes: Scientific Philosopher.* Vol. 2: Philosophy of Physics, Theory Structure, and Measurement Theory. 1994 ISBN 0-7923-2553-2
235. P. Humphreys (ed.), *Patrick Suppes: Scientific Philosopher.* Vol. 3: Language, Logic, and Psychology. 1994 ISBN 0-7923-2862-0
Set ISBN (Vols 233–235) 0-7923-2554-0
236. D. Prawitz and D. Westerståhl (eds.), *Logic and Philosophy of Science in Uppsala.* Papers from the 9th International Congress of Logic, Methodology, and Philosophy of Science. 1994 ISBN 0-7923-2702-0
237. L. Haaparanta (ed.), *Mind, Meaning and Mathematics.* Essays on the Philosophical Views of Husserl and Frege. 1994 ISBN 0-7923-2703-9
238. J. Hintikka (ed.), *Aspects of Metaphor.* 1994 ISBN 0-7923-2786-1
239. B. McGuinness and G. Oliveri (eds.), *The Philosophy of Michael Dummett.* With Replies from Michael Dummett. 1994 ISBN 0-7923-2804-3
240. D. Jamieson (ed.), *Language, Mind, and Art.* Essays in Appreciation and Analysis, In Honor of Paul Ziff. 1994 ISBN 0-7923-2810-8
241. G. Preyer, F. Siebelt and A. Ulfig (eds.), *Language, Mind and Epistemology.* On Donald Davidson's Philosophy. 1994 ISBN 0-7923-2811-6
242. P. Ehrlich (ed.), *Real Numbers, Generalizations of the Reals, and Theories of Continua.* 1994 ISBN 0-7923-2689-X

243. G. Debrock and M. Hulswit (eds.), *Living Doubt*. Essays concerning the epistemology of Charles Sanders Peirce. 1994 ISBN 0-7923-2898-1
244. J. Srzednicki, *To Know or Not to Know*. Beyond Realism and Anti-Realism. 1994 ISBN 0-7923-2909-0
245. R. Egidi (ed.), *Wittgenstein: Mind and Language*. 1995 ISBN 0-7923-3171-0
246. A. Hyslop, *Other Minds*. 1995 ISBN 0-7923-3245-8
247. L. Pólos and M. Masuch (eds.), *Applied Logic: How, What and Why*. Logical Approaches to Natural Language. 1995 ISBN 0-7923-3432-9
248. M. Krynicki, M. Mostowski and L.M. Szczerba (eds.), *Quantifiers: Logics, Models and Computation*. Volume One: Surveys. 1995 ISBN 0-7923-3448-5
249. M. Krynicki, M. Mostowski and L.M. Szczerba (eds.), *Quantifiers: Logics, Models and Computation*. Volume Two: Contributions. 1995 ISBN 0-7923-3449-3
Set ISBN (Vols 248 + 249) 0-7923-3450-7
250. R.A. Watson, *Representational Ideas from Plato to Patricia Churchland*. 1995 ISBN 0-7923-3453-1
251. J. Hintikka (ed.), *From Dedekind to Gödel*. Essays on the Development of the Foundations of Mathematics. 1995 ISBN 0-7923-3484-1
252. A. Wiśniewski, *The Posing of Questions*. Logical Foundations of Erotetic Inferences. 1995 ISBN 0-7923-3637-2
253. J. Peregrin, *Doing Worlds with Words*. Formal Semantics without Formal Metaphysics. 1995 ISBN 0-7923-3742-5
254. I.A. Kieseppä, *Truthlikeness for Multidimensional, Quantitative Cognitive Problems*. 1996 ISBN 0-7923-4005-1
255. P. Hugly and C. Sayward: *Intensionality and Truth*. An Essay on the Philosophy of A.N. Prior. 1996 ISBN 0-7923-4119-8
256. L. Hankinson Nelson and J. Nelson (eds.): *Feminism, Science, and the Philosophy of Science*. 1997 ISBN 0-7923-4162-7
257. P.I. Bystrov and V.N. Sadovsky (eds.): *Philosophical Logic and Logical Philosophy*. Essays in Honour of Vladimir A. Smirnov. 1996 ISBN 0-7923-4270-4
258. Å.E. Andersson and N-E. Sahlin (eds.): *The Complexity of Creativity*. 1996 ISBN 0-7923-4346-8
259. M.L. Dalla Chiara, K. Doets, D. Mundici and J. van Benthem (eds.): *Logic and Scientific Methods*. Volume One of the Tenth International Congress of Logic, Methodology and Philosophy of Science, Florence, August 1995. 1997 ISBN 0-7923-4383-2
260. M.L. Dalla Chiara, K. Doets, D. Mundici and J. van Benthem (eds.): *Structures and Norms in Science*. Volume Two of the Tenth International Congress of Logic, Methodology and Philosophy of Science, Florence, August 1995. 1997 ISBN 0-7923-4384-0
Set ISBN (Vols 259 + 260) 0-7923-4385-9
261. A. Chakrabarti: *Denying Existence*. The Logic, Epistemology and Pragmatics of Negative Existentials and Fictional Discourse. 1997 ISBN 0-7923-4388-3
262. A. Biletzki: *Talking Wolves*. Thomas Hobbes on the Language of Politics and the Politics of Language. 1997 ISBN 0-7923-4425-1
263. D. Nute (ed.): *Defeasible Deontic Logic*. 1997 ISBN 0-7923-4630-0
264. U. Meixner: *Axiomatic Formal Ontology*. 1997 ISBN 0-7923-4747-X
265. I. Brinck: *The Indexical 'I'*. The First Person in Thought and Language. 1997 ISBN 0-7923-4741-2
266. G. Hölmström-Hintikka and R. Tuomela (eds.): *Contemporary Action Theory*. Volume 1: Individual Action. 1997 ISBN 0-7923-4753-6; Set: 0-7923-4754-4

267. G. Hölmström-Hintikka and R. Tuomela (eds.): *Contemporary Action Theory.* Volume 2: Social Action. 1997 ISBN 0-7923-4752-8; Set: 0-7923-4754-4
268. B.-C. Park: *Phenomenological Aspects of Wittgenstein's Philosophy.* 1998 ISBN 0-7923-4813-3
269. J. Paśniczek: *The Logic of Intentional Objects.* A Meinongian Version of Classical Logic. 1998 Hb ISBN 0-7923-4880-X; Pb ISBN 0-7923-5578-4
270. P.W. Humphreys and J.H. Fetzer (eds.): *The New Theory of Reference.* Kripke, Marcus, and Its Origins. 1998 ISBN 0-7923-4898-2
271. K. Szaniawski, A. Chmielewski and J. Woleński (eds.): *On Science, Inference, Information and Decision Making.* Selected Essays in the Philosophy of Science. 1998 ISBN 0-7923-4922-9
272. G.H. von Wright: *In the Shadow of Descartes.* Essays in the Philosophy of Mind. 1998 ISBN 0-7923-4992-X
273. K. Kijania-Placek and J. Woleński (eds.): *The Lvov–Warsaw School and Contemporary Philosophy.* 1998 ISBN 0-7923-5105-3
274. D. Dedrick: *Naming the Rainbow.* Colour Language, Colour Science, and Culture. 1998 ISBN 0-7923-5239-4
275. L. Albertazzi (ed.): *Shapes of Forms.* From Gestalt Psychology and Phenomenology to Ontology and Mathematics. 1999 ISBN 0-7923-5246-7
276. P. Fletcher: *Truth, Proof and Infinity.* A Theory of Constructions and Constructive Reasoning. 1998 ISBN 0-7923-5262-9
277. M. Fitting and R.L. Mendelsohn (eds.): *First-Order Modal Logic.* 1998 Hb ISBN 0-7923-5334-X; Pb ISBN 0-7923-5335-8
278. J.N. Mohanty: *Logic, Truth and the Modalities from a Phenomenological Perspective.* 1999 ISBN 0-7923-5550-4
279. T. Placek: *Mathematical Intiutionism and Intersubjectivity.* A Critical Exposition of Arguments for Intuitionism. 1999 ISBN 0-7923-5630-6
280. A. Cantini, E. Casari and P. Minari (eds.): *Logic and Foundations of Mathematics.* 1999 ISBN 0-7923-5659-4 set ISBN 0-7923-5867-8
281. M.L. Dalla Chiara, R. Giuntini and F. Laudisa (eds.): *Language, Quantum, Music.* 1999 ISBN 0-7923-5727-2; set ISBN 0-7923-5867-8
282. R. Egidi (ed.): *In Search of a New Humanism.* The Philosophy of Georg Hendrik von Wright. 1999 ISBN 0-7923-5810-4
283. F. Vollmer: *Agent Causality.* 1999 ISBN 0-7923-5848-1
284. J. Peregrin (ed.): *Truth and Its Nature (if Any).* 1999 ISBN 0-7923-5865-1
285. M. De Caro (ed.): *Interpretations and Causes.* New Perspectives on Donald Davidson's Philosophy. 1999 ISBN 0-7923-5869-4
286. R. Murawski: *Recursive Functions and Metamathematics.* Problems of Completeness and Decidability, Gödel's Theorems. 1999 ISBN 0-7923-5904-6
287. T.A.F. Kuipers: *From Instrumentalism to Constructive Realism.* On Some Relations between Confirmation, Empirical Progress, and Truth Approximation. 2000 ISBN 0-7923-6086-9
288. G. Holmström-Hintikka (ed.): *Medieval Philosophy and Modern Times.* 2000 ISBN 0-7923-6102-4
289. E. Grosholz and H. Breger (eds.): *The Growth of Mathematical Knowledge.* 2000 ISBN 0-7923-6151-2

290. G. Sommaruga: *History and Philosophy of Constructive Type Theory*. 2000 ISBN 0-7923-6180-6
291. J. Gasser (ed.): *A Boole Anthology*. Recent and Classical Studies in the Logic of George Boole. 2000 ISBN 0-7923-6380-9
292. V.F. Hendricks, S.A. Pedersen and K.F. Jørgensen (eds.): *Proof Theory*. History and Philosophical Significance. 2000 ISBN 0-7923-6544-5
293. W.L. Craig: *The Tensed Theory of Time*. A Critical Examination. 2000 ISBN 0-7923-6634-4
294. W.L. Craig: *The Tenseless Theory of Time*. A Critical Examination. 2000 ISBN 0-7923-6635-2
295. L. Albertazzi (ed.): *The Dawn of Cognitive Science*. Early European Contributors. 2001 ISBN 0-7923-6799-5
296. G. Forrai: *Reference, Truth and Conceptual Schemes*. A Defense of Internal Realism. 2001 ISBN 0-7923-6885-1
297. V.F. Hendricks, S.A. Pedersen and K.F. Jørgensen (eds.): *Probability Theory*. Philosophy, Recent History and Relations to Science. 2001 ISBN 0-7923-6952-1
298. M. Esfeld: *Holism in Philosophy of Mind and Philosophy of Physics*. 2001 ISBN 0-7923-7003-1
299. E.C. Steinhart: *The Logic of Metaphor*. Analogous Parts of Possible Worlds. 2001 ISBN 0-7923-7004-X
300. To be published.
301. T.A.F. Kuipers: *Structures in Science Heuristic Patterns Based on Cognitive Structures*. An Advanced Textbook in Neo-Classical Philosophy of Science. 2001 ISBN 0-7923-7117-8
302. G. Hon and S.S. Rakover (eds.): *Explanation*. Theoretical Approaches and Applications. 2001 ISBN 1-4020-0017-0
303. G. Holmström-Hintikka, S. Lindström and R. Sliwinski (eds.): *Collected Papers of Stig Kanger with Essays on his Life and Work*. Vol. I. 2001 ISBN 1-4020-0021-9; Pb ISBN 1-4020-0022-7
304. G. Holmström-Hintikka, S. Lindström and R. Sliwinski (eds.): *Collected Papers of Stig Kanger with Essays on his Life and Work*. Vol. II. 2001 ISBN 1-4020-0111-8; Pb ISBN 1-4020-0112-6
305. C.A. Anderson and M. Zelëny (eds.): *Logic, Meaning and Computation*. Essays in Memory of Alonzo Church. 2001 ISBN 1-4020-0141-X
306. P. Schuster, U. Berger and H. Osswald (eds.): *Reuniting the Antipodes – Constructive and Nonstandard Views of the Continuum*. 2001 ISBN 1-4020-0152-5
307. S.D. Zwart: *Refined Verisimilitude*. 2001 ISBN 1-4020-0268-8
308. A.-S. Maurin: *IF Tropes*. 2002 ISBN 1-4020-0656-X
309. H. Eilstein (ed.): *A Collection of Polish Works on Philosophical Problems of Time and Spacetime*. 2002 ISBN 1-4020-0670-5
310. Y. Gauthier: *Internal Logic*. Foundations of Mathematics from Kronecker to Hilbert. 2002 ISBN 1-4020-0689-6
311. E. Ruttkamp: *A Model-Theoretic Realist Interpretation of Science*. 2002 ISBN 1-4020-0729-9
312. V. Rantala: *Explanatory Translation*. Beyond the Kuhnian Model of Conceptual Change. 2002 ISBN 1-4020-0827-9
313. L. Decock: *Trading Ontology for Idealogy*. 2002 ISBN 1-4020-0865-1

SYNTHESE LIBRARY

314. O. Ezra: *The Withdrawal of Rights*. Rights from a Different Perspective. 2002
ISBN 1-4020-0886-4

Previous volumes are still available.

KLUWER ACADEMIC PUBLISHERS – DORDRECHT / BOSTON / LONDON

GPSR Compliance
The European Union's (EU) General Product Safety Regulation (GPSR) is a set of rules that requires consumer products to be safe and our obligations to ensure this.

If you have any concerns about our products, you can contact us on

ProductSafety@springernature.com

In case Publisher is established outside the EU, the EU authorized representative is:

Springer Nature Customer Service Center GmbH
Europaplatz 3
69115 Heidelberg, Germany

www.ingramcontent.com/pod-product-compliance
Lightning Source LLC
Chambersburg PA
CBHW072243240926
51846CB00012B/155
* 9 7 8 9 0 4 8 1 6 1 2 7 0 *